ON CAPITOL HILL

ON CAPITOL HILL

Studies in the Legislative Process

Second Edition

John F. Bibby
University of Wisconsin-Milwaukee

Roger H. Davidson
University of California, Santa Barbara

The Dryden Press Inc.
901 North Elm
Hinsdale, Illinois 60521

To Lucile and Nancy

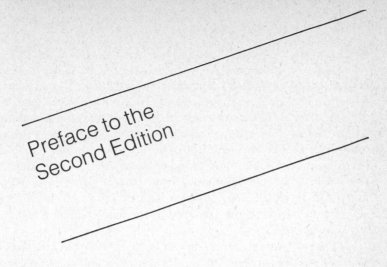

Preface to the
Second Edition

In introducing a revised edition of this book, it is appropriate to explain to new readers (and to remind old readers) of the philosophy and objectives that led us to undertake this work. We are convinced that, to comprehend fully the life of our national legislature, one must encounter it directly and at first hand. This kind of encounter can occur in a variety of ways: from work or study on Capitol Hill, from legislative internship programs, or simply from observing or interviewing senators, representatives, staff aides, journalists, and others close to the legislative process. Whatever the method, it should provide an opportunity to experience the drama (and boredom) of congressional activities at close range. But not all teachers, and certainly few students, are actually able to travel to Washington and to spend an extended period of time on Capitol Hill.

This book is designed to bring to the reader this element of experience. In our professional careers our paths have frequently led us to Capitol Hill in various roles: as interviewers, as committee witnesses, as director of a party committee in the House, as academic critics, and mostly as inquiring students seeking to learn what goes on and why. We consider ourselves representative of a generation of scholars who, in the words of congressional journalist Neil MacNeil, have frequented the committee rooms, lobbies, and corridors of Congress to "lay siege to the congressmen to have them explain their actions and motives."

We came naturally upon the "case" method as a way of implementing our objective in this book. As students we were exposed to the vivid narratives in Stephen K. Bailey and Howard Samuels' *Congress at Work*; even the photographs were memorable: How could one forget Senator George W. Norris' magnificent arched eyebrows, which spoke volumes about the "outsider" role in the Senate?

Although not consciously modeling our work on Bailey and Samuels' volume, we hoped to be able to fill some of the gap left when it went out of print. In the years since *On Capitol Hill* first appeared in 1967 we have all benefited from an impressive outpouring of scholarly literature on Congress and other legislative systems. Perhaps in no other corner of political science has research been so fecund and the results on the whole so fruitful. Still the need for accessible case material continues undiminished, if for no other reason than to illustrate and enrich both the literature and pedagogy on Congress. We are aware, for example, that some of the most fascinating writing about Congress has come from journalists like Richard Harris, Elizabeth Brenner Drew, and Larry King—who have managed to overcome the tendency of their profession to give short shrift to legislative events.

What we have attempted in this book is neither a "textbook" nor a series of anecdotes. We have tried to summon whatever journalistic skills we possess, in combination with the best current scholarly findings, to describe patterns of individual and institutional behavior typical of Capitol Hill. Because we are mindful of the particularity of the case approach and the imperative for political scientists to move cautiously toward broader generalizations about the political system, we have tried to combine narrative with analysis. We thus seek to describe not only the particular events and behaviors embodied in a case but also to suggest what is unique about them, what is typical, and what variables underlie them. We can express the hope only that readers will find as much information and enjoyment in the book as we have gained from the research that went into it.

We have eschewed a polemic approach to discussing Congress. Inevitably, perhaps, our narrative gives prominence to what might be called the "insiders' " point of view. This emphasis is not an establishmentarian plot being perpetrated by us. Rather, we have deliberately tried to let the reader see how things appear from where the actors stand. Legislators, like the rest of us, act upon mixed motives—some laudable, others objectionable, and still others the result of merely following paths of least resistance. We may properly criticize political actors for their deeds, and, for that matter, we may find fault with the system of relations in which these political actors are ensnared. We would hardly expect our readers to view the legislative process as an entirely benign phenomenon, guided by some hidden hand of reason or justice. It is flawed, biased, cumbersome, and often insensitive—just as individual politicians frequently are. But the prerequisite of intelligent criticism is a deep and even sympathetic understanding of the actors and the system in which they operate. We therefore invite readers to form their own evaluations of the events that we portray.

The basic format of the book remains little changed from the first edition. In order to describe the most recent actors, we have prepared entirely new materials for more than half this edition and have updated and revised large portions of the remainder. Chapters 2, 3, and 4 are completely new, though they parallel chapters on similar topics in the first edition. We have added a history of the 1970 Legislative Reorganization Act (Chapter 8) and have extended the concluding chapter (Chapter 9) to reflect the important, though still uncompleted, changes taking place in the wake of the Vietnam war. In other instances we have contented ourselves with updating, having concluded that the original cases should be retained.

Writing a book of this type is a matter of people as much as of ideas. We have thus incurred many debts along the way, some of which cannot be publicly acknowledged, and few of which can be adequately repaid. We are continually struck by the sufferance that legislators and staff people display toward "those professors" and their infernal questions.

Representative William Steiger allowed us to describe his 1970 reelection campaign and even to accompany him on the campaign trail in Wisconsin. Frederic A. Seefeld, Representative Steiger's district secretary, and Peter Kohler, former Sixth District Republican chairman, were most helpful. M. Albert Figinski, campaign director for former Senator Joseph Tydings, was extremely candid and perceptive in helping us assess Tydings' last campaign, as were Ernest Lotito, Albert G. Salter, and Mrs. Leah Freedlander. Representative John Anderson allowed us to describe his daily schedule of activities. Senator Abe Ribicoff was equally generous in permitting us to follow him on his rounds during a particularly dramatic and busy day in the Senate. Special thanks must be directed to John Koskinen, Senator Ribicoff's administrative assistant, Miss Vergie Cass, his personal secretary, and virtually every member of his staff—who opened their offices to our inquiries. The description of the House leadership contest (Chapter 4) would have been impossible without the close cooperation of Representatives Morris K. Udall and James G. O'Hara and their staffs. In our studies of the Area Redevelopment Act (Chapter 5) and the Economic Opportunity Act (Chapter 6) we are indebted to Dr. Sar A. Levitan, now director of the Center for Manpower Studies of George Washington University. Our account of the Legislative Reorganization Act of 1970 (Chapter 8) is based on the help and comments of many people, as befits description of a law with so long and complex a history. We wish to thank especially Representative Thomas M. Rees; Richard Conlon and Linda Kamm of the Democratic Study Group; Nicholas Masters of the Joint Committee on Congressional Operations; and Walter Kravitz, senior specialist in the Congressional Research Service, all of whom taught us much and saved us from many an error.

Finally, we would surely seem ungrateful if we did not express our appreciation to the readers of the first edition of our book. Their reactions and comments encouraged us to do the job again, and we hope that they will not be disappointed.

John F. Bibby
Roger H. Davidson

Milwaukee, Wisconsin
Santa Barbara, California
September 1971

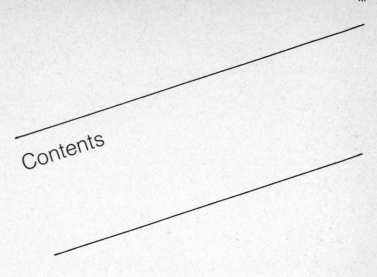

Contents

On Capitol Hill

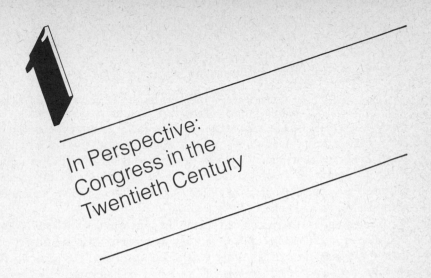

In Perspective:
Congress in the
Twentieth Century

As each session of Congress grinds to a close amid adjournment parties, eulogies for retiring members, and intense partisan and policy maneuvering, it has become traditional in Washington to assess the work of the session. Witness the following evaluations made about the 91st Congress (1969-1970). Senate Majority Leader Mike Mansfield (D.-Mont.) said that the Congress had acted in a "responsible" manner, and Speaker of the House John W. McCormack (D.-Mass.) claimed that Congress had seized the policy initiative and produced innovative legislation. President Richard M. Nixon, however, issued a statement blasting the Congress' record. He said that this Congress would be remembered for "what it failed to do" and that the legislative body apparently "had lost the capacity to decide and the will to act."

These diverse comments illustrate the fact that Congress is a focal point in the continuing struggle to determine the future of the United States. The President's statement gives evidence of the autonomy of Congress in our political system. It is not controlled by the executive branch: His basic criticism was that Congress had failed to act upon the major policy initiatives that he had recommended as essential domestic reforms. The political independence of Congress is also manifest in new assertiveness on foreign policy and military issues. Its crucial role in decision making was aptly expressed by Ralph K. Huitt: "Whoever tries to weave a seamless web of American . . . [public] policy will find soon enough that all threads lead ultimately to Congress."[1]

Why Be Concerned about Congress?

Although there appears to be general agreement that Congress plays a significant role in shaping public policy, there is little consensus, as the assessments of the 91st Congress illustrate, on its capacity to meet the challenges of the twentieth century and on its proper role in shaping policy. Precisely because of its importance in policy making, disagreements over its proper role, and persistent questions about its ability to meet present and future challenges, Congress is a constant object of reform proposals from people representing a wide spectrum of opinion.

For example, liberals tended during the post-World War II period to view Congress as an "obstacle course," a body determined to prevent or to delay unduly the enactment of necessary government programs. The generally liberal executive, which seemed capable of developing comprehensive and aggressive programs, appeared to be thwarted by a decentralized and conservative Congress, which permitted small but determined minorities to kill presidential programs. Particularly distressing to many liberals was the death in Congress of key segments of President John F. Kennedy's legislative program. People of liberal persuasion therefore frequently advocated reorganizing Congress so that it would be more responsive to proposals of the President and would be guided by stronger and better-disciplined political parties.

By contrast, conservatives—less impressed with the federal government's capacity to deal effectively with social problems—typically sought to strengthen the autonomy of Congress, which they saw as the last and best hope for preventing enactment of measures that they considered foolish, dangerous, and nearly always wasteful.

This ideological alignment obtained through most of the post-1945 period, but it shifted with the political forces dominating the presidency and Congress. After Nixon's election in 1968 and the advent of a more conservative administration, many liberals became less interested in ensuring that Congress would respond to presidential initiatives, whereas conservatives looked more hopefully to the executive branch.

Opinions on the extent to which Congress should be involved in foreign policy have also undergone dramatic shifts. As is discussed in Chapter 9, during most of the post-World War II era the President was considered the source of prudent and progressive foreign policy, whereas most observers thought Congress almost hopelessly parochial and sometimes even isolationist. As a result, such attempts to restrict presidential powers and prerogatives in national security matters as the proposed Bricker amendment of the 1950s were quickly condemned by opinion leaders, particularly those in academic circles.

But recently the controversy raging over American involvement in Southeast Asia has caused a dramatic realignment of political forces on the issue of presidential versus congressional prerogatives in foreign policy. Groups that used to argue most forcibly for presidential preeminence in foreign affairs now see in Congress their best hope for policies they deem prudent and responsible; former advocates of congressional involvement in foreign policy are now less certain of Congress' capacity in this sphere and are more inclined to follow presidential leadership.

The Functions of Congress

Article I, Section 1, of the U.S. Constitution declares that "All legislative Powers herein granted shall be vested in a Congress of the United States, which shall consist of a Senate and House of Representatives." This constitutional provision and those that follow it say relatively little, however, about the nature and functions of a legislative body. The basic question thus remains: What are the functions of a legislature? We suggest that they include deliberation and lawmaking, legitimizing governmental decisions, representation, resolving conflicts and seeking consensus, public education, and overseeing the administration.

Deliberation and Lawmaking

In the late nineteenth century Woodrow Wilson characterized the American government as "congressional government." Congress not only enacted the laws, but it also initiated legislative proposals and, through its committees, dominated the administration of the laws that it passed.

The *lawmaking* powers of Congress remain impressive. There is hardly an aspect of American public policy—foreign or domestic—that is not significantly affected by congressional action (or inaction). Among the major legislatures of the Western world, it alone is still capable of initiating major legislation (see the history of the depressed-areas bill in Chapter 6). More important, Congress has proved that it can modify or alter those measures proposed by the executive that it chooses to enact. No one would assert today, however, as Wilson did, that Congress dominates the executive branch, even when the President is not aggressive in leading the legislature, as President Dwight D. Eisenhower was not.

The nineteenth century was characterized by the doctrines of laissez-faire, social Darwinism, and "strict constructionism" in constitutional law. Government was a passive instrument that imposed minimal restraints on an economy thought to be largely self-regulating and that provided relatively few services (few were demanded). Accommodation of interests, of course, had to take place. It could be accomplished by relatively simple statutory enactments—legislation developed primarily by Congress itself. The government was so small and the sums of money involved were so restricted that Congress, through its various committees, could with reasonable efficiency draw up the entire federal budget; the Budget and Accounting Act of 1921 transferred this function to the executive. Nor had the executive branch's role in foreign policy yet given it the influence that it exercises over total national policy in the 1970s. The United States' role in world affairs, even in the expansionist era of the late nineteenth and early twentieth centuries, was relatively modest. Congress could still interject itself forcibly, if somewhat spasmodically, into basic foreign-policy concerns, as when the Senate rejected the Treaty of Versailles and the League of Nations.

The role of Congress has changed markedly, however. David B. Truman, commenting on the current state of national legislatures, has observed that this century has been marked by "parliamentary crisis." National legislatures have been compelled to cope with the "complexities of increasingly urbanized, industrialized, and irrevocably interdependent societies."[2] This is a different world from the one Wilson was writing about in *Congressional Government*, and, correspondingly, the passive government of yesterday has today become a massive "service state," providing assistance in varying degrees to all segments of society and assuming responsibility for maintaining a prosperous economy. In order to provide necessary services to an interdependent society and to guide an economy with an annual gross national product (GNP) of approximately $1 trillion, Congress has been forced to rely increasingly on the expertise of the executive branch. The successful implementation of today's extensive, and expanding, governmental programs requires continuous administrative supervision and flexibility. Congress is not equipped to administer the day-to-day demands of a "service state." It does not have the time, the manpower, or the knowledge required. Nor can Congress act quickly enough to modify existing laws to bring them into accord with conditions that change almost daily. As a result, Congress has delegated to the executive branch vast amounts of discretionary authority over public policy. This delegation has been accompanied, of course, by an increase in the political power of administrators and by concomitant shifts in the locus of political conflict. How a bill is administered by the discretion of the executive bureaucracy is today as important as the actual content of the bill originally enacted by Congress.

The expanding scope of administrative activity and the accumulation of technical expertise in the hands of administrators has resulted in marked attrition of congressional power to initiate new legislation. The President, with superior informational and technical staff, and publicity resources, has emerged as the chief legislator. It is he who is expected to provide Congress with a comprehensive legislative program. Contemporary pundits and future historians will judge him on the scope and adequacy of his proposals. His batting average in getting his program adopted by Congress will be computed and compared (perhaps unfairly) with that of other Presidents. Gone are the days when Congress could, with wounded pride, castigate a Cabinet officer for the "effrontery" of having his department draft a bill for submission to Congress, as it did to the Secretary of Interior in 1908. Now it is considered the job of high executive officials to supervise the drafting of bills and then to steer them through Congress.

The formulation of legislative proposals within the executive branch is, however, an extremely complicated and often lengthy process, not unlike the one that operates within the legislative branch. The "war on poverty" proposals, for example, directly affected several administrative departments and agencies, each of which represented, in the councils of the administration, powerful and often conflicting interests within the country. It was therefore necessary for the President to exert strong leadership, if a bill was to emerge from the executive branch. The final package was in reality a treaty negotiated among the various factions within the administration (see Chapter 7 for further discussion).

The massive involvement of the United States around the world and the delicate nature of the present balance of international power have meant that the government must deal with situations—like the 1962 Cuban missile crisis, the Berlin Wall, Arab-Israeli confrontations, and war in Korea and Vietnam—that may arise suddenly and require decisive action based upon detailed information and on an understanding of the impact of any proposed action on other governmental policies. The conduct of foreign affairs also requires the ability to engage in confidential and delicate negotiations—for example, on the nuclear-test ban, the Strategic Arms Limitation Talks (SALT), the Middle East truce, the return of Okinawa to Japan. As in domestic affairs, the exigencies of American world involvement have thrust upon the executive initiative in policy making along with its traditional responsibility for execution.

The functions of the executive and the legislature have come to be the reverse of those that the Founding Fathers intended. Congress was expected to propose and enact new programs, with the President acting as the restraining agent armed with a veto. Today the President initiates most major legislation, while Congress frequently exercises the veto power by defeating or drastically changing the President's proposals.

While this may be what some have called an "executive-centered" age, one can excessively depreciate the role of Congress. The President's resources for influencing and leading Congress are great indeed. But it should be remembered that it is still Congress, and not the President, that passes the laws. The centers of power may have shifted in the twentieth century, but the legislative process remains one of bargaining, consensus seeking, and compromise, as people strive to find a majority on each issue. Alternating between docility and hostility, Congress has impressed this realization on all modern Presidents from Truman to Nixon.

Indeed, the congressional role in initiating legislative proposals is probably much more extensive than many commentators (including political scientists) would have us believe. James Sundquist found, for example, that most of President Kennedy's legislative program was developed for him by his party's policy activists in the Senate in the 1950s.[3] Similarly, Lyndon B. Johnson's legislative program was "incubated" in Congress and gathered support there before it was "hatched" by the President. A major Nixon administration initiative in domestic policy—revenue sharing—was also nurtured in Congress by such leaders as Congressman Melvin Laird (R.-Wis.) and Senator Edmund Muskie (D.-Maine) before it was presented as part of the President's program of domestic reform to a nationwide television audience. It may well be that the best route to placing a bill on the President's legislative agenda "is occasioned by a series of thoughtful congressional hearings and sponsorship by respected senators who have already begun generating publicity and support for the 'new' proposal."[4] (In Chapter 3, the role of Senator Abraham Ribicoff [D.-Conn.] as such a policy entrepreneur is described in detail.)

In those instances in which the policy initiative does clearly rest with the executive, as it did in the development of the "war on poverty," Congress, as a representative and intensely political institution, quickly responds to the forces unleashed by new programs. The speed and vigor with which it reacted to the changed political environment occasioned by the enactment of antipoverty legislation are described in Chapters 4 and 7.

Apart from Congress' vitality in initiating and incubating new policy directions and in responding to presidential proposals, the President and the executive bureaucracy have extensive influence on the legislative process. Despite constitutional separation of powers, officials in the executive branch are participants in the work of the legislative branch. The role and strategies adopted by the Nixon administration in its relations with the House of Representatives are explored through a series of "case studies" in Chapter 4.

In the sphere of foreign policy a President cannot act without money, matériel, and manpower, both civil and military. To a large extent Congress controls the amounts and quality of these resources. As a result of the Vietnam war, Congress has sought to use these powers to gain a larger voice in the conduct of foreign policy. For example, during Senate consideration of proposals to extend the draft in 1971, an amendment calling for an end to American military involvement in Vietnam within nine months (provided that North Vietnam would release American prisoners of war) was approved. (Congress' overall response to the Vietnam war is considered in more detail in Chapter 9.)

Legitimizing Government Decisions

Congress thus remains, as it has been from the beginning, the official lawmaker of the nation. It is, however, more than a "bill and resolution factory" whose members are to be graded on a "piecework basis."[5] As a representative assembly, it includes among its functions the legitimation of political leadership and political decisions. A minimum requirement for every stable governmental system is that its decisions be accepted by the vast majority of the citizenry. At one time the doctrine of the divine right of kings was used to induce the necessary public acceptance. The explosion of that myth and the development of democratic ideologies vesting ultimate political power in the hands of the people meant that new justifications for the exercise of political power were required. Theories and devices of representation (like popular election of delegates to a national assembly and decisions by a majority vote in the assembly) provide citizen control over governmental decision makers in accordance with the dictates of democratic theory. Representation thus converts a "leader" into a "representative" and "power" into legitimate "authority."[6] An institution that can induce acceptance of its decisions, no matter how controversial (as were the Civil Rights Act of 1964 and the Medicare Act of 1965), is indispensable to a stable political system.

The policies emerging from our national legislature may not necessarily be the best solutions to particular problems (though this kind of question is difficult to judge objectively), for the process of decision making in Congress normally involves an almost endless process of negotiation and compromise. Bargaining produced, as is demonstrated in Chapter 6, a far different depressed-areas bill than its sponsors originally intended. Indeed, it can be argued that pork-barrel features incorporated to ensure passage considerably lessened the desired economic impact of the program. But, once enacted, the program was accepted as a piece of the "national consensus." And, although the administrative instruments and techniques have been modified over the years, the policy commitment to aid depressed areas seems firmly fixed. The depressed-areas legislation thus illustrates one of the continuing dilemmas of democratic and majoritarian politics. How does a society achieve policies that are both "good" and accepted? However responsive to citizens' preferences it may be, democratic decision making holds forth no assurance that "good" policies will be forthcoming; it is simply based on the assumption that no policy will be viable unless it is considered legitimate and worthy of support.

Representation

Certainly contributing to the ability of Congress to have its decisions accepted is the widespread assumption by the public and the legislators that Congress represents the wishes of the people. *Representation* of society's interests is therefore an important function of Congress. But beyond its significance for inducing acceptance of governmental decisions, a representative assembly is essential to a free society because it keeps the government sensitive and responsive to the society's needs and concerns. Indeed, Congress is "psychologically as well as politically a representative body."[7] The mystique of the President, as Chief of State, and that of the Supreme Court set them apart and protect them from much criticism: Both institutions operate in an aura of dignity and high purpose, unlike congressmen and senators. Plainly visible and expected to handle willingly even the petty problems of their constituents, congressmen are obviously mortal, reflecting our own weaknesses and strengths. Such a body of men and women is a ready-made target for criticism.

Representation is, of course, a complex phenomenon.[8] For one thing, legislators may perceive the interests of their constituents in quite different ways. Witness the divergent manner in which Senators Jacob Javits and James

Buckley represent the same geographic area, New York. Legislators also exhibit a diversity of representational *styles*. A recent survey of House members, for example, revealed that 23 percent consider themselves *delegates*, reflecting their constituents' sentiments, whereas 28 percent have adopted the *trustee* role, exercising their own judgment. A more common (46 percent) representational style is that of the *politico*, who seeks to balance both the delegate and trustee roles. The practice of representation is further complicated by the fact that congressmen have more than one *focus* for their representational activities. Some try to represent what they consider a national interest, many more focus upon their districts, and still others seek to represent both national and district interests.[9] Although legislators can perceive their representational roles variously and can even respond differently to the same constituency, it is important to note that no less than 82 percent of a sample of congressmen interviewed in the mid-1960s declared that their most important task was "determining, representing, and protecting the interests of the people."[10]

Furthermore, insecurity of job tenure arising from the system of popular elections also encourages (perhaps "forces" is a better word) sensitivity to social and constituent needs, especially in an electoral system so decentralized that each member must rely in considerable degree upon his own resources to stay in office (see Chapter 2, which deals with the elections of a senator and a representative). In addition, the procedures of Congress permit widespread participation in its decisions. Members encourage their constituents to express their views on public policy and spend vast amounts of time, money, and energy maintaining lines of communication with them (Chapter 3 describes how Senator Ribicoff and Congressman John Anderson [R.-Ill.] have organized their offices for this purpose).

With its loosely organized party system, its specialized committees that further decentralize power, and its lengthy and almost unbelievably complex procedures, there are multiple points of access and influence within Congress. Virtually all interests have an opportunity to influence Congress or, to borrow a phrase used in another governmental branch, "to have their day in court." This openness of the procedures also makes it possible for Congress to function as a legitimizing agent.

It should never be assumed, however, that because Congress accords virtually everyone an opportunity to be heard, everyone has an *equal* opportunity to exert influence. For example, one effect of the Founding Fathers' decision to permit equal state representation in the Senate (in an attempt to pacify the fears of small states) has been to increase the influence of interests located in sparsely populated areas—for example, farmers, mining industrialists, and southern segregationists. Nor is the seniority system for choosing committee chairmen neutral in impact. Rather, as is illustrated by the analysis of the Senate Banking, Housing, and Urban Affairs Committee in Chapter 5, it enhances the influence of legislators from safe one-party areas because chairmen are chosen for having served continuously on particular committees longer than other members of the majority party. When the Democrats control Congress, the southern members of the party are thus apt to hold a high proportion of the committee chairmanships; when the Republicans are in power, these positions are occupied primarily by members from midwestern areas. The extent to which the seniority system bolsters southern influence in Congress can be seen by the fact that in the 92nd Congress (1971-1972) southerners chaired eight of twenty-one House committees and nine of seventeen committees in the Senate.

Congressional procedures, with many built-in opportunities for delay and obstruction, make it easier to defeat a bill than to pass one. Even a handful of people strategically located on the right committee or subcommittee can do it. Groups or forces that are on the defensive thus have an advantage in Congress.[11] In addition, it has been argued that, because of the way in which legislators are elected, they are particularly responsive to local elites and thus inject a strong parochial influence into national policy making.[12] Congress is obviously not a perfect reflection of the political forces in American life, but people do accept its decisions. One contemporary scholar has therefore defended it in these terms:

> Congress has the strength of the free enterprise system; it multiplies the decision makers, the points of access to influence and power, and the creative moving agents. It is hard to believe that a small group of leaders could do better. What would be gained in orderliness might well be lost in vitality and in sensitiveness to the pressures for change. Moreover, Congress resembles the social system it serves; it reflects the diversity of the country. There is much to be said for a system in which almost every interest can find some spokesman, in which every cause can strike a blow, however feeble, in its own behalf.[13]

Public Education

The activities of Congress are "news," and Congress is a prime subject for coverage in the national news media. Because of this capacity to generate publicity, Congress performs the function of *public education*. That is, Congress through its deliberations informs the public on issues and raises the level of public interest in current problems.

Because of well-publicized committee hearings and floor debates and the press releases that flow constantly from members' offices, there are few matters that do not receive congressional publicity. Often the publicity surrounding congressional activities has helped to crystallize public opinion on issues and has thus facilitated the passage of new legislation.

The vocal efforts of congressional Democrats, for example, helped to mobilize the public support needed to pass the depressed-areas bill of 1961 (see Chapter 6). Similarly, the publicity given to persistent criticism of American Southeast Asian policy at hearings of the Senate Foreign Relations Committee no doubt played a role in changing public opinion and governmental policy on this vital issue. Congress provides an effective channel of communications even for its most junior members. In 1971 two freshman members of the House—Robert H. Steele (R.-Conn.) and Morgan F. Murphy (D.-Ill.)—dramatized the magnitude of drug addiction among GIs in Vietnam. Their activities resulted in stepped-up efforts by the Department of Defense and the Veterans Administration to deal with the problem.

Congress is thus more than an object of public opinion. Its relation to the electorate is reciprocal. Although influenced by the voters, it is also constantly engaged in stimulating public interest in current issues and in influencing public thinking.

Resolving Conflict and Consensus Building

Politics invariably involves conflicts of varying intensity. Conflict is the dynamo of politics; yet, though indispensable, it can destroy a political system when passions are too intense or ideological positions too inflexible. An institution for resolving conflict and consensus building is required. Congress is such an institution. It must do more than make decisions of staggering proportions; its decisions must be made so that in the process the political system is not torn apart. A political system, then, cannot be judged solely on the basis of the speed with which it deals with matters of public concern; there is also the question of how well the system is maintained in the process. It is simple to condemn the 1964 Senate for having spent eighty-seven days in a filibuster against the civil rights bill. (The administration is less often condemned for taking two years to draft and send to Congress a comprehensive civil rights bill.)[14] But such criticism ignores the fact that the resulting bill had the overwhelming support of both Democrats and Republicans, along with a scattering of southern and border-state representatives. Although at first there seemed to be no agreement on the need for certain provisions, like the ban on discrimination in places of public accommodation, by the end of the deliberations the divergent factions had agreed that such a ban was indeed necessary. This bill, like most that emerge from the tortuous legislative halls, was too weak to satisfy some and too strong to satisfy others. But it did represent a broad area of agreement on probably the most controversial domestic issue of our time. The conflict had been blunted; a temporary consensus had been reached.

Congress is well adapted to serve the functions of conflict resolution and consensus building because it is an arena of decentralized power in which each participant has some means of influencing the outcome of its deliberations. Because in our democratic system political parties cannot impose rigid discipline upon their members, Congress' decisions are normally the result of extensive bargaining and compromise, as various congressional leaders—committee chairmen, party leaders, subject-matter experts, state delegation leaders, bloc leaders—negotiate the outcomes of the legislative process. These outcomes are seldom entirely satisfactory to all, but they are usually sufficient to mitigate conflict until the issue can again be raised in any or all three branches of the government. For legislative enactments are seldom clear-cut or final resolutions of important issues. Rather, they are the verbal formulas that "a majority of congressmen find adequate as a basis for their continuing policy struggle."[15] A new law reflects a different balance of forces and provides the ground rules under which the political struggle will continue. Chapters 4 and 6 provide evidence of the continuing nature of battles over public policy, in the intense struggles over "war on poverty" programs, from their inception within the executive branch through the biennial attempts in Congress to change (or abolish) the Office of Economic Opportunity (OEO).

Conflict resolution is frequently facilitated because even the losing side is seldom so weak that it cannot gain certain concessions, and it seldom has to accept a decision of Congress as unalterable. For example, in 1961, House Appropriations Committee Chairman Clarence Cannon (D.-Mo.) could not accept "back-door financing" for the depressed-areas bill. Although he lost on this issue when the bill was originally before the House, he was ultimately successful, in a later appropriations bill, in eliminating "back-door financing" (see Chapter 6).

Overseeing the Administration

Long before the rise of the modern "service state," John Stuart Mill expressed reservations about the capacity of legislative assemblies to legislate. He nonetheless believed that these deliberative bodies have an essential contribution to make to the protection of liberty. In 1878 he wrote:

> The proper office of a representative assembly is to watch and control the government; to throw the light of publicity on its acts; to compel a full exposition and justification of all of them which any one considers questionable; to censor them if found condemnable, and if the men who compose the government abuse their trust, or fulfill it in a manner which conflicts with the deliberative sense of the nation, to expel them from office . . . . This is surely ample power, and security enough for the liberty of the nation.[16]

The function to which Mill was referring is commonly called *legislative oversight of administration*. It is a legislative function that most observers believe has taken on renewed significance with the rise of the "service state" and the executive's assumption of wide discretionary powers to make policy within the framework of broad congressional mandates contained in the statutes. Some believe that oversight is now and will continue to be the principal function of Congress as long as mammoth administrative establishments are required. Congress itself formally recognized the importance of this role by placing a provision in the Legislative Reorganization Act of 1946 directing each of the standing committees of Congress to exercise "continuous watchfulness" over the agencies under their jurisdiction. This section of the law reflects a fearful recognition in Congress that this century's changes in legislative-executive relations have resulted in presidential encroachment on congressional power. Conscientious attention to the oversight function, it was thought, might at least halt the diminution of congressional power.

Although important decisions are increasingly being made by federal administrators rather than by Congress, these decisions are no less political in character. Only the locus for the decisions has changed. Congressmen and senators therefore retain a concern about the administration of laws; it is good politics to know how the administrators are treating interests and constituents.

The power of Congress to control administrative activity rests ultimately on its authority to pass laws affecting an agency: granting an agency the right to exist at all or to perform given functions; prohibiting certain agency actions; arranging the administrative structure of the agency; and granting or withholding funds. These powers augment such other, less formal techniques as committee hearings and investigations, instructions or criticisms in committee reports or floor statements, committee clearance of administrative actions, and informal communications between congressional and agency personnel. The existence of such formal and informal methods of influence forces administrators to develop a sensitivity to congressional thinking and to try to make their decisions as palatable as possible to those members of Congress interested in agency programs. Congress has become a "court of appeals" in which citizens and interests adversely affected by administrative decisions seek redress for their grievances with the bureaucracy.

The standing committees are the principal agents for performing the oversight function. There is, however, considerable variability from committee to committee in aggressiveness as overseers. Some, like the Joint Atomic Energy Committee, are extremely active and powerful.[17] Others, like the Senate Banking, Housing and Urban Affairs Committee, described in Chapter 5, are more passive.

Understanding Congress

There is good cause for concern about the operation of Congress. Congress has a profound influence on public policy and performs functions essential to a stable democratic order. Its future is also the nation's future. Concern about this future is widely apparent in the readiness of scholars, politicians, and commentators to prescribe reforms for congressional behavior. The views of the reformers and the actual process of congressional reform are analyzed in Chapter 8.

But, although there may be a surfeit of reform proposals, there is also a dearth of models for how a legislature should operate that take into account all its manifold functions and parts. Perhaps even more important is the absence of a model for describing how legislatures do operate. Without knowledge about an institution beyond superficial conventional wisdom there can be little useful reform.

In the past failures to understand adequately the congressional context have resulted in reforms with unintended consequences. For example, the reduction of the number of congressional committees and the clearer statement of their jurisdictions in the Legislative Reorganization Act of 1946 were intended to make the system more efficient and to reduce jurisdictional conflicts among committees over control of particular bills. Jurisdictional conflicts were indeed reduced, but an unintended consequence of the change was to reinforce further the seniority system (the problems posed for political parties by this system are considered in Chapter 4). Furthermore, the leadership structure was decentralized through reduction of the discretionary powers of the presiding officer in each chamber to assign bills to those committees in which they would receive the kind of treatment that he favored. Consolidation of standing committees also resulted in a proliferation of subcommittees in response to certain basic needs of the legislators: specialization in committee deliberations and additional power centers at which members might pursue their legislative goals.

To be practicable, reforms must be adaptable to various aspects of the congressional environment. They must help the institution and its participants to meet their needs. It makes little sense, for example, to propose reforms taken from British parliamentary practice if the American political system lacks the prerequisites to make them work—such as a parliamentary form of government rather than a presidential form, or a disciplined and responsible party system rather than a decentralized party system. Therefore, adequate knowledge of the institution is basic to sensible reform.

Elections: The Threat to Tenure

The ultimate basis of a congressman's or senator's power is his ability to satisfy his constituents at election time. The nature of the process of recruiting, nominating, and electing candidates for Congress obviously has a profound effect upon the behavior of legislators. The tendency of the Senate to be more liberal than the House is on most issues (civil rights legislation has been an important exception), for example, can be explained largely by the different constituencies and electoral problems faced by congressmen and senators. Senators represent whole states, most of which contain diverse interests and at least one major urban center each. They must therefore show concern for urban interests, particularly the active minorities—labor unions, racial minorities, religious-ethnic groups—that can critically affect elections. No senator from a large state, for example, dares to appear antilabor or anti-civil rights if he wants to survive. Because they come from smaller and more homogeneous constituencies, a much larger percentage of representatives can be expected to be conservative.[18] This example is only one of many showing how the intentions of the Founding Fathers, who expected the Senate to serve as a conservative check on the popularly elected House, have been reversed by the political developments of the twentieth century.

The electoral process also contributes to one of Congress' most salient characteristics: its decentralized power structure. The campaigns of Senator Joseph Tydings (D.-Md.) and Representative William Steiger (R.-Wis.), to be discussed in Chapter 2, illustrate the loosely structured nature of the party system. Upon each was thrust the major responsibility for acquiring and utilizing the resources necessary for victory at the polls. Both Tydings and Steiger developed personal campaign organizations and conducted campaigns of highly localized character, reflecting their own personal backgrounds and legislative interests.

The decentralized nature of the American party system is nowhere more apparent than in nominations for Congress, in which the national party plays virtually no role. Rather, as V. O. Key pointed out, each state or congressional district "exercises complete autonomy in the designation of nominees for Senate and House."[19] Because of the national party's inability to coordinate nominations and to select compatible candidates to run under the party's banner, there is little potential for unified and disciplined party organization within the national legislature. To be sure, in some places the state or local party organization is so strong that it can cast its mantle upon a man and designate him as the party's nominee. The usual pattern of congressional nominations, however, is for the candidate to build a personal organization and base of support—one that can sustain him through times when his party is in disfavor with the voters or when its leaders may oppose him.

Not only the party system but also the present legal system of making nominations—the direct primary, which is used in all but a handful of states— works against centralized control of the selection process. The primary was evolved in the early years of this century in reaction against the machinations of party conventions and legislative caucuses; it was intended to permit more citizen participation in party affairs and to provide meaningful popular elections in those areas where single-party domination had rendered general elections mere formalities.

The effects of the system, however, have not fulfilled the reformers' hopes. Participation is lower at the primary level than at the general election level. Furthermore, factional lines within the majority party are often highly fluid from year to year, which has meant that incumbents can usually expect to win renomination. The primary has often tended to diminish competition between the parties, as voters and party workers channel their energies into the majority party, where the crucial electoral battles take place. The primary nomination procedure has also weakened party organizations by making it more difficult for them to control and influence nominations. The dependence of a representative or senator upon the party organization for his political survival has thus been reduced. Representatives and senators with strong personal followings have been able to flout state or local organizations by defeating organization candidates in the primaries. The winners then force the organizations to accept them as bona fide party candidates in the general elections. The Tammany Hall organization of New York, for example, failed miserably in its attempt to purge Democratic Congressman Adam Clayton Powell because of his support of President Eisenhower, a Republican, in 1956. But for the candidate and his organization the primary may mean an expenditure of money and other resources in two contests, as Senator Tydings discovered in 1970.

The decentralizing impact of the nominating process is partially offset, however, by the centralizing tendencies of the general election. Here, traditional party affiliations, national issues, and, in presidential years, the presidential ticket, can exert powerful influence on the fate of congressional candidates, who may be hurt or helped by grasping the coattails of their parties' presidential candidates or by national swings in voter sentiment.

National trends are most important in Senate races, for party competition has become increasingly intense at the state level and in some highly competitive congressional districts. Most House seats are, however, safe for one party or the other. Indeed, there has been a trend during this century toward fewer and fewer House districts that are truly competitive between the two parties. Relatively few seats are apt to change hands even when a party's presidential nominee wins by landslide proportions. Even in Lyndon Johnson's sweep of the presidential election in 1964, by the widest margin in this century, the Democrats registered a net gain of only 38 of 435 House seats (8.7 percent).

Despite the strong pull of national trends, candidates may be able to fight the current and survive politically by building strong personal followings or perhaps by dissociating themselves from their national parties. For example, in 1968, though Richard Nixon carried Indiana with 65 percent of the major-party vote, Democratic Senator Birch Bayh was able to withstand the trend. Equally impressive were the 1964 victories of Republican Senators Hiram Fong and Hugh Scott in Hawaii and Pennsylvania, where President Johnson received 78.7 and 64.9 percent of the vote respectively.

Given the importance of satisfactory constituency relations, it is small wonder that legislators spend vast amounts of time, money, energy, and staff resources on the "care and feeding" of their states or districts. The activities of Congressman Anderson of Illinois and Senator Ribicoff of Connecticut, discussed in Chapter 3, and the campaign of Congressman Steiger (Chapter 2) show that a legislator's mind is seldom far from those who have elected him. For the incumbent legislator, the campaign actually never ends.

A resourceful member of Congress can frequently use the advantages of incumbency—publicity, constituency service, newsletters, and questionnaires mailed to his constituents—to consolidate his hold on his seat. Indeed, the advantages of incumbency are so great that more than 80 percent of all representatives and senators win reelection, which means, of course, that Congress is a highly stable institution not normally given to sudden shifts in policy.

No two members of Congress face the same electoral problems. Steiger, for example, has a reasonably safe district in which party organizations are weak; others, like Ribicoff and Tydings, have had to operate in more competitive environments and in Ribicoff's example within the framework of cohesive and well-organized parties (see Chapters 2 and 3).

The very uniqueness of electoral situations within the various states and the absence of cohesive and disciplined national party organizations to control candidate recruitment and nomination mean that the leadership of Congress must be loose, for it cannot ensure a member's job security. The harsh truth of congressional politics is that if a member is rejected by his constituency he cannot, in our system, be given another and safer district in which to run.

The Party in Congress

Although the decentralized American party system thus produces legislators who are basically "ambassadors" from their respective districts and states, the congressional party should never be considered insignificant or impotent. By virtue of its being the most inclusive group within either chamber, it operates as the major unifying force within Congress. When a party controls the White House, its congressional contingent has a special focus and unity, as is demonstrated in the discussion of the Republicans during the Nixon administration in Chapter 4.

Party membership is for members of Congress a source of personal identity and a matter of emotional attachment and loyalty. Furthermore, the party supplies each member with benefits that he cannot do without, including all-important committee assignments, leadership positions, office space, cues on how to vote, reliable political information, campaign assistance, and friendly associations within the chamber. Formal leadership positions in the party hierarchy in Congress are considered of sufficient importance and power that men will risk a great deal in terms of their standing with their colleagues to gain such positions, as was shown in the struggle for positions of strength among Democratic senators and representatives in 1971 (see Chapter 4).

Objective proof of the importance of party in congressional decision making has been furnished by studies of roll-call votes in each chamber. They show that though each party is torn by internal disagreements, there is a sharp difference between the parties on major issues of public policy.[20] That is, on issues usually classified as indexes of liberalism and conservatism, the Republicans are clearly more conservative and less liberal than are the Democrats. One test of liberalism or conservatism is the extent to which members of Congress vote in accordance with the views of Americans for Democratic Action (ADA), an interest group widely recognized for its liberal ideology.

The general policy divergence between the two parties is graphically por-

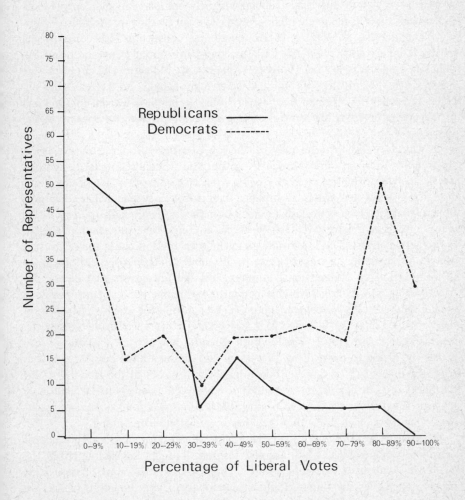

Figure 1
The Overall Liberalism Scores of Members of Congress on ADA rated roll calls.

trayed in Figure 1. The Republicans tend to cluster toward the conservative side of the scale, whereas the Democrats' predominant sentiments are more liberal. This difference can also be found in the individual scores of senators. Of the eleven senators scoring 90 percent or higher, ten were Democrats and only one a Republican; of the seventeen senators with scores from 0 to 3 percent thirteen were Republicans and four Democrats.

Of course, Figure 1 also demonstrates the diversity of views within each party, particularly within the Democratic Party, which has a sizable conservative bloc (primarily, but not exclusively, composed of southerners) in both chambers as well as its significantly larger liberal wing. By comparison, the congressional Republican Party is relatively homogeneous, though far from monolithic.

Leading the heterogeneous groupings that constitute both congressional parties is an extremely delicate task, as complaints about Democratic and Republican leadership in the 1960s (see Chapter 4) indicate. The problems are manifest in the difficulties that Congressman Gerald Ford (R.-Mich.) encountered when he assumed the post of House Republican Leader in 1965 and in the plight of John McCormack during his lengthy tenure as Speaker of the House.

Whatever the obstacles may be, the job of a party leader in Congress is to try to hold divergent party elements together and to create a majority on each issue. This task often requires picking up votes from the other side of the center aisle that divides the parties. In building majorities, party leaders have few sanctions available. There is no lash to crack over the heads of recalcitrant members who know that the basis of their positions as congressmen or senators is satisfying their districts. The leader must bargain with his colleagues and rely on his powers of persuasion, a sense of party loyalty among his troops, superior sources of information on congressional business, and the few favors that he can distribute: help in securing favorable committee assignments, assistance in scheduling important bills for debate, and public recognition for worthwhile service in the Congress. That party leaders lack vast formal powers was made clear by the late Speaker of the House Sam Rayburn when he remarked: "You cannot lead people by trying to drive them. Persuasion and reason are the only ways to lead them. In that way, the Speaker has influence and power in the House."[21] But the Speaker is in a position to hinder or advance the careers of his colleagues through the favors that he can bestow. "Mr. Sam" was fond of reminding the junior members of his party that "you have to go along to get along."

Robert A. Dahl has called the congressional party a "loose alliance of individual congressmen."[22] In similar fashion, Truman has characterized the legislative party as a "mediate group": That is, from the point of view of its members it does some things of importance for them; and though its failures are of consequence to them, the retention of their status as members of Congress does not completely depend upon it.[23]

The Committee System

The work load of the Congress is enormous. Almost 30,000 measures were introduced during the 91st Congress (1969 to 1970). Many of them involved problems of great complexity. Congress has found it necessary to delegate substantial portions of its responsibilities to smaller units: its standing committees. These committees sort out the bills worthy of serious consideration, a small fraction of which are reported out for final consideration on the floor of the House or Senate. The content of congressional decisions is largely shaped in these committees. Such vast powers have made the committees strategic points of influence in the legislative struggle. A corollary result has been that they have become specialized and semiautonomous power centers, further fragmenting power within each chamber. The power of the committees and their leaders over the fate of legislation under their jurisdiction has meant that party leaders must frequently try to reach accommodation with individual committee leaders.

How a committee functions depends largely upon its chairman and how he chooses to use the prerogatives of his office. These prerogatives include the power to call meetings, to set the agendas for meetings, to appoint committee staff, to control the expenditure of committee funds, to create subcommittees and to appoint their members, to control appointments to joint House-Senate conference committees, and to formally report bills approved by the committee. These powers must be used within the confines of what a committee majority will tolerate, for ultimately every chairman's power rests upon the support of his committee. The styles of committee leadership analyzed in Chapter 5 clearly show the reciprocal relations that exist between a chairman and his committee colleagues. The powers of a chairman are extensive enough, however, to make committee members reluctant to alienate him lest he withhold favors and help from them.

The different styles of committee leadership exhibited by the Senate Banking, Housing, and Urban Affairs Committee's recent chairmen provide impressive evidence of how a chairman can affect the operations of his committee. If he so chooses, he can weld it into an active and aggressive unit for developing legislation and overseeing administration, or he can use his powers to restrain his committee and prevent it from acting. The range of possible committee behavior patterns is suggested in Chapter 5.

This specialized and decentralized committee system is well adapted to the needs of relatively independent politicians who might be called "free enterprisers," or "political entrepreneurs," for each is engaged in operating a political enterprise for whose prosperity he is primarily responsible. A member with special competence or interest in a certain policy area is allowed to concentrate on that area on the appropriate committee—that is, provided that he manages to be assigned to the committee that he desires. Serving on a committee dealing with the interests of the people who elected him is one way for a congressman to help solve the problems of his constituency. Furthermore, the committee system, with its many chairmanships, subcommittees, and subcommittee chairmanships, gives a substantial number of members opportunities to win prestige, publicity, experience, and influence within Congress. (Senator Ribicoff's use of his subcommittee chairmanship on the Government Operations Committee is discussed in Chapter 3.)

Because committees can provide these services to individual members, and because of their pervasive influence on governmental policy, they are arenas of intense conflict. Committee rooms are battlegrounds in which propaganda can be generated, substantive and political information gathered, decisions made or postponed, and conflicts resolved. A committee can also perform a cathartic function by allowing various competing groups to express their views and feelings in a forum that conforms to the expectations of people nurtured on democratic values.[24] The committee can also be used as a device to control administrative agencies as they carry out the laws passed by Congress. How well a committee performs any of these functions is dependent upon various factors: the chairman and his style of leadership, the subcommittee organization, the nature of the membership, the ways in which the members view their jobs on the committee, the subject matter before the committee, the committee staff, and unwritten norms of committee behavior. The interplay of these factors is discussed in Chapter 5, which deals with the politics of the Senate Committee on Banking, Housing, and Urban Affairs.

The Job of a Member

Membership in Congress is no sinecure. Each representative or senator must vote on a series of complex issues of consequence for the nation and the world. Seldom are the alternatives before him entirely clear in their implications. The legislator is rarely satisfied with the information on which he must base his decisions. Yet decide he must, often in the face of conflicting demands from party, interest groups, constituency, and colleagues. In addition, he must attend to the business of his committee or committees; serve his constituents (answering torrents of letters that may run as many as 1,000 a day for a senator from a large state, returning to the district regularly, meeting visitors to the Capitol, and acting as personal travel agent and guide for some of them); handle satisfactorily his relations with party leaders, pressure groups, constituents, colleagues, and reporters; and properly discharge personal responsibilities like those to his family. These aspects of congressional life are apparent in the detailed portraits of Congressman Anderson and Senator Ribicoff in Chapter 3.

Despite the demands upon him, a member of Congress belongs to a "free profession"; that is, he makes his own work schedule, defines the content of his job, and sets its standards of achievement.[25] There are many different ways of being a congressman or senator, depending upon the individual's objectives and styles. Some, for example, choose to concentrate on providing prompt and efficient service to their constituents and on acting as agents of local and state interests; others choose to emphasize the planning and development of legislation; still others specialize in legislative tactics in the well-known fashion of Lyndon Johnson or the late Senator Everett Dirksen of Illinois. Some, like Senators Ribicoff and Barry Goldwater (R.-Ariz.), engage in educating external publics through various forums; some build and maintain powerful state or local political organizations (for example, the Virginia political "dynasty" of the late Democratic Senator Harry Flood Byrd, Sr.); and others use Congress to advance their presidential ambitions, as John F. and Robert F. Kennedy and Hubert H. Humphrey did. Each member chooses the kind of job that he wants to do and the kind of legislator that he wants to be.[26] Made up as it is of persons elected from separate and quite autonomous electoral districts, Congress is very tolerant in permitting a wide range of interpretations of the legislator's role. There is no one "right" way to be a representative or senator, though there are limits even in this highly permissive environment. For example, the Senate publicly condemned the late Senators Joseph McCarthy (R.-Wis.) and Thomas Dodd (D.-Conn.) for behavior unbecoming a senator. Other "deviants" may be ignored or discriminated against in more subtle ways, but such instances are rare.

Every member of Congress is forced to be highly selective in what he chooses to do because he lacks the resources to do all the things normally associated with his office. These resources include time, energy, staff assistance, information, and good will, all of which are in short supply. They must therefore be used where they will do the most good: that is, in helping the member to maximize his individual objectives from the legislative process. One of the most important decisions any congressman therefore makes is that of how and where he will use his scarce resources of influence.

Senator J. William Fulbright (D.-Ark.), for example, has chosen to devote most of his attention to foreign policy, whereas his Arkansas colleague, Democrat John McClellan, has stressed investigation of crime and corruption. Congressman Anderson and Senator Ribicoff (discussed in Chapter 3) have tended to be policy "generalists," periodically seizing the initiative on various issues.

To attain any objective a congressman must depend upon the assistance, or at least the acquiescence, of other members who are equally busy. What develops within Congress, therefore, is a complex set of relationships that require a great deal of bargaining, cooperation, compromise, and self-restraint if any member is to achieve even a portion of his objectives.

The environment is one of considerable strain for the individual member. There are the uncertainty of his tenure and the constant threat of having to find a new occupation or to return to a long-neglected one. This problem of tenure is made more difficult by the ambiguous relationship a member has with his party—one that makes demands upon him and to which he has an emotional commitment, but which cannot guarantee his tenure in office. There are also the conflicting pressures imposed on him by a constituency that does hold the key to job security, but whose sentiments he cannot comprehend fully, no matter how much energy he expends.[27] He must also bear the strains of the great work load and the continuous burden of performing errands for his district, which often force him to slight weighty legislative issues.

The pressures of politics are further intensified because Washington, D.C., is essentially a political city. Not only its values and standards of success but also the personalities with whom a legislator comes in contact are political in nature. There is no reprieve from the demands of the job. Even a social event is not without political overtones, for the congressman is usually in the company of other legislators, administrators, lobbyists, and reporters. Such pressures might be eased somewhat if the congressman thought that his was a profession revered and respected in American society, but unfortunately many do not think so. Rather, the average congressman considers that he is criticized and even ridiculed by people who do not understand his problems or his accomplishments. Even so, the satisfactions are many: seeing a cause in which he believes enacted into law, helping people, using power, and participating in exciting and important events.

This discussion is intended neither to justify nor to condemn present congressional practices, though the reader has no doubt accurately detected that the authors are basically friendly toward Congress. Rather, the discussion is designed to encourage understanding of why Congress functions as it does. The following chapters depict and analyze significant phases of congressional life—the campaign, the daily work load, floor activity, committee assignments and committee work, the impact of procedural rules, intraparty activity, the shaping of legislation, oversight of administration, and the role of the administration. These aspects of congressional life are presented through discussions of recent and specific events in the lives of congressmen.

NOTES FOR CHAPTER 1

1 Ralph K. Huitt, "Congressional Organization and Operations in the Field of Money and Credit," in Commission on Money and Credit, *Fiscal and Debt Management Policies* (Englewood Cliffs, N.J.: Prentice-Hall, 1963), p. 408.

2 David B. Truman, "Introduction: The Problem and Its Setting," in David B. Truman (ed.), *Congress and America's Future* (Englewood Cliffs, N.J.: Prentice-Hall, 1965), pp. 1-2.

3 James L. Sundquist, *Politics and Policy: The Eisenhower, Kennedy, and Johnson Years* (Washington, D.C.: Brookings, 1968), pp. 396-415.

4 Thomas E. Cronin, "The Textbook Presidency and Political Science" (Paper delivered at the Sixty-sixth Annual Meeting of the American Political Science Association, Los Angeles, September 1970), p. 32.

5 Huitt, "The Outsider in the Senate: An Alternative Role," *American Political Science Review,* 55 (September 1961), 566-575.

6 Theodore J. Lowi, *Legislative Politics*, U.S.A. (Boston: Little, Brown, 1962), p. ix.

7 Huitt, "What Can We Do About Congress?" *Milwaukee Journal*, December 13, 1964.

8 For an excellent analysis of how the process of representation actually operates, see Warren E. Miller and Donald E. Stokes, "Constituency Influence in Congress," *American Political Science Review*, 57 (March 1963), 45-57.

9 Roger H. Davidson, *The Role of the Congressman* (Indianapolis: Bobbs-Merrill, 1969), pp. 110-142.

10 *Ibid.*, p. 80.

11 Truman, *The Governmental Process* (New York: Knopf, 1951), p. 353.

12 See, for example, Thomas R. Dye and L. Harmon Zeigler, *The Irony of Democracy* (Belmont, Calif.: Wadsworth, 1970), chap. 10.

13 Huitt, "Congressional Organization," p. 494.

14 See Huitt, A Congressional Reorganization: The Next Chapter" (Paper delivered at the Annual Meeting of the American Political Science Association, Chicago, September 8-12, 1964), p. 3.

15 Raymond A. Bauer, Ithiel de Sola Pool, and Lewis Anthony Dexter, *American Business and Public Policy: The Politics of Foreign Trade* (New York: Atherton, 1963), p. 426.

16 John Stuart Mill, *Representative Government* (London: Longmans, 1878), p. 42.

17 Harold P. Green and Alan Rosenthal, *Government and the Atom: The Integration of Powers* (New York: Atherton, 1963).

18 See Lewis A. Froman, Jr., *Congressmen and Their Constituencies* (Chicago: Rand McNally, 1963), pp. 69-84.

19 V. O. Key, *Politics, Parties, and Pressure Groups* (5th ed.; New York: Crowell, 1964), p. 435.

20 Julius Turner, *Party and Constituency: Pressures on Congress* (Baltimore: Johns Hopkins University Press, 1951); and Truman, *The Congressional Party: A Case Study* (New York: Wiley, 1959).

21 "Rayburn is Dead; Served 17 years as House Speaker," *The New York Times*, November 17, 1961, p. 28.

22 Robert A. Dahl, *Congress and Foreign Policy* (New York: Harcourt, 1950), p. 51.

23 Truman, *The Congressional Party*, pp. 95-96.

24 Truman, *The Governmental Process*, pp. 369-377.

25 Bauer, Pool, and Dexter, *American Business and Public Policy*, p. 409.

26 *Ibid.*, pp. 409-410.

27 *Ibid.*, pp. 403-413.

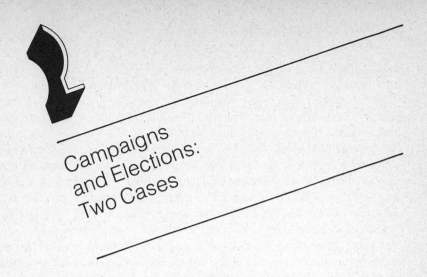

Campaigns
and Elections:
Two Cases

"I GUESS I WAS JUST TOO LIBERAL":
JOSEPH TYDINGS OF MARYLAND

Just before 3:00 in the morning Joseph Tydings, accompanied by his wife, Ginny, left his election night hideaway and walked the eight blocks to the Sheraton Belvedere Hotel in downtown Baltimore. He had made the hike twice before—once at around 9:00 P.M. and again at 11:30 P.M. Standing before the television cameras, he had twice thanked hundreds of youthful volunteer workers for their help in his reelection campaign for the United States Senate. Both times he had counseled them to ignore the lead of his opponent, freshman GOP Congressman J. Glenn Beall, Jr., and to await the Baltimore City returns.

All evening Tydings and his closest associates had been examining the returns. The night had been long and disappointing, but Tydings was repeatedly urged to delay any concession until heavily Democratic Baltimore, which was late in reporting its votes, had been heard from; perhaps the city vote would tip the election in Tydings' direction. Finally, the city returns were tallied and showed a Tydings margin of 57,000 votes—too little and too late to overcome Beall's edge in twenty-one of Maryland's twenty-three counties.

Walking through the rainy streets toward election night headquarters, Tydings mused to reporters: "I guess I was just too liberal . . . or at least they thought I was." Tydings went before the dwindling crowd of supporters. conceded that Beall had won, and offered his congratulations. His face betrayed the strain of the disappointing vigil, as he recalled the sentiments uttered by Adlai

Stevenson and Abraham Lincoln in similar circumstances: "I'm too old to cry, but it hurts too much to laugh." Many of Tydings' workers were unable to follow his example. One thirty-year-old staff aide, a veteran of the 1968 Eugene McCarthy campaign, stood helplessly in the hotel lobby with tears streaming down his face.

Five months before that November night Tydings had stood unchallenged in his 1970 reelection bid. And two months before the election his opinion-survey analysts, though detecting a certain "softness" in his support, had assured him that he was in no trouble. The ironies do not stop there. His eventual opponent was the son of former Senator J. Glenn Beal, Sr.—whom Tydings himself had whipped by 276,000 votes to win the Senate seat in 1964.

The Tydings campaign illustrates that incumbents in public office, despite the enormous advantages that they enjoy, are not assured of easy reelection. Obviously officeholders are expected to take stands on a wide variety of contro-versial issues. The more issues there are, the greater is the chance of alienating various segments of the electorate. (Meanwhile, challengers—if they are in private life or less prominent public posts—enjoy the luxury of avoiding such decisions or at least of making them in comparative obscurity.) Senators are more vulner-able than representatives in this respect; not only are they expected to master a wider range of issues, but they normally also have larger and more diverse constituencies to please. And, when they take positions, they usually receive greater publicity in the media than do their colleagues in "the other body."

For these reasons the Senate is more competitive than the House of Rep-resentatives; that is, elections tend to be closer, and incumbents are more fre-quently "bumped off."[1] In 1970, for example, seven, or 20 percent, of the thirty-five incumbents up for reelection were defeated either in the primaries or in the general elections. Four other senators retired, bringing the total turnover to almost one-third.[2] In Tydings' case the ordinary hazards of senatorial re-election were compounded by his nature and that of his constituency.

Politics in the Old Line State

The Old Line State illustrates the variety of constituent interests facing an office holder with a statewide constituency. Maryland is a state with three major regions. Tidewater Maryland, comprising the Eastern Shore and the southern portion of the Western Shore, is flat country, characterized by tobacco farms, resorts, fishing villages, and the traditions (and politics) of the rural South. Along the so-called "fall line," running approximately from Washington, D.C., to Baltimore and then to Wilmington, Delaware, lie large urban concentrations and piedmont farms. About 80 percent of the state's people live along this line: Baltimore City and Baltimore County; Harford, Howard, and Anne Arundel Counties; and the District of Columbia's bedroom counties, Montgomery and

Prince George's Counties. The population runs the gamut of urban areas everywhere: black ghetto dwellers, lower-middle-class white and ethnic concentrations, and affluent suburbanites. The third region of the state is the western, mountainous segment, dominated by mining and small farming.

Maryland lies south of the Mason-Dixon Line, and before the New Deal its politics had a distinctly southern complexion. After 1932 the conservative, southern-oriented "Bourbons" of Tidewater Maryland found themselves in uneasy alliance with the more or less liberal Baltimore party, composed of laborers, immigrants, and blacks. This urban party was also more than 50 percent Roman Catholic, in contrast to the rural Protestants of the Tidewater, whose opinions were rooted in the antebellum South.[3] When undisturbed by disunity or scandal, this fragile coalition of urban and rural Democrats usually prevailed over the minority GOP, whose major source of strength was the mountain population of western Maryland, nonslaveholding, pro-Union during the Civil War, and still strongly Republican.

Of all the variables used in analyzing state party politics, the one most favored by political scientists is "interparty competition," that is, the "normal" distribution of popular votes and public offices between Republicans and Democrats. Maryland has usually been classified as a "modified one-party Democratic" state: Most voters have identified with the majority (Democratic) party, though a significant minority have identified with the GOP.[4] Democrats have held more than a two to one edge in Maryland voter registration; in 1970, of 1,577,944 registered voters, 1,112,072 (70 percent) were Democrats and 421,409 (27 percent) Republicans.

Voter-registration figures (or even survey measures of party identification) do not tell the whole story, however. The rise of the GOP has been perhaps the most dramatic development of recent years in the border and southern states. In Maryland this trend can be attributed largely to two factors: the phenomenal growth of the suburban areas surrounding Baltimore and Washington, D.C., and the progressive estrangement of the Tidewater Bourbons and other traditional Democratic voters from the liberal tendencies of the national Democratic Party.

In Maryland, as in most border and southern states, "Republicanization" of office has taken place from the top down. Because grass-roots organization is difficult for a subordinate party to build, local and state legislative offices remain largely in the Democrats' hands. Statewide and national elections, on the other hand, can be won through publicity and media campaigning and are therefore more competitive. Although the Maryland legislature is invariably Democratic, elections to federal offices are competitive. In 1970 the state's congressional delegation was split evenly between the two parties, whereas more than four of five state legislators were Democrats. From 1946 through 1970 three Republicans and four Democrats had been elected governor, and in U.S. Senate races during the same period there had been five Republican and three Democratic victors. The state had cast its electoral votes for GOP presidential candidates three times and for Democrats three times. In 1968, the year of the state's last Senate election, Republican Charles "Mac" Mathias had ousted the incumbent Democrat, Daniel Brewster, by winning 55 percent of the two-party vote cast.[5] Clearly party competition in Maryland is bifurcated: competitive in statewide contests, mostly Democratic in local contests.

The Democratic Party organization is centered in Baltimore but has counterparts in other areas. It is oiled by local and state patronage; its politics, insofar as it concerns itself with issues, is relatively conservative. In 1970 the organization was represented in the governor's mansion by Marvin Mandel, a longtime state legislator who had proved unusually popular in his two years as governor. Running for his first full term, he was conceded to be far ahead of any challengers. In the Shore counties party organization consisted essentially of the "courthouse rings" so familiar in the South; in western Maryland there was little effective party organization, but Democratic interests were promoted by labor unions.

"He Never Ducks the Tough Ones"

The Tydings name had been important in Maryland politics for half a century. The late Millard Tydings had been a senator for twenty-four years before his defeat in 1950. President Franklin D. Roosevelt had tried to "purge" the senior Tydings in 1938 for opposing major New Deal legislation; but it was a vicious Joseph McCarthy-era campaign depicting him as "soft on communism" that finally ended his political career. (The campaign featured a "doctored" photograph, purporting to show him with Communist Party leader Earl Browder.)

Joseph Davies Tydings, his son, was thus raised in prominence and affluence, taking his B.A. and law degrees from the University of Maryland and starting law practice in Baltimore in 1952. But a fierce independence dominated "Young Joe" Tydings' entire political career. After his appointment by President John F. Kennedy as U. S. Attorney for the District of Maryland, he had gained prominence by obtaining, in 1963, convictions of the popular Speaker of the Maryland House, A. Gordon Boone, and former Representatives Thomas F. Johnson (D.-Md.) and Frank W. Boykin (D.-Ala.) on charges of conspiracy and conflict of interest in Maryland savings-and-loan deals. Tydings, a friend of President Kennedy, had served as his campaign manager for the 1960 Maryland presidential primary. Then in 1964 Tydings had successfully challenged the organization's senatorial candidate, State Comptroller Louis L. Goldstein, and had gone on to score a victory over Beall, a twelve-year veteran of the Senate. Tydings had campaigned as a reform candidate who, as he said, wanted to "revitalize Maryland from slot machines, savings and loan, and Cambridge [an Eastern Shore town notorious for racial violence]."

In the Senate Tydings had continued his independent ways. He was a strong supporter of civil rights legislation and fought attempts to overturn the U.S. Supreme Court's reapportionment rulings. He was active in opposing President Richard M. Nixon's nominations of Clement Haynsworth and G. Harrold Carswell to the high court in spring 1970. He described the population explosion as "probably the greatest threat to mankind" aside from nuclear war and called for federal aid for voluntary family-planning programs—sentiments not likely to endear him to some of his state's more traditionally minded Roman Catholics. In August 1967 he broke with the Johnson administration over the Vietnam war and later became one of the first senators to endorse his friend, the late Senator Robert F. Kennedy, for the presidency. (Later still he supported Senator George McGovern but ended up working for the Humphrey-Muskie ticket in 1968.)

Tydings' most controversial role—ironically, as 1970 was supposed to be a good year for "law and order" candidates—was that of crime fighter. He had been active in the passage of the Omnibus Crime Control and Safe Streets Act (P.L. 90-351) in 1968. He had also sponsored a gun-control bill (P.L. 90-618) and had led an unsuccessful fight to include in that bill a provision for federal gun registration and licensing of gun owners. This activity had aroused the wrath of many gun owners—including hunters and marksmen—and in 1970 Tydings was "number-one target" of a national gun-lobby drive.

Crime control led Tydings into a different kind of controversy two years later. In 1969 the Senator had become the youngest Senate committee chairman when he was put in charge of the District of Columbia Committee. Although not an attractive assignment for most legislators, it intrigued Tydings because more than a million Marylanders lived in the suburbs of Washington and many of them worked in the city. The nation's capital, whose population is more than 70 percent black, arouses fear in suburbanites because of high crime rates and racial unrest, which erupted in rioting in April 1968. In his first major test on the Senate floor Tydings steered a controversial D.C. crime bill to passage; it was signed by President Nixon in July 1970.[6] The law's most celebrated section authorizes "no knock" searches under specified circumstances, allowing policemen to enter premises without notice. The act also authorizes the use of wiretapping evidence and pretrial detention of individuals charged with dangerous crimes. Civil libertarians fought a prolonged battle to defeat the bill; the leader of their forces, courtly and conservative Sam J. Ervin, Jr. (D.-N.C.), called the law "a sellout of constitutional liberties" to what he termed the "expediency of law and order." Tydings pronounced the bill "sound and constitutional."[7]

Tydings had compiled a record on a broad range of issues. As chairman of the Subcommittee on Improvements in Judicial Machinery, he was a recognized authority on the judicial system. Urban and consumer programs, intercity transit, tax reform, drug abuse, education, and maritime matters also received his attention. Although not a specialist in foreign policy, he had a record of opposition to the Vietnam war and defense spending that had earned him the label "dove." Clearly the Tydings record would be a major factor in his reelection campaign, for good or ill.

Tydings prepared to run a campaign centered around the issues and attempting to make a virtue of his controversial stands. The theme was "He never ducks the tough ones." By the end of the campaign some staff members were heard to mutter ironically, "Well, he should have ducked a few of the tough ones."

The Senator's independent ways had also prevented him from seeking a détente with the regular Democratic organization in his state. In his first senatorial campaign in 1964 he had run explicitly as a "reform" candidate. Two years later he had supported Representative Carlton Sickles in the gubernatorial primary against Attorney General Thomas B. Finan, the organization candidate. The primary winner had been neither Sickles nor Finan but perennial candidate George Mahoney, whose campaign had been noteworthy for attacks on open housing; his slogan: "Your home is your castle—Protect it!" In the election itself, frightened by Mahoney's appeals, hordes of moderate and liberal Democratic voters had been driven to the GOP candidate, a relatively unknown Baltimore County executive, Spiro T. Agnew. Both regular Democrats and Tydings forces blamed each other for the victories of Mahoney and then Agnew.

Mahoney, a sixty-eight-year-old Baltimore paving contractor who had run unsuccessfully in eight statewide races since 1950, was hardly an innocuous figure. He had received more than 40 percent of the vote against Agnew in 1966, and he appealed strongly to the conservative rural population and to blue-collar workers, both of whom were politically restless in 1970. After declaring for governor in January 1970, he had changed his mind in June and had said that he would oppose Tydings in the September 15 Democratic primary.

The Republicans, meanwhile, were having trouble finding a candidate to oppose Tydings in the general election. Speculation first centered on Rogers C. B. Morton, a popular Eastern Shore congressman and chairman of the Republican National Committee. Although Morton was considered the strongest opponent, surveys showed Tydings far ahead.[8] Whether for this or some other reason, Morton took himself out of the race on December 16, 1969, after a talk with President Nixon in which he promised to remain as GOP chairman.

For several months no Republican candidate appeared, though attention had turned to J. Glenn Beall, Jr., a freshman congressman from western Maryland and former minority leader of the state's House of Delegates. As the son of a two-term senator, he had a well-known name. His lack of identification with any particular issue could prove an advantage against Tydings, though in his short tenure in Congress he had been a loyal supporter of the Nixon administration. When in June he announced his candidacy for the Senate, it was reported that Vice-President Agnew had been instrumental in persuading him. The White House took an unusually active role in recruiting senatorial contenders in 1970 and was partly responsible for the choice of candidates in North Dakota,

Utah, and Nevada, as well as in Maryland. Although Beall insisted that his decision had been his own, it had certainly been strongly urged by the White House. And it brought concrete support from the White House as the campaign went along.

A final entrant in the race was Harvey Wilder, a fifty-eight-year-old engineer and minister from Hagerstown, who was running for the right-wing American Party. Wilder characterized both Tydings and Beall as "extreme liberals," adding that "there's not a dime's worth of difference between the two political parties." He called for winning the Vietnam war and curtailing big-city aid programs; he also joined Mahoney in opposing the "no knock" and preventive-detention features of the D.C. crime bill. Although he was a long way from the major-party candidates, Wilder was not regarded as a crackpot; in a period when "middle America" was believed to be militant, Wilder's showing could affect the outcome of the senatorial race.

The Campaign Organization

It is difficult to say when the Tydings campaign really began, but his Senate staff aides place the time somewhat after the 1968 presidential election. The campaign started with "a few very elementary and offhand things" like viewing sample campaign films and attending seminars sponsored by the Senate Democratic Campaign Committee. During the summer of 1969 the advertising agency that had handled the first Tydings campaign started filming sequences with the Senator "on location" around the state. The first official event of the campaign was a carefully planned Salute to Senator Joe Tydings dinner at the Baltimore Civic Center in October 1969. At $100 a plate, it grossed several hundred thousand dollars and provided important early money. A smaller fund-raising dinner was soon held in Washington.

On May 4, 1970, his forty-second birthday, Senator Tydings held a Baltimore news conference to announce, to no one's surprise, that he was a candidate for reelection. His campaign theme was stated early in his remarks: "In the Senate I have not ducked the tough issues. I do not believe the people of Maryland send their men to Washington to be a rubber stamp for any party, any President, or any special interest."

Behind every senatorial candidate is an extensive organization, which must perform many indispensable functions: It must probe voter opinion, raise money, handle publicity and advertising, schedule the candidate's appearances, and mobilize the vote on Election Day. Some of these functions are performed by groups outside the candidate's own organization, occasionally beyond his control entirely. But the core of the work must usually be done by the candidate's own people.

An incumbent, of course, has an office staff that continues to work on his behalf throughout the campaign. Often staff members are enmeshed in essentially campaign matters, but their day-to-day responsibilities for the senator do not lessen. Tydings' administrative assistant, Ken Gray, was consulted on major campaign decisions, but, because the Senate was in session during most of the campaign period, Gray and the office staff had very little time to think about the campaign. For one thing, they had to protect Tydings from distractions so that he could discharge his Senate duties, including steering the D.C. crime bill through the Senate.

Once Tydings had announced his candidacy, a central campaign head-quarters was opened in a storefront in downtown Baltimore. Seven or eight workers, the only paid staff, worked there. The state campaign chairman was Victor Cushwa, who oversaw strategy and coordinated the statewide effort. The operating head of the campaign was Executive Director M. Albert Figinski, a Baltimore lawyer who had served as staff director of Tydings' Subcommittee on Improvement in Judicial Machinery before switching to working full time on the campaign. Figinski saw to it that all the pieces of the campaign effort fit to-gether and took charge of liaison with the regular Democratic organization. Others who came from the Senator's office were Jo Ann Orlinsky, who handled scheduling, and Ernest Lotito, the press assistant.[9]

The volunteer precinct organization was in the hands of Mrs. Leah Freed-lander, an experienced political worker who occupied what was called the "war room" at headquarters. Voter registration was directed by Robert J. Fitzpatrick, a young man on leave from teaching at a private school in Baltimore. This campaign was "basically a young people's operation," with more than 200 col-lege and high-school students working as volunteers at one time or another.

Fund raising was headed by Irving Blum, a Baltimore mortgage banker. About seventeen separate committees were set up for fund-raising purposes. Most of the general funds were channeled through two groups called Tydings for Senator in 1970 and Marylanders for Tydings. The other committees were single-purpose groups set up to raise money for local advertising, opening and maintaining local Tydings headquarters (about six outside Baltimore), and so on. The only professional group, Lawyers for Tydings, was created mainly to raise money for a single advertisement in the *Baltimore Sun.*

The seed money for the campaign, as mentioned earlier, was raised late in 1969 at the Salute to Tydings dinners. Although fund raising received no special emphasis after that, it played a part in virtually every activity during the cam-paign: canvassing, advertising, personal appearances, and private solicitations. Just before the November election a large amount of money poured in, largely unsolicited and stimulated (so the staff speculated) by reaction to Vice-President Agnew's campaigning against Tydings. As this late money had not been planned for, it could not be put to the best use. The funds did help to finance last-minute saturation radio advertising, but most prime television time had been bought by that time. "If we'd had the money, or known we were going to have it, a week earlier, it would have had four times the impact," Figinski declared. The last-minute influx did, however, ensure that the campaign could be completed without a deficit.

As treasurer of the campaign, Joseph H. H. Kaplan kept all financial records and filed the reports required by state and federal law. The total cost of the campaign exceeded half a million dollars, of which slightly more than 10 percent came from labor unions, issue groups, and the Democratic Senatorial Campaign Committee.

Campaign organizations are not neat, logical structures. They are messy and many-headed, and they almost defy careful description. The Tydings organization was no exception. As long as the Senate remained in session, Tydings' personal office staff remained closest to him and tended to control his time. The Baltimore office was the nerve center, but the workers had a great variety of tasks and were often out in the field. Tydings' advertising agency was separated from both the personal and campaign staffs and worked only part time on the Tydings account. Still other contributions to the effort were local volunteer groups, regular Democratic clubs, and various interest groups (including friendly labor committees).

Probing the Electorate

A year before the formal campaign began Tydings hired Oliver Quayle, an experienced survey analyst whose political accounts were primarily Democrats, to undertake an intensive public-opinion survey. The report gave Tydings and his aides a detailed picture of the electorate that they would have to work with.[10]

Maryland voters were concerned about a variety of issues, mostly domestic but some foreign. High taxes and government spending were the most frequently mentioned problems, followed by crime and law enforcement (including gun registration), the Vietnam war, racial problems, and campus disorders. Of course, the *direction* of attitudes on such questions could either coincide or disagree with those of the Senator. Quayle and the Senator's staff concurred, however, that an issue-oriented campaign emphasizing Tydings' six-year record would prove advantageous.

The survey also engendered some uneasiness about the Senator's prospects. When voters were asked to rate Tydings' performance as a senator, they gave positive but not fervent assessments. Most were vague about the reasons for their ratings. (Twice as many people claimed to agree with his position on gun registration as to disagree with it.) When interviewers asked voters to rank both themselves and Tydings on a liberal-conservative scale, however, the results were as follows:

	"Liberal"	"Moderate"	"Conservative"
"Sen. Tydings is"	52%	31%	17%
"I am"	27	46	27

Marylanders obviously considered themselves much more conservative than their senior senator. One-quarter of them agreed with the proposition that "Joseph Tydings is too liberal."

These findings seemed no more than small clouds on the horizon, for the survey showed generally favorable attitudes toward the Senator. And, although no formal opposition had materialized, the survey showed that Tydings would be the probable victor against every likely challenger.

Some Tydings people, however, wanted to learn more about the Senator's public image. The advertising agency's research director decided to adapt a technique from marketing analysis and to stage a series of nine panel interviews throughout the state to probe attitudes toward Tydings. These in-depth discussions with representative groups of voters confirmed the intuitive conclusions of many political observers: Tydings was considered aloof, and he had an "image problem" among many voters. These feelings were echoed in a survey taken for another candidate in April 1970 by the John F. Kraft organization. Although Tydings was "not necessarily in trouble," he had a lower rating than did Governor Mandel. Voters either liked Tydings or they did not; there were few "in-between" feelings. This fact posed a difficult strategic problem, because so many people already had opinions about him. He was disliked, the survey found, for stands that he had taken on specific issues. In addition, the report noted that he was "not a personal senator" and that in his image there was "a certain remoteness."

Attitude surveys thus played a somewhat ambiguous role in helping to chart the course of Tydings' effort. For most people in his camp the findings reinforced the notion that, however controversial their senator, he was still a fairly sure bet for reelection. The surveys also strengthened the inclination to wage a fight directly on the issues in the Senator's record, on the theory that the gains would outweigh the losses. A few Tydings aides grew uneasy about the image problem revealed by some of the surveys, and they set about trying to personalize the campaign appeals.

The Media Campaign

Communications media are increasingly relied upon for the footwork of a campaign, for reaching into voters' homes with the candidate's message. Basically, three types of media materials are available (though in practice they may be difficult to distinguish): professionally produced materials like radio and television announcements and campaign brochures, press releases that report the campaign's progress and describe the candidate's role in events, and media coverage of the campaign. This last element is crucial, even though the candidate and his staff have imperfect control over it.

In the spring of 1970 W. B. Doner & Co., an advertising agency with offices in Baltimore and Detroit, was formally engaged to produce the campaign materials. Albert G. Salter, the firm's executive vice-president, had handled Tydings' 1964 advertising and was again designated as account executive.

Salter and his associates sat down with key Tydings aides sometime in the spring to talk about the campaign. Drawing upon findings from its panel interviews, the agency staff drew three ideas that they wanted to stress in advertising materials: Tydings' personal concern about individuals, his ability to "get things done," and his toughness of mind. These themes, it was believed, would build on the candidate's strengths—experience and independence—while dispelling suspicions about his "aloofness." The themes were accepted and embodied in media advertising, but they by no means constituted the overarching structure of the campaign. A campaign strategy, whether well conceived or not, may not actually be carried into daily decisions that shape speeches, press releases, and the like. Furthermore, events during the campaign may demand shifts in strategy.

Five sixty-second "spot" announcements were prepared for television, and they were crucial to the tone of the campaign. One, called the "needs" spot, featured a series of film clips illustrating Tydings' contributions to the state: a stoplight at a dangerous intersection, treatment for the elderly and chronically ill, and the preservation of Assateague Island for recreation. Then, as the camera showed Tydings listening intently to an out-of-focus figure in the foreground, the scene froze, and the announcer concluded: "Joe Tydings cares. And he listens to people. Then he does something. Constructive and positive."

Another sixty-second spot, generally conceded to be among the most effective, featured film footage of Tydings talking to voters in various campaign settings. Meanwhile the Senator's wife was heard to say:

> That's my husband . . . Joe Tydings. *[Noise from campaign scene heard under Mrs. Tydings' voice]* And this is another campaign. And that means early breakfasts. And late dinners. Eighteen hours a day. Hundreds and hundreds of people to meet. But he seems to thrive on it. He loves the chance to get out of the office and meet people. And hear about what they're thinking. He loves the chance to be able to respond to people. Firsthand.
>
> *[Location noise swells, then goes under as Mrs. Tydings continues]* We've talked about it. And I know he's in a tough fight this year. But that's all right. It's times like these when he's strongest. He's taking his record to the people. Because he believes in the truth of what he's accomplished in the past six years. For all the people of Maryland. I think I'd admire a man like that. Even if he weren't my husband. Besides, he's my Senator. Too.

A third spot featured a crowd of children singing the state song, "Maryland, My Maryland." Between stanzas the sound track went silent as the camera cut to scenes of Tydings around the state, talking to a policeman, greeting a crowd of people, sailing on an oyster boat. All three of these spots were designed to illustrate Tydings' personableness, forthrightness, and ability to "get things done."

The issue of crime and gun control was the object of two other sixty-second announcements. In the first, which was used early in the campaign, the names and ages of Marylanders killed by gunshot wounds were rolled across the screen, slowly and inexorably. Meanwhile Tydings' voice was heard explaining that these were "honest, law-abiding Maryland citizens—cut down by guns of violence." As the camera shifted to a close-up of Tydings, he ended with an appeal for his gun-control bill. A second spot, prepared later in the campaign, used film footage of riots and a tough message from Tydings condemning violence. Salter decided that Tydings' voice came across somewhat stridently in this spot and curtailed its use, but in the last week of the campaign, as Tydings' staff became panic-stricken over the probable outcome of the race, it was used again.

Other television ads were also produced. There were ten-second "get out the vote" announcements and one five-minute film of Tydings discussing the state of the economy with two "average" voters. (Originally, two more of these films, one on crime and one on an undecided topic, had been planned, but the press of time and shortage of funds prevented them from being produced.) Heavy reliance on relatively long announcements caused a problem, for it is harder to place a sixty-second (or longer) spot in prime time than it is to place a thirty- or ten-second spot.

Television advertising is staggeringly expensive, and many observers have proposed ways of reducing costs to candidates—including subsidized time, time donated by the stations, and limitations on allowable expenditures. The Tydings campaign had a fairly adequate television budget, which was used mainly on major Baltimore and Washington stations. But advertising time is bought and sold in the marketplace, where the political candidate is at a disadvantage in competing for prime time with the commercial advertiser, who has a much larger budget and will be advertising for a long time.

Media audiences can be pinpointed to a degree—that is, messages can be directed to special demographic groups. The spot featuring the Senator's wife was thus run frequently on daytime television. Radio stations in particular tend to attract more distinctive audiences. An appeal to workingmen was used on stations featuring popular or country-and-western music early in the morning (6:00-8:00 A.M.) and in midafternoon (3:00-5:00 P.M.), when working-class people are most likely to be commuting to and from work. An endorsement from a successful black candidate for State's Attorney was used extensively on stations catering to blacks. In many people's judgment the most effective parts of the media campaign were television and radio endorsements by Brooks Robinson, the Baltimore Orioles' stellar third baseman and Most Valuable Player in the World Series that year. A unique disclaimer—"Brooks Robinson wasn't paid for by anybody. He just said what he believes"—enhanced the appeal of the endorsement.

The Doner agency also produced brochures and posters and procured special materials (buttons, bumper stickers, and the like) from suppliers. The initial brochure, entitled "Joe," was intended to introduce prospective precinct workers to the candidate's record. It unfolded to explain the Senator's contributions to various parts of Maryland; it could then be used as a poster on the wall of campaign headquarters. The major canvassing brochure also had a double use. Along with a standard political message, it included a return envelope so that the person could indicate whether or not he could contribute to the campaign in any way. There were also a brochure on gun control—"The Guns of Crime and Violence"—and a four-page rotogravure insert that appeared in Maryland papers two Sundays before the election.

As in its television and radio spots, the Doner agency tried in its prepared campaign materials to emphasize Tydings' personality. Sometimes the Senator's personal staff balked at the informality. One bumper sticker, "He's a good Joe," was rejected as not dignified enough. A number of letterheads, buttons, and other materials with the simple name "Joe" were produced, but they were not usually reordered.

With the exception of the videotaped television spot on crime, the media campaign was produced more or less as a package. That is, it was conceived beforehand and altered very little as the campaign progressed. Nor was there much change in the materials used before and after the September 15 primary. Limitations on time and money seemed to preclude major shifts in emphasis, but some campaign aides were later to regret this lack of flexibility. "If we had been more flexible in responding to new issues as they arose," Salter said, "we would have served the Senator's interest better." Among other things, there could have been more use of videotaped spots, which can be produced more quickly than films.

Some flexibility was provided, however, by Lotito's day-to-day press copy. (Routine press notices continued to be turned out by the Washington office, where a second press aide was left in charge.) Few days passed without some offering, including verbatim press-conference statements, news stories based on speeches, challenges to opponents, endorsements, and "backgrounders." Besides supplying a constant stream of copy to various newspapers around the state, Lotito had the task of overseeing general relations with the press—assisting reporters who were covering the campaign and seeing that the candidate was available for interviews.

As the campaign progressed, Tydings received a large share of newspaper endorsements. Especially gratifying was that of the *Washington Star*, a Republican paper that opinion surveys showed would have the most influence on the vote for a Maryland candidate. The leading Baltimore paper, the *Sun*, also backed Tydings, and even the liberal *Washington Post*—still angry over the D.C. crime law—gave a backhanded endorsement. The *News-American*, a Hearst paper, came out for Beall. "We got all the endorsements that counted," Lotito declared.

The media campaign is an integral part of everything that happens during the campaign period. In many statewide elections electronic media have become the primary channels for reaching the voters, so important that their effectiveness and enormously high costs have become hotly debated issues of political theory and practice. For all its importance and fascination, however, the media campaign has not entirely supplanted the traditional techniques of organization and personal contact.

The Grass-Roots Campaign

To reach voters requires organization. There are only two ways for a candidate to secure an organization: He can build one himself, or he can latch onto an existing structure. Actually a candidate must usually combine these two techniques because, though political structures (however anemic) exist almost everywhere, they are seldom geared to his particular needs.

Democratic organization is strong in Maryland's central counties and especially in Baltimore City. But Tydings, whose entire career had been as a political reformer, was no favorite of most organization Democrats. Only in Montgomery County were Tydings forces in control of the regular organization. He therefore had to build his own volunteer precinct organization while trying to remain friendly with what his people called the entrenched "regular organization." The Tydings precinct organization, headed by Mrs. Freedlander, was the campaign's good right arm. The left arm, in Figinski's charge, consisted of relations with the regular organization. "You might say that the left arm and the right arm were never brought together," Figinski explained, "and any help we got on the left-hand side we considered over and above what we had expected."

Organizations are spun out of lists of names. Top prospects were those who had worked for Tydings in his first statewide campaign six years earlier. All these people were sought out; if they were still living in the state they were asked about volunteering. A second list of prospects, supplied by the Washington office, consisted of those people whom the Senator had helped in some way or another during his six years in office. Other names were taken from forms passed out at campaign meetings, from word of mouth, and from people who telephoned or stopped by the office. When names reached headquarters they were distributed to county precinct chairmen.

The key figures in the Tydings organization were presumably the chairman and chairwoman for Tydings in each county. These people were selected to contribute leadership and prestige to the campaign effort; sometimes they were figureheads, sometimes active participants. One of their main jobs was to cooperate with the county precinct workers' chairman, who was charged with overseeing all grass-roots workers under Mrs. Freedlander's direction. Other volunteer workers included headquarters managers, Election Day chairmen and workers, finance chairmen, and chairmen of various civic and professional groups for Tydings. This organization extended down to the precinct and even the block level.

A meeting of precinct leaders was held on July 30, as the primary election drive started, in a room above the storefront headquarters. It drew 800 people to receive instructions and to hear Tydings speak. It was hot, the air-conditioning broke down, and the floor literally sagged under the weight of the crowd, but almost everyone agreed that it was the psychological high point of the campaign.

All precinct leaders received a manual, "Very Important People," which described the duties of various types of workers; told how to conduct mailings, telephone canvassing, and registration drives; listed Election Day activities; and explained the state election laws. Each worker received a shopping bag emblazoned with "Win with Tydings" and filled with campaign materials. Literature, bumper strips ("expensive and must be utilized effectively," the manual warned), buttons, and other paraphernalia were included. The packets remained basically unchanged throughout the campaign, both before and after the primary. When canvassers prepared to make their rounds a second time after the primary election, they asked for fresh materials, but the original brochures were simply reprinted. "Perhaps we couldn't have afforded two sets of materials," one worker said, "but I don't think the decision was made consciously."

In addition to the door-to-door canvassing, telephone canvassing was used as the general election approached. A bank of telephones was installed in the central headquarters, where volunteers worked under the direction of a young man recruited from Tydings' staff. Callers used prepared scripts of essentially two kinds. One, designed for Democratic registrants, was direct and partisan: "I'm calling for Joe Tydings, and I hope you'll give him your support." The other was designed also to elicit information and was more circumspect. "I am polling for the senatorial race," the caller would say, "and I am wondering who you are planning to support." Whenever the person indicated support for Tydings, the caller tried to make certain that he would reach the polls, that he had a ride, babysitting service, or whatever else might be needed.

The precinct organization stressed the state's populous central corridor. "In practice," Mrs. Freedlander explained, "this meant little work in western Maryland and none at all on the Eastern Shore." On the whole, the precinct organizations were judged a great success. In one county, though, things were going so badly that two full-time campaign workers had to be dispatched to open a new headquarters, bypass the people originally chosen to lead the local campaign, and put the effort on its feet again.

The regular Maryland Democratic organization, fueled largely by state patronage and favors, was temporarily in the hands of Governor Mandel. Relations between Tydings and Mandel were described as "cordial"; they consulted several times during the campaign, but the Senator never pressed the Governor to come out with support before the primary. Mandel maintained public neutrality in the primary battle, though he claimed to have worked for the Senator behind the scenes, trying to prevent local Democratic leaders from coming out publicly for Mahoney. Meanwhile Figinski worked constantly to improve the

Senator's standing with regular Democrats, and by primary time there was some Tydings support within the regular organization in virtually every locale.

Once the primary had certified Tydings as the party's official candidate, relations with regular Democrats were more friendly, at least in public. Schedules were meshed so that Tydings and Mandel could campaign together wherever possible. The names of Tydings and the local congressional candidate sprouted at the bottom of Mandel billboards, and most organization Democrats appeared to support Tydings, even though many did little in his behalf. For their part, the Tydings strategists tried to cater to local Democratic leaders and to schedule their candidate at as many officially sponsored affairs as possible. But this task was difficult because Tydings had already built his own volunteer organization. "After all, we couldn't suddenly tell our own people to go fly a kite," Figinski said.

Although relations between the two major candidates were friendly, they were not always echoed down in the ranks. The two camps basically distrusted each other, and the Senator's fiercely independent career had done little to resolve this problem. There was a fundamental hostility between an entrenched paid organization and one manned by volunteers and reformers. "We aren't their kind of people, and they aren't our kind of people," one Tydings worker summed it up.

The Candidate Himself

Scheduling, handled out of the Baltimore headquarters by Mrs. Orlinsky, was best described as a "three-ring circus." Not only did the long congressional session often prevent the Senator from keeping campaign appointments, but also Maryland's proximity to the nation's capital meant that people throughout the state expected the Senator to be on hand at every campaign affair. "Maryland is too accessible," one staff person mused, "and constituents always expect you to show up at midweek functions." Scheduling was therefore an exercise in timing and high diplomacy, with private airplanes often required to shuttle the candidate to far corners of the state.

Tydings' geographic strategy was nowhere more evident than in scheduling. The thirty-two days of campaigning scheduled before the primary were divided into eight days in Baltimore City, eight in Montgomery and Prince George's Counties, eight in the Baltimore suburbs (Baltimore, Anne Arundel, Harford, and Howard Counties), and eight in the rest of the state. The staff counted on five campaigning days each week, with Thursdays reserved for senatorial business and Mondays set aside for rest, relaxation, study, and campaign planning. Bids from local chairmen for the Senator's time came to Figinski and Mrs. Orlinsky, who granted them according to overall priorities. Local chairmen were urged to plan appearances so that the candidate would reach the largest number of people. ("Remember, 20 minutes in a crowded shopping center may be as effective as 90 minutes attending and speaking to a local service or political club," the manual counseled.)

On the road, the candidate traveled by car, accompanied by a driver and someone from the locality that he was visiting. Early mornings were usually spent greeting workers at plant gates (workers are less anxious to go to work than they are to go home in the afternoon), followed by mid-morning coffees or shopping-center tours. For the latter a campaign car with a loudspeaker system would be used; "Tydings girls" might also be on hand to distribute literature. Or the Senator might be accompanied by athletic stars from the Baltimore Colts or Bullets. While aides distributed literature, Tydings himself would make the rounds shaking hands. The day would conclude with appearances at one or more meetings.

Personal appearances had to be meshed with other events—interviews, television tapings, and Senate duties. Along with most candidates, Tydings complained that his staff worked him too hard, but an hour or so of rest was usually planned each day.

The Senator's wife, Ginny, also kept a relatively full campaign schedule after the Tydings children had returned to school in September. Somewhat reluctant to campaign at first, she soon developed into a "really terrific" campaigner. Besides, she could keep her schedule better than her husband, who was often tied down with Senate business. After seeing the children off to school in the morning, Mrs. Tydings would start out with a shopping-center tour or a women's *kaffeeklatsch*. A luncheon, perhaps with a women's group, might be followed by a stop at the local Tydings headquarters to meet the volunteer workers and have pictures taken. In the evening she would usually join her husband for a big event, or they would appear separately and meet later. As one staff member said admiringly, "She went everywhere—she even worked plant gates."

People who observed Tydings in his personal appearances sometimes commented on his seeming lack of enthusiasm for meeting large crowds of people. "Joe is best in small groups of friends," a person who knows him well confessed. "He's just not relaxed in a large group of strangers." After standing directly opposite the Senator in a receiving line, one worker said, "He was invariably looking off in the distance while greeting people." Even loyal supporters were occasionally miffed. "I gave a thousand dollars to his campaign," one of them remarked, "but, you know, I don't think he ever knew who I was." The Senator's closest associates found it hard to believe that their boss was considered cold and unresponsive, but local campaign workers remarked on it, and the belief surely provided a rationale for many who wanted to vote against him. Meanwhile the affable Beall was touring the state, and his ads described him as "a man you can walk up to and talk to."

Cannon to the Left, Cannon to the Right

Elections are invariably localized affairs, stubbornly resisting the efforts of journalists and other outsiders to turn them into national referenda of one kind or another. This observation was true of the 1970 Tydings campaign, though the influence of outside forces was in evidence.

During the campaign Tydings wore a small American-flag pin in his lapel and told people that he owned eleven shotguns. But, as chief sponsor of gun-control legislation, he was anathema to many gun owners and others who failed to see gun control as essential to any war against crime. Tydings claimed that he was "the number-one target of the nation's firearms lobby."

Most of the anti-Tydings campaign was the responsibility of Citizens Against Tydings (CAT), a group formed a year before the election by Michael J. Parker, a thirty-year-old Washington-area lawyer. Parker saw the battle against gun control as a "civil liberties issue." "We made our feelings on his gun control legislation known to him many times," he explained. "It gets to the point where letter writing just won't work."

CAT's membership, according to Parker, amounted to only 300 or 400 at its peak, with perhaps twice as many people over the entire thirteen months of its existence. But it was nevertheless responsible for a prodigious amount of activity in the campaign: Members passed out 150,000 bumper stickers ("If Tydings Wins, You Lose"), mailed out 35,000 brochures and distributed 150,000 others, ran 30 full-page ads, and paid for dozens of radio spots on 26 stations. Two waves of telephone canvassing were also sponsored. ("Remember," callers urged, "if Tydings wins, he'll have six more years to work toward destroying the right to own firearms.") The group's drive boosted Mahoney, Tydings' primary opponent, and then Beall, the Republican challenger.

CAT's budget of $50,000-$60,000 was supplied by gun owners throughout the nation. "*Gun Week* kept us alive," Parker has said, referring to his advertisements in a weekly whose gun-owner subscribers provided a steady flow of small contributions. One $750 contribution came from a California group called Firearms and Individual Rights (FAIR), which had raised it by raffling scores of rifles and gun accessories, some donated by arms manufacturers.

Although CAT was a local organization, it symbolized the influence of such national groups as the National Rifle Association and the Firearms Lobby of America. The one-million-member NRA, which, as a "social welfare" organization, is prohibited by tax statutes from engaging in political campaigns, remained discreetly in the background, though its publication, *The American Rifleman*, gave some publicity to CAT's work. FLA, not under such restraints, worked to raise money to defeat "those irresponsible lawmakers who would deprive us of our rights to keep and bear arms." Finally, the conservative Liberty Lobby contributed $7,000 to a group composed of Mahoney workers, called Voters Opposed to Tydings' Election (VOTE).

Tydings' response was typically direct. His statements and press releases cited crime rates and death tolls from firearms, in contrast to law enforcement officials' support of firearms legislation and the role of such measures as California's gun law in facilitating capture of criminals. Most of all, however, Tydings portrayed himself as the object of "bullying" tactics by out-of-state gun interests. In a tour of western Maryland in early August, the Senator pursued the topic whenever he could, explaining the provisions of his bill. At one point, Tydings patiently described his proposals to a group of farmers in a livestock shed at the Allegheny County Fair in Cumberland while nearby a cow noisily poked her newborn calf to its feet and began to lick it clean. He told a group of striking road workers that, "To be quite honest, gentlemen, I had two very close friends assassinated by lunatics," referring to the deaths of John and Robert Kennedy. Repeatedly he accused what he called "the national gun lobby" of distorting and lying about his bill. Surveys showed that his position on guns was opposed by a minority, but the opposition of this minority was intractable. One of his workers told him during his Allegheny County visit: "Your gun bill. That's the only trouble we're having. People don't understand you on the gun thing."

Both of Tydings' main opponents benefited from the gun issue, but they took somewhat different positions on the matter. On announcing his candidacy for the Senate, Mahoney declared that he was "bitterly opposed to registering or taking guns away from the people of Maryland." Beall, who described himself as a middle-of-the-roader, opposed gun legislation as a useless exercise ("criminals won't register their guns anyway") that would merely create "another federal bureaucracy at the expense of the taxpayers." After the primary Tydings tried to paint Beall as the gun lobbyists' candidate, accusing him of "snuggling up" to them. While the gun groups openly campaigned for Beall, the GOP contender himself tried to avoid the posture of a one-issue candidate.

The gun issue had been fully anticipated, but late in August there occurred one of those unpredictable events that are impossible to plan for. Late in June a writer named William Lambert asked to interview Senator Tydings about his relationship with the Charter Company, a Jacksonville, Florida, firm of which Tydings was a major stockholder and former director. The interview covered a variety of topics, and at one point the reporter asked whether or not Tydings and an officer of the firm had once met with an official of the Agency for International Development (AID) to help secure a $7 million loan (subsequently approved) for a Charter operation in Nicaragua. Tydings denied that the meeting had taken place while he was a senator and subsequently asked his secretary to unearth his old appointment books to verify his claim. The notebooks pinpointed the meeting at December 1, 1964—after Tydings' first election but before he had become a senator—rather than in early 1965, as the reporter's sources had indicated.

After the interview Tydings' aides thought that the matter was finished. "We really didn't take the matter very seriously," one of them said. When, in early August, the reporter reappeared for a second interview, the appointment book was shown to him. He seemed doubtful, so Tydings offered to submit the entry to an "ink-freshness test" to determine whether it had been written in 1964 or added later. Tydings' aides understood the reporter to say that, if the chemical test came out in the Senator's favor (which it did), he would scrap the article. At any rate, they believed that it would not be printed even if submitted.

The article actually appeared in *Life*'s August 28 issue. It charged that Tydings had "repeatedly lent his personal and senatorial prestige to the urgent promotion of his own greatest financial interests."[11] The story itself hardly justified such sweeping language, for among the many innuendos was only a single verifiable fact, the AID meeting. Perhaps it is idle to speculate on the reporter's reasons for writing the piece or his magazine's reasons for publishing it. Tydings believed that high administration officials had put the reporter onto the story and had then egged him on. The motivations of *Life* management were somewhat different: Most weekly photo-feature magazines had suffered declining circulation and had turned, *Life* with them, to "investigative reporting" in an effort to boost sales.

Once the article seemed certain to appear, Lotito and several other staff members undertook a crash investigating job in order to prepare a lengthy rebuttal. Press releases and a detailed tabloid-style flier were prepared. The Senator himself held two Baltimore news conferences to deliver prepared statements and to answer reporters' questions. Labeling the charges "wholly untrue and terribly unfair," Tydings told the newsmen that "In no way, shape or form, directly or indirectly, have I ever used my office as a United States Senator to advance the interests of the Charter Company or of any other company in which I have a personal stake."[12] He refuted the various insinuations of the *Life* article and strove to leave the impression that "persons in the White House itself" were behind the article and had fabricated the charges.

The charges and countercharges were given large play in the local press, but what would the voters' reaction be? The candidate said that he noticed no changes in the way voters received him during his tours, and his final opinion survey, taken two weeks after the *Life* article had appeared, seemed to confirm that the public reaction was minor: 62 percent of the voters reported that they had "heard something about the *Life* article," and of those people 94 percent had heard about Tydings' denial. Of those who had heard of both the article and the denial 52 percent believed Tydings' denial, 23 percent (or 13 percent of all voters) doubted it, and 25 percent were not sure. When asked whether or not they had changed their minds about whom to support because of the *Life* revelations, 4 percent admitted that they had, and 4 percent were undecided. The rest said that they were unchanged in their intentions. Tydings' survey firm concluded that the *Life* article would have little bearing on the outcome. But in a close election who could tell?

The *Life* episode represented an enormous drain on staff time at a crucial point just before the primary. The event was ironic because Tydings had advocated full financial disclosure by senators and himself made a practice of going beyond the disclosure requirements of Senate Rule 44.[13] The injustice of the accusation was highlighted when, exactly ten days after the November election, the U.S. State Department announced that its investigation had found no evidence that Tydings had influenced AID's loan to the Charter Company. In a forty-five-page report, the department concluded that nothing indicated "there was any variance in the processing of the projects as a result of any Congressional interest or contact."[14] The controversial AID meeting, it appeared, had actually taken place after the loan decision had been reached, and it was even possible that the loan application had not been discussed. Then it was revealed that Senate Foreign Relations Committee Chairman J. William Fulbright had asked the State Department to look into the matter immediately after the *Life* article had appeared and that his office had hounded the department's chief inspection officer throughout October to unveil its report. The department's explanation (that the investigation had taken a long time and that, even so, to have released the results before the election would have "stirred up the whole thing,"[15] convinced no one.

The Primary

Observers might well have missed the fact that Tydings had primary opposition had they relied wholly on his campaign materials for evidence. "The campaign wasn't pitched against anyone until after the primary election," an aide explained. "We took a couple of potshots at Mahoney, but not very many."

Mahoney nevertheless received more votes than he had ever garnered in a Maryland election. His 174,000 votes represented 38 percent of the Democratic primary voters. Tydings won with 238,624 votes, or 52 percent of the primary votes cast. Two minor candidates between them gained almost 45,000 votes, which could be interpreted as reflecting efforts to find an alternative to Tydings. Furthermore, nearly 60 percent of the state's registered Democrats failed to vote.

For Tydings the results were disheartening but not necessarily disastrous. Although he had received only 44 percent of the votes in his home county, Harford, he had done relatively well in most other areas of the state. The Eastern Shore, of course, went strongly for Mahoney, but the total vote there was small. The Tydings margin was impressive in the Washington suburban counties, indicating that the D.C. crime bill was working in his favor, and the three to two edge in Baltimore City suggested that the measure had not completely alienated the black neighborhoods. Baltimore County was lost by a somewhat narrower margin than his advisers had expected. In the smaller western counties Tydings did surprisingly well. On the whole, grounds for concern but not alarm. Governor Mandel, whose primary vote was the largest ever received by a Maryland candidate, would be leading the party's ticket, and with the Democrats' 2.5 to 1 edge in voter registration it was conceded that Tydings was still well ahead.

Meanwhile Beall, with only token opposition, had received his party's nomination. He told reporters that he saw encouraging signs in Tydings' primary-vote totals, but he admitted that there was "no question" that he remained the underdog.

The cautious optimism pervading the Tydings camp was reinforced by an extensive survey taken by the Quayle organization.[16] It appeared that voters' attitudes toward the problems facing them had changed somewhat since the first Tydings poll fourteen months earlier. Crime and law enforcement had become the number-one problem, and issues of inflation and jobs loomed somewhat larger. The Vietnam war continued to be mentioned frequently, but it was clearly not foremost in the voters' minds. Campus disorders had receded in importance, and environmental problems had assumed new significance. In discussing the candidates, the voters predictably revealed more sharply focused ideas than before; after the barrage of electioneering fewer voters were uninformed or undecided. The Senator's stand on gun control was the major reason cited for liking or disliking him, but the percentages still seemed to run in his favor. Indeed, Quayle found that crime and narcotics were Tydings' strongest vote-getting issues.

Voter perceptions of the candidates also gave little cause for alarm. According to the Quayle survey, Beall was considered by voters "an honest and hard-working young man of a fine background who speaks well."[17] Few negative comments about Beall were heard. Tydings was considered "an honest and outspoken man who has the courage of his convictions and who works hard." A solid majority rejected the proposition that the Senator was unapproachable and did not spend enough time in the state, though his accessibility was apparently viewed as an issue. In sum, the surveyors concluded that "on the whole, Tydings' profiles are sound" and that he was far ahead in the race: with 57 percent, as opposed to 31 percent for Beall, 9 percent undecided, and 3 percent for other candidates.

Once the primaries were behind them and with the surveys as encouragement, Tydings' workers plunged into the last seven weeks of the campaign.

The Stretch Drive

The seven weeks between the primary and general election were a time of frantic campaigning and tough charges. Tydings' speeches and press releases began to hit directly at the GOP contender, portraying him as a "do-nothing" congressman and an "unthinking rubber stamp" of his party. Beall responded by calling Tydings a "lackey" for "ultraliberal" groups. Both candidates exchanged accusations of absenteeism at congressional floor votes, not to mention those related to issues like aid to the elderly, school busing, foreign aid, and the economy. Tydings worked continually to emphasize his crime-fighting record as opposed to that of Beall and criticized unceasingly the Nixon administration on such issues as unemployment, inflation, and environmental protection.

On seven occasions during this period Tydings, Beall, and Wilder (the American Party candidate) appeared for television debates, which were broadcast by nearly every major station in the state. Tydings strategists were not enthusiastic about the debates: By giving exposure to the lesser-known candidate (Beall), they could harm the better-known candidate (Tydings). Once the television stations had made their offer, however, it was difficult for any candidate to refuse to participate. "We weren't going to let Beall do the empty-chair bit," one Tydings aide said. So the Senator showed up for all the taping sessions, which were held in mid-afternoon, when dozens of campaign appearances were also scheduled. As usual, he went on the offensive in these debates: "Joe went for the jugular and tried to cut up Beall," one of his aides recalled. Beall, for his part, made a good impression; although not as aggressive as Tydings, he came through as intelligent and personable.

As the campaign went into its final phase, the candidates were inevitably drawn into national controversies. Beall sought and received help from Maryland's popular senior senator, Charles "Mac" Mathias (though Mathias told reporters that his voting record was generally closer to Tydings' record than to that of Beall). Tydings' polls told him that only one outsider, Edmund Muskie of Maine, could help him, and Muskie was brought in for an appearance and a press conference at Baltimore's Friendship Airport. Other outsiders were shunned, though Senator Gaylord Nelson (D.-Wis.), a leader on environmental issues, appeared at a reception for Tydings to which many Maryland conservationists had been invited.

The big drawing cards of the 1970 elections were President Nixon and Vice-President Agnew, the latter, of course, a native son. Soon after the primary Agnew appeared at a Washington fund-raising dinner for Maryland candidates; a month later, in late October, he delivered a hard-hitting speech at another fund-raising dinner in Baltimore. He attacked the incumbent as a "radical liberal" willing to take "all the advice he can get from Hyannis Port" while ignoring his own constituents. Few aspects of Tydings' career were overlooked in the Agnew speech: his "arrogance," his "intransigence," his "business interests," and his role in the state Democratic Party.

Hardly had Agnew's words been uttered than Tydings fired off a counter-attack on the "White House purge," which, he said, was part of the administration's dream of filling the Senate with "faceless, colorless, and spineless . . . mechanical puppets." He tried to align himself with his Maryland Senate colleague, the popular Mathias, whom he described as a "radical liberal" in Agnew's own party.

A few days after the Agnew speech, President Nixon helicoptered to Baltimore's working-class area of Dundalk to appeal for GOP votes. Rather than attacking Tydings directly, the President devoted most of his time to an appeal for senators who shared his views, a theme that led Tydings to renew his charge that Beall would be a rubber stamp for the administration.

At about that time Tydings was the target of a large newspaper ad in the *Washington Post* and *Baltimore Sun*[18] charging that he was in league with radicals and extremists. "What Kind of Man Is Joe Tydings?" it asked in bold type. Smaller headlines declared: "The extremists need Joe Tydings. Maryland does not." The text of the ad then cited out-of-context quotations purporting to link Tydings and other Democrats with radical sympathies.[19] It appeared that virtually identical ads had been placed in sixty-one papers in six states and directed against various Democratic candidates.[20] The ads were signed "Committee for a Responsible Congress—Carl Shipley, Treasurer." Shipley, GOP national committeeman from the District of Columbia, commented only that "The ad speaks for itself," but his two local cosponsors denied responsibility for the ad. Tydings' press aides had a field day, trotting out a letter of praise that the Senator had earlier received from Shipley.

The last weeks of the campaign meant nonstop appearances for all the candidates, particularly after Congress finally adjourned in mid-October. They and their managers pushed themselves without mercy, knowing that they would have time to recuperate once the election was over. On the Sunday before the voting Tydings showed up at five church services, an oyster roast at Polish Hall in southeast Baltimore, and the second half of the Baltimore Colts' football game. At night he appeared with R. Sargent Shriver at a large rally at the Baltimore Civic Center.

Little about Beall's campaign caused alarm in the Tydings camp. "Beall's campaign never got off the ground," one Tydings aide remarked. The GOP contender seemed to be drawing smaller crowds than Tydings did, and in most formal aspects of the campaign effort—especially face-to-face debates and press releases—the staff felt that, as Figinski put it, "we clobbered the Republicans." Until the final week, when he began to pick apart Tydings' record, Beall ran a fairly bland campaign. But that could prove an advantage against a controversial incumbent: "We were running against our record, but Beall had very little record to run against," a Tydings assistant declared. Furthermore, without the burden of an expensive primary fight, Beall had saved most of his funds (estimated at $425,000) for the general election effort and was able to outspend Tydings in the stretch drive.

The Tydings camp became jittery toward the close of the campaign. Telephone surveys taken for Mandel, though showing Tydings in the lead, revealed a "softness" in the Senator's support and a large proportion of undecided voters.[21] Tydings' own telephone canvassers also turned up large numbers of undecided voters. Were these people truly undecided, or were they against Tydings but reluctant to admit it? With hindsight some Tydings strategists confess to having felt a growing sense of panic. "We could feel the slippage," said one. "We were all desperate."

The weekend before the voting Mrs. Freedlander went into Figinski's office at headquarters. "I think we're losing," she said. "Well, what can we do about it?" Figinski responded. The answer was: "Nothing. It's too late."

Election Day

The campaign does not end once the polls open; rather, a final and quite different phase begins. The candidate's image is fixed in the voters' minds, and his message has been disseminated. Now the effort is simply to bring out the vote. But the effort is selective, focusing on areas of greatest return. For Tydings this selectivity meant concentration on strong Democratic areas with high turn-out possibilities.

The large corps of precinct chairmen was charged with keeping an eye on polling places to check on registered Democrats who had failed to vote. By midday precinct workers had begun calling these people to lure them to the polls. Rides, babysitting services, even volunteers to watch the roast in the oven—all were offered to persuade voters to the polls. By then it mattered little which candidate the voter chose, though the targeted districts were expected to yield high Tydings votes.

In many Baltimore areas Election Day work is unique. In place of unpaid volunteers there are people who walk up and down the blocks, bringing the vote out. Most of these workers are paid for their services with what is called "walking-around money." Both parties hire such Election Day workers, and the bidding is sometimes fierce. The money, which ostensibly goes for printing sample ballots, is distributed to the various Baltimore organizations, from which it filters down to precinct chairmen and precinct workers. From the Tydings point of view, this process was risky because it was in the hands of old-line organizations, which were not always enthusiastic boosters of the Senator. Tydings volunteers were thus sent into some of these areas to check up; usually Tydings literature was being distributed fairly, and his name appeared appropriately on the sample ballots. There were some exceptions, however.

Other Election Day workers, called "challengers," were briefed in state election law and stationed at the polling places to protect the party's interests and to challenge dubious opposition voters. A corps of Lawyers for Tydings stood ready in many areas to rush to polling places to back up challengers in serious disputes.

In bellwether precincts the same organizations that were responsible for bringing out the vote also relayed the returns to Baltimore headquarters. The results were tallied on a large board, where Tydings and key strategists came to learn the most up-to-date statistics on election evening.

In the end Tydings lost by about 25,000 votes, out of about 950,000 cast. He received 48 percent to Beall's 51 percent (the American Party's candidate received 1 percent). Tydings took only two counties, Montgomery and Prince George's, in addition to Baltimore City. His margins of victory in the former were not as large as had been hoped, and the Baltimore turnout was not as large as it should have been. In Baltimore Tydings led two to one, but Democratic registration was considerably higher than that. Elsewhere in the state Tydings trailed.

Indeed, an extraordinarily light vote in the city—only 46 percent of the registered voters, compared with a 60 percent turnout in previous nonpresidential elections—was perhaps the key factor in Tydings' defeat. In almost all white areas of the city, participation was low, perhaps reflecting lack of enthusiasm for the Senator coupled with lack of interest in the gubernatorial election, which was a forgone conclusion. The black vote was also light, except in the Seventh Congressional District, where Parren J. Mitchell was elected the state's first black congressman. A heavy rain may have helped to keep voters away, though outside the city the turnout was about normal.

Beall ran best in outstate areas, where political conservatism was no doubt reinforced by dislike of Tydings' stance on gun control. Tydings' margins in the suburban and urban areas were simply insufficient to overcome Beall's advantage.

When asked to give the underlying reasons for Tydings' defeat, Figinski said, "Well, the left-handed Lithuanian vote didn't go for him." That is, the margin was so thin, and the deciding factors so numerous, that it would be impossible to isolate a single explanation. Tydings himself tended to blame the gun lobby, which in turn was quite willing to take the credit. "Nobody in his right mind is going to take on that issue again," one Tydings strategist admitted. The D.C. crime bill had no doubt alienated liberals and blacks. Certainly the Senator's image of remoteness, whether warranted or not, gave many people a rationale for disliking him. So did the *Life* article (though few voters had probably read it, much less understood its import), which unquestionably contributed to controversy over the candidate. "We all felt," one campaign strategist said, "that Tydings himself was the primary issue. And I don't think we ever learned how to deal with this issue properly."

Tydings was whipsawed by a combination of these issues, each of which affected a segment of the population deeply enough to persuade it to oppose the incumbent. The absence of any one of these factors might have altered the ultimate outcome of the election; taken together, however, they contributed to a general antipathy toward the candidate. Pleasant, uncontroversial, and possessed of a familiar name, Beall offered a convenient alternative—or, at least in Baltimore, an excuse to stay home. Beall was helped not only by his own attributes but also by the right-wing American Party's failure to capture the imagination of more than a few Maryland voters. Their candidate, Wilder, claimed only about 10,000 votes; had he garnered more, they probably would have been at Beall's expense.

Even though the evidence of the last weeks had been increasingly disquieting to Tydings, the final result was still a surprise to him, his staff, the newsmen, and the pollsters. "Every one of us walked away that night thinking we had let the Senator down," one worker said.

The surveys were particularly puzzling, for they had all shown Tydings well ahead. Their shortcomings illustrate the difficulties of using and interpreting survey findings. First, the final depth survey was taken during the week of the primary, or seven weeks before the November election. During that period Beall's recognition factor improved markedly, doubtless attracting some of the many undecided voters. Furthermore, the surveys may not have captured the full extent of anti-Tydings sentiment; opposition voters may have ended up in the undecided column. More fundamentally, probable turnout, so crucial in Baltimore, is exceedingly difficult to measure. If he is to predict elections, the survey analyst must not only fathom respondents' attitudes but also determine the likelihood that they will act upon those attitudes and go to the polls. Although commercial survey analysts devote enormous energies to solving this problem, it remains more complex than is the actual content of attitudes.

Tydings wanted to concede at 11:00 P.M. on election night, but his staff, still banking on the Baltimore vote, persuaded him to hold off. A reporter, walking with the Senator to the site of his concession statement, asked him what his immediate plans were. "Find jobs for my staff," he answered. His concession statement, written on yellow legal paper and stuck in his pocket, was finally read at 3:00 A.M. Then he left and drove away with his wife, Ginny, in the family station wagon.

INCUMBENCY AND REELECTION: WILLIAM STEIGER OF WISCONSIN

At 10:40 P.M. on election night, November 3, 1970, Franklin Utech, a lanky art professor, emerged from his storefront campaign headquarters on Main Street in Oshkosh, Wisconsin. Behind him was a group of supporters saddened by the early returns, which indicated that Utech had lost by a wide margin in his first bid for public office. Their destination was the jubilant headquarters of the incumbent Republican congressman for the Sixth District of Wisconsin, William A. Steiger, whom challenger Utech was about to congratulate.

With television commentators droning in the background, offering their views on the impact of law and order, the economy, the environment, and the Vietnam war, the candidates assessed the campaign for the local reporters. Their perspectives were quite different. Steiger commented:

> [This victory] is attributed to all of the people who worked so hard. There were 700 persons who circulated my nomination papers and hundreds more who were on the telephone plus others who put on bumper stickers and distributed literature. This is the only way this kind of victory comes about. . . . It was easier this time from the standpoint of the fact that more people knew me. . . . I'm not sure that Professor Utech developed a pivotal issue.

In contrast Utech observed:

> I think the biggest thing that probably made the difference was that I was running against a name, and it overpowered the issues; so, the reasons for my losing were kind of vague. I think my campaign was run on about $8,000 and this certainly is a handicap when one is low on funds, especially when one is not a household word. . . . The issue was economics, but it didn't jell here. . . . [Steiger] wasn't identified with what is wrong.

Scenes similar to the one in Oshkosh were replayed hundreds of times across the country on election night 1970, and in all but a handful of districts the outcome was the same: The incumbent won.[22] Who wins and who loses in the 435 congressional districts is determined by a variety of factors: the partisan distribution of the voters in the district, national and state trends operative in a given year, and the resources available to the respective candidates.

In exploring Representative William Steiger's reelection, it is important to examine the impact of each of these factors, paying particular attention to the resources and advantages available to the incumbent compared with those of his challenger. The nature of the respective campaign organizations, tactics, and strategies will also be considered. Finally, an effort will be made to interpret the campaign and vote, as well as the relationship between the Congressman's legislative career on Capitol Hill and the campaign.

The Setting

The Struggle for Control of Congress, 1970

The 1970 midterm elections for control of Congress were unusual in partisan intensity, bitterness, and heavy involvement of administration and national party leaders seeking to influence the outcomes. Both the President and the Vice-President toured the country on behalf of Republican candidates; both parties bought sizable chunks of television time (for example, between halves of the professional football games on the Sunday before election and on election eve), and candidates attacked each other on the issues of permissiveness, law and order, unemployment, peace, high interest rates, and inflation.

The national news media focused on the critical contests for the Senate, in which the Republicans believed that they had at least a chance to wrest control from the Democrats. Incumbents and challengers fought their more lonely battles to decide the future of the House of Representatives in relative anonymity. This anonymity and lack of public attention are not only characteristic of congressional campaigns; they are also characteristic of life in the House itself— which is part of the difference between being a member of Congress and a U.S. senator.[23] (The differences between the Washington activities of a senator and a representative are examined in Chapter 3.)

The Sixth District of Wisconsin

Wisconsin's Sixth District is a seven-county area in east-central Wisconsin stretching along Lake Michigan from the growing northern suburbs of Milwaukee north to the port and industrial city of Sheboygan and west to the papermaking centers in the Fox River Valley (see Figure 2). The district is dominated not by any one urban concentration but by four medium-sized urban centers (Oshkosh, Fond du Lac, Sheboygan, and Neenah-Menasha), ranging in population from approximately 30,000 to 50,000, and many small cities and villages. The non-urban areas of the district are characterized by intensive agriculture.

All but two of the counties have higher than the state average (39.2 percent) of population employed in manufacturing. Yet no single industry dominates the district. Located here are the home offices and major plants of such corporations as Kimberly-Clark (which makes Kleenex), Bergstrom Papers, and Kohler. In addition, there are important manufacturers of machine tools and heavy machinery, plastics, cooking ware, motors, washers and dryers, packaging materials, wearing apparel, leather goods, and foundry products. This industrialization also means that the area contains a large concentration of labor-union

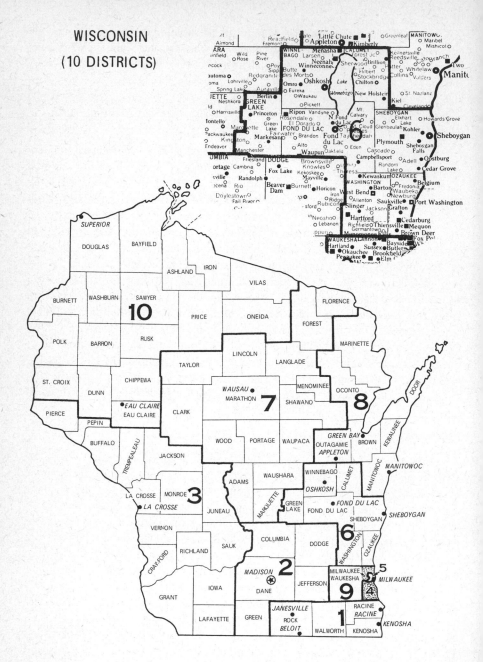

Figure 2
Wisconsin's Congressional Districts and the 6th District.

members. In this highly productive dairying area the average value of products sold per farm is well above the state average.

The voters of the district are predominantly of German descent—"frugal homeowners with savings accounts," as Representative Steiger has described them. As is true of most House constituencies, nonwhites (there are fewer than 200 in the whole district) constitute a tiny fraction of the district population.

The Sixth District has a long history of voting Republican. Only during the Depression and in the 1964 Johnson landslide have the Democrats won the congressional seat. Table 1 summarizes congressional election results in the district since 1952.

TABLE 1   The Vote for Congress, Sixth District of Wisconsin, 1952-1970

Year	Total Vote	Republican	Democratic	Plurality	Percentage Republican
1952	144,374	103,464	40,910	62,554 (R)	77.3
1954	109,844	68,653	41,191	27,462 (R)	62.5
1956	144,062	96,783	47,277	49,506 (R)	67.2
1958	116,521	61,490	55,031	6,459 (R)	52.8
1960	163,892	91,450	72,442	19,008 (R)	55.8
1962	120,538	71,298	49,238	22,060 (R)	59.1
1964	190,426	82,103	84,690	1,587 (D)	49.2
1966	129,706	67,941	61,761	6,180 (R)	52.4
1968*	174,940	111,934	60,059	51,875 (R)	64.0
1970*	145,531	98,587	44,794	54,893 (R)	67.7

* In 1968 the American Party candidate received 2,947 votes (1.68 percent), and in 1970 it received 2,150 votes (1.41 percent).

The key local party organizations in Wisconsin are the county units. In each Sixth District county the Republicans are adequately financed and have volunteer organizations that are capable and experienced in mobilizing the party's vote. Unlike most congressional districts, where party organizations are rudimentary at best and normally moribund, the Republican Party in the Sixth District operates in a coordinated manner.

In sharp contrast, the Democratic Party is poorly organized and lacking in personnel, funds, and campaign experience. Even candidates have been in short supply, and the party has frequently failed to field full slates for county offices. Democratic congressional campaigns in the district have been largely the responsibility of the candidates, with whatever auxiliary support they have been able to obtain from organized labor. Indeed, a state leader of the AFL-CIO's Committee on Political Education (COPE), noting the weakness of the district Democratic organization, commented wryly, "In the Sixth there's a well organized Republican Party, and then you have the independents plus COPE."

Further weakening the Democrats in the district have been lingering animosities from the bitter 1968 intraparty fights between the followers of Eugene McCarthy and the more traditional "organizational" Democrats, who supported either Hubert H. Humphrey or Robert F. Kennedy.

The Contestants: Recruitment and Nomination

The Incumbent: "At 32 an Old Political Pro"

After following a Steiger caravan through Sheboygan County, a local reporter headlined his feature story, "Steiger: At 32 an Old Political Pro." It was an apt description. Steiger is much younger than the typical representative (whose average age is fifty-two), and his appearance and manner emphasize this fact. His slender build, blond hair, unwrinkled face, ready smile, and tendency to run rather than to walk have led many to assume that he is even younger than he is.[24] Despite his youth, Steiger's political experience was extensive—two terms in Congress; three terms as a state legislator, including service as a committee chairman; and service as a Nixon delegate to the 1968 Republican convention.

The Steiger family has long been prominent in Republican state politics, and the Congressman started his own career early. By the time that he had finished at the University of Wisconsin, he had already served two years as national chairman of the College Young Republicans and had been president of the University of Wisconsin Young Republicans and vice-president of the student body. After graduation in 1960 he immediately ran and was elected to the Wisconsin Assembly. Early in 1966 Steiger announced his candidacy for the Republican congressional nomination against Representative John Race, a freshman Democrat, who had narrowly ousted a long-term GOP incumbent in 1964.

A key factor in winning a Republican nomination for Congress in Wisconsin is endorsement by the district party organization. This endorsement is decided at a spring caucus. The candidate who receives caucus endorsement also receives financial and organizational support in the September primary. Party endorsement thus gives a formidable advantage to the preferred candidate and normally discourages competition in the primary.

From January to May 1966 Steiger waged a virtually full-time campaign to win endorsement at the Republican Sixth District Caucus. He met personally with delegates and party leaders in the various counties and sought speaking engagements—particularly at service clubs like Kiwanis and Rotary—to make himself better known, especially in areas outside his own legislative district. His intensive drive for caucus-delegate support paid off when he won a 277 to 99.5 vote victory over his nearest rival, who then pledged Steiger his support, thus eliminating a primary fight.

Winning party endorsement in 1970 was far easier for Steiger, who as a two-term incumbent was well known and generally popular with organization people (though there were occasional complaints among some workers that Steiger was a bit liberal for a Republican). Although there was no opposition to Steiger's renomination, he did not take endorsement and renomination for granted. Accompanied by the Sixth District Republican chairman, Peter Kohler, he toured the district in the spring, in order to meet with the executive committees of each Republican county organization and to assess the party's prospects. In each county he pledged himself to assist local leaders in their efforts to elect Republicans to county and state legislative offices.

As there was no opposition Steiger received the party's endorsement at its spring caucus in Oshkosh by acclamation while a band gave him a rousing salute and green-and-white banners bearing a "Steiger tiger"—his campaign emblem—were unfurled.

The Challenger: "Democrats Seek Willing Loser"

As Table 1 suggests, Steiger's electoral position had improved dramatically between 1966 and 1968, from a 6,180-vote plurality (52.4 percent) to a 51,875-vote plurality (64 percent). Indeed, he was thought to be so strong that the Democratic Party had difficulty in recruiting a candidate. One news story describing the Democratic problems carried the headline "Democrats Seek Willing Loser." The story went on to say that the Democrats were looking for a candidate with sufficient wealth to finance his own campaign and who would be willing to run twice—once in 1970 to become known and again in 1972 when prospects for victory, it was hoped, would have improved.

Early in 1970 Franklin Utech, a forty-year-old art professor at the University of Wisconsin at Oshkosh, had been urged by the Sixth District Democratic chairman, Gordon E. Loehr, a Fond du Lac labor leader, to make the race. The Democrats were seeking an attractive candidate capable of winning over independents and uniting the diverse elements of the Democratic coalition: organized labor (which tended to be "hawkish" on the Vietnam war and concerned about "bread and butter" economic issues) and issue-oriented, ideological liberals (who tended to be "dovish" on the Vietnam war and less interested in "pocketbook" matters than in such questions as reorienting priorities). Loehr thought that Utech's background as a laborer—he had been both a butcher and a railroad worker—and his issue-oriented liberalism would help to unite both liberal-ideological Democrats and organized labor. Recognizing that a race against Steiger would be extremely difficult to win, Utech wrote to Loehr in January declining the opportunity to be a candidate.

The United States' incursion into Cambodia in May 1970 caused Utech to reconsider his decision. Both he and his wife, Sandra, had been leaders of the peace movement in the Oshkosh area and had participated in marches and demonstrations to protest the war in Vietnam. They had also worked tirelessly for Senator Eugene McCarthy in the Wisconsin presidential primary in 1968, and Mrs. Utech had been chosen a McCarthy delegate to the Chicago Democratic

convention. Utech, deeply concerned about the Cambodian incursion, suc-
cumbed to Loehr's continued urging and agreed to make the race, even though
Loehr could promise little in the way of campaign support.

The Democrats do not endorse candidates in the primaries, so that, in
contrast to Steiger in his first race for Congress, Utech did not have to woo
delegates to the district caucus. In any event, he was unopposed for the nomination.

The American Party—an outgrowth of Alabama Governor George Wallace's
1968 campaign for the presidency—had built a small statewide organization in
Wisconsin, reflecting the unrest within both the Republican and Democratic
Parties. As in 1968 it also entered a candidate against Steiger, Mrs. Rani Davidson, a housewife from a prosperous suburban area north of Milwaukee. She had
been an active Republican before becoming chairman of the Ozaukee County
American Party in the belief that the Republicans and Democrats had moved
closer and closer together and were leading the nation down the road to social-
ism. A pleasant, attractive, and articulate woman in her mid-forties, with many
friends in Republican ranks, Mrs. Davidson was considered likely to be effective
in drawing normally conservative Republican votes away from Steiger, the prime
target of her campaign.

Two Uncontested Primaries

Political scientists have frequently commented on the failure of the direct-
primary method of nomination to stimulate voter turnout and intraparty competition for nominations in the manner envisioned by its proponents. Incumbents normally can discourage competition in their party primaries, and the
prospect of likely electoral defeat stifles interest in minority primaries.[25]

The Sixth District primary election, held on September 8, 1970, followed
the pattern outlined almost perfectly. Steiger, Utech, and Mrs. Davidson each
won nomination with no primary opposition. Turnout was extemely low; less
than one-third as many people voted as had voted in the 1968 presidential
elections. Here is a comparison of Sixth District voter-turnout rates in the 1966
midterm general election, the 1968 presidential election, and the 1970 primary:

Election	Vote
1966 midterm general election	129,706
1968 presidential election	174,940
1970 primary election	43,929

In the primary Steiger polled almost twice as many votes as did Utech and
Mrs. Davidson combined, though his total was down 6,500 votes from that of
the 1966 primary, and that of the combined opposition was up 300 votes.

1970 Primary: Sixth District of Wisconsin

Candidate	Vote	Percentage
Steiger	28,641	65.2
Utech	14,915	34.0
Davidson	373	.8
Total	43,929	100.0

No candidate saw in the results of the primary any unusual or unexpected trends. As had been the normal pattern, the GOP vote far exceeded that of the Democrats. Nor did the candidates view the results from the limited turnout as accurate indicators of probable general-election votes—though the percentages of the vote for Steiger and Utech in the primary did finally closely parallel those of the general election.

The Campaign Organizations

Congressional constituencies are not normally shared by other office seekers for the simple reason that they are usually not coterminous with other governmental jurisdictions. State party organizations are normally geared to statewide campaigns, whereas county and city organizations compete for offices within their jurisdictions. This tends to leave congressional candidates in districts that encompass several counties without permanent party organization on which to rely. The common pattern therefore is to build highly personal campaign organizations.[26]

The Steiger campaign organization was something of an exception. In each of his three campaigns for Congress Steiger has relied heavily on the regular party organization within each of the seven counties in his district. He and his first campaign manager, Peter Kohler—president of Kohler General Corporation—shared a belief that it is important not only to win the election at hand but also to sustain Republican victories for Congress and all other offices. This requires permanent, well-organized parties, rather than personal loyalties and followings.

In addition to the Steiger for Congress committee chairman, campaign manager, treasurer, and secretary-legal counsel, Steiger also appointed a county coordinator in each county after consultation with (and with the approval of) the respective GOP county chairmen. Such a coordinator's function was to supervise all Steiger campaign activities in his county, to help arrange speaking engagements, meetings, caravans, and distribution of literature on behalf of his candidate. In all their dealings with county coordinators Steiger, his campaign manager, and his staff kept the respective county chairmen fully advised. Because of Steiger's commitment to assist the county chairmen in their own campaign activities, his staff and the county coordinators scheduled joint appearances for him and county candidates, as well as joint distribution of campaign literature.

One of the first campaign decisions in Steiger's initial campaign (1966), which was repeated during the first reelection campaign in 1968, was to hire a firm to make depth surveys of voter sentiment in the district. The surveys conducted in 1966 (in June 1966, after Steiger became the endorsed candidate, and in September) and in 1968 were considered by the candidate and his campaign manager absolutely essential to ensure that the campaign organization would function with maximum effectiveness. It was important to know voter sentiment on issues, which issues were salient, and voters' perceptions of the relative strengths and weaknesses of Steiger and his opponent, John Race. By 1970 Steiger was well established in the district and familiar with issues and district attitudes. It was decided that a major expenditure for a survey would therefore not be justified.[27]

In his first campaign Steiger had hired a prominent Milwaukee public-relations firm to handle his media campaign. In 1970 this expenditure was also deemed unnecessary, and the budget for media advertising was substantially reduced. A small advertising firm in Fond du Lac was retained to handle the candidate's limited television and radio advertising during the final week of the campaign. The firm also helped to design the newspaper advertising and the "Steiger for Congress" brochure that was distributed to virtually every household in the district.

The 1966 Steiger congressional campaign had cost approximately $70,000. The National Republican Congressional (Campaign) Committee in Washington had contributed $15,000 through its Booster Club because the district was considered one of its prime targets. The Republican state committee had also placed a high priority on regaining the Sixth District and had therefore allocated substantial funds to the Steiger campaign. A testimonial luncheon at which former Wisconsin Congressman Walter Judd had spoken and solicitations within the district had also helped to raise funds.

The 1970 campaign budget was much lower—approximately $30,000. Because he was considered a relatively safe incumbent Steiger received only $2,500 from the National Republican Congressional Committee and no money from the Republican state committee. Rather, he helped to raise $5,000 beyond his own campaign budget for the state committee to use in meeting its own obligations. Steiger explained: "I strongly believe that incumbent congressmen should not be a drain on the party financially. They should be paying their own way and should actually help the party raise money."

The largest segment of his 1970 campaign funds was raised early in June at a $25-a-plate testimonial dinner attended by Governor Warren Knowles and other state officials. Secretary of Labor James Hodgson was the principal speaker. Securing his presence had been facilitated by Steiger's membership on the House Education and Labor Committee, which has jurisdiction over

Hodgson's department. The dinner netted the Steiger for Congress Committee approximately $15,000. The timing of the dinner was important because it provided the "early money." With money in the bank early in the campaign, the candidate could reserve prime television and radio time and "firm up" his campaign plans. There was no need to spend the critical weeks immediately before the election trying to raise necessary funds.

Any candidate for major office must be informed on the issues. Here the advantage of incumbency was particularly great. For four years Steiger had been dealing with the major national issues on a day-to-day basis. Although a junior member of the House, he had been a prominent advocate of a volunteer army, reform of manpower training, congressional reform, and revenue sharing. By virtue of his mail from constituents, frequent visits to the district, and his mail survey of the district, he was also familiar with the matters on the minds of his constituents. Furthermore, his Education and Labor Committee assignment had put him in a favorable position to speak on issues of special importance in the 1970 elections: employment, job training, and education.

In summary, the Steiger campaign was well organized and functioned with the support of the regular Republican organizations in each of the seven counties in the district. Although not lavishly funded, the Steiger for Congress Committee had sufficient financial resources to run the type of campaign that he had chosen. In addition, Steiger entered the campaign well informed on national and district issues.

The Democratic challenger's organizational resources were in sharp contrast to those of Steiger. The Democratic organization in virtually every county was rudimentary at best; it had neither personnel nor funds to mount a sustained campaign. Utech therefore followed the familiar pattern among congressional candidates. He sought to create his own personal organization. Steiger had still another advantage: He was well known to voters of the Sixth District. A 1968 survey conducted after Steiger had been in office less than two years revealed that 70 percent of the electorate could correctly identify him as their congressman and 38 percent had met or seen him; 52 percent reported reading about him in the news several times a month. Not only was Steiger well known; he was also favorably known to his constituents, as these data from the 1968 campaign survey indicate:

	Total	Republican	Ticket Spliters	Democrats
Approve	66%	78%	67%	51%
Disapprove	8%	2%	9%	19%

Although these figures reflect an expected partisan bias in evaluations of Steiger as a congressman, more than half the Democrats approved of the job that he was doing.

Running a seven-county campaign required a central headquarters staff, as well as coordinators and "field workers" in each county. All of them were difficult to find. The Lots of People for Utech Committee lacked the financial resources to hire a staff. Utech's campaign manager, Richard Flintrop, was a former student at the University of Wisconsin-Oshkosh who received only a nominal salary and found it necessary to live in the Utech home to hold down his expenses.

In attempting to work with the county Democratic units, Utech encountered considerable resentment because of his former involvement in the McCarthy campaign and the peace movement. Many of the regular Democrats thought that the McCarthy supporters had failed to support Hubert H. Humphrey in 1968 and had thus contributed to his defeat. In other sections of the state the McCarthy, Humphrey, and Kennedy partisans had been able to make common cause against the Republicans. But that was not the case in the Sixth District. As an art professor, McCarthy supporter, peace activist, and resident of only three years in the district, Utech remained suspect among many active Democratic leaders.

Frequently cut off from effective organizational support within the party organization, Utech sought to work through his contacts from the McCarthy movement of 1968. Although many McCarthy followers did work in his behalf, the fire had gone out of that movement, and their help was an insufficient substitute for an effective party apparatus. Furthermore, some prominent individuals who had worked in behalf of McCarthy were reluctant to be identified with a Democratic congressional candidate running against a popular and non-doctrinaire Republican.

Utech's basic campaign organization consisted of himself, his wife, the campaign manager, and approximately 100 volunteers—mainly from his hometown of Oshkosh—who manned the headquarters that he rented, distributed literature, prepared press releases and position papers, arranged speaking engagements, and canvassed for votes.

The total budget for the campaign was approximately $9,000, raised mainly through small contributions from individuals (there was one $1,000 contribution and another for $400 from a faculty colleague), a few labor-union locals, and county party organizations. The candidate himself spent approximately $800-$900 out of his own pocket. There were no contributions from the state Democratic administrative committee and none from such national groups as the Democratic Congressional Campaign Committee and the Committee for an Effective Congress. As in the senatorial election described in this chapter, the national Democratic organizations tried to concentrate their dollars where they would do the most good.

Because of the modest organizational and financial resources available to him, Utech had to rely heavily on personal contacts with voters at plant gates and shopping centers, distribution of literature, and billboards. He did no television and little radio advertising—other than the free time he could obtain on interview and call-in programs.

A serious limitation on his campaign was his failure to receive endorsement by the AFL-CIO's political arm, COPE, which had supplied the bulk of the money and organization for previous Democratic campaigns.

The unequal distribution of resources was also apparent with regard to issue research and information. Utech was relatively new to the district and therefore lacked detailed knowledge of its economy, especially agriculture. Furthermore, he had not been dealing with national issues constantly over a four-year period as Steiger had. Consequently he and his recruits had to spend a great deal of time studying the issues. He had to rely rather heavily on background materials and press releases sent to him by the Democratic National Committee in Washington, D.C.

Lewis A. Froman has suggested that as districts become more competitive between the parties, inequality of resources becomes more important.[28] The previous history of the district confirms that it is potentially competitive. In a 1965 survey respondents were asked, "In politics, do you usually consider yourself a Republican or Democrat?" When a voter responded with "I don't know" or declared himself independent, he was asked, "Well, do you think of yourself as closer to the Democratic Party or the Republican Party?" The results were as follows:

	Total
Republican	48%
Democrat	45%
Independent	7%

Even though the district could have been highly competitive, the resources available to the candidates—both young, energentic, and articulate—were hardly equal. Neither in organization, financing, nor research was the Utech campaign on a level with that of Steiger. Nor was Utech as well known as Steiger. The importance of the distribution of resources will be explored in later discussion of the actual conduct of the campaign.

Labor Endorsement

An important element in the Democratic coalition nationally and in Wisconsin is organized labor, particularly COPE. It is especially important in the Sixth District, with its relatively high concentration of manufacturing and union memberships.[29]

Steiger was aware of the actual and potential strength of organized labor in the district. He was also intimately involved in many issues of concern to labor because of his membership on the Education and Labor Committee and his service on its Select Labor Subcommittee. Although COPE had sought to defeat him in both 1966 and 1968, Steiger had not during his four years in Congress become known as one of labor's arch enemies. He had worked actively for passage of the federal Construction Safety Act—a measure of special importance to the building trades. He had also assumed leadership among House Republicans on manpower legislation. Although not agreeing to all the provisions sought by labor, Steiger had worked effectively in committee with labor-oriented Democrats to produce a compromise manpower bill that contained a labor-endorsed public-service-employment provision. Steiger then took the lead in selling the bill to his fellow Republicans on the committee and in the Nixon administration.

While thus demonstrating that he could work constructively with the labor movement, he had also demonstrated that he could be an effective tenacious opponent. In coordination with the administration and the House GOP leadership, he had fought the labor-endorsed version of the Occupational Health and Safety Act. He had introduced a substitute bill, which had been defeated in committee, and he had then pledged to carry his fight to the floor.[30]

Steiger's record therefore was mixed as far as COPE was concerned. He had cooperated on some important labor issues, but he had also been a resourceful opponent on others. At the end of the first session of the 91st Congress, however, Steiger could claim a 70 percent COPE rating—the highest among the state's Republican delegation.[31] This rating contrasted sharply with the results of a 1966 private survey, showing that the only negative aspect of Steiger's image among the voters was lack of identification with labor.

The Sixth Congressional District COPE committee met in spring 1970 to interview candidates. For the first time Steiger was invited along with the Democratic candidate. This setting was extremely unfamiliar to Steiger, who broke the ice by remarking, "Unaccustomed as I am to speaking at COPE meetings . . ." The reception was warm and friendly, and the interview extended well beyond the customary time. While it continued, Utech sat outside the meeting room awaiting his turn. When it came, the reception was extremely cool and the interview brief. The committee then voted by an overwhelming majority not to endorse a candidate in the Sixth District.

This outcome was precisely what Steiger had sought. Endorsement of Utech would have given the latter funds and part of the organizational machinery needed for an effective campaign. A COPE endorsement of Steiger, on the other hand, might have alienated some staunch Republicans. No endorsement meant that Republicans would not be offended and at the same time that the maximum possible Democratic vote in the district would probably not be mobilized. COPE's decision was thus a critical early blow to the Utech campaign.

There were four reasons behind the COPE decision. First, Steiger had developed support among the influential local building-trades leaders, particularly in Winnebago County, where both he and Utech lived. As a result, when the Sixth District COPE met, Utech was without support from his home county, while Steiger had such support.

Second, Steiger had the formal endorsement of the national building-trades unions, which meant that a COPE endorsement of a Democrat in the Sixth District would have caused disunity within the ranks of labor. Although building-trades endorsement of the Congressman was certainly a factor in preventing COPE from endorsing Utech, it should be noted that such an endorsement of Steiger in 1968 had not prevented COPE from mounting a heavy campaign to defeat him and to elect former Congressman Race. But Race was himself a union member who had been elected right out of the shops in 1964, a candidate whom COPE could easily sell to its members as deserving their support. This approach would have been more difficult with Utech.

Utech's relations with the forces in the Democratic coalition were a particularly important factor in the COPE decision. As mentioned previously, he had been a leader of the 1968 McCarthy for President movement. Among labor leaders there was resentment about the adverse effect of the McCarthy campaign on Humphrey's presidential bid. In the minds of labor leaders Utech was closely identified with what they considered the divisive McCarthy faction. One leader said:

> You have to understand that Hubert H. Humphrey is the patron saint of the labor movement. We love him. He has always been for us and helped us. A lot of our people can't forget the way those McCarthy people hurt Hubert and failed to support him after the convention.

Utech was not, in short, the type of candidate that the COPE leaders in the Sixth District thought that they could effectively persuade their members to support. At the same time, Steiger's own record on issues of importance to organized labor did not seem too bad. In describing COPE'S attitude toward Steiger, a labor leader said:

> Every so often on the political scene you find a candidate that seems to fit the needs of a district pretty well. He's young, attractive, works hard, and has shown a certain independence. He's not necessarily opposed to us—we can work with him. Of course, he's not like Clem [Zablocki] or Henry Reuss [Democrats from Milwaukee], but he's not automatically against us either the way a lot of Republicans are. There's some hope for Steiger.

County-level COPE organizations in Sheboygan and Fond du Lac Counties later did endorse Utech, but this support was of limited value. Major financial contributions come from COPE's state and national bodies, and Utech's county endorsements were worth only a few hundred dollars.

In addition to the favorable policies of COPE and the building trades,

Steiger was successful in gaining the endorsements of the Teamsters and the railroad brotherhoods. These endorsements had many advantages for his candidacy: Utech's charges that he was antilabor could be refuted by citing his endorsements and his role in manpower legislation. Furthermore, Steiger was invited to speak to union meetings, whereas Utech met rather cool reactions to most of his attempts to find union speaking engagements.

By neutralizing the major campaign resource normally available to a Democratic candidate and actually winning limited labor support himself, Steiger widened the advantage that he already held as an incumbent.

The Campaign

Congressional campaigns are normally considered to begin in the spring or summer of even-numbered years and to intensify after Labor Day. For the resourceful incumbent, however, the campaign has no real beginning or end. It is a year-round activity essentially indistinguishable from his official congressional duties.

A congressman must make decisions and statements on issues of national and district concern; they in turn generate news stories about him in the district. Steiger has benefited in this regard because the newspapers and radio-television outlets in his district are not primarily located in large metropolitan areas represented by several congressmen. Rather, the papers and stations are in small or medium-sized cities and are in a position to focus attention on *their* congressman and to give his activities extensive coverage. For example, all the papers in the district promptly carried accounts of Steiger's call for speedy congressional action on antibombing legislation proposed by President Nixon in the aftermath of the August 1970 bombing at the University of Wisconsin, which had killed a young physicist. In addition to such news coverage of his activities, Steiger also writes a weekly column which is printed in several newspapers in the district. Several papers also frequently carry the full text of his major speeches. His television and radio reports to the district are also given considerable play.

Incumbency also provides opportunities for personal contact with the voters. During the year Steiger makes frequent weekend trips to the district. These visits are filled with speeches to local organizations and "office hours" in post offices, city halls, and courthouses. These activities enable the Congressman to learn at first hand about district problems and the personal difficulties that constituents may be having with federal programs. Steiger and his staff spend a large portion of their time dealing with all these problems (see Chapter 3 for a more detailed account of congressional service to constituents).

In an effort to provide effective constituent service to individuals, organizations, and local governments, Steiger has a full-time home secretary, Fred Seefeldt. Seefeldt operates out of Steiger's home office in the Oshkosh post office; he travels widely in the district, meeting people who wish some contact with the Congressman.

Without regard to partisanship, the conscientious and resourceful incumbent can thus project an image of himself as a dedicated, concerned, and effective legislator. He does so as part of his job, not simply as a campaigner in the fall of an election year. The way in which official duties and campaigning activities merge and mutually reinforce each other can be illustrated by Steiger's work during the two-week congressional Labor Day recess.

Steiger and his family flew back to the district immediately after adjournment. There followed an intensive schedule of engagements—some openly campaign oriented but most as part of his congressional duties. Steiger held office hours in nineteen different communities (in addition to being available in his home office in Oshkosh on many days). Particular attention was paid to the smaller communities that he had not been able to visit during earlier weekend visits. Often Steiger would include in these trips handshaking tours of the main streets, stopping for brief chats with local merchants, tradesmen, and shoppers.

When he visited a community for office hours he usually also spoke at noon and in the evening to the local service clubs. In all he made thirteen service-club appearances during the two-week recess. Such appearances were relatively easy to arrange. Often all that was involved was accepting a standing invitation from the local Lions, Rotary, or Kiwanis Clubs.

Although the Sixth District has one of the highest rates of industrial growth in the state, agriculture continues to be an important part of its economic base. The county fairs of August and September are therefore important events. During the recess Steiger made thirteen appearances at county fairs, frequently at the county Republican organizations' booths. Steiger also met with and spoke to local chapter meetings of the American Farm Bureau Federation and the National Farmers' Organization (NFO).

As an incumbent congressman he also received invitations to speak and participate in significant local events: the centennial celebration of the Fond du Lac newspaper, a graduation ceremony for practical nurses in Neenah, the ground-breaking for a new industrial park in Germantown, and the Jaycee Fall Festival parade in Berlin.

Because of Steiger's commitment to working with and strengthening Republican Party organizations in the district, he also attended and spoke at GOP fund-raising events in three counties.

Steiger's intensive schedule of office hours, speeches, ceremonial functions, personal appearances, and public statements on current issues all received detailed coverage in the district media. Most of the coverage was as "hard news" (rather than political or partisan in tone).

Steiger's opponent was not idle during this period. Utech was also meeting voters in shopping centers, at plant gates, and at fairs; attending coffee hours in

friends' and supporters' homes; and fulfilling a limited number of speaking engagements. He was also trying to issue at least one major press release each week
attacking Steiger and the Nixon administration. But as the nonincumbent his
activities generated little public attention or press coverage. Coverage of his
statements was frequently found in the last paragraph of a major story about
Steiger—often complete with headlines about Steiger and Steiger's picture. When
Utech did receive separate coverage, it was usually in a format that aroused little
attention. In addition, his news stories nearly always portrayed him in an electioneering role, whereas Steiger's stories seldom did.

On September 9 Congress ended its Labor Day recess and resumed regular
sessions that lasted until October 16. The necessity of being in Washington and
his duties connected with the manpower occupational health and safety legislation limited Steiger's campaign activities during September and October. But
during this period he returned home on four weekends. Whereas the Labor Day
recess had been devoted primarily to activities that would be considered non-
political by the general public, the post-Labor Day activities were much more
oriented toward campaigning. The weekend visits, however, still included time
for office hours in various cities and villages, service-club speeches, and ceremonial functions like a school dedication.

There were frequent visits during these weekends to local radio, television,
and newspaper offices for discussions with editors and interviews with reporters.
Steiger also went out to shake hands on main streets and at shopping centers.

When Congress recessed in mid-October to give its members time for full-
time campaigning, Steiger returned to maintain a continual round of activities
that again included both regular congressional work and campaigning. On a
typical day, Tuesday, October 20, Steiger spent 8:30-10:30 A.M. in his Oshkosh
office. He first read the Wisconsin newspapers and answered congressional mail,
dictating replies or making notes on the letters informing the staff how matters
should be handled. It was also necessary to call his office in Washington: to give
directions for work that he wanted done in preparation for House consideration
of the manpower bill; to consult administrative assistant Maureen Drummy
about office administration and political developments in Washington; and to
work out details of his postelection schedule.

When the lengthy call to Washington was completed, Steiger and his executive assistant, Ted Cormaney, turned their attention to a water-and-sewage grant
application that a city in the district had made to the Department of Housing
and Urban Development (HUD). When the Congressman had been campaigning
in the city earlier in the fall the mayor had sought his help in determining the
status of this application. Cormaney was assigned to check further with HUD on
the status of the application.

Before leaving for the day's round of campaign appearances, Steiger took
several telephone calls from constituents seeking help on matters that involved
federal programs. He also reviewed various aspects of his media campaign with

his campaign staff. Finally, he asked the staff to make certain that "Thank You for Your Support" billboard signs had been ordered to be used after the election, regardless of whether he won or lost.

Campaigning in a multicounty district involves many hours on the road. As he traveled to his first stop—a radio station in Fond du Lac, which had invited Steiger and Utech to appear on a call-in show—Steiger worked in the front seat while an assistant drove. He scanned a variety of materials sent him from the Washington office, reviewed a speech to be given later in the day, and gave an interview to a reporter.

The call-in program began with three-minute statements by the candidates. Utech led off. As he had done throughout the campaign, he attacked the Nixon administration on economic issues—blaming it for the rise in unemployment and inflation, for a misdirected set of priorities placing too great an emphasis on national security and not enough on human needs, and for continuing the Vietnam war. Utech did not focus on Steiger or his record, though his attack was an implicit criticism of Steiger for supporting Nixon's administration.

Steiger gave three principal reasons why he was running for reelection: (1) to facilitate the Nixon administration initiatives in scaling down the war in Vietnam, beginning the transition from a wartime to peacetime economy and changing national priorities so that more was spent on human resources than on defense programs; (2) to continue the legislative projects on which he had been working but which could not be accomplished in a short time-creation of an all-volunteer army, establishment of a comprehensive child-care program, reform of vocational-education and manpower programs, and improvement of higher-education programs; and (3) to continue the fight to achieve passage of administration reform programs (like the Family Assistance Plan and revenue sharing) which he claimed had been thwarted by a Democratic Congress.

The campaign themes of the two candidates were clearly different. Steiger, as the incumbent, stressed his own record and his support for the policies of the administration. Utech, as the challenger, sought to discredit Steiger indirectly by running against the Nixon administration, which Steiger openly supported.

Virtually all the questions telephoned to the contestants dealt with "bread and butter" economic issues—the income tax, rising property taxes, interest rates, inflation, and unemployment. For each of these problems Utech blamed the Nixon administration. He also consistently advocated reduced defense spending and elimination of Defense Department waste with resulting savings to be spent on domestic problems like mass transit. During much of the debate Steiger explained the issues for the listeners. The advantage of familiarity with issues that comes from day-to-day involvement with them was apparent throughout the interview program.

When he challenged John Race in 1966, Steiger had effectively exploited Race's refusal to debate and to appear with Steiger in a public forum. This tactic is rather common when incumbents refuse to give publicity to their opponents.

Because Steiger was willing to make several joint radio or television appearances with Utech during the course of the campaign, Utech was denied this sort of campaign ploy.

Following the hour-long interview program with Utech, Steiger had lunch at a local restaurant operated by a Republican supporter. In the restaurant Steiger shook hands with friends and customers; many people stopped at his table to greet him. He was obviously known by sight to many of his constituents.

After a quick lunch the Congressman went to the Fond du Lac Odd Fellows Hall to speak to the local chapter of the American Association of Retired Persons (AARP). Steiger's brief remarks summarizing the status of bills affecting the elderly were met by a barrage of critical questions related to the financial plight of older Americans living on fixed incomes. Although it was apparent that the AARP members were deeply troubled and even angry about their situation, most later demonstrated that they did not blame Bill Steiger. One member who made a hostile comment about Steiger and his record received a tart response from an elderly lady and cold stares from others. During the coffee hour that followed the meeting, most members of the group made it a point to tell Steiger that they thought that he was doing a good job and that they appreciated his telling it to them straight and not making them a bunch of promises. Many people seemed to take an almost parental interest in the young representative. One elderly man said: "The first time I saw you, I thought you were just some little kid running across the street. You've done lots since then." Others made it a point to ask about Steiger's year-old son, William, and his wife, Janet.

From the AARP meeting Steiger traveled back to Oshkosh to speak at the annual dinner of the Wisconsin Rehabilitation Association. Steiger's Education and Labor Committee assignment had involved him rather heavily in vocational-rehabilitation legislation, and legislative and campaign activities once again merged. The meeting provided an opportunity to discuss informally with national and state vocational-rehabilitation leaders the legislative proposals that would be acted upon during the next session of Congress. Steiger also had another forum from which to make contact with the voters.

He left the dinner early to drive sixty miles to Sheboygan to attend a candidates' forum sponsored by the League of Women Voters. Utech and Mrs. Rani Davidson, the American Party candidate, had also been invited to attend. Parked outside the YMCA, where the meeting was to be held, was Mrs. Davidson's Liberty Bell float. The red, white, and blue float carried a replica of the Liberty Bell and a large banner with the words "Support the Liberty Amendment"—a major theme of her campaign.

Steiger and Utech made opening statements very similar to the ones that they had made earlier in the day on the radio in Fond du Lac. Mrs. Davidson, in a carefully prepared statement, stressed that she was an "ex-Republican" who had become disillusioned with her party and candidates like Steiger because they did little to stop the growth of "big government"—including government competition with business and government infringement of individual liberties. She called for either winning in Vietnam or getting out, curtailment of trading with the enemy, and defeat of the Nixon welfare-reform plan. She made a strong plea for the "liberty amendment"—repeal of the income tax.

Whereas the discussion at the radio station had chiefly centered around economic issues, the League of Women Voters' session, probably reflecting the middle-class nature of the League, tended to be much more wide-ranging. There were questions about the President's veto of Labor-HEW appropriations, the seating of Adam Clayton Powell (D.-N.Y.), law and order, the D.C. crime bill, arts and humanities appropriations, electoral and congressional reform.

As in the morning debate Steiger's familiarity with a wide range of issues was immediately apparent. It was frequently necessary for him to devote time to explaining the contents and status of legislation. He again had the advantage of being able to cite his record when asked a question. When a woman asked about reform of Congress—especially the seniority system—Steiger responded that he had been a leader of a bipartisan group that had achieved a series of major reforms in the House (see Chapter 8) and that he had served on a Republican House task force whose recent proposal for a change in seniority had been accepted by the GOP House leadership.

Throughout the forum Utech tended to give rather lengthy, unfocused answers that did not directly criticize Steiger. Mrs. Davidson, after Steiger's exposition of an issue and his activities connected with it, would frequently comment, "I agree with Bill on that one."

The League of Women Voters meeting concluded at about 10:00 P.M. Steiger stayed on to talk informally with those in attendance and to confer briefly with Peter Kohler, the Sixth Congressional District leader. They discussed the potential impact of Mrs. Davidson on conservative GOP voters. Kohler reported on efforts that were being made to counteract her campaign in Ozaukee County.

Steiger left Sheboygan at about 10:30 P.M. for a drive through heavy fog back to Oshkosh, where he arrived at midnight.

Saturdays were devoted to county-caravan tours (usually made in about twenty cars or trucks sporting various Republican cartops and signs) with other GOP candidates through rural areas and small towns. Along with other Republican candidates, Steiger would start with breakfast at a local restaurant. Then there would be a handshaking tour of the village—chats with people on the street and visits to stores, barbershops, and gas stations to meet the townspeople and pass out green and black Steiger for Congress matchbooks. This routine would be followed in each town on the tour.

These county caravans brought Steiger excellent press coverage. The *Sheboygan Press* reported on his caravan tour of that county:

That topic [highways taking farmland out of production] came up again in Smitty's Sweet Shop in Cedar Grove. And again Steiger sat down and patiently explained his position, took notes for future use and told those with whom he was talking to write him in Washington about the issue.

Steiger's natural quality is readily apparent. In spite of his hurried pace between stores and business places at which he made his political calls, he always seemed to have ample time not only to meet people but to listen to what they had to say.

He seemed right at home with both young and old . . . .

As a press assistant to the Congressman commented after reading this news story, "You just can't do better than that. I'd be embarrassed to write a press release that was that favorable to Bill. You can't beat news coverage—it's better than ten press releases."

During the final week Steiger stepped up his media campaign by running a series of spot announcements on the Green Bay television station (which services most of the district), "spots" on all the district radio stations, and advertisements in the district papers.

In keeping with his campaign theme—"A Congressman You Can Talk To"—the climax to the Steiger campaign was a television call-in program emanating from a Fond du Lac station, the first time that the technique had been used by the Congressman. The response to the advertisements requesting that people call collect to talk with their congressman was greater than the Steiger organization had anticipated. The Congressman fielded a steady stream of calls for an hour without a break.

The opening call set the program off to a sensational start. The caller was the father of a Vietnam veteran, who said that he was calling because he "just wanted to say thank you" to the Congressman for help while his son had been a patient in a military hospital. The father had been concerned that his son had not been receiving proper care, and Steiger had been instrumental in seeing to it that proper care was provided. There were, of course, critical callers, but generally it was thought that the Congressman was able to respond to the questions and that he handled himself well.

The Utech campaign contrasted sharply with that of Steiger. There was no occasion to hold office hours, no reason for anyone to be in touch with him about local problems or personal problems relating to federal programs. Nor were there many invitations to attend ceremonial events and parades. Rather Utech had to solicit nearly every speaking engagement that he received, which was often difficult. The service clubs—most of whose members were Republicans—manifested no enthusiasm for his speaking at their meetings.

In addition, Utech's limited staff and money meant that he could generate little more than perfunctory publicity and attention for his candidacy. A survey of newspaper coverage of the two candidates between October 26 and 31, 1970, showed that there were twenty major news stories on Steiger's activities—often including pictures—but only five short stories about Utech, one a hostile editorial in a small-town weekly.

Utech and his campaign manager were the mainstays of the organization; Utech frequently had to drive himself to campaign engagements. By contrast, Steiger, because his assistant drove for him, could use travel time for study, work, and press interviews. Given Utech's shortage of personnel and his heavy personal investment of time and energy in routine campaign duties, it is not surprising that he was unable to develop a consistent set of campaign themes that would attract public attention.

Utech's personal campaigning consisted of such speaking engagements as could be generated, coffee hours at supporters' homes, and many hours shaking hands and passing out literature at plant gates and shopping centers.

Conclusion

On the morning after the election, Sixth District voters were greeted by special bold signs reading "Thank You for Your Support" on the black-and-green Steiger for Congress billboards. These signs had been quickly put up by youthful volunteers late on election night, reflecting the well-organized basis from which the Steiger campaign operated and the Congressman's belief that campaigns do not end on election eve.

Whereas other Republican congressional incumbents from Wisconsin had closer races than expected or were defeated, Steiger won his largest plurality (54,893 votes) and his highest percentage of the vote (67.7), increasing it in each of the seven counties in the district. In no county did he receive less than 65 percent of the vote.

Given Steiger's incumbency, his organization, financial and reputational advantages, and the Republican traditions of the district, his victory was expected. The margin of victory, however, was impressive, given the statewide adverse trend against the GOP. The Democratic candidate for governor received 54 percent of the statewide vote, and Democratic Senator William Proxmire won 71 percent of the vote in his reelection. Most observers believed that Proxmire, who was on the ballot just above the congressional candidates, had a major coattail impact on congressional races in the state, but he apparently had little effect on the Sixth District, reflecting the ability of voters to make sharp differentiations in the polling booth when there is a well-known incumbent with a positive image.[32] Only in the Sixth District, where Steiger's name was just above those of legislative candidates, did the GOP fail to lose state legislative seats.

The campaign also demonstrated the close relation between congressional duties and campaigning. Indeed, it was virtually impossible to make a sharp distinction between the two kinds of activity. This fact of congressional life may mean that a shift to four-year House terms, which some have advocated, would not significantly change the ways that congressmen spend their time and enable them to devote more time to legislative work. Steiger used his position and his obligations in a way that reinforced the image of a concerned, active, and responsible legislator. He drew heavily on his involvement in Labor and Education Committee issues in his discussions with voters. This involvement continued to be intense during the "lame duck" session that followed the election. Steiger acted as GOP floor manager in the House for both the Occupational Health and Safety Act and the Manpower Act. He also served as a conferee on the joint Senate-House conference committee that attempted to develop a compromise between the House and Senate versions of the latter legislation. When the conference failed, in the judgment of Steiger and his Republican colleagues, to develop a compromise adequately reflecting the contents of the House version, Steiger recommended a presidential veto of the legislation. On December 16, 1970, President Nixon vetoed the bill.

Steiger's role in this congressional-executive battle involving a major economic-employment issue was a major news item in the Sixth District. The stage was thus already being set and the issues being developed for Steiger's 1972 reelection campaign.

The advantages of incumbency, which Steiger used so effectively, are not without implications for the functioning of Congress. These advantages cause stability in the membership of the House (and the Senate, where approximately 80 percent of incumbents win reelection). The ability of incumbents to be reelected and even to withstand powerful adverse trends generated by opposition presidential candidates prevents dramatic shifts of sentiment within the House. Low turnover in congressional seats has also tended to "professionalize" the congressional job, turning it into a full-time occupation and potentially a lifetime undertaking. Stability of membership makes certain norms of the House, like seniority, attractive to members and strengthens other norms like apprenticeship, bargaining, negotiation, and compromise. Advancement within the chamber is relatively slow, as members are evaluated and reevaluated by their peers. This slow pace is reflected in the increasingly long tenure required before a congressman can achieve major leadership positions (in the nineteenth century Henry Clay was chosen Speaker as a freshman congressman).

The ability to use congressional office to consolidate one's electoral position also means that a representative will probably maintain a constant involvement and interest in local problems and local orientation toward many issues. The nature of his electoral situation will probably have considerable influence on the roles that he adopts in Congress.[33]

NOTES FOR CHAPTER 2

1 See Barbara Hinckley, "Incumbency and the Presidential Vote in Senate Elections: Defining Parameters of Subpresidential Voting," *American Political Science Review*, 64 (September 1970), 836-842; and V. O. Key, Jr., *Politics, Parties, and Pressure Groups* (5th ed.; New York: Crowell, 1964), pp. 546-556.

2 The total turnover (including retirements and defeats) in the House of Representatives was only about 13 percent in 1970.

3 John H. Fenton, *Politics in the Border States* (New Orleans: Hauser, 1957), p. 148. Although Fenton's observations are now somewhat dated, they were perceptive for their time and form the basis for much of this discussion.

4 Austin Ranney, "Parties in State Politics," in Herbert Jacob and Kenneth Vines (eds.), *Politics in the American States* (Boston: Little, Brown, 1965), pp. 63-67. Ranney's index score for Maryland was .7137, which means, in approximate terms, that the state was about 71 percent Democratic. Ilis index took into account the proportion of success for each party, the duration of success, and the frequency of divided control of state government. The measure was, however, based wholly on state offices (governor and state legislature) and limited to the period 1946-1963.

5 Richard M. Scammon (ed.), *America Votes 8* (1968) (Washington, D.C.: Governmental Affairs Institute, 1970), pp. 164-172.

6 District of Columbia Court Reorganization and Criminal Procedure Act of 1970 (P.L. 91-358).

7 Robert F. Levey, "Senate Liberals Outgunned on Crime Bill," *Washington Post*, July 24, 1970, p. A-8.

8 A survey by John F. Kraft, Inc., in April 1970 showed the following preferences: for Tydings 49 percent, for Morton 31 percent, unsure 20 percent.

9 Lotito was the only campaign aide who remained on the Senate payroll during the campaign. Tydings had questioned the Senate Ethics Committee, which ruled that as a press aide's job is to publicize and further a senator's interests, his professional role could not be distinguished from his role in the campaign.

10 Oliver Quayle, Inc., Study 1219 (May 1969). Results are cited with the permission of Senator Tydings.

11 William Lambert, "What the Senator Didn't Disclose," *Life* (August 28, 1970), pp. 26-29.

12 A text of the statement appeared in the *Washington Post*, August 21, 1970, p. A-20. See also *The New York Times*, August 25, 1970, p. 28.

13 Financial reports submitted to the Clerk of the Senate are confidential, but some senators make public some or all of their reports. Tydings was one who issued such a

disclosure, with an accompanying press release that stated that "such [public] disclosure is the best protection against both actual conflicts of interest and public suspicion of partiality for private gain in the writing, execution and judicial interpretation of the laws."

14 Ronald Kessler, "Sen. Tydings is Cleared of Loan Charge," *Washington Post*, November 14, 1970, p. B-1.

15 Quoted in Kessler, "Tydings Loan Figure Quits State Dept.," *Washington Post*, November 17, 1970, p. C-1.

16 Oliver Quayle, Inc., Survey 1354 (September 1970). Findings are cited with the permission of Senator Tydings.

17 So many voters referred to Beall's experience that the survey analysts speculated that he was being confused with his father, a two-term senator.

18 Ironically, the Republican *Washington Star* refused to print the ad.

19 Here are sample quotations: "You have the God-given right to kick the government around—don't hesitate to do so" (Edmund Muskie); "Instead of intimidating the public dissenter, we ought to welcome his independence and give his views a careful hearing" (George McGovern).

20 The ads were used against Muskie, Gale McGee (Wyoming), Joseph Montoya (New Mexico), Harrison Williams (New Jersey), John Tunney (California), and Tydings. All but Tydings won reelection.

21 The last of the four surveys, taken by the Joseph Napolitan organization, showed the following breakdown: Tydings 37.7 percent, Beall 30.0 percent, undecided 32.3 percent. Of the undecided voters 17.1 percent were "leaning toward" Tydings, 5.9 percent were leaning toward Beall, and 77 percent were still undecided. Telephone surveys, without face-to-face contact, tend to turn up larger portions of undecided respondents and are therefore not reliable.

22 In the 1970 congressional elections only thirteen incumbent congressmen were defeated in the general election. Ten lost in the primaries. Fifty had no opposition in the general election. For further information on the theme "incumbents win," see Charles O. Jones "Inter-Party Competition for Congressional Seats," *Western Political Quarterly*, 17 (September 1964), 461-476; Milton C. Cummings, Jr., *Congressmen and the Electorate* (New York: Free Press, 1966), chap. 3; and Hinckley, "Incumbency and the Presidential Vote in Senate Elections," *American Political Science Review*, 69 (September 1970), 836-847.

23 In 1970 sixteen members of the House relinquished their seats to bid for seats in the "upper chamber."

24 In the 1966 congressional campaign the incumbent, John Race (D.-Wis.), sought unsuccessfully to exploit Steiger's youth by frequently referring to him as "the kid" or "Billy."

25 See William J. Keefe and Morris Ogul, *The American Legislative Process: Congress and the States* (Englewood Cliffs, N.J.: Prentice-Hall, 1968), pp. 107-108.

26 On party organization at the congressional district level, see Key, *Politics, Parties, and Pressure Groups*, p. 448.

27 For a discussion of polling in political campaigns see Dan Nimmo, *The Political Persuaders: The Techniques of Modern Election Campaigns* (Englewood Cliffs, N.J.: Prentice-Hall, 1970).

28 Lewis A. Froman, Jr., *Congressmen and Their Constituencies* (Chicago: Rand McNally, 1963), p. 53.

29 Former Congressman John Race, whom Steiger defeated in 1966 and 1968, had relied heavily on labor for funds and organization. For a detailed consideration of the role of organized labor in financing Wisconsin political campaigns, see H. Gayland Greenhill, *Labor Money in Wisconsin Politics, 1964* (Princeton: Citizen's Research Foundation, 1967); and David Adamany, *Financing Politics: Recent Wisconsin Elections* (Madison: University of Wisconsin Press, 1969).

30 In the "lame duck" session of Congress called after the 1970 elections, Steiger led the successful floor fight for House passage of the Steiger-Sikes substitute to the committee reported version of the Occupational Health and Safety Act.

31 When in August 1970 COPE published its preelection rating of congressmen, Steiger's voting record was not as favorable to labor. On the twelve issues before the 91st Congress that COPE based its ratings on, Steiger had voted "right" four times and "wrong" eight times.

32 See Lewis Anthony Dexter, *The Sociology and Politics of Congress* (Chicago: Rand McNally, 1969), pp. 211-216.

33 For a detailed discussion of congressional roles, see Roger H. Davidson, *The Role of the Congressman* (Indianapolis: Bobbs-Merrill, 1969).

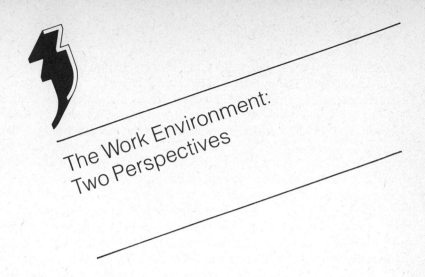

The Work Environment:
Two Perspectives

A DAY WITH JOHN B. ANDERSON OF ILLINOIS

It was April 1968. Martin Luther King was being buried in Atlanta. Federal troops ringed the Capitol Building in riot-torn Washington, D.C., as the House Rules Committee met in its ornate third-floor chambers to consider the Civil Rights Act of 1968, with its controversial open-housing provisions. After the witnesses had been heard the committee went into executive session. A crowd of reporters and others interested in the fate of the legislation waited in the hall outside the committee room for the decision. When members emerged later they announced that, by a narrow 8 to 7 vote, the committee had granted the bill a rule. The decisive vote was cast by a junior, generally conservative, and until then relatively anonymous Illinois Republican, John B. Anderson.

The following day, to what *Newsweek* called "thundering applause," the young Representative delivered a short (he had been allotted one minute under House procedures) but eloquent speech urging passage of the act. Within an hour the bill had passed the House by a 250 to 171 margin.[1] Anderson's vote in the Rules Committee had made a difference, and his eloquence in debate had been noticed by his colleagues and the often cynical Washington press corps.

More than two years later at approximately 7:30 A.M. on an unusually mild Tuesday morning in August 1970, the five-term Congressman from Rockford left his home in suburban Bethesda, Maryland, and drove along River Road and Rock Creek Parkway toward Washington.

At forty-nine Anderson was a youthful looking and vigorous man with a distinguished shock of gray hair. Like most of his House colleagues, he had begun his career in elective office in local and state government. In 1956 he had been elected state's attorney of Winnebago County (including Rockford), and in 1960 he had won election to the House of Representatives when the incumbent Republican, Leo Allen, had retired. In making his successful bid for the GOP congressional nomination Anderson had had the advantage of being a major officeholder in the county in which the Sixteenth Congressional District's population is concentrated. The Republican Party has dominated this seven-county "downstate" area during most of the period since the Civil War. It is an area of prosperous farms (dairy, corn, soybeans), small and medium-sized cities, and one major industrial center—Rockford. Partly because of the Republican advantage in voters' party identification, Anderson easily won general-election victories in 1960 and in each successive campaign.

Although still a relatively junior member of the House, Anderson has risen rapidly in an institution that operates under what Richard Fenno has called the "seniority-protégé system," which emphasizes gradual and well-modulated ascent to positions of formal leadership.[2] In 1965 he was assigned to the powerful Rules Committee, primarily thanks to the support of the ranking Republican member of the committee, Clarence Brown (R.-Ohio). The late Representative Brown was then also the dean of the Ohio Republican delegation and controlled that state's sizable bloc of votes in the Republican Committee on Committees, which makes committee assignments. Brown took a special interest in Anderson because he had been impressed with the young man's work on the Government Operations Committee, on which Brown also served. Anderson also received the united support of the large Illinois Republican delegation; the vacant position had previously been held by an Illinois congressman, which also helped. Furthermore, Anderson's predecessor, Leo Allen, had served as chairman of the committee.

In 1969, four years after Anderson's assignment to the Rules Committee, Melvin R. Laird (R.-Wis.) vacated his post as chairman of the House Republican Conference (the third-ranking House Republican leadership position) to become Secretary of Defense. The Republican membership then elected Anderson conference chairman.

Anderson's rather rapid rise in the House hierarchy reflects a favorable assessment by his peers and broad support from important segments of the party. His appointment to the Rules Committee demonstrates that the party elders had identified him early in his career as a future leader. He was considered highly intelligent (Anderson had been elected to Phi Beta Kappa at the University of Illinois) and a reliable party man who could work effectively with the party leadership. Membership on the Rules Committee greatly enhanced his visibility in the House, for he became involved in a wider range of issues and spoke with increasing frequency on the floor. His skills in public speaking and debate (important skills for a leader) became widely recognized, especially after the passage of the 1968 Civil Rights Act. A further measure of Anderson's increasing stature among House Republicans was his being invited into SOS, a Republican social group of considerable prestige. The SOS membership provided an important base of support among many Republican state delegations when Anderson campaigned for the conference chairmanship in 1969. Anderson also benefited from a second assignment to the Joint Committee on Atomic Energy. Finally, his bid for a leadership post was strengthened by the support of the large state delegations, particularly his own Illinois group and that from California.

Farm-Bill Politics

Normally at 7:30 on Tuesday morning Anderson's destination would have been the White House, where he would have entered via the southwest gate and gone directly to the Cabinet Room for a weekly meeting with the President, key administration officials, and the Republican congressional leadership. At these meetings Republican legislative leaders were given advance briefings on administration legislative and administrative programs. The meetings also afforded an opportunity to review the status and prospects for the President's legislative program, as well as to exchange views on certain policies and strategies.[3] But, because the President had been out of the city until late the previous night, no leadership meeting was being held on the Tuesday under examination.

Anderson's official day started at the U.S. Post Office Department instead. Postmaster General Winton Blount was sponsoring an informal coffee hour for congressmen in conjunction with the issuance of a commemorative stamp for General Dwight D. Eisenhower. At the reception Anderson was photographed with Blount next to a special Eisenhower display. The photograph was later used in press releases for his district, the newsletter that he sends to his constituents, and a campaign brochure.

While at the Post Office Department Anderson conferred with House Republican Leader Gerald R. Ford (R.-Mich.) on the farm bill (H.R. 18546) that had been removed from the Tuesday agenda of the House late the previous afternoon by the Democratic leadership. Anderson was anxious to know more about the status of the bill because later in the morning he was to preside at a Republican Conference (of all GOP House members) called to consider this legislation. The 1971 farm bill had been a subject of eighteen months of negotiation and maneuvering between the Department of Agriculture and the members of the House Agriculture Committee. The most controversial issue was limitations on the amounts of payments that a farmer could receive under price-support programs. The existing law contained no limitations, and some large-scale farmers were receiving annual price-support payments greater than $1 million. On two previous occasions the House had voted to limit payments to $20,000, but these provisions had been eliminated in conference committees at which Senate conferees (with the support of the Department of Agriculture) had been adamant against payment limitations.

Sensing rising public and House opposition to unlimited payments, the Agriculture Committee and Secretary of Agriculture Clifford Hardin had agreed to a provision in the 1970 bill limiting them to $55,000 per crop. The limitation would primarily affect large cotton farms in Mississippi, Texas, Arizona, and California.[4] Farmers in these areas and their representatives were therefore opposed to the limitation, but they were even more apprehensive that the House might again vote for the lower $20,000 limitation.

Concern over this possibility had intensified when the *Wall Street Journal* had reported that the White House was not firmly committed to the $55,000 figure.[5] Commodity groups and southern and southwestern congressmen feared that unless the administration firmly backed the $55,000 figure, the lower payment limitation would again be approved on the House floor. They were also worried about rumors that some House GOP leaders planned to support a floor amendment imposing $20,000 limits. As the Senate had reversed its position of previous years and had approved payment limitations, the opponents of limitations believed that it was imperative that they hold the line in the House.

Against this background Speaker John W. McCormack (D.-Mass.) had been prevailed upon by Congressman B. F. Sisk (D.-Calif.), whose district contained many large cotton farms, and by other Democrats with substantial cotton producers among their constituents to postpone House consideration of the Agriculture Act of 1970 until the administration position on payment limitations had been clarified.

In discussing this situation with Anderson, Ford said that he had met the previous afternoon with Congressman Page Belcher (R.-Okla.), the ranking Republican on the Agriculture Committee, and Bryce Harlow, a key adviser to President Nixon on legislative matters. Harlow, Ford related, had planned to see the President late Monday night after his return on Air Force One from California. It was hoped that the result of this meeting would be a letter from the President to read to the conference, which would clear up any misunderstandings concerning the President's views on payment limitations. Ford said that he and Belcher would advise Anderson about the presidential letter before the conference.

Suite 1101 Longworth Building

After his talk with the Minority Leader and pleasant exchanges and banter with other colleagues, the Illinois Congressman left for his office. Suite 1101 is one of the larger and most coveted suites in the Longworth House Office Building.[6] It contains a small reception room, a large room for staff, a private office for the Congressman looking out on Independence Avenue and the Capitol,[7] plus a small workroom adjoining the Congressman's office. A particularly desirable feature of the office is its close proximity to the Capitol—a special advantage when the bells summon representatives from their offices for quorum calls and votes on the House floor.

After greeting his staff the Congressman immediately immersed himself in the morning newspapers. He has described himself as "an avid newspaper reader" who finds the papers much more useful as a source of information than television, which his schedule rarely permits him to view. Having already read the *Washington Post* at home, Anderson started with *The New York Times* and then turned to the *Wall Street Journal*. Time is one of a congressman's most precious resources, and most are therefore anxious to use it to maximum advantage.[8] One of the fastest ways for members of Congress to pick up information that they need is through careful reading of the morning papers. The press is thus an important source of information for Washington's official decision makers as well as for ordinary citizens.

Because congressmen must also keep up with developments and points of view in their constituencies, Anderson also reads the *Chicago Tribune* and the *Rockford Morning Star* daily. His staff reviews and marks for his attention items of interest in other district and Chicago newspapers. The Congressman's daily reading also includes the *Congressional Record* and the Washington *Evening Star*, which he reads at home in the evening.

Anderson's attention to the newspapers has often been a source of amazement and embarrassment to his staff. He frequently calls aides' attention to items of legislative or political significance that they have overlooked and asks them to do additional work on topics that he has identified. On the day in question, for example, he noted with concern a Gallup survey predicting GOP House losses in 1970. A staff member was therefore directed to ask the National Republican Congressional Committee which GOP members might be facing difficult challenges so that he might, as a member of the leadership, volunteer his assistance.

Anderson's interest in the electoral fortunes of his colleagues reflects an often overlooked aspect of the responsibilities imposed upon party leaders in Congress—campaigning for colleagues in their districts and helping to raise funds for the party's campaign war chest. Since January he had journeyed from California to Massachusetts speaking on behalf of GOP colleagues at various testimonial and party dinners and on behalf of the congressional committee to help raise funds for the 1970 election. The demanding national speaking schedule of leaders takes time away from legislative and constituency responsibilities, as well as from their families. Campaign assistance for the party is, however, expected of people in leadership positions. From such activities leaders build support among their colleagues for legislative battles and contests for leadership positions (which are considered in Chapter 4).

As Anderson was completing his review of the morning papers, his administrative assistant, Howard Moffett (a former editor of the *Yale Daily News* and foreign correspondent for *Newsweek*), brought in the morning mail. While sorting the mail Moffett normally assigns routine letters (like requests for government documents) to other members of the staff, but Anderson personally reads the bulk of his mail. He dictates responses to some letters and others he assigns, with instructions, to members of the staff. As do many congressmen, Anderson attaches considerable importance to the mail that he receives from his constituents and is anxious to read personally about their problems and views.

The Congressman's review of his mail was interrupted several times by telephone calls and visitors. Following a brief conference with an official of the Atomic Energy Commission and a fifteen-minute discussion with a student intern about his summer duties with the Republican Conference, Anderson called the staff director of the conference to arrange a luncheon in the Capitol for the twelve students working in that office on various research projects for Republican members.

Another call was from a longtime friend and supporter from Rockford, who asked if the Congressman was free to have lunch with him and his son that day. Anderson readily agreed to the luncheon appointment. Joe Fisher, a former Washington reporter for the *Rockford Morning Star* who was serving as an aide to Senator Ralph T. Smith (R.-Ill.), then called requesting information on administration policy in Southeast Asia. As a member of the leadership, Anderson was frequently in a position to obtain information more easily than were some of his colleagues and therefore was often treated as a source by others working on Capitol Hill. In this instance Anderson was able to provide the information needed by Senator Smith.

There was also a call from the American Farm Bureau Federation's Washington representative about the farm bill. The Farm Bureau (which is well organized and influential in Illinois) opposed the bill because it did not go far enough toward a free-market policy on agricultural commodities. The lobbyist asked Anderson about the status of the bill and whether or not it was likely to be scheduled for floor consideration that day. He also asked about Anderson's and the administration's attitudes toward the legislation. Administration and House GOP leadership doubts about the payment-limitation issue, which had been revealed in the *Wall Street Journal* on the previous day, were important to the farm organization in determining its strategy on the bill.

The conversation between Anderson and the lobbyist was amiable and conducted on a first-name basis, as each sought to gain additional information and to outline his own position. Anderson explained why the Speaker had postponed consideration of the bill and his hopes for clarification later in the morning after Harlow's meeting with the President. He also said that he planned to vote for the bill, despite Farm Bureau opposition, because it was absolutely essential that Congress pass a farm bill in that session. Otherwise the old 1958 farm law would take effect again—a totally unacceptable alternative because of the likely adverse impact on farmers and the U.S. Treasury.[9] He also noted that out of loyalty to his party and the administration he wanted to support the bill. He said that he was not yet committed to the $55,000 payment limitation and noted current doubts about administration policy on the matter. No farmers in his own district were receiving payments close to the $55,000 figure, and it would therefore be much more popular for him to vote his convictions, as he had in the past, and to support an amendment providing for a payment limitation of $20,000.

Despite the importance of agriculture in Illinois' Sixteenth District, which contains rich and intensely cultivated farm acreage, Anderson had received relatively little mail or pressure on this issue, apparently because the dairy section of the act was satisfactory to northern Illinois dairy interests, the most important single commodity group in the district. Although House action on the measure was imminent, only twelve letters from constituents—mainly Farm Bureau members expressing opposition to the bill—had been received. Of major concern to Anderson was the possible impact of payment limits on soybean growers in his district. He had noted the claims of the members from cotton-producing areas that, if payment limitations were approved, cotton farmers would diversify and raise other commodities, particularly soybeans. He naturally wanted to prevent such an occurrence.

House Republicans and the Farm Bill

After the telephone calls Anderson continued with his mail and then at 9:50 A.M. walked across Independence Avenue to the House chamber for the Republican Conference. Conferences are called before House consideration of major legislation when in the judgment of the leadership discussion among all Republican members is necessary. Because the House schedule is extremely flexible—bills are often postponed or quickly scheduled—GOP Conferences must be called on relatively short notice and often therefore conflict with regularly scheduled committee hearings and meetings. On August 4, eighteen full committee or subcommittee meetings were being held, including a meeting of the Rules Committee, on which Anderson served. Committee responsibilities often prevent members from attending conferences or staying for the full meetings, as each must decide for himself which meeting is more important in terms of his own priorities. Because this conference was dealing with a complex and controversial major bill that could have significant impact on the electoral futures of many members, attendance was relatively high—approximately 120 GOP members.

As members drifted into the House chamber, Anderson greeted his colleagues and made a special point of seeking out members of the Agriculture Committee. By custom, members of the committee that has reported the bill under consideration are accorded the first opportunity to speak. Anderson therefore prepared a list of committee members who wished to be heard. Party leaders and others known to be very interested in agricultural matters were also consulted. As he moved among the Republican congressmen, many of whom were chatting informally in small groups or quietly reading the *Congressional Record* of the previous day, he received a message that Representative Belcher wanted to speak to him on the telephone. He left the chamber and took the call on one of the fifteen phones in the Republican cloakroom.[10]

Belcher advised Anderson that he would be a little late for the conference because the anticipated letter from the President was at that moment being delivered by messenger from the White House. When Anderson returned to the floor, a group of congressmen seated around one of the large oak tables was engaged in good-natured banter over whether Representative Silvio Conte (R.-Mass.) or Paul Findley (R.-Ill.) would be the principal sponsor of the year's $20,000 payment-limitation amendment. Both were strong advocates of such amendments, and in the past they had been rivals for sponsorship of such provisions.

Payment limitation was a continuing issue for the members. Legislators on both sides of the issue had been arguing and maneuvering for years, and each side understood the arguments and tactics of the other. Although each side tended to feel strongly, as often happens among congressmen who work in the environment of controversy, these differences of view did not usually cause personal animosities and resentments. There was also friendly chiding of some Agriculture Committee members who, after years of opposing farm bills proposed by Secretary of Agriculture Orville Freeman during the Kennedy and Johnson years, now in a change of roles found themselves supporting a farm bill and acting as spokesmen for the Nixon administration.

With approximately 100 members present at 10:15 A.M., Anderson called the conference to order and recognized the ranking Republican on the Agriculture Committee, Belcher, who had just entered the chamber. Belcher, a crusty senior member given to pointed and frequently amusing comments in debate, declared that during the previous twenty years farm bills had been the focus of intense partisan and interest-group battles, with the Secretary of Agriculture and the Agriculture Committee frequently locked in fierce struggle. He noted, however, that this year was an exception. The 1970 farm bill had been worked out over a period of eighteen months of negotiation between the committee, whose chairman was W. R. Poage (D.-Tex.), and the department. Twenty-five meetings of the Secretary and the full committee, as well as numerous smaller and more informal sessions, had been held before the compromise had been achieved. Much of Belcher's statement dealt with payment limitations, which he believed to be wrong. He was, however, willing to support the $55,000 figure because it would not unduly disrupt the farm economy. In answer to questions raised the previous day about the administration's position on the bill, Belcher read a letter from the President urging enactment of the bill "with a minimum of change." The President said further:

The proper payment limitation would seem to me to be peculiarly within the province of Congress, and I will, of course, abide the Congressional judgement . . .

Secretary Hardin and a bipartisan majority of your Committee . . . recommend $55,000 as the limitation. I am aware of the widespread desire for a much lower figure, . . . However, I must agree with Secretary Hardin that in present circumstances this could be harmful to the constructive farm program which your Committee and the Department have so painstakingly evolved.

You may, therefore, inform your colleagues that . . . I must prefer the limitation proposed by your Committee.

One of Belcher's major arguments was that, unless the bill was passed, the federal farm programs would revert to the old 1958 law which, he said, would be bad for farmers and therefore bad for Republicans. Belcher also noted that the major farm organizations did not like the bill. Both the so-called "coalition groups," led by the National Farmer's Union and the Farm Bureau respectively, were opposing the bill. The dissatisfaction of these groups reflected the compromises that it contained.

Minority Leader Ford then praised Belcher and the committee members for their work on the bill and urged members to support it. He too stressed the adverse consequences of failing to pass any farm bill during the 1970 session. He said that the House schedule was such that it would be virtually impossible to prepare an alternative bill if this one was rejected. He also emphasized that the 1958 law simply could not be allowed to take effect because it would mean vastly greater farm surpluses and necessitate larger federal appropriations for price supports. If increased appropriations were required, he said, they would probably include a $20,000 payment limitation.

A series of shorter speeches by members from farm areas, whose views on the bill tended to reflect the differing impacts of the legislation on their respective constituencies, followed. The most vigorous opponent of the bill was Congressman Robert Price (R.-Tex.), whose district stood to lose more than any other if the $55,000 limitation were enacted. In Price's cotton-growing constituency nineteen million acres of land were under cultivation, and his district alone received more money in payments than nineteen states did in a single year.

Among the last people to speak were Congressmen Conte and Findley, each of whom urged support of their amendment to impose a $20,000 limitation. Both claimed that the wording of the President's letter indicated that he would sign a farm bill containing a limitation figure below $55,000. As Findley finished his remarks, Anderson adjourned the meeting, noting that it was necessary to vacate the chamber at 11:45 A.M., in order that it might be made ready for the regular session of the House at noon.

As is customary at GOP Conferences there was no vote to determine the point of view of the Republican members of the House or to bind them to a particular position on the legislation. These meetings are primarily informational, providing opportunities for members not on the committees reporting major bills to benefit from their colleagues' opinions and to learn the view of the leadership and the administration on both the substance of the legislation and the importance both attach to it. Because the leaders always have an opportunity to speak, the conferences give them a chance to rally partisan support for their positions. In this instance, although it was clear that the leadership and the administration wanted the Poage-Belcher bill to pass, it was also apparent that this bill was not as important to them as were some other measures—for example, extension of the surtax and the presidential veto of the Department of Health, Education, and Welfare appropriations in 1969 (see Chapter 4).

While the Republicans were discussing the bill in conference, Democratic leaders learned of Nixon's letter and completed a Whip check, which showed enough Democratic votes to pass the bill with a $55,000 limitation. They then decided to call up the farm bill for debate that afternoon and advised the GOP leaders of their decision. This decision necessitated a series of hurried strategy huddles at the rear of the chamber during the conference, among Minority Leader Ford, Minority Whip Leslie Arends (R.-Ill.), Belcher, and GOP Rules Committee members.

Anderson's final duty as conference chairman was to brief members of the congressional press corps, who were waiting for him in the Speaker's Lobby, a long red-carpeted hallway directly behind the Speaker's rostrum. On its walls are portraits of past Speakers, and off the lobby are a series of reading rooms where members may read the latest newspapers from across the country, check the Associated Press and United Press International news tickers, and receive the latest National Weather Service bulletins.

The press was already aware, through the Speaker's regular morning press conference, of the Democratic leadership's decision to schedule debate on the farm bill that afternoon. It was therefore primarily interested in what position the GOP had taken on the bill. Anderson replied that the members seemed impressed with the work of the committee in achieving an unusual amount of agreement for a farm bill. He also said that he believed that the President's letter had had a persuasive effect on Republicans. When pressed by a correspondent, he noted that there appeared to be no consensus on the payment limitation issue among Republicans yet and that Representatives Conte and Findley continued to be firm in their resolve to seek House approval for a $20,000 limitation.

As he moved through the Speaker's Lobby toward the elevator, one reporter cornered him and asked his own personal views on payment limitations and how he planned to vote. Anderson noted that he personally would prefer a lower limitation but that he had not yet made up his mind on the issue. He felt somewhat constrained because of his leadership position, White House interest in the legislation, and possible adverse consequences of a lower limitation level for his district.

Because of his position, his role as a frequent "swing vote" in Rules Committee controversies (like those over open housing in 1968 and consumer protection in 1970), and his acknowledged abilities as a speaker, Anderson received more attention from the Washington press corps than do most representatives. Yet even so, except for the politically aware in northern Illinois and those who follow the House of Representatives with special care, he is not a well-known political figure. The news media tend to concentrate attention on the Senate and the White House and to leave members of the House to labor in relative obscurity, even though many representatives have ability at least equal to that of senators and often greater expertise and influence in their legislative specialties.

The House Rules Committee

While Anderson was presiding over the Republican Conference, the Rules Committee was holding hearings on two bills—H.R. 17809, to establish a system to fix and adjust rates of pay for federal employees, and H.R. 18434, to impose limitations on the amounts that political candidates could spend for radio and television advertising. By the time that Anderson had slipped into his brown-leather swivel chair near the head of the table next to H. Allen Smith (R.-Calif.), the ranking Republican on the committee, the hearing on the federal pay bill was over and the committee was listening to testimony by Representative Lionel Van Deerlin (D.-Calif.), a principal sponsor of the campaign-advertising bill.

Most committee hearings are held in large rooms with committee members looking down from elevated podiums at witnesses seated at tables before them. Witnesses and members use microphones to communicate with each other, and there is normally a good deal of commotion at the press tables and in the spacious areas set aside for the public.

By contrast the Rules Committee meets in a small third-floor room of the Capitol. Members are seated about a large, green, felt-covered table—the chairman at the head and Republicans and Democrats on opposite sides in order of seniority on the committee. Witnesses are seated opposite the chairman; reporters, spectators, and other interested members of Congress are seated on folding chairs amid the staff desks. The atmosphere is informal. Witnesses (usually senior members of standing committees that have reported bills for which they want Rules Committee clearance in order to gain full House consideration) rarely read prepared statements but rather summarize their bills. They also specify the type of rule that they prefer. In approving a resolution, or authorizing House consideration of legislation, the committee specifies the conditions under which the bill will be considered by the House: the length of time for debate, whether or not the bill can be amended, and whether or not points of order against a bill may be waived.

In commenting on H.R. 18434, Van Deerlin noted that it was based on a growing concern that "we are pricing ourselves out of democracy" and that it would impose what he considered reasonable limits on campaign spending ($20,000 for congressional candidates) for radio and television. Van Deerlin also said that the bill would not apply to the 1970 elections because many candidates had already purchased media time. He stressed the importance of timing and urged that the bill be passed in 1970 because he thought there would be opposition to a campaign-spending bill as the presidential elections drew closer.

When Van Deerlin finished his remarks Chairman William Colmer (D.-Miss.), in a soft southern accent, commended the Interstate and Foreign Commerce Committee for presenting legislation on a major problem but noted that he opposed federal regulation of campaign spending for state offices. He also expressed his displeasure at some provisions of the bill, which seemed dictated by a parliamentary situation which required accepting a Senate version of the bill in order to avoid the delays involved in a Senate-House conference. Reflecting the belief of many House members that the Senate does not delve deeply into problems and that its legislative products reflect this failure, Colmer and others commented on the inferior quality of Senate-initiated legislation.

When it came Anderson's turn to question the witness, he asked Van Deerlin how the bill would deal with the many committees that are created (some to avoid campaign-spending limitations) to support candidates and how candidates who run on a slate would be affected by the proposed bill. Several times during the discussion there were somewhat heated exchanges across the table as members traded partisan gibes. Ray Madden (D.-Ind.), the elderly second-ranking Democrat, launched at one point into a long harangue about the cost of newspaper advertising (a topic not covered by the bill) and then proceeded to cite instances to prove his claim that Republicans were buying up elections. Representative David Martin (R.-Nebr.) then noted wryly that Madden had forgotten to mention any alleged failings of the McKinley administration in the campaign-finance field, a reference to Madden's penchant for blaming all the nation's ills since 1896 on the GOP. Martin's remark won approving smiles and comments, particularly on the GOP side of the table.

Colmer then turned to the specifics of the rule being requested. Van Deerlin said that his committee wanted two hours of general debate and an open rule (amendments to any section of the bill would be in order). As there were no further questions, Colmer recognized the next witness, Representative James Broyhill (R.-N.C.), the ranking Republican member of the subcommittee that had considered the bill. Broyhill made a short statement indicating that GOP members of the subcommittee were supporting H.R. 18434.[11]

The chairman thanked Van Deerlin and Broyhill for their testimony and proceeded to recognize Chairman Wright Patman (D.-Tex.) of the Banking and Currency Committee. Patman and the ranking Republican of his committee, William Widnall (R.-N.J.), had been waiting about an hour for their turn to testify on H.R. 17795, the Emergency Community Facilities Act of 1970.

Patman had just begun his testimony when Colmer noted that only six committee members were present and suggested that someone might want to raise a
point of order that a quorum was not present. Martin made the point of order.
Colmer sustained him, adjourned the meeting, and advised Patman, an elderly
and frequently erratic populist with whom Colmer has had frequent differences,
that his testimony would have to be put over until the next meeting of the
committee.

During the course of deliberations four members of the committee had left
the meeting to be present on the House floor to present the rule calling up the
farm bill for House consideration. Their departure prevented the committee not
only from hearing the community-facilities presentation but also from meeting
in executive session to vote on whether or not to grant a rule to the legislation
on which it had just heard testimony. Rescheduling the farm bill had a further
impact on the deliberations of the committee. When word of this development
reached the committee there was considerable scurrying about as members responsible for presenting the rule made the necessary preparations to be on the
floor at noon.

Later in the day an Illinois political science professor came to Anderson's
office to interview him about his Rules Committee responsibilities and the role
of the committee in the House. At that time Anderson explained to the interviewer that he believed that the committee's powers should be procedural in
character and that it should not be primarily involved in substantive issues,
though he acknowledged that its powers over scheduling for the House inevitably involve it in substantive matters. The most recent example, he believed,
was its vote to permit bringing the Senate version of the voting rights bill (which
included a provision permitting eighteen-year-olds to vote in federal elections)
directly to the House floor for a vote instead of requiring differences between
the House and Senate versions to be resolved in a conference committee. Anderson had departed from the position taken by the House Republican Policy
Committee (of which he is a member) and the Minority Leader and had supported granting eighteen-year-olds the right to vote by statute rather than by a
constitutional amendment.

He explained that he had not followed the party position on this issue
because it was one on which he had strong personal convictions. This proclivity
to independence and occasional straying from party leadership positions on
issues has caused problems for Anderson. During the 91st Congress there were
rumblings among the more conservative House Republicans (who once considered Anderson one of their number) that he was becoming too liberal and was
insufficiently reliable on party issues. There was a strong but unsuccessful campaign to unseat him as chairman of the conference at the beginning of the 92nd
Congress in 1971. (For more information on Republican and Democratic leadership contests in the House, see Chapter 4.)

Although noting his own departure from party policy on an occasional issue, Anderson told his interviewer that as a general rule he believed that the constituency of a Republican Rules Committee member was the GOP membership and the GOP leadership. For the House to function, he said, there must be close harmony between the Rules Committee and the leadership. He also noted his belief that the committee had lost influence since it had been expanded from twelve to fifteen members in 1961 in order to enable the Democratic leadership to secure the appointment of enough cooperative Democrats to ensure a majority on most issues.

As the Rules Committee meeting was breaking up, the bells in the Capitol rang twice, summoning House members to a quorum call on the floor. As Anderson emerged from the elevator and was about to enter the Speaker's Lobby, he was stopped by a UPI reporter. Over the previous weekend the reporter had written a story about the Ford Motor Company's leasing of luxury cars to some prominent congressmen at the modest annual rate of $750. "I'm told," the reporter commented, "that the only trouble with my story is that I didn't identify all the members who received the special leasing arrangement." Anderson retorted that the story had indeed caused a great deal of comment in the cloakrooms; members had been teasing one another about apparently not being sufficiently important to have been offered leased Continentals. The reporter then became more direct. He said, "I've been told, John, that the chairman of the conference and your Democratic counterpart each have such leased cars." Anderson replied that the accusation was not true and that he had never been approached on this matter by an auto maker. Because of his Rules Committee meeting and the reporter's questions, Anderson missed the first reading of his name by the House reading clerk and had to wait in the chamber about fifteen minutes before the names of those who had not answered the first time were read again. This wait allowed him to check the news ticker off the Speaker's Lobby and to discuss provisions of the campaign-finance bill with Van Deerlin and his Rules Committee colleagues, Martin and James Delaney (D.-N.Y.). Anderson then reentered the chamber, chatted casually with several colleagues, answered when his name was called, and headed toward his office at about 12:50 P.M.

In the office Anderson first talked with the caseworker on his office staff about a young man from his district who was seeking assistance in transferring to a different Army Reserve unit. He also took another call from the Farm Bureau representative, who asked about developments at the conference and about the status of the farm bill. By the time that Anderson had briefed his caller, his friends from home (one of them vice-president of a major corporation in the district) had arrived for their lunch appointment, and the three walked back to the Capitol to the House Restaurant on the first floor. The restaurant was crowded with congressmen, many of whom were with constituents or their families. Others, including the Speaker, were obviously discussing business with administration officials, staff, and colleagues.

Much of Anderson's conversation centered around economic conditions in the Rockford area. His friend's report was not encouraging. He noted that unemployment was rising and that further cutbacks were anticipated in the machine-tool industry. Anderson observed that the Democrats were becoming increasingly partisan and irresponsible on economic issues—speaking of "Nixonomics" and blaming the President for the current rise in the cost of living and downturn in the economy. They also discussed the implications for the Rockford area of the pending occupational health and safety legislation. His friend was strongly opposed to the committee bill, and Anderson assured him that he was supporting the Steiger substitute (see Chapter 2). After lunch Anderson made arrangements for his staff to assist his guests in their afternoon sightseeing.

On the House Floor

By that time the House had approved the Rules Committee's resolution calling up the farm bill for consideration and was in the midst of general debate on the bill. Under House procedures general debate is a fixed amount of time (four hours for this farm bill) which is controlled and allocated among members wishing to speak by the chairman and ranking minority member of the committee that reported the legislation. On that day the time was controlled by Chairman Poage and Belcher. Anderson did not request an opportunity to speak during general debate. He planned to make his comments on the following day, when the House would consider and vote on amendments to the bill while sitting as the Committee of the Whole on the State of the Union—a procedural device that enables the House to expedite its business and restrict individual speeches to five minutes for each amendment. (The work of the House while in the Committee of the Whole is discussed in more detail in Chapter 8, which deals with the legislative reform bill of 1970.)

To the unpracticed eye the proceedings of the House are frequently chaotic and disconcerting. Some members are intent on participating in and listening to the debate, while others often read, confer with their colleagues, and move about the floor and cloakrooms. Members constantly scurry in and out of the chamber. This commotion and seeming inattention to debate reflects the role of the House chamber as an important communications center. It is the one place where one is likely on any given day to be able to see any colleague with whom one must speak. Like other members, Anderson has found it essential to spend considerable time on the floor, not only because of official proceedings but also because he needs information on legislative and other political developments that only his House colleagues can provide.

Anderson himself frequently also serves as a source of information for other members because of his leadership position and his membership of the Rules Committee. Members often ask him about the status of legislation in the committee and when bills are likely to be brought up for House action.

Such information helps them to plan their activities. Anderson's help is frequently sought by colleagues anxious to have the committee either open or bar the door to House action on legislation.

On that particular day most of the informal floor discussion revolved around the farm bill. Among those with whom Anderson conferred was Thomas Railsback (R.-Ill.). Railsback, a young second-termer who represented a west-central Illinois district similar to that of Anderson, discussed the bill's probable impact on his district and noted that the Farm Bureau (the most powerful of the organized farm interests in their respective districts) opposed the current bill. Railsback said that he planned to offer an amendment on the following day calling for increased long-term land retirement. He thought that this amendment would strengthen the bill and also make it more acceptable to his constituents and Farm Bureau members. Anderson agreed to speak and vote for the amendment when it was offered by Railsback.[12]

Anderson also met with another Republican colleague from Illinois, Edward Derwinski, a House member of the conference committee seeking to resolve House and Senate differences on the Postal Reform Act. They discussed an amendment Anderson had offered to the act during House consideration. The amendment (which was designed to prevent "featherbedding" and resistance to the installation of new technology in the post office), Derwinski advised, had been deleted from the bill in conference. The conferees had been informed by union representatives that Anderson had lost interest in the amendment. Anderson told Derwinski that this was a misrepresentation of his comment that he would not object to perfecting language being added to his amendment in conference. He therefore urged Derwinski to move reconsideration of his amendment in conference and sought out H. R. Gross (R.-Iowa), a senior Republican conferee, and Thaddeus J. Dulski (D.-N.Y.), the chairman of the Post Office and Civil Service Committee, to urge their support of his amendment. (These efforts later proved unsuccessful when the conference emasculated the amendment.)

Anderson's interest and involvement in floor action on legislation covering a wide range of subjects is somewhat atypical of members of the House, who normally tend to specialize in the work of their respective committees. Unlike most of his colleagues, however, Anderson's principal committee assignment is to a committee almost totally lacking in substantive jurisdiction.[13] The Rules Committee's power, though extensive, extends primarily to determining if, when, and under what circumstances legislation will reach the floor, and not to the actual provisions of bills. Therefore, if Rules Committee members are to make their mark on legislation personally, they must usually do it on the floor. John Anderson's ability to operate in this arena is enhanced by his familiarity with legislation derived from his Rules Committee membership, his leadership position, and his acknowledged ability as a public speaker and debater.

The Role of the Staff

While the Congressman was engaged at the conference, in committee, and on the floor, the work of his office proceeded in a rather institutionalized manner as his seven staff members (plus four college student summer interns) performed their assigned responsibilities. The organization of congressional offices varies greatly depending on the interests, constituency, style, and administrative abilities of the individual member. There are, however, positions and functions common to most offices—a receptionist to greet visitors and answer the steady stream of phone calls; a personal secretary to the Congressman who handles his correspondence, accounts, and schedule; legislative and press assistants to help with analysis of legislative issues and publicity; an administrative assistant who is in general charge of the office, particularly district-oriented business; and a caseworker to handle constituent requests and problems.

Anderson's personal secretary, in his absence, had typed the letters he had dictated earlier in the day, prepared replies to letters (mainly invitations to speak) assigned her by the administrative assistant, Howard Moffett, and helped to work out Anderson's schedule for the balance of the week. Among the necessary arrangements were reservations for a trip back to the district on Thursday for a Winnebago County GOP fund-raising event. Normally the Congressman went home every second weekend. Occasionally, however, Anderson had made as many as four quick trips to Illinois in a single week, while still attending all major votes and meetings of the House.

Moffett had started his morning by reviewing mail to be sure that matters requiring immediate attention or consideration by the Congressman would be on his desk when he arrived. He also prepared draft replies to constituents' letters, in accordance with Anderson's instructions. Moffett, a former newsman, also wrote several press releases for the district press. He talked on the telephone with the Congressman's district office in Rockford to coordinate the handling of casework problems at the state or local level. Moffett personally took care of several major services to constituents, including helping to arrange appointments at the Office of Education for Rockford area school officials seeking Elementary and Secondary Education Act funding for a remedial-learning program. In the Congressman's absence Moffett also took telephone calls from constituents in Rockford and met people who came to the office to see Anderson.

During the course of the day, three families from the district visited and were assisted by the receptionist and Moffett. Because Anderson was tied up in meetings virtually all morning he was unable to meet these people. Normally he saw as many of his constituents as possible and often had his picture taken with them on the steps of the Capitol. An autographed picture was then sent to each family and a copy to its local newspaper. The office also arranged tours of Washington landmarks and government offices. In effect, Anderson—and most congressmen—operated a modest travel bureau from his office for constituents.

While work related to the constituency and the more personal aspects of the Congressman's job were being handled in Suite 1101, in another office—Room 1129—three staff members were handling legislative assignments. Charged with responsibility for this office was Don Wolfensberger, the Congressman's legislative assistant. Wolfensberger and his assistants were responsible for preparing analyses of bills scheduled for Rules Committee or general House consideration, drafting press releases on issues that the Congressman deemed worthy of statements, answering mail from constituents on legislative issues, and preparing background information and suggested positions (including draft language for bills and amendments) on issues likely to be the focus of future House action. The press of daily business, however, permitted relatively little time for anticipating and developing such future issues.

On that Tuesday Wolfensberger was analyzing the President's emergency strike legislation, which had stimulated an increasing amount of mail from Illinois members of the Teamsters' Union. He also drafted a series of replies to constituents who had expressed opposition to the 1968 gun-control legislation. One sportsmen's organization had requested a statement from Anderson to read to its next meeting. This statement obviously required special care, and Wolfensberger conducted a thorough review of the 1968 act, which Anderson had supported.

Another legislative aide, David Stockman—a young former graduate student from Harvard University—was completing an analysis of the farm bill. He also drafted a press release on the bill, which he would review with Anderson the next morning before the House vote on the bill. (The House passed the farm bill with a $55,000 payments limitation. Anderson voted for the bill but also supported the Findley-Conte amendment calling for a $20,000 payment limitation.)

Legislative analyses like those prepared by Anderson's assistants normally involve careful study of committee reports on legislation plus telephone conversations with the party's counsel to the standing committees reporting the bills. If these sources fail to yield adequate information on a piece of legislation, the assistant may telephone executive agencies, the White House congressional liaison staff, and occasionally trade associations vitally interested in the legislation.

Back to the Office

Congressman Anderson stayed on the floor until about 3:00 P.M. listening to the debate and conferring with his colleagues. Then he returned to his Longworth office and resumed his review of the day's mail, which had accumulated in his absence because of the numerous daily deliveries made by the House post office.

Among the letters that attracted special consideration was a "Dear Colleague" letter from Congressmen Clarence Brown, Jr. (R.-Ohio) and Brock Adams (D.-Wash.), members of the Interstate and Foreign Commerce Committee, urging support of H.R. 8298, The Water Carriers Mixing Rule—a complex bill pertaining to the regulation of barge lines on the nation's waterways. The bill was extremely controversial among the groups concerned: regulated and unregulated barge lines. Anderson was therefore anxious to obtain additional information, particularly from a colleague like Brown, whom he respected, before the bill came before the Rules Committee. Writing a note on the letter, he referred it to his legislative assistant, with instructions to analyze the issue in depth.

Constituents were also urging different courses of action on the controversial occupational health and safety bill (H.R. 16785). There were letters and wires from businessmen in the district urging him to oppose the bill. Anderson directed his legislative assistant to prepare letters expressing agreement with their views and indicating his support of the Steiger substitute. There were also, however, letters from labor unions in the district asking him to support the bill. Anderson asked the staff to draft a friendly but firm letter explaining his preference for the Steiger bill. In addition to such letters on legislative issues, there were eight requesting the Congressman's assistance. For example, an unemployed man was seeking help in finding a job, and a soldier in Vietnam wanted a transfer to a combat-infantry unit. Such requests were referred to the caseworker, who would make the necessary preliminary inquiries at various federal and state government offices. Anderson would then follow up as required.

At 3:15 P.M. the Illinois political scientist whose interview with Anderson has been described arrived for his appointment. That interview was completed at 4:00 P.M., and Moffett brought in a series of memorandums prepared by staff members. The first pertained to a national health-care proposal that had recently been introduced in the Senate by a group of senators, including Edward Kennedy (D.-Mass.) and two Republicans, John Sherman Cooper (Ky.) and William Saxbe (Ohio). The measure had received a great deal of press attention at the time of its introduction and was being aggressively pushed by the new president of the United Auto Workers, Leonard Woodcock. Recognizing that health-care issues were likely to be the topic of congressional debates as the session became more partisan in its closing days, Anderson was anxious to have additional information on them. He also wanted the information for use in his own reelection campaign and because, as a party leader known to have rather independent views on some issues, he was likely to be under considerable pressure from various sources to sponsor health-care measures in the next Congress.

Other memorandums dealt with casework matters requiring either personal follow-up by the Congressman or his approval before further staff action. In the midst of these matters a call came in from the Washington representative of the building-trades unions of the AFL-CIO inquiring about the status of the farm bill. Anderson recited the morning's developments and his conviction that it was absolutely essential that a farm bill be passed in 1970. Although the building-trades unions had no direct interest in farm legislation, the inquiry reflected the frequent efforts of politically active and well-organized groups to be certain that they have up-to-date information on all major bills. They can then sometimes provide lobbying assistance to other groups whose support they may need on legislation of direct concern to their own members.

There was also another call from Joe Fisher of Senator Ralph Smith's office. A campaign rally was being held in Anderson's district in September for 5,000-10,000 people, and Smith's office was anxious to secure Senator Robert Dole (R.-Kans.) as the main speaker. Anderson's assistance was being requested because the rally would be in his district and because he and Dole had been friends when the latter had served in the House. Anderson agreed to talk to Dole. (Although Anderson had campaigned hard to secure for himself the senatorial appointment that had gone to Smith upon the death of Everett M. Dirksen, he had subsequently committed himself to help in the 1970 Smith campaign.) He immediately called Dole. They first discussed the farm bill. Anderson was anxious to hear Dole's views on the measure, for Dole had specialized on farm matters during his service in the House and was now a member of the Senate Agriculture Committee. Dole said that he would like to speak in Illinois and would readjust his schedule to accommodate Anderson and Smith.

Then one of the regular congressional rituals occurred—the signing of the day's mail. Anderson's personal secretary brought in the letters that he had dictated the previous day and those drafted by his staff. Most of these letters he approved and signed, but several he sent back to the staff with notes to give more factual information and more direct answers to the constituents' questions or requests.

When the mail had been completed, Anderson called the Republican cloakroom to inquire about developments on the House floor. He was advised that the time for general debate on the farm bill had almost expired and that the House would be adjourning shortly.

Assured that no further legislative business would be transacted on the floor that day, Anderson loaded his briefcase with reading material and headed for the office of a Republican colleague who was hosting an SOS meeting. SOS is an informal Republican club that meets every week in a member's office for social reasons, as well as to discuss legislative and party issues. Such clubs are more common on the Republican side of the aisle (the most famous is the Chowder and Marching Society, originally organized in the 80th Congress by Representatives Richard Nixon of California and Glenn Davis of Wisconsin). One of the items discussed at SOS was the work of the Seniority Task Force appointed by the leadership during the previous spring. Barber Conable (R.-N.Y.), chairman of the task force, discussed some of the ideas for modifying the selection of committee leaders that were under consideration. He noted that the task force was seriously considering a plan under which the Republican Committee on Committees would nominate people to serve as ranking committee members, with Republican Conference approval required for selection. Reaction to this idea was mixed, but Anderson, who had urged his GOP leadership colleagues to appoint the task force, was pleased that a recommendation providing for change in seniority appeared to be forthcoming.

After the SOS gathering broke up at about 6:00 P.M., Anderson headed for his car in the garage of the Rayburn Building. His schedule for the evening included meeting his wife at home and returning to Washington for dinner with a Rockford constituent at a downtown restaurant.

A DAY WITH ABRAHAM RIBICOFF OF CONNECTICUT

The late-summer day was already becoming hot and humid as a gray Thunderbird eased into parking place number 11 on Delaware Avenue just west of the Old Senate Office Building. The driver of the car, Connecticut's Democratic Senator Abraham A. Ribicoff, walked briskly to his office on the third floor of the building, entering at exactly 8:45 A.M. It was to be a varied and dramatic day in the Senate.

When he arrived at his office Ribicoff was met by his executive secretary, Vergie Cass, a Capitol Hill veteran who had been with him since he came to the Senate in 1963. Miss Cass had already sorted the first of four daily mail deliveries, holding out items for the Senator's personal attention and routing the remainder to other staff members. They discussed the scheduling of a speech that the Senator was to deliver three months later. Of more immediate concern was an invitation from President Nixon to attend a meeting the next day at the summer White House in San Clemente, California. The session was being called to devise ways of rescuing the President's family-assistance bill from the Senate Finance Committee, one of Ribicoff's committees. Ribicoff was interrupted by a call from Republican Senator Jacob Javits of New York, who was concerned about a hearing to be held before Ribicoff's Government Operations Subcommittee, of which Javits was ranking GOP member, later in the day. After a short discussion Ribicoff agreed to talk with Javits on the Senate floor later that morning.

Ribicoff picked up his first newspaper of the day (he usually reads five, not to mention clippings from other newspapers). Then, glancing at his watch, he pressed three buzzers beside his desk to summon several key aides. The Senate was convening at 9 A.M. (its normal hour is noon) because a six-week debate over military procurement had left it hopelessly behind in its business, and in an election year the senators were especially anxious to go away for a brief Labor Day holiday.

Ribicoff's foreign-affairs assistant, Morris Amitay, began with a rundown of the issues to be voted on that day. The most notable was the so-called "end the war" amendment proposed by Senators George McGovern (D.-S.D.) and Mark Hatfield (R.-Ore.). Presented as an amendment to the military-procurement authorization bill, the McGovern-Hatfield proposal was to order complete withdrawal of American troops from Vietnam by the end of 1971. Although it had little chance of passage, the amendment quickly offered a symbolic referendum on the Vietnam war and was the subject of intensive lobbying by peace groups, students, and others opposed to the war. Ribicoff and Amitay did not discuss this amendment, for it had been publicized for months, and Ribicoff already planned to vote for it. Another amendment, offered by William Proxmire (D.-Wis.), was intended to prohibit the use of draftees in Vietnam unless they volunteered to serve there. When Ribicoff asked his staff for opinions on this proposal he provoked a mild argument. Amitay insisted that, as long as the draft was operative, the army should be free to send draftees wherever necessary. To do otherwise would be "a hell of a way to run an army." "I'm far out on this issue," countered Taggert Adams, who as legislative assistant was responsible for keeping the Senator abreast of floor debates. Normally he served as Ribicoff's listening post, briefing the Senator on the issues to be voted upon and suggesting what votes would be consistent with the Senator's general positions ("He doesn't always follow my advice," Adams has said). This time Adams urged voting for the amendment as an antiwar protest. Many antiwar amendments were being defeated on the Senate floor by large votes, he said, and it was just possible that the administration had not received the message about the war. Ribicoff was noncommital but observed that he was convinced that the administration was serious about "winding down" the war.

Without pause the discussion turned to Robert Wager, general counsel and acting staff director of the Senator's Government Operations Subcommittee on Executive Reorganization. The subject was the Senator's upcoming conversation with Javits about the subcommittee's hearings on an administration-proposed reorganization plan. Javits, who was being prodded by the White House, wanted to be assured that Ribicoff still favored the plan. Wager and the Senator briefly discussed the wording of the subcommittee's projected report on the plan. Quickly they shifted to another subcommittee issue, a consumer-protection bill sponsored by the Senator. "Have we got a majority on the subcommittee for this bill?" Ribicoff queried. Wager answered in the affirmative, then spoke about problems in getting the bill through the full committee. Ribicoff said that he would check the matter with other senators.

Just then bells rang for the vote on the McGovern-Hatfield amendment, and the Senator left for the floor.

"You Can't Keep Very Far Ahead"

Senators are treated like sovereigns in their Capitol Hill domain. Staffs and services are organized to cushion them from the minor hardships that plague the everyday lives of ordinary citizens. This care is no more in evidence than when the bells ring for a vote on the floor. The elevator button is pressed quickly three times, and an elevator appears immediately; a car on the world's shortest subway stands waiting; policemen and pages clear the way.

Ribicoff, a short, wiry man, always seems to walk briskly, He is ruggedly handsome and possesses a unique presence. He recalled that while he was still a representative from Connecticut, he had asked financier Bernard Baruch for a contribution to his political campaign. Baruch had turned him down with the following advice: "Get out and get around. Let them see your face, and you won't have any trouble." Indeed, Ribicoff's political fortunes had been built on his face and personality and his knack for projecting them. One of his staff people liked to think that the Senator has a little television camera inside his head that monitors whatever he is doing, leading him to strike the correct pose and say the correct word for the moment.

As he made his way to the Senate chamber, Ribicoff reflected on the job of U.S. senator. The Senate was for him the capstone of a career that had kept him in public life for thirty-two of his sixty years.[14] His life has been a traditional success story made up of hard work and an uncanny instinct for politics. The son of Jewish immigrants from Poland, he was graduated with honors from law school during the Depression, returning to his native Connecticut to open a law office. In the same building worked a rising young politician named John Bailey, under whose tutelage he ran successfully for the state legislature as an antimachine Democrat. Two years later he was defeated in a purge of the young antiorganization legislators—this time he was opposed by Bailey, who had made his peace with the local political machine. After six years away from electoral politics as a Hartford police-court judge, Ribicoff was persuaded by Bailey to run for Congress in 1948. It was a good year for Democratic congressional candidates, and Ribicoff won. "At the end of those six years I was untouched by turmoil," Ribicoff has recalled of his years as a judge. "The fact that I had been out of politics was a great asset to me as I ran for Congress."

Ribicoff remained in the House for four years, retiring in 1952 to run unsuccessfully for the Senate. While a freshman representative, Ribicoff had struck up an acquaintance with a sophomore congressman from Massachusetts named John F. Kennedy; in writing to a friend he had predicted that Kennedy would become the first Roman Catholic President of the United States. As Kennedy went on to national prominence, Ribicoff's career also prospered. In 1954 he defeated the incumbent Republican governor of Connecticut, John Davis Lodge, by a little more than 3,000 votes; four years later he was reelected by the largest plurality in the state's history. Meanwhile he continued his friendship with Kennedy, by then junior senator from Massachusetts; Ribicoff nominated him for the vice-presidency at the 1956 Democratic convention and, after Kennedy had been defeated by Senator Estes Kefauver, worked toward securing the 1960 presidential nomination for him. Until 1960 Ribicoff was virtually the only prominent political figure to support Kennedy for President. After Kennedy's nomination, Ribicoff also played an important role in his campaign.

When Kennedy was elected, Ribicoff could have chosen virtually any job in the new administration. He chose to become the fourth Secretary of Health, Education, and Welfare—even though as a congressman he had voted against a proposal to create the department. He made this choice because, as he explained, "everything about HEW is affirmative. Everything about it is directed toward the betterment of individuals and . . . society." As a recent amalgam of established agencies, however, HEW has resisted the efforts of secretaries who have struggled to coordinate it, before and since. It proved an unruly assignment and, in any event, Ribicoff grew restless away from elective office. In 1962 he resigned to run for the Senate, winning by a narrow margin. Six years later he won re-election by a much larger margin. He chose that year also to underscore the independence that has marked his political career. At the Democratic convention of 1968 he angrily faced Chicago's Mayor Richard J. Daley from the stage and charged the police with "Gestapo tactics" in the streets. Back in his home state he also proclaimed his independence from Bailey's Democratic organization.

Ribicoff's political creed stresses optimism and independence. "I consider myself as having followed an independent course in politics," he has declared. "I am not doctrinaire. I am not extreme. That is why liberals are often after me." There has been an intriguing mixture of recklessness and prudence in his career. He has plunged with abandon into issues or courses of action and has often talked about "breaking your lance" on an issue. Yet he has also seemed reluctant to commit himself fully; he has been called the "cautious crusader." Critics point out, for example, that his behavior in 1968 was as shrewd politically as it was bold. After the Chicago convention young people had a reason to work on Ribicoff's campaign, and his break with Bailey came at a time when the latter's organization had pretty much disintegrated.

Even as a newcomer in the Senate, he was treated as an elder statesman: "You're not a 'freshman' senator, Abe. Don't bother to act like one," advised Vice-President Lyndon Johnson, long a proponent of the Senate "folkways," one of which specified that freshman senators should be seen and not heard. Coming to the Senate with a long public career behind him, Ribicoff was able to follow Johnson's advice. Rather than specializing in a narrow range of issues, he preferred to explore widely and sought out problems of broad concern. Soon Ribicoff was able to make his Executive Reorganization Subcommittee a forum for documenting and dramatizing a wide range of highly visible problems. He plunged into the matters of air and water pollution, pesticides, auto safety (it was a Ribicoff hearing that propelled Ralph Nader into the public view), cities, and consumer protection. Ribicoff has offered no profound explanation for his political success. "You've got to have a feel for it," he has said. "It's a visceral feeling, right inside you. You don't think about it, you just know."

Commenting on day-to-day issues, Ribicoff has confessed that "you can't keep very far ahead of floor issues." A senator must rely heavily on his staff to keep him abreast of those issues, and Ribicoff has freely acknowledged his debt to a bevy of bright young assistants. "Then, too, you have to have a feel for the issues."

The Senator stopped in mid-sentence to speak to a young couple from New Haven who were visiting the Capitol. He greeted them cordially, telling them to obtain gallery passes from his office. Then, without a pause, he continued his train of thought: "You have to have a very agile mind in this job. You are shifting gears all the time."

In the Senate chamber Ribicoff seated himself at his desk in the back row on the majority side and began to ruffle through the stack of pending bills on his desk.[15] Meanwhile, John Stennis (D.-Miss.), as chairman of the Armed Services Committee, was speaking in defense of the military-procurement authorization bill. Stennis was pleading emotionally with colleagues to defeat the McGovern-Hatfield amendment. "It is a historic vote. For the first time, if this amendment is adopted, we will have voted to change direction in the midst of a war." He concluded on the theme that, if the Senate was going to reverse the judgment of the President on the war, "then I do not have the heart to continue to tell those boys that they are fighting for something worthwhile."[16]

Two desks away from Ribicoff Senator McGovern then made a final appeal for his amendment. His flat monotone belied his harsh words. The amendment, he stated, "presents us with an opportunity to end a war we never should have entered," a war that he called

the cruelest, the most barbaric, and the most stupid . . . in our national history. . . . Every Senator in this Chamber is partly respon-sible for sending 50,000 young Americans to an early grave. This Chamber reeks of blood. . . . And if we do not end this damnable war, those young men [who are still living] will some day curse us for our pitiful willingness to let the Executive carry the burden that the Constitution places on us.

As the vote began, the din became noticeable, for the galleries and the floor were both crowded and restless. In the press gallery journalists used long tally sheets to record the votes. The clerk called the roll with disconcerting slowness. Sen-ator Richard Russell (D.-Ga.), dean of the Senate, wheezed his response: "Nay." There were few surprises: The first senator called, George Aiken (R.-Vt.), voted "nay." Although he had been an early opponent of the Vietnam war, he was also a senior Republican and reluctant to tie the hands of his President. Another "nay" came from Albert Gore (D.-Tenn.), a foe of the war but up for reelection and under attack for his liberalism.

Ribicoff voted "aye," then retired to the cloakroom to meet Javits and discuss various items of subcommittee business. Meanwhile, the McGovern-Hatfield amendment was defeated 39 to 55. The White House quickly issued a statement interpreting the outcome as "a solid vote of confidence in [the Presi-dent's] policy of working toward peace in Vietnam." McGovern, in an interview after the vote, observed that "it is remarkable that for the first time in history more than one-third of the U.S. Senate has voted to cut off funds for a war while we are still in battle."

Committee Business: Ecology and Welfare Reform

After discussing committee matters with Javits, Ribicoff made his way through the subway to Room 3302 of the New Senate Office Building, where his subcommittee was to convene at 10:30 A.M. It was the third and final day of public hearings on President Nixon's Reorganization Plan Number 4, in which the administration had proposed to create a National Oceanic and Atmospheric Administration in the U.S. Department of Commerce. The topic sounds innocent and perhaps a little dull, but at the heart of the administrative proposal was one of the most salient contemporary political issues: preservation of the natural environment.

The Executive Reorganization Subcommittee was Ribicoff's personal domain. The committees of Congress are the workhorses of the Hill, but often they are singled out as the most undemocratic parts of the legislative process. Although it is true that the committee system disperses power and often vests it in unrepresentative individuals or committee cabals, it must also be said that recently the Senate has used the committee system to disperse power to an extent not known in the House of Representatives.[17] Since the 1950s Senate Democrats have followed the so-called "Johnson Rule," enunciated by former Majority Leader Lyndon Johnson. This principle means that no Democratic senator will hold two major committee assignments until all senators have at least one. The Republican leadership has also tried to ensure that all GOP senators have an advantageous committee assignment. Second, the small size of the Senate means that relatively more members can serve as committee or subcommittee chairmen: In the 91st Congress, no fewer than fifty-three of the fifty-seven Democratic senators were chairmen of at least single committees or subcommittees!

The subcommittee served the Senator as a base of operations. A not inconsiderable contribution was the additional staff leverage it afforded him. Three professionals employed by the subcommittee were chosen by Ribicoff and served for all practical purposes as extensions of his personal staff. (A fourth professional served at the pleasure of the ranking Republican on the full committee.) A constant path was beaten between the third-floor office and the subcommittee offices in the basement of the Old Senate Office Building. But committee personnel were in a better position to explore legislative issues without the constant interruptions that make up the daily work load of Ribicoff's personal staff. At the time of this hearing the three committee aides were working on consumer protection, environmental agencies, the role of the General Accounting Office, and the problems of providing medical care to all citizens.

Besides the additional staff, allowing a senator to engage in such issue entrepreneurship, a subcommittee offers a forum for publicizing issues—for advancing its chairman's views and enhancing his reputation. Ribicoff's Executive Reorganization Subcommittee was a conspicuous example of this phenomenon. Although its formal mandate might seem to have been confined to organizing the executive branch, Ribicoff had adopted the spacious interpretation that "executive reorganization" embraces any functions that are, or could be, performed by the federal government. To the charge that the subcommittee exploited publicity but failed to follow through on issues, the staff pointed out that the Senator did not have equivalent influence over the legislative committees that have direct authority to act in these matters. (This charge, incidentally, has been leveled at all government operations subcommittees, which inevitably touch upon substantive issues handled by other committees.) In recent years, however, Ribicoff's subcommittee staff had displayed increasing ingenuity in framing substantive legislation that could be referred to the subcommittee and acted upon.

Of course, the subcommittee was not entirely free to select its agenda, and the hearing in question was an example of this limitation. In July 1970 President Nixon had issued, as part of his "environmental package," Reorganization Plan Number 4 for creating a National Oceanic and Atmospheric Administration (NOAA) in the Commerce Department. The agency was to combine several existing governmental agencies, mainly the Environmental Science Services Administration (already in Commerce), the Bureau of Commercial Fisheries (in the Department of the Interior), the marine sports-fishing program of the Bureau of Sports Fisheries and Wildlife (in Interior), and the sea-grants programs (under the National Science Foundation). Under the terms of the Reorganization Act of 1939 and its successors, the President had limited power to reorganize executive agencies by redistributing functions and overhauling structures. His initiatives went into effect if they were not disapproved by either house of Congress within sixty days. In other words, although Congress was empowered by the Constitution to establish executive departments, it had decided to allow the President to make minor administrative adjustments subject to legislative veto.

Once the President had transmitted his reorganization proposal, Congress could disapprove it or simply do nothing. Within three weeks of the plan's announcement Senator Gaylord Nelson (D.-Wis.) had introduced Senate Resolution 433: "RESOLVED, That the Senate does not favor the Reorganization Plan Numbered 4 transmitted to the Congress by the President on July 9, 1970." The resolution was then referred to Ribicoff's subcommittee. In most instances committees have discretion over whether or not they will report, or even consider, matters referred to them, but the Reorganization Act provides that the legislator introducing a resolution of disapproval may petition for a discharge from the committee within ten days of the introduction of his resolution.

Ribicoff's reaction to the reorganization issue illustrates the interrelatedness of a legislator's concerns. Most observers would have preferred that the government's environmental activities be housed in an independent agency or at least in the Interior Department, rather than in the Commerce Department; indeed, the President's own organizational advisers had originally taken this view.[18] The President, however, had decided on Commerce, whose traditional business orientation is generally distrusted by conservationists. Although Ribicoff shared this distrust, he did not feel strongly enough to make an issue of it;

still, he was not unhappy to give Senator Nelson the forum to argue against the proposal and perhaps even to raise the possibility of congressional disapproval. For lurking behind the proposal was the much larger issue of coastal development. Environmentalists feared that the Commerce Department would tend to designate scenic or recreational coastal zones for industrial purposes, in response to pressures from its business clientele. The reorganization hearings offered an opportunity to "build a record" on the impending coastal-zones question and to alert the administration that future activities would be closely scrutinized. Perhaps assurances would be required from the Commerce Department that environmental considerations would be given weight in decisions on coastal zones, or maybe even the expected removal of the coastal-zone question from the Interior Department to Commerce could be prevented.

The hearings were proving useful to Ribicoff for quite another reason. For more than a year his staff, directed by Adams, had been studying the long-range environmental problems of Long Island Sound, a body of water that embraces almost all of Connecticut's coastline. According to a plan devised by the staff and approved by the Senator, the New England River Basins Commission would undertake a three-year ecological study of the sound. At that moment Ribicoff and his staff were campaigning for $100,000 in federal money to finance the first year of the study.

The administration's reorganization plan and Senator Nelson's resolution had produced, quite by accident, a new chance to press for the Long Island Sound project. The actual negotiations had so far taken place in the offhand fashion familiar in Washington: A Ribicoff staff aide had telephoned the Office of Management and Budget (OMB) to express the Senator's interest in funding for the Long Island Sound research; in passing he had suggested that the President's reorganization plan would probably be approved by the subcommittee but that its chances would be even brighter if the Long Island Sound appropriation were forthcoming. The OMB man had spoken to a Commerce Department man, who had telephoned the Ribicoff man to express the department's solicitude about Long Island Sound and to say that the matter of funding would certainly be taken up. That is where the matter stood as the final day of hearings began.

That morning perhaps two dozen spectators—and no reporters—were on hand. At the front of the hearing room, facing the audience and the witnesses' table, is a raised semicircular dais for the senators; behind it are seats for the numerous staff aides who were milling around. The only senator on hand so far was Ribicoff himself. Wager spoke to him for a minute or so; because two previous hearings had been held on the administration's "environmental package," the Senator was already well briefed. The present hearing had been delayed and rescheduled several times: There had been problems in arranging for witnesses to appear before the sixty-day cutoff period was over. Ribicoff's staff took the position that, as originator of the resolution, Senator Nelson—even though he was not a member of the subcommittee—had the major responsibility for procuring witnesses. But Ribicoff's people had stipulated that the number be limited and that there be no overlap in testimony. The arrangements for the hearing had thus actually been made by Senator Nelson's staff under conditions laid down by the subcommittee staff.

When Senator Nelson arrived at 10:40 A.M., Ribicoff immediately rapped his gavel and intoned, "The Committee will be in order." Ribicoff observed that Nelson was sitting with the subcommittee that morning "to develop his view." After reading a brief statement explaining Reorganization Plan Number 4, he yielded to Nelson for a statement. Nelson explained that he favored the first part of the administration's environmental package (Reorganization Plan Number 3) but that a developmental agency like the Commerce Department should not have responsibility for making decisions on the marine environment. Above all, he said, it was necessary to learn the administration's intentions on the pending crucial problem of designating coastal zones before acting on the present proposal.

Ribicoff called the first witness, Andrew M. Rouse, executive director of the Ash Commission. Because the commission was known to have advised against the present plan, the tactic was to make Rouse admit as much in public. He was in a delicate spot, and the exchange that followed was tentative and halting. Nelson did persuade Rouse to admit that "the administration of pollution standards should not be in a resource users' or development agency." When Ribicoff asked whether or not the already-established independent Environmental Protection Agency should take precedence over NOAA, Rouse demurred, but later Ribicoff was able to say, "Then you agree with Senator Nelson." When Rouse thought that he had gone too far, the questioning bogged down. Rouse was dismissed, and a panel of conservationists was called.

The first panel member, an official of the National Audubon Society, spoke succinctly and effectively. He argued that the Interior Department was biologically oriented whereas Commerce was not; therefore it would make sense to leave fisheries research and coastal-zone management to the former agency. When the second witness, a man from the National Wildlife Federation, repeated this theme, Ribicoff cut in impatiently: "Do you think that the Commerce Department is incapable of balancing development with a concern for the environment?" The witness replied that the department had traditionally been involved in exploitive activities. "But we've all been exploitive," Ribicoff countered, adding his view that society is finally "turning around" on the environmental question. He challenged the witnesses to say whether or not they believed that the Commerce Department would dare to act in conflict with presidential and congressional policy. "Frankly, yes," one witness responded. The third witness, from the Izaak Walton League, summed up the arguments of the other two.

When the buzzer sounded for a floor vote at 11:15, Ribicoff turned to

Javits, who had just joined the group. Rather than question the witnesses, Javits produced a short statement in defense of the administration's proposal. As soon as he had finished, Ribicoff adjourned the subcommittee. The floor vote was on the Proxmire amendment to prohibit the use of draftees in Vietnam; he voted in favor of it (the amendment lost 22 to 71). Ribicoff and Nelson reviewed the NOAA issue on the way to the Capitol, with Javits and Senator Theodore Stevens (R.-Alaska) trailing along. Ribicoff assured Nelson of his concern for the environment, mentioning the Long Island Sound project. Although he would have preferred that environmental-protection activities be centralized in an independent agency, he thought that he could "live with" the President's plan. He suggested putting strong language about the responsibilities of the Commerce Department in the committee's report.

Minutes later the senators were back, and the hearing was resumed. Having had time to regroup forces, the panel commented on the Javits and Ribicoff rejoinders. Ribicoff wanted to help the environmentalists, but he could not see enough of an issue to justify opposing the President on this proposal. Then Stevens questioned the panel sharply. He spoke for the ship-construction and fishing interests, who thought that they would receive better service from NOAA in Commerce than they did from the Interior Department. As a former Interior official himself, he proved a knowledgeable spokesman for the administration. In passing he gave Secretary Maurice Stans' assurance that the Bureau of Commercial Fisheries would not be tampered with in the Commerce Department. Finally, he argued that the new NOAA, like all governmental bodies, would be subject to the provisions of the Environmental Protection Act of 1969. "Do you fear that the Commerce Department won't comply with the 1969 Act?" he asked.

The witnesses hesitated before this onslaught. They had clearly been outfought, though they had succeeded in making the key point that the coastal-zone question—still unresolved—remained the fundamental issue. Impatient with the impasse, Ribicoff yawned and closed his file folder, a signal that he was about to end the hearing. Stevens finished making his points and noted that Javits wanted to insert further comments in the record. Ribicoff assured him that the record would be kept open for statements from absent members and that the subcommittee report would not be published until it had received the approval of all the senators. Then he adjourned the meeting subject to "the call of the chair." As the senators left the committee room, Javits bounced in and was reassured that the record would be kept open for "your eloquent statement." In the hall they met another subcommittee member, Charles Percy (R.-Ill.), also with a statement to introduce; he too was assured that the record had been kept open. As Ribicoff and Nelson parted at the "Senators Only" elevator, they arranged to have "your man and my man get together" on the contents of the subcommittee report.

After the hearings the subcommittee would be polled on the reorganization plan; a letter on the subject would be ready for Ribicoff's signature later that day. Over the next couple of weeks the subcommittee staff would work on the report and, once the Senate had reconvened following its Labor Day vacation, obtain "sign-offs" (approvals or disapprovals) from the subcommittee members. Next the matter would go to the full Government Operations Committee for discussion and resolution, and then to the Senate floor.

Ribicoff decided to look in on the Finance Committee, his second committee assignment. There was a fair-sized crowd, including a half-dozen or so reporters. The subject of these hearings was the President's Family Assistance Plan (FAP), designed to reform the chaotic welfare system by setting an income floor for every citizen. It was perhaps the administration's most far-reaching legislative proposal and the keystone of the President's New Federalism. Having passed the House of Representatives, it was lodged in the Senate Finance Committee, where it was meeting resistance from the chairman and from some senior Republican conservatives on the committee. As a former HEW Secretary Ribicoff took a special interest in FAP. Earlier in the year Tag Adams had convened a group of welfare experts to advise the Senator on the plan; their discussions had resulted in a series of fifteen Ribicoff amendments, introduced on April 20. As the year passed Ribicoff was still trying to incorporate job-creation provisions in the bill and, most of all, to help pry it loose from the skeptical committee.

The witness on the stand was Mayor Carl Stokes of Cleveland, speaking for the powerful urban lobby: the National League of Cities and the U.S. Conference of Mayors. As the television cameras moved in to get footage of Stokes, Ribicoff, as the second-ranking Democrat in attendance, moved from his usual place near the end of the semicircular dais into the seat next to Chairman Russell Long (D.-La.). Attending on the Republican side were flinty John Williams of Delaware, Carl Curtis of Nebraska, and Len Jordan of Idaho. All were foes of the Family Assistance Plan.

Stokes began by recalling that his family had been on welfare until he was seventeen years old. "Welfare state" programs—public assistance, the GI bill, and state-subsidized college and law school—had made it possible for him to go as far as he had. He was urbane and articulate, but he spoke from personal experience, ending on a sharp note: "I come here not as a supplicant; I come as a mayor to speak to the federal government, which is taking our money but not spending it on the proper priorities." He said that he had been told that the Department of Labor could not even determine an accurate cost-of-living index for various cities. "I just don't believe that," he declared. "But it's true," Ribicoff rejoined. "The fact is that we have been more interested in technology than in human beings."

Then Ribicoff launched into a favorite line of questioning: He believed that jobs were the key to the assistance problem, but the administration bill had no provision for creating jobs (though it included money for job training).

Stokes testified that in Cleveland 3,000 men could be placed in municipal jobs immediately. Could these welfare recipients be used to help clean up the city? "Unquestionably," replied Stokes—clearly a friendly witness. Ribicoff moved easily from question to question, using no notes. He became the instinctive politician, drawing on all his experience, knowledge, and wit to make his point. He believed that job incentives without jobs would be meaningless; "people do not need to drift in this life," he said. But he also realized that the public was reluctant to accept welfare programs without work-incentive provisions, so important is work in the gallery of American values.

Finally, he cautioned that "we oversell every piece of social legislation we pass. I want a workable piece of legislation. But it will not solve all our welfare problems."

The Senator's Office

Shortly after 1:00 P.M. Ribicoff left the committee hearing for a luncheon engagement with a former staff aide in the senators' private dining room in the Capitol. Within half an hour he was back in his office to sign mail prepared by Miss Cass and to return several telephone calls that had come in his absence.

During the Senator's freewheeling activities on the Senate floor and in committee hearings his office staff had been functioning as his alter ego. The complex of crowded offices, of which Suite 321 formed the apex, reflected Ribicoff's institutional position and personal habits. In turn it conditioned his operations on the Hill. His staff was organized to complement his background, style, and legislative interests in performing the office of U.S. senator. Indeed, staff members were trained to play many of these roles with minimum personal intervention by Ribicoff. The Senate is an intimate institution in comparison with the larger House of Representatives, but the senators' offices have just the opposite characteristics. Whereas the average congressman can exercise strong direction over his small staff, a senator heads an institution that must run largely on its own steam. Yet the larger Senate staffs yield dividends in additional research and the policy entrepreneurship that they can generate.

The full dimensions of Senator Ribicoff's job can thus be measured only after exploration of the nooks and crannies of Suite 321 and auxiliary offices. It is necessary to look carefully at the functioning of Ribicoff's staff organization, which is in fact the formal structure arising from the Senator's job perceptions and performances.

Casual visitors, including constituents seeking tourist information about the nation's capital and visitors' passes to the House or Senate galleries, penetrate no farther than the outer office, which is large enough to accommodate only a receptionist-secretary and a small waiting area. The receptionist must be from Connecticut because, as she says, "everyone who comes in asks me where

I'm from." (Besides, she must be able to pinpoint the location of visitors' hometowns.) One wall is devoted to political cartoons featuring the Senator, another to photographs supplied by the Connecticut Historical Society.

To the right of the reception room is an inner office, which serves as an anteroom to the Senator's own chambers. A cubicle to the rear is the office of John Koskinen, a young lawyer serving as Ribicoff's administrative assistant. As the Senator's chief aide, he performed a variety of functions, including management of the fifteen or so people who worked in the office. "The Senator should not have to worry about running the office at all," Koskinen said. He estimated that about 20 percent of his time was devoted to tasks that included simply being available to serve as a backstop and buffer for the other staff people.

Koskinen also played a role in steering people and mail through the office. In cooperation with Miss Cass, who also had her desk in this segment of the suite, he helped to decide which visitors should actually see the Senator. And when Ribicoff was unavailable, Koskinen himself tried to satisfy visitors' expectations. A special problem occurred in May 1970, when hordes of students and others came to Capitol Hill to protest the Cambodian invasion. To handle the crowds Ribicoff scheduled open meetings once or twice a day for Connecticut students, about 400 of whom were seen by the Senator. Out-of-state students talked to other staff members. Of course, it helped that Ribicoff was already identified as a foe of the Vietnam war, and he and the staff thought that these young people should not be turned away without talking to someone in the office.

In addition to these tasks, Koskinen had a tough, ambivalent, and often unrewarding assignment, perhaps the most difficult in the office: to serve as "devil's advocate," jurist, critic, and confidant to Ribicoff as the Senator experimented with new ideas, plans, speeches, and policies. It is, as one Senate staffer put it, "a job that requires inordinately good judgment, an ability to see issues through the Senator's eyes, not your own, and a sense of timing—you have to know when to speak and when to be quiet."

In order to keep abreast of current issues, Koskinen also tried to look at most of the incoming mail before it was routed to the appropriate staff members for reply. Once the letters had been opened by machine they went to Miss Cass, who initialed them for various staff people. If a letter indicated that the writer had corresponded with the Senator earlier, she added the word "previous" so that the earlier correspondence could be pulled from the files for reference. After Koskinen had checked the mail, it was distributed to the desks of various people in the office. There was a rule that letters had to be answered within a week; if delays were anticipated the letters were acknowledged immediately and detailed responses sent later. Like all people in the public spotlight, Ribicoff received all manner of correspondence, a small portion of it crackpot in nature. But most mail fell into several distinct categories.

"Legislative mail" involved current issues and was handled by Adams and a veteran staff member, Katherine Komfala. They prepared replies for everyone who wrote to express views on pending legislation or related issues (out-of-state letters, however, were usually left unanswered). Each reply expressed the Senator's appreciation of the constituent's sentiments, explained the bill's status, and finally assured the writer that his views would be kept in mind. Whenever possible, Ribicoff's position on the issue was also explained.

If a large volume of mail on a particular subject was received, form letters were composed and typed by tape-fed automatic typewriters called "robotypes." Even the Senator's signature could be affixed automatically by means of a template device called an "Auto-Pen." Sometimes even robotyping proved too cumbersome. After the Cambodian invasion of May 1970, the Senator received 15,000 letters, not counting petitions with thousands of additional names affixed to them. Even the robotypes would have required several months to churn out enough of the two-page responses prepared by the Senator. So all the general letters, pro and con, were answered with a two-page letter printed by offset. Even so, a great many individual responses had to be prepared for letter writers who had taken special positions, which consumed a great deal of time.

Other letters came from constituents who had problems: the so-called "casework mail." Casework includes every kind of request for assistance: servicemen's requests for transfer of assignments, citizens with social-security claims, ex-GIs' efforts to establish eligibility for veterans' benefits, requests for help in bringing friends or relatives into the country under immigration quotas, and thousands of similar demands. Although some legislators talk disparagingly about "running errands" for constituents, most (including Ribicoff) are convinced that casework is well worth the effort. As he said, "A senator or representative is often the only person to whom a citizen can turn to receive fair and prompt treatment from the impersonal federal bureaucracy." In an increasingly complex and bureaucratized world citizens often need a "friend at court" in dealing with the government. Ribicoff's office had several people with long experience in particular fields.

Sometimes the petitioners were not individual citizens but rather local government units: for example, a municipality applying for model-city funds, a school district seeking a library grant, or a village protesting the planned route of a federal highway. Such requests were directed to the "Connecticut desk" presided over by Brian McGovern, who was familiar with state problems and maintained liaison with city and state agencies. He often met with their representatives, directed them to the appropriate federal officials, and even accompanied them to appointments with these officials. When agencies of local or state governments were involved, the Senator's office assumed an advocacy role on constituents' behalf.

Quite the reverse approach was taken to the requests of private firms. The office would provide information or make inquiries to obtain that information, but the staff made a point of not assuming an advocate role. "We opt for doing less rather than more," explained Koskinen. "All we ask is fair and equal treatment for Connecticut firms: no more and no less." Needless to add, most firms are not without resources in dealing with the federal government: They can hire Washington representatives or rely upon their trade associations to voice their interests; the largest firms have their own Washington offices.

Beyond the day-to-day assistance given to constituents, the office staff pursued a limited number of more ambitious projects. The Long Island Sound research program has already been mentioned. Another was an effort to create a Connecticut River National Recreation Area, which would preserve the scenic and historic value of that great New England waterway. Both projects had involved several staff members in extended work stimulating local support, writing legislation, and steering that legislation through the Washington labyrinth.

Foreign policy was the province of Morris Amitay, whose desk was located in a small cubicle behind the reception room. Like many senators, Ribicoff was expected to develop a foreign-policy image. Furthermore, he had once served on the House Foreign Affairs Committee and, as a Jew, he was especially concerned about the problems of the Middle East. A longtime critic of the Vietnam war, Ribicoff had abandoned support of President Johnson on the war issue several years before. And, as acting chairman of the Senate Investigations Subcommittee, he had conducted inquiries into foreign-aid programs. That afternoon Ribicoff was to deliver a speech on the Middle East prepared by Amitay, a former foreign-service officer.

The Attack on Northern Segregation

His relatively large staff gives a senator the opportunity, if he is so inclined, to engage in policy entrepreneurship—the searching out and cultivation of issues. These issues need not be directly related to the senator's committee assignments or even to his constituency. More frequently than the House member's staff, the senator's office staff can untangle itself from everyday responsibilities to do research, write speeches, and draft bills. Of course, Ribicoff's subcommittee provided an important staff resource, but even on his personal staff virtually everyone could become involved, in one way or another, with policy questions.

Speeches provided one avenue for developing policy issues. Ribicoff was in great demand for speaking engagements around the country; ever since his bitter exchange with Mayor Daley at the 1968 Democratic convention in Chicago he had been a popular figure on college campuses. He relished his campus appearances, preferring to engage in discussion with students, in addition to presenting his prepared remarks. He scheduled outside speeches rather frequently—twelve to fifteen in the spring of 1970 and virtually the same number the following fall. Speeches for those appearances were given careful attention by Ribicoff and his staff. When the Senator was asked to speak on a certain subject, his staff started from scratch, though if a Ribicoff speech on that subject was already on file, they could begin with that. When the topic was left open, however, the audience would doubtless be treated to an exposition of whatever issue Ribicoff was developing at the moment. The issue of segregation in the North—a dominant Ribicoff theme during 1970—serves as an example.

The occasion was Senate consideration of an HEW-Labor appropriations bill (H.R. 514) to extend various educational programs for four years. In two weeks (February 4-19, 1970) of floor debate, controversy centered almost wholly on an amendment introduced by Senator Stennis of Mississippi to require that school racial standards be applied uniformly throughout the country "without regard to the origin or cause of such segregation." This innocent-sounding amendment was designed to eliminate the distinction between de jure segregation (required or supported by law) and de facto segregation, which is not specifically established by law but results from segregated residential patterns. Such an amendment was calculated to touch the raw nerves of almost everyone. Northerners charged that Stennis was merely trying to deflect the government's integration efforts in the South by focusing attention on the North, and southerners argued that the government had already indulged its own bias by concentrating on one region.

Meanwhile Ribicoff was slowly coming to the belief that, for the sake of consistency, he ought to support the amendment. From his subcommittee's hearings on the urban crisis (in 1966-1967) he understood that many of the problems of northern cities arose from the increasing alienation of the black-dominated core cities from the white, middle-class suburbs. As the Senate took up the Stennis amendment, an incident occurred which led Ribicoff to a decision. Before an audience of 2,000 students at the University of Texas, where he spoke on the topic of de facto segregation, he remarked during the question period that it was indefensible that a university of 35,000 students had only 400 blacks and 200 chicanos in its student body. The audience responded with thunderous applause. "I decided it would also be a form of hypocrisy if I were afraid to vote in the Senate the convictions I voiced on the campus," Ribicoff recalled.

As soon as he returned to Washington, he summoned several staff aides to a Sunday morning meeting at his office to discuss the problem. First they searched the *Congressional Record* to find out what the Stennis amendment really specified and to review how the issue had developed. Then they discussed Ribicoff's possible responses and the likely political repercussions. By 8:00 P.M. Ribicoff had decided to support the amendment, and his staff had prepared a speech for delivery on the Senate floor the next afternoon. As Ribicoff had made up his mind, little time was spent mulling over the matter. "There were no memos, no exchanges of information, no comments from people outside," one staff member recalled. "It was just a gut reaction on the Senator's part." As the speech was being drafted, his press secretary was called in to prepare a press release on it. That evening, shifts of secretaries typed, mimeographed, and collated the speech for distribution to the press the next morning.

On February 9 Ribicoff declared:

> The North is guilty of monumental hypocrisy in its treatment of the Black man. Without question, northern communities have been as systematic and as consistent as southern communities in denying the Black man and his children the opportunities that exist for white people.

Northerners, he continued, regard southern desegregation with a "sense of revenge." In the North, he said, the races are resegregating, as whites flee to the suburbs and blacks are concentrated in inner-city ghettos. Unless such de facto segregation could be stopped, "we are never going to solve the problem of education in a racist society."

Ribicoff's staff anticipated that the press would show some interest in the issue, but it was not prepared for the flood of articles that followed on the heels of the speech. Along with many of Ribicoff's liberal Senate colleagues, many editorial writers charged that the Senator was giving aid and comfort to the southerners and attempting to sidetrack desegregation efforts by focusing attention on de facto segregation elsewhere. Others were more philosophical, linking the speech with the discouraging progress of integration since the 1954 Supreme Court decision. Tom Wicker of *The New York Times* produced a column entitled "The End of Integration"; David Broder, the *Washington Post*'s respected political writer, wrote a gloomy piece concluding with a reference to "the end of the American dream." Many Connecticut editorial writers, on the other hand, seemed pleased by what they interpreted as a courageous stand by their senator, considering the residential segregation in Connecticut.

The Senator's mail, furthermore, was overwhelmingly (and surprisingly) favorable: Of 5,000 or so letters only about 10 percent were opposed. Half the critical writers complained of Ribicoff's "capitulation" to the southerners. The National Association for the Advancement of Colored People wrote to all its Connecticut members: "The bigoted, conservative southern whites, especially their politicians, continue to be our enemies. . . . And they've got helpers like Senator Abraham Ribicoff." Others who opposed the Senator were whites who feared that he was proposing to move blacks into their northern neighborhoods. Those who sided with him also had mixed motivations: Some thought as he did that if integration is good for the South, it must be good for the North as well, but others saw the amendment as a means of thwarting integration.

The Senator's staff had failed to anticipate so much publicity, and they certainly had not expected the Stennis amendment to pass. Yet pass it did, by a 56 to 36 roll-call vote. Before the vote Ribicoff proposed adding to its language a specific reference to de facto and de jure segregation; this provision was accepted 63 to 24 on roll call.

Having won so much publicity, Ribicoff was convinced that he had an obligation to develop the issue further and in particular to recommend legislation designed to reduce de facto segregation in the North. Two forums for developing this issue presented themselves. First, Ribicoff was asked to address the American Society of Newspaper Editors' annual meeting in San Francisco; in that speech he outlined a series of educational proposals. Then he was asked to write an article on the subject for *Look*, though it actually did not appear until early fall.[19] During the autumn speaking season Ribicoff planned to develop the issue still further. (Later in the session he introduced a pair of bills designed to subsidize educational and residential desegregation in urban areas.)

Although the issue of de facto segregation was clearly the major preoccupation of Ribicoff's staff during this period, it was by no means the only one. During a single day, for example, the Senator was busy promoting the idea of public-service employment (in the Finance Committee) and later the Middle East question (in a floor speech). Lurking under the surface at the morning's environmental hearing had been still another Ribicoff issue, the Long Island Sound project. Meanwhile, down in the subcommittee offices one staff member was working on a Ribicoff consumer-rights bill, another on a bill to strengthen the powers of the General Accounting Office as an overseer of executive agencies, and still another on a book by Ribicoff on the inadequacies of medical care in the United States.

The selection of a staff is one of the most important sets of decisions that a legislator makes. Good, aggressive staff work can raise the stock of even a mediocre legislator; unimaginative staff support can drag down the most talented legislator. Ribicoff's principal staff people tended to be young activists. "My job," one of them explained, "is to try to push the Senator in certain directions, raising issues until he buys one, and then working on them—but not beyond the Senator's attention span." Particularly when he is new on the job a staff member can expect to work very hard on an issue and then have the Senator reject it. As one staff aide put it, the best strategy was to speak out strongly and then "save your influence for another day." Even when the Senator decided to accept a staff initiative, the person who had thought up the idea had to be content with having his labors advertised under someone else's name.

Clearly, senators are not merely creatures of their staffs. It is they, after all, who must decide whether or not to adopt the bright ideas of their aides, and it is they who must bear the consequences of such decisions. Ribicoff was an experienced and instinctive politician, and his decisions were neither prolonged nor agonized. In weighing staff initiatives, he was concerned mainly with political impact and the likelihood of eventual success. "He works instinctively and alone," one aide remarked. "He senses a headline and then leaps at it. When he decides to move, he moves quickly."

The Senator and the Press

"I'm really a half-time press aide," said Fred Asselin, a young former newspaperman who served as Ribicoff's press assistant. Neither Asselin nor his boss had much use for organized press agentry, which was just as well because the Senator knew how to make the front pages on his own. "The Senator is usually his own best press agent," Asselin confided. "My job is to adjust to his needs—to catch up to him and learn at least a part of what he knows instinctively about politics." Ribicoff instructed his subordinates: "Stay away from handouts. Nothing gives warmth and personality to something as much as each reporter writing his own story."

The office only rarely put out a newsletter and in fact did not even have the up-to-date state mailing list that would be necessary to distribute such a newsletter. (Most senators' staffs regularly distribute newsletters and spend much time expanding their mailing lists.) But a biweekly column entitled "All to the Good" was distributed to Connecticut newspapers. Its title and its optimistic theme reflected the Senator's own character. ("I hate to knock anyone," he has been quoted as saying. "Be positive. Tell people what you are doing, not what someone else isn't doing. I don't like to take the negative approach ever.") The column was designed primarily for weekly newspapers and small dailies, though larger newspapers occasionally picked up individual items for their pages. Several newsmen included Ribicoff's office in their regular "beats." Among them were the Washington reporters for two Hartford papers, as well as for papers in Stamford and Bridgeport. The Senator received attention from *The New York Times* and from reporters in the Washington offices of the two major wire services, AP and UPI.

Ribicoff prepared no regularly scheduled radio spots or television programs. In answer to special requests he might tape an interview, and he readily accepted requests from Connecticut radio stations for telephone "bleeper" interviews. Some of the more prominent Washington reporters were personal friends and spoke with him directly. And the office itself was relatively open to inquiries from reporters, who were encouraged to consult appropriate staff people directly.

Although Asselin's press assignment was not overburdening, he had other responsibilities to take up his time. He was involved in the Long Island Sound study and the Connecticut River National Recreation Area, projects that had demanded large investments of time in arousing and organizing local interests. Asselin also served as Ribicoff's liaison with the staff of the Permanent Investigations Subcommittee of Government Operations. At the request of Senator John McClellan (D.-Ark.), chairman of both the subcommittee and the full committee, Ribicoff had served as acting subcommittee chairman for investigations of commodity-imports programs in Southeast Asia and later of the black market in American currency in Asia and the abuses of nonappropriated funds in Vietnam and elsewhere. This last issue was a continuing one; irregularities in the operation of American servicemen's clubs throughout the world had turned up. The investigation was far from closed and had taken Asselin on several foreign trips.

The Day Draws to a Close

Meanwhile, floor debate on military procurement had been droning on, and at 2:15 P.M. the bells rang for another roll-call vote. This time the issue was an amendment by Senator Edmund Muskie (D.-Maine), which would require that the prime contractor for a new series of navy destroyers divide the construction work with at least one major subcontractor. Ribicoff, whose state has shipbuilding interests (as does Maine), favored the provision, but when his name was called he answered: "On this vote I have a pair with the Senator from Nevada [Mr. Cannon]. If he were present and voting, he would vote 'nay'. If I were at liberty to vote, I would vote 'yea'. I withhold my vote." This procedure is what is known as a "live pair" and arises from legislators' desires to be recorded on certain issues when they are not on hand to vote. The majority and minority clerks try to oblige absent legislators by arranging "pairs"—one in favor of the proposition and one against—whose votes would cancel out if they were present. In a live pair one partner is on hand but withholds his vote in deference to the absent legislator.

Following this vote Ribicoff lingered on the floor because the next amendment would directly affect the welfare of Israel. Ostensibly the proposal, made by J. William Fulbright (D.-Ark.), would merely protect the jurisdiction of his Foreign Relations Committee over the controversial question of arms sales to foreign powers. But it would also hold up implementation of a section of the military-procurement bill, which, among other provisions, permitted the United States to sell aircraft and ancillary equipment to Israel. After being recognized for two minutes to speak against the Fulbright proposal, Ribicoff read a speech that Amitay had composed earlier in the day and that they had discussed that afternoon. Explaining the complicated procedural context of the Fulbright proposal, Ribicoff noted that approval of Fulbright's amendment would "establish that the Senate favors insufficient credit resources for Israel, deferred too far into the future, and on terms inconsistent with Israel's critical financial problems." As others spoke up in opposition to the proposal, several senators made their way to Ribicoff's desk to ask questions about the Fulbright proposal; he attempted to answer and urged them to vote against the amendment. When the vote was taken ten minutes later, the amendment was defeated 7 to 87, with only a handful of the most adamant opponents of arms sales following Fulbright on the issue. At 4:30 P.M. the military-procurement bill was ready for a final vote. It passed by a tally of 84 to 5.[20] It authorized funds for military procurement for the fiscal year 1971 (which had begun two months earlier on July 1, 1970).

As Majority Leader Mansfield and Minority Leader Hugh Scott (Pennsylvania) discussed the schedule for subsequent sessions, Ribicoff headed for his office to finish the day's chores. As he left the chamber, he was buttonholed by an old friend who had been waiting to talk to him about the President's Family Assistance Plan. The friend was Wilbur Cohen, former Secretary of Health, Education, and Welfare and one of the nation's foremost experts on welfare policies. He had several ideas for amendments that might help pry the bill out of committee, and he had already been lobbying with Chairman Long. (Later in the session the committee rejected the bill but approved an experimental test of the program proposed by Ribicoff.)

Back in his office Ribicoff savored with Amitay the victory over the Fulbright amendment and returned telephone calls that had come in during the day. Staff members wandered in and out of his office, consulting with him on various matters. Ribicoff and Adams conferred briefly on the proposed FAP amendments. The Senator said that he was willing to cooperate with Cohen and Long on anything that might ensure the bill's passage that year. As he was going to San Clemente the next day, Adams promised to have memorandums on the Ribicoff amendments ready by that time.

A few minutes later Ribicoff called for Asselin. At last the Senator was making progress in reading the daily papers, and he had found an article in the *Hartford Courant* headlined "Ribicoff Growing in Stature." The Senator was pleased with this article and one in another Connecticut paper that pursued the same theme.

The Senator returned a call from "downtown" and heard some good news that could hardly be coincidental. He emerged to announce to the staff that the administration had suddenly uncovered $100,000 in the current Army Corps of Engineers' budget to finance the first year's study of the Long Island Sound. The veiled implications of the subcommittee's hearings on the environmental-reorganization plan had not been lost on the administration. A semifestive air prevailed as some departing staff lingered to discuss this accomplishment.

Shortly before 6:00 P.M. the bells summoned Ribicoff to the floor for a final vote. The leadership, pressing to clear up business before the Labor Day recess, wanted to dispose of an uncontroversial appropriations bill for the Treasury and Post Office Departments, the Executive Office of the President, and several independent agencies.[21] The vote was 68 to 0.

Most of the staff had departed by the time that Ribicoff returned to his office once more to finish his newspapers and make a few telephone calls. His face showed weariness from the day's activities. The day had been a memorable one but in one respect quite typical: The wide range of topics thrown at the Senator had required unflagging mental agility. In contrast to bureaucrats and scholars, legislators cannot afford the luxury of prolonged concentration on single problems. The next day would offer Ribicoff no respite: In the afternoon he would board a jet for San Clemente and intensive talks on the Family Assistance Plan. The sun was low in the sky when he got into his car for the brief trip across town to his Watergate apartment, where he would fix himself a simple dinner (his wife was in Connecticut), read, and be in bed by 9:00 P.M.

NOTES FOR CHAPTER 3

1 For Anderson's personal account of these events see his *Between Two Worlds: A Congressman's Choice* (Grand Rapids, Mich.: Zondervan, 1970), chap. 1.

2 Richard F. Fenno, Jr., "The Internal Distribution of Influence: The House," in David B. Truman (ed.), *Congress and America's Future* (Englewood Cliffs, N.J.: Prentice-Hall, 1965), p. 72.

3 For example, at one August leadership meeting in 1970 the legislators and the President had a lengthy discussion of what action the President should take on the HUD and Office of Education appropriations for fiscal 1971, as well as on railroad-retirement and veterans' disability-compensation legislation.

4 For a summary of the bill see U.S., Congress, House, Committee on Agriculture, *Agriculture Act of 1970*, 91st Cong., 2d sess., 23 July 1970, H. Rept. 91-1329.

5 Burt Schorr, "Nixon Stand May Produce $20,000 Ceiling on Farm Payments" *Wall Street Journal*, August 3, 1970.

6 The three massive House office buildings are named after powerful, almost legendary twentieth-century Speakers of the House—Joseph "Uncle Joe" Cannon (R.-Ill.), Nicholas Longworth (R.-Ohio), and Sam Rayburn (D.-Tex.).

7 In common with most members of Congress, Anderson's office is lined with framed autographed photographs of prominent national leaders, fellow congressmen, mementos of his political career (for example, pens used by the President to sign major pieces of legislation), and symbols of his state and constituency. Careful study of these office decorations frequently tells a great deal about the occupant. For example, Anderson's deep religious convictions and concerns are apparent in pictures and artifacts.

8 On how congressmen use their scarce resources, including time, see Raymond A. Bauer, Ithiel de Sola Pool, and Lewis Anthony Dexter, *American Business and Public Policy: The Politics of Foreign Trade* (New York: Atherton, 1963), pp. 406-413.

9 On the importance of Congress' passing *some* legislation on critical issues, see Bauer, Pool, and Dexter, *American Business and Public Policy,* pp. 426-428.

10 The cloakroom, an informal gathering place for members, is a narrow, L-shaped room off the back of the House chamber; it contains a bank of telephones, a snack bar for sandwiches and coffee, a conference table, and leather-upholstered chairs and couches.

11 The bill later passed the House but was vetoed by the President, who said that it would

regulate campaign finance in piecemeal fashion and inadequately. The President's veto was sustained in a subsequent vote.

12 The Railsback amendment was defeated by a voice vote on the following day.

13 The major bill prepared by the Rules Committee in the 91st Congress was the Legislative Reorganization Act of 1970 (See Chapter 8).

14 The best portrait of Ribicoff is found in Ben H. Bagdikian, "Honest Abe–The Vote-Getter," in Lester Tanzer (ed.), *The Kennedy Circle* (Washington, D.C.: Luce, 1961), pp. 213-236. We have drawn from this article to round out our account of the Senator's background and views.

15 In contrast to House members, senators, except for floor leaders and Whips,are assigned individual desks by seniority.

16 The floor debates for the day are recorded in U.S., Congress, Senate, *Congressional Record* daily ed., 91st Cong., 2d sess., 1 September 1970.

17 The resistance of the House Democratic leadership to a "committee bill of rights" is described in Chapter 8.

18 It was the position of the President's Advisory Council on Executive Organization, known as the Ash Commission, after its chairman, Roy L. Ash.

19 Abraham Ribicoff, "Do Most Americans Secretly Want Segregation?" *Look*, 34 (September 8, 1970), 11-13.

20 Opposed were Fulbright, Charles Goodell (R.-N.Y.), Hatfield, McGovern, and Nelson.

21 This day's votes included the two major types of legislation considered by Congress: authorizations and appropriations. In theory the distinction is not always meaningful, for both kinds of bills may deal with broad policy questions and both may have dollar amounts attached to them. But in practice the distinction is clear enough: Authorizations like the military-procurement bill emanate from substantive committees and state the intention of Congress in substantive, or policy, terms. Appropriations like the Treasury and Post Office bill are the province of the appropriations committees and actually allow the expenditure of money for purposes and programs that have been previously authorized.

Party Leaders and Followers

With its localized process of member recruitment and election and its strong committee system, Congress is among legislatures of the Western world a classic case of fragmented power and decision making. Such centralization of power as exists in Congress comes about primarily through the actions of political party groups. Party organizations draw their strength from being the most comprehensive groups within Congress, groups that for most members offer important sources of support and identification, as well as focuses for loyalty. Parties are organized and influence decision making across committee lines and at many stages in the legislative process. The parties' activities, internal practices, composition, and leadership are thus critical factors in the legislative process.

Although they share many common characteristics, the Democratic and Republican Parties in Congress are significantly different and will therefore be treated separately in this chapter. The first two case studies consider the role of parties, their internal pluralism, and their responses to the competitive environment in which they operate. Special emphasis is placed on struggles for leadership posts among the Democrats. In discussion of the Republicans the stress is on legislative strategy and especially on the impact of the White House. Among the most important leaders of both parties are the committee chairmen and the ranking minority members, who hold their positions largely through seniority. The third case study reveals how the two parties have dealt with the consequences of the seniority system.

DEMOCRATS: CHANGING THE GUARD

The Telephone Call to Boston

Just before Christmas 1968 a young western representative asked himself for the last time, "What do I have to lose?" He then picked up his telephone and called Boston, thus launching a series of events that led to House Democratic leadership changes in 1971. The 1968 elections had put the Democratic Party in opposition to the White House but still in control of both houses of Congress. The party would need vigorous and articulate leadership on the Hill. As long as Democrats had held the White House in the Kennedy and Johnson years program leadership had emanated from the President, and congressional leaders had frequently served only as tactical lieutenants. Richard M. Nixon's election would force upon the leadership quite different functions: criticizing the administration, formulating and publicizing alternative policies, and helping to build strength for the next presidential contest. In such instances of divided government the congressional majority is called "truncated," for it lacks the potential "chief legislator." Such a majority can achieve partnership in policy making, Randall B. Ripley has argued, either by consistently cooperating with the President or by maintaining enough strength to force presidential acceptance of some of its initiatives. The narrowness of Nixon's margin of victory, not to mention many Democrats' intense dislike of him, seemed to rule out a strategy of cooperation in 1969. In such hostile circumstances the tendency is for congressional opposition to crystallize around a strong leader.[1]

To members of the majority party in the House of Representatives "the leadership" means the Speaker of the House and the House Majority Leader, who work in tandem to wield decisive influence on the highly structured House. The Speaker is normally the single most influential individual on Capitol Hill. As the presiding officer of the House, he possesses an array of formal powers that permit him to control the course of legislation, including the powers of recognizing members on the floor, voting to break tie votes, referring bills to committees, and appointing conferees, members of select and joint committees, and chairmen of Committees of the Whole. An even larger proportion of the Speaker's powers is unwritten, dependent upon his personality and skill. In particular, he influences the assignment of members to committees, strives to guide the semiautonomous activities of the committee chairmen, and takes the lead in scheduling legislation for floor consideration.

The Speaker's work is augmented by that of the House Majority Leader, who traditionally succeeds him when he retires or dies. (All six Democratic Majority Leaders since 1931 have become Speakers of the House.) Although there are no written directives for the Majority Leader, he usually functions as the chief floor spokesman for his party, scheduling bills for floor action and working to maximize voting strength on the floor. He is assisted by the Majority

Whip and his deputies, who notify members of pending business and endeavor to have them on the floor at the right time to vote on important party issues.

Party leaders play a crucial part in bringing together the scattered work groups in Congress and orchestrating their efforts to produce legislative results. As might be expected, these tasks are extremely demanding. Ripley has summarized the functions of majority leadership: taking the initiative in organizing the congressional party, making basic decisions about scheduling House business, promoting desirable attendance on the floor, collecting and distributing information, and persuading members on legislative matters.[2] Since the revolt against the dictatorial powers of Speaker Joseph G. Cannon in 1910-1911 and the attendant close of an era of strong Speakers, leaders of majority parties in Congress have tended to rely most on their informal powers, and individual leaders have thus varied strikingly in effectiveness.

Vigorous and attractive leadership was something that House Democrats sorely lacked in the 1960s. The Speaker was seventy-seven-year-old John W. McCormack, a cigar-chomping thirty-three-year veteran of the House. Although he had served for two decades as deputy to Speaker Sam Rayburn of Texas (seventeen years as Majority Leader and four years as Whip when the Democrats were in the minority), McCormack nonetheless had acquired a surprisingly low reputation as a legislative leader. As one reporter wrote, "It was Rayburn who listened, turned on his sixth sense, and made the crucial decisions."[3] When Rayburn went home to Texas late in the 1961 session McCormack was named Speaker Pro Tempore, and the House was in recess when cancer finally claimed the legendary "Mr. Sam." The speakership thus fell to McCormack without challenge, even though many of his colleagues were unenthusiastic.

McCormack's tenure as Speaker, it was assumed, would be brief, but after he had outlasted two Presidents (he was next in the presidential succession for more than a year after President John F. Kennedy's assassination) complaints began in the Democratic ranks, especially among younger members. Richard Bolling (Mo.), a former Rayburn associate and frequent critic of his successor, made the first public call for McCormack's retirement in 1967 and repeated his challenge frequently.

Because of uncertain direction from the aging McCormack, the brunt of the leadership burdens was carried by sixty-year-old Carl B. Albert of Oklahoma, the Majority Leader. Although colleagues testified to Albert's dedication and Herculean efforts, he consistently declined to upstage the Speaker. His job was rendered more difficult by the uneven performance of Whip Hale Boggs of Louisiana. For his efforts Albert was rewarded with relative obscurity for almost a decade and, in 1966, a severe heart attack.

These considerations were in the mind of Representative Morris K. Udall of Arizona as he telephoned McCormack's Boston home in 1968 to announce that he would challenge the Speaker at the January 1969 Democratic Caucus. At forty-six years of age, Udall had occupied since 1961 the House seat that his brother, Stewart, had vacated to become Secretary of the Interior in the Kennedy Cabinet. Mo Udall, as everyone calls him, is a lanky and informal westerner (he once played for the Denver Nuggets of the National Basketball League) with plenty of ambition, a ready wit, and a Mormon appetite for hard work. One of his committee assignments—Post Office and Civil Service—was not attractive, but he made the most of it. He helped to obtain new rules, retire an ineffectual chairman, obtain two pay raises for congressmen, and place the 2.5 million federal civil servants on a semiautomatic pay scale. "Give Mo a lemon," one of his admirers observed, "and he'll make lemonade."

Like many younger Democrats, Udall became increasingly restive under McCormack's leadership. But he took inspiration from Senator Eugene McCarthy's (D.-Minn.) challenge to President Lyndon B. Johnson: "He made it respectable to break with the establishment—he helped show us the way." Udall himself had broken with the President over the Vietnam war and was unhurt in his reelection bid in Arizona's cautious Second District.

As legislators drifted back to the nation's capital after the 1968 elections, liberal Democrats searched for a coalition that could ensure installment of new leadership. Northern organization members were heavily in favor of McCormack, and the liberals therefore turned to the southerners. Wilbur Mills (Ark.), the influential chairman of the Ways and Means Committee, was asked whether or not he would run against McCormack on a southern-liberal "ticket" that would include a programmatic liberal—probably Udall—for Majority Leader. Although not ruling out this possibility, Mills was reluctant to come into the open without demonstrated support. Inquiries were made, and the ticket notion faded as opposition materialized, even among Mills' fellow southerners. Some northern liberals were also against the idea, thinking that Mills would build a conservative coalition and ignore the liberals once in office. Even earlier Majority Leader Albert had been urged to run against McCormack but, ever cautious, he refused. Although Albert reportedly complained to friends that he had been forced to compensate for the weaknesses of McCormack and Boggs, he continued to counsel the dissidents against making a challenge.

When these negotiations proved fruitless, several liberals—led by Udall's old friend Frank Thompson, Jr. (N.J.)—urged Udall to make the race. "What do I have to lose?" Udall finally asked himself. In the short run "lightning might strike, and I might just get elected Speaker." More likely, if McCormack could be induced to step down and someone else elected in his place, the major objective would have been achieved. In the long run Udall hoped at least that people would remember his courage.

Two days before Christmas Udall placed his call to McCormack in Massachusetts. ("I really didn't expect this kind of thing from you," the Speaker responded.) A final touch was a formal press release and a six-page "Dear Colleague" letter to be sent to all House Democrats the day after Christmas. The letter stated that Udall's name would be placed in nomination the following week at the initial party caucus of the 91st Congress. Although he had consulted "a very few trusted colleagues," Udall said that the decision was his alone. "I am the candidate of no individual member or group of members." The letter showed repect for the delicacy of the situation, even sounding a bit wistful: "I would welcome your suggestions, advice, criticisms, or expressions of support. It's lonely out here in orbit; say something!" Conceding that "many who want a change would prefer someone other than myself," he promised that if he prevailed in the balloting he would treat the victory only as a decision that change was desired and would ask the caucus to open the nomination to other candidates. Although professing "genuine respect and affection" for McCormack, he recounted the reasons why new leadership was needed in the House: growing GOP strength, a Republican in the White House, and shifting political and sectional alignments and loyalties.

Hardly anyone gave Udall any chance of unseating the Speaker, but a number of insurgents soon surfaced. McCormack himself flew back to Washington to take personal charge of his reelection battle. Following the 1968 election McCormack had sent congratulatory letters to winning candidates, asking for their support for the speakership. Most had pledged their support routinely, and McCormack and his friends now marshaled these pledges to ensure votes. (A number of Democrats were annoyed that they had thus unwittingly committed their votes, and not a few resolved to be more careful in the future.) McCormack loyalists also intimated that the Speaker planned to retire in two years, though McCormack later denied this possibility.

At the January 2 caucus Udall's name was presented by Thompson, who told his colleagues: "Change is the great law of life. Men and institutions must change as they adapt to the ever-changing conditions of human existence." McCormack was nominated by Philip J. Philbin, acting dean of the Massachusetts delegation, and his name was seconded by a cross section of members including Mills. When nominations were closed caucus chairman Daniel Rostenkowski (Ill.) directed the clerk to distribute ballots, thus ending fears of Udall forces that a secret ballot would not be adopted.

McCormack was chosen as the Democrats' candidate for Speaker; in a straight party-line vote in the full House, he later prevailed over the GOP candidate, Minority Leader Gerald Ford. The vote was 178 to 58 (Udall had counted 81 commitments), with 4 votes for Mills. The prior commitments of most Democrats to support McCormack no doubt played a key role, and the Speaker and his lieutenants had worked diligently to sew up their support. Senior northerners had contacted the big-city delegations, and Mills had spoken to many of his southern colleagues. Outgoing Johnson staff members at the White House spread the word that Udall had "run out on the President" on the Vietnam issue. A host of other reasons—personal as well as political—helped to determine the outcome.

At first the liberals despaired. But as one-third of his colleagues had voted against him, McCormack had suffered a fairly eloquent no-confidence vote. Furthermore, several parts of a reform package proposed by the liberal Democratic Study Group (DSG) Executive Committee had been accepted by McCormack before the caucus. Chief among them was an agreement to hold regular monthly caucuses to give Democrats, young and old, a chance to voice their opinions and to strengthen an earlier precedent that rank-and-file members could pass on committee assignments. Other concessions authorized scheduling holidays and vacations in advance, allowing members to plan trips to their districts and time with their families; a study of electronic and mechanical voting systems for the House; and enlarged committee staffs. Two proposals made by Thomas M. Rees (Calif.) were blocked on procedural grounds: to place the Democratic Campaign Committee under caucus control and to require that any amendment of more than twenty-five words be printed and distributed to members before the vote on it. Most members credited Udall's candidacy with inducing the leadership to agree to changes.[4] "The roof didn't fall in," Udall said, "and in fact some good things happened as a result of the challenge."

Rising Discontent in the 91st Congress

Complaints about the Democratic leadership did not subside in the 91st Congress; indeed, they grew bolder and more open. On several occasions—most notably the failure to override President Richard M. Nixon's veto of the Health, Education, and Welfare appropriations bill early in 1970 (see p. 163)—the leaders' prior head counts were disastrously off the mark. Congressional doves resented the leaders pushing the so-called "Peace with Justice" resolution (H. Res. 613), passed late in 1969, in which the President's efforts in Vietnam were commended. Especially galling was the four-hour, no-amendment rule under which the resolution was debated. Ninety-nine Democrats and thirty-three Republicans opposed the rule on the floor, and later eighty-two legislators signed a statement of protest.

Then, late in 1969, it was publicly charged that McCormack's longtime administrative assistant and a New York lawyer had used the Speaker's offices as a base for influencing certain federal agencies. Although McCormack himself was not directly implicated, the charges clearly threw a cloud over his stewardship. In response to questioning from the press, he bristled and announced that he would seek reelection as Speaker in 1971. "I don't think he'd have run again if it hadn't been for this," said his nephew, Edward J. McCormack.

Behind closed doors there were bitter exchanges between the Speaker and his liberal antagonists.[5] At the first caucus of 1970 a number of Democrats criticized the party's limp record of opposition to the Nixon administration. At the next caucus a two-term California congressman, Jerome Waldie, offered a resolution of no confidence in the Democratic leadership. Most of Waldie's potential allies, though admiring his courage and sharing his anger, deplored his timing. They predicted that a challenge would only produce an overwhelming vote of confidence for the leadership and force many Democrats to commit themselves for the coming year's contest before they wished to. After a strong defense of the leadership from Albert, Bolling therefore moved to table Waldie's motion, in order to prevent a resounding defeat in a direct test. The motion to table prevailed by a 192 to 23 vote. The caucus revolt was only symptomatic of continuing restlessness in the ranks. Although McCormack claimed 167 pledged votes, an unpublished survey taken by *National Journal* in May indicated that the old man would have serious opposition if he chose to run again.

Personal as well as political factors forced McCormack to reconsider his earlier decision to run. In 1969 his administrative assistant for twenty-five years had died; his own wife's health was failing. By the end of 1970 McCormack would have served nine years as Speaker, longer than anyone in history except Rayburn. Amid mounting rumors McCormack called a press conference on May 20 to announce his retirement from Congress after forty-two years of service. As his successor, he endorsed Albert, who was standing at his side. The sixty-two-year-old Albert's election as Speaker was virtually assured, and potential leadership candidates quickly lined up behind him. Although he had been Democratic Whip and then Majority Leader since 1955, Albert had successfully evaded most of the critics' barbs. For years he had labored at his posts in relative obscurity, winning a reputation for being soft-spoken, diligent, and accessible to all factions of the party. As he himself explained:

> I guess you could say that the main element in my climb to the leadership is the fact that I've heard more speeches than anyone else and called more people by their first names. I've always been fascinated by [people]. There are so many variances and eccentricities. I got so that I could guess within a few votes how they vote on any given issue.[6]

Albert also profited from his record as a border-state moderate and from the tradition by which eleven of the twelve preceding twentieth-century Speakers had been recruited from their parties' floor leadership, either Majority or Minority Leaders.

As automatic succession to the speakership was ensured, the competition, immediately centered on the Majority Leader's post being vacated by Albert.[7] Udall and James G. O'Hara (Mich.) promptly announced their candidacies; Boggs, the incumbent Whip, eventually entered the contest, and several other hopefuls hovered just outside the ring.

The Contenders and Their Strategies

The Democratic Party in the House, like ancient Gaul, is divided into three approximately equal parts. The northern, urban wing, epitomized by McCormack, is composed largely of New Deal liberals who support federal involvement in economic and social programs. As often as not, however, these members fail some of the litmus tests of the newer liberalism on such issues as environmentalism and reduced defense commitments. A second wing of the party, fallen somewhat from its former glories but nonetheless still strategically strong, includes southern and border-state conservatives and moderates. In the 91st Congress its ranks included chairmen of twelve of the twenty-one standing committees. A third group, scattered geographically, embraces younger, issue-oriented liberals like those in the activist core of the Democratic Study Group.[8] Traditionally the first two groups have controlled the party in the House through a coalition represented by McCormack and Albert and earlier by Rayburn and McCormack. These three factions are by no means neat, coherent groups, and there are many crosscurrents of personal and political loyalties and animosities. But any campaign for a leadership position would have to reckon with this basic configuration.

Campaigning for an internal legislative post is unique because the constituency is unlike any other. "It boils down to a tiny little electorate," one of the contenders remarked, "of only 250 people who are very sophisticated and who, moreover, have nearly a 100-percent turnout." Or, as one staff member put it, "the boys go around and massage one another's egos." The campaigns are thus personal affairs in which outsiders tread, if at all, very lightly. "It's a hard thing to lobby," explained a labor-union spokesman. "People who would go along with us on an issue which they thought concerned us directly, might not listen to us at all—or even be turned off—if we tried to push them on this thing. So it's definitely the soft sell."

It would be misleading to conclude, however, that caucus members are intimately acquainted with the virtues and vices of all the candidates and are thus able to cast their votes on the basis of unimpeachable information. The size of the House and demanding personal schedules militate against close human relations. Members of the House, like the rest of us, often base their evaluations of colleagues not only on personal observation but also on rumor, reputation, and appearance. The circumstances of the voting also impede the flow of information. Balloting occurs at the first caucus of the new session on the day before Congress itself convenes. Most members are just returning to the nation's capital after months in their districts; virtually all have been preoccupied with their constituencies during the months before the November elections. (In 1970, however, Congress reconvened in a "lame-duck session" after the election to complete its work.) As the balloting is secret and relatively few outsiders are interested, the individual legislator has incentives to remain secretive about his inclinations. Information is scarce; rumor, inference, and outright falsehood are rife.

A contest for the majority leadership in 1962 had pitted Albert against Bolling, who had finally withdrawn before the balloting. Nelson Polsby has characterized the race as a rivalry of "inside" versus "outside" strategies:

The inside strategy is likely to define situations as "family matters," and to feature face-to-face interaction among members. The outside strategy is likely to evoke a more ideological, issue-oriented definition of the situation. Interaction among members is more likely to take place through third persons, lobbyists, and the press.[9]

Party-leadership contests, Polsby has argued, are essentially insiders' games, which explains the victory of Albert's "inside" strategy over Bolling's "outside" approach.

Applying this typology to the 1971 leadership struggle, one might expect the "inside" strategy to have been emphasized by Boggs, who as incumbent Whip had superior contacts and could argue that he, like his predecessor Albert, was entitled to advancement. The "outside" strategy would have been open to a liberal challenger like Udall, whose narrower contacts on the Hill might be offset by strong and vocal support from interest groups. Dark-horse or compromise candidates would hope to capitalize on a stalemate between Boggs and the liberal forces. This explanation fits the events of 1970-1971 imperfectly, however, because none of the leading candidates pursued an exclusively inside- or outside-oriented strategy.[10] Elements of both strategies were combined because leadership contests are insiders' games in which the players are hampered by imperfect information, much of which comes from outside sources.

Boggs had been a member of the House since 1947 and Democratic Whip since 1962. A solidly built, florid-faced man, he is known as a genial and skilled legislator and, on his better days, one of the more agile minds in Washington. Although a southerner, he has a voting record that can be classed as moderate: representing urban New Orleans, Boggs has supported civil rights measures since the mid-1960s and even voted to reduce by 5 percent the oil-depletion allowance—despite the importance of the oil industry to his home state. He gained national visibility as a member of the Warren Commission and later of the National Commission on the Causes and Prevention of Violence. At the behest of President Johnson, he had taken on the thankless job of heading the Platform Committee for the 1968 Democratic convention. That year he also faced the most difficult reelection fight of his career and won with a bare 52 percent of the vote. Perhaps these stresses were to blame for his noticeably erratic personal behavior during that period, not to mention his indifferent performance as Majority Whip.

Boggs' campaign was thus initially wobbly. He had not been notified of McCormack's impending retirement announcement and had to elbow his way through the press-conference crowd. At first, McCormack avoided supporting him as Albert's successor, and Boggs and Albert did not endorse each other. In fact, Boggs did not make his candidacy official until the November 1970 election had yielded him a comfortable majority at home. Despite his slow start, Boggs had obvious advantages if he could overcome his sagging reputation among his colleagues: As a southerner, he might be expected to win most of the sixty-seven votes from the eleven states of the old Confederacy; his moderate views and Roman Catholic faith would attract many urban northerners. On the other hand, some southerners claimed that his record was too liberal, and issue-oriented liberals suspected his establishment ties. Above all, Boggs would have to prove himself by steadiness on the job.

Once his leadership drive had been launched, Boggs wooed his supporters with a combination of sociability, personal contact, and subtle pressure. He and his family are socially active, and they proceeded to entertain those whose votes were on the fence. One of their celebrated garden parties, featuring a Dixieland band imported from New Orleans, drew more than 1,000 guests, including most representatives. Three smaller affairs were also held for House members, grouped according to their committee assignments. Before the election Boggs' office sent 140 nonincumbent House candidates copies of the 1968 party platform, suggesting that they might find the document useful in their campaigns. Messages of congratulations were sent to the winners, and a later letter openly discussed his credentials.

Boggs and his friends argued that, having served as deputy and then chief party Whip, he deserved to be promoted to the higher office. He wrote to his colleagues:

> As whip, I have often filled in as acting majority leader and I have worked hard for the progressive programs of our party—many times at great peril to my own seat. During my eight years of service, the whip organization has worked effectively and I have been able to advise the majority leader and the Speaker with great accuracy as to the success or failure of legislative proposals. The whip organization has also been extremely useful in making your views known to the leadership.

To northerners and liberals, Boggs stressed his record as a "national Democrat"; he reminded fellow southerners and hawks of his "responsible" posture toward such House traditions as seniority and of his support of defense efforts, including the Vietnam war.

A concrete asset in Boggs' effort was his seat on the Ways and Means Committee, which also serves as the Democrats' Committee on Committees. After twenty years on the committee Boggs ranked just behind Chairman Mills in seniority. He assured new members—and anybody else who hankered for a change of assignment—that he was interested in seeing them assigned to the committees that they preferred. Several intriguing assignments later suggested that Boggs' influence had been at work.

To sway his more senior colleagues, those who knew him best and who had no need of new committee assignments, Boggs worked to cultivate an image of diligence as Whip. He was on the floor with unaccustomed frequency and presided over the House during important debates in the summer of 1970.

(Speaker McCormack's belated support came in handy, for the Speaker designates members to serve as chairman of the Committee of the Whole.) In floor votes Boggs' party-unity score rose six points between 1969 and 1970 to 82 percent, which was eighteen points better than the Democratic average and thirty-eight points above those of his southern colleagues.[11]

The Boggs campaign also included elements of an outsider's strategy. Oil, tobacco, textile, and maritime interests worked in Boggs' behalf. Extensive contacts among the Washington press corps were called upon to elicit favorable comment. Conservative columnists like Joseph Alsop and William S. White pronounced Boggs the overwhelming favorite, pointing approvingly to his record as a Vietnam hawk. "The stop-Boggs movement was primarily a movement of the anti-Vietnam, anti-national defense brand of liberal Democrat," Alsop told his readers. "For that very reason, it has been a flop."[12] Most other Washington columnists decided to sit on the fence, influenced either by Boggs' charm or by the thought that they would have to remain on good terms with the winner, whoever he turned out to be. Boggs' opponents charged that the Louisianan had "gotten to" the publishers of such papers as the *Washington Post* and *The New York Times* to prevent hostile editorials from being run. Whatever the reason, the general-circulation press published few if any critical words about Boggs.

Udall's campaign, like that of Boggs, was based primarily upon personal contacts and lobbying among colleagues. The single most important premise of his efforts—so fundamental that it seldom had to be repeated—was that the Arizonan represented youth, vigor, and change. After his unprecedented challenge to Speaker McCormack, in fact, Udall had the burden of proving that he was not a "bomb thrower." "I'm not a 'damn Yankee' and my ADA record isn't 100 percent," he reminded conservatives. To show the congressional elders that he was a regular guy, he played down his ties with the Democratic Study Group and applied his best backslapping technique, playing paddle ball in the House gym with his ideological opposites and showing up regularly at congressional prayer breakfasts. And in the closing days of the 91st Congress he steered through the House a federal pay increase (H.R. 13000) that allowed representatives to increase the salaries of their staff aides by 6 percent or to use the equivalent sums to hire more staff.

As did Boggs, Udall and his lieutenants gave particular attention to the thirty-three Democratic freshmen. Aware that earlier successful GOP insurgent challenges had accompanied influxes of new members, he assumed that newcomers would naturally gravitate to his cause. He therefore lavished attention on them, actually campaigning for several. One freshman, who reported that as many as two-thirds of the newcomers were in the Udall camp, said that he had received brief communications from the other candidates but "a flood of material from Udall and Udall supporters."

This flood of communications started long before the elections. Copies of Udall's book, *The Job of the Congressman*,[13] were sent to candidates; letters of encouragement went to primary victors and to especially promising candidates. Telephone calls and congratulatory letters were directed to winners, followed by memorandums explaining the intricacies of the Democratic Caucus. Not long after newcomers had been installed in their Hill offices, they would be treated to a whirlwind visit by Udall, who proffered advice and explained the mysteries of Hill life.

If Udall's campaign was more conspicuous than those of the others, it was because it involved a great many representatives. Udall's old friend Thompson served as campaign manager and chief adviser, assisted by almost thirty others. By late summer these members were talking to their colleagues on Udall's behalf. Each had informal assignments of contacts to make, based on geography, committee assignment, and personal friendship. But Udall himself bore the brunt of the personal campaign. As the 91st Congress drew to a close, he sent letters to twenty-six colleagues whom he had been unable to see. He asked each for a few minutes to talk or at least time for a brief telephone conversation. "I promise no threats, promises, arm-twisting or anything else but frank talk between friends," he wrote. Several waves of letters went out to all colleagues; the exact form of the letters depended upon whether the member was an announced supporter, a probable supporter, a person considered undecided, or a likely supporter of someone else.

The outsider part of Udall's campaign was subordinated to these basic efforts. Attracted by his conservation efforts (he was a member of the Interior and Insular Affairs Committee), several environmental lobbyists offered to canvass their supporters and, through them, members of Congress. "I only ask," Udall told them, "that you do what you reasonably can without detracting from your main assignments." Representatives of the Izaak Walton League, the National Wildlife Federation, the Wilderness Society, and other groups talked up the Udall cause. Other supporters included liberal writers, lawyers, and activists in Washington and elsewhere.

Programmatic liberals had a second candidate, Michigan's James G. O'Hara, representative from suburban Macomb County near Detroit. Known for his close ties with the United Auto Workers and the AFL-CIO's Industrial Union Department (IUD), O'Hara had won a reputation as a legislative strategist and tactician, a master of parliamentary procedure and the art of legislative compromise. More than once he had bested southerners in parliamentary maneuver, a talent usually considered a southern specialty. For almost a decade O'Hara had been an acknowledged congressional expert on federal antipoverty and manpower-training programs. As immediate past chairman of the DSG, he was known as an advocate of reform legislation.

"Jim is the brightest man I know in Congress," one of his colleagues said of him, adding however that "O'Hara comes off as a diffident super-intellectual, but I think he's really very, very shy." This comment seemed to sum up O'Hara's qualifications and liabilities as a candidate for the leadership. A frequent comment from Hill liberals was, "O'Hara's great, but he's no good in front of the TV cameras." O'Hara himself said: "If they decide it on charisma, I'm afraid I won't fare well. If they're looking for someone who's been active on the floor, in debate and so on, maybe I'll make it."

O'Hara's campaign was in a deliberately low key. During the fall he was preoccupied with shepherding manpower and occupational-safety bills through the House. Even had his schedule been freer, it is difficult to believe that his campaign would have been very different. O'Hara, a private man, harbors a deep-seated aversion to backslapping and is reluctant to pressure his colleagues on matters of self-advancement. Letters, telephone calls, and personal conversations were thus almost always handled by O'Hara himself. Everyone assumed that he was organized labor's candidate for the leadership. As one union lobbyist explained: "Jim knew that whatever happened, people would claim his campaign was directed by organized labor. So he said, in effect, 'Come on in; the water's fine.' " Actually, not all labor representatives were in O'Hara's corner: The conservative Construction Trades Division of the AFL-CIO, convinced that Boggs was in line to win, sat out the race, and scattered union support went to other contenders. IUD lobbyists were mostly O'Hara supporters, but they were experienced in working on social issues and fully appreciated the delicacy of their assignment. Labor representatives were sometimes accused of denigrating Udall, who had once voted against repeal of the so-called "right to work" provision—Section 14(b) of the Taft-Hartley Labor Relations Act of 1947. Another outside O'Hara supporter was the Leadership Conference on Civil Rights, an umbrella group of civil rights organizations.

O'Hara's strategy was based on the premise that ultimately he might command wider appeal as a liberal candidate than Udall would. True, Udall was the front-runner among programmatic liberals, but many big-city northerners were unbendingly hostile to him. Perhaps O'Hara would be the kind of candidate that these members could support. A private memorandum issued to O'Hara supporters a few days before the caucus outlined his strategy and included several accurate observations.

> Neither Sisk nor Hays have taken off. . . . Udall can't get most of the uncommitted or most of the Hays-Sisk strength. *We have identified 50 or more of these 75 votes who simply will not go for Udall under any circumstances.* . . . By the time it's fish or cut bait, they will be fishing in O'Hara waters.
>
> The Udall bandwagon rumors may start most anti-Udall people moving toward Boggs. . . . *If it boils down to Boggs versus Udall, it will be Boggs who will win.*

O'Hara's base of support was his own seven-member Michigan delegation

(William Ford of Detroit served as his campaign chairman), most of the Black Caucus (which had interviewed all the candidates), and a few personal friends. It was widely assumed that O'Hara and Udall had worked out an arrangement so that their support would ultimately be pooled in the balloting to maximize the votes of the programmatic liberals. No such agreement actually existed, but their support clearly overlapped.

O'Hara also argued that he was the most liberal of all the candidates for the majority leadership. Voting records released by his office showed that other candidates (including Udall) had less solid records of opposition to militarism and support of social-welfare programs. On December 18 members received a letter from Cesar Chavez, head of the United Farm Workers Organizing Committee in Delano, California (O'Hara had visited striking grape- and lettuce-workers on several occasions and subsequently in the 92nd Congress became head of a new subcommittee on agricultural labor): "Jim O'Hara has been the farm worker's strong friend," Chavez wrote, "always in the forefront of the struggle to win economic and social justice for the farm worker and his family."

Two other candidates represented the efforts of more conservative Democrats to find an acceptable alternative to Boggs. One, peppery conservative Wayne Hays, from a rural Ohio district, explained why he had decided to run: "Well, last summer when Hale Boggs was drinking and making a horse's ass of himself, he asked me to talk him up. I drew a blank. People didn't want him. They didn't want Udall and his bunch of clowns. I figured what the hell, it was wide open."[14] Admittedly a dark-horse candidate, Hays nonetheless bet his colleagues $100 that he would not be low man in the balloting (nobody took him up on it). His strength was centered in his two committees—Foreign Affairs and House Administration—though he also had scattered support among the Ohio and West Virginia delegations.

Some southerners and committee elders were still wary of Boggs, and after the start of the lame-duck session in mid-November an informal talent search in the California delegation turned up a fifth candidate, B. F. (Bernie) Sisk from the San Joaquin Valley. Sisk's main sponsors, Chet Holifield, dean of the California delegation, and Rules Committee Chairman William M. Colmer (Miss.), hoped to rally southerners, border-state members, westerners, and moderate northerners in a coalition that would sidetrack Boggs' candidacy. Sisk was a bona fide southerner, having grown up in Texas, and he represented an agricultural district. After beginning his congressional career as a liberal, he had become more conservative through the years, but he had won unanimous praise for his work on the Legislative Reorganization Act of 1970 (see Chapter 8). "I have friends in all camps, and that's the strength of my candidacy," he told reporters.

Other candidacies were rumored. Northeasterners, in particular, were combing their ranks for a candidate. They were bothered by the prospect of losing representation within the top leadership, and their indecision gave them a pretext for evading the clutches of the announced candidates. Discussion most frequently centered on Edward P. Boland of Massachusetts, a close friend of both the McCormacks and the Kennedys and a man with some appeal to the liberal camp. Another Massachusetts liberal, Thomas P. O'Neill of Cambridge, was also testing the waters. A midwestern possibility was Dan Rostenkowski, leader of the Chicago delegation and a protégé of Mayor Richard J. Daley. He would draw his support from urban members, beginning with his Daley-directed Chicago colleagues. Rumors also linked his name with his good friend Boggs, who presumably wanted a deal that would place the Chicagoan in the Whip post in exchange for having supported Boggs for Majority Leader.

Albert maintained strict neutrality throughout. Privately he told colleagues that he could work with any of the candidates mentioned. "After all," Representative Sam Gibbons (Fla.) observed, "he's made a career out of not offending people and not getting involved in other people's affairs." Another personality trait that dictated neutrality was his inborn and chronic caution. A worrier by nature, Albert knew that the speakership was finally in his grasp and was determined not to ruin it by alienating anyone. He told some of his close associates:

> O.K. I understand there's going to be a fight for the majority leadership. There's no way it can be avoided. And if I take sides I can't do anything but lose support. If I would have picked this guy, this guy would have had enemies and the other guys would have had friends and those friends would have gotten their feelings hurt.[15]

Albert's strategy was safe, but in the long run it could have been the most costly. If he had indicated his choice of successor, that man would probably have won the contest, thus assuring the Speaker of a deputy committed to working with him. As long as Albert remained silent, the winner of the contest would owe him nothing.

Boggs was the obvious victim of Albert's neutrality, for the two had served together in leadership posts for years. Boggs himself claimed that "the liberals got to Albert," meaning that they had scared him away from a commitment to Boggs. DSG leaders argued that Albert's neutrality merely masked his antipathy toward Boggs. "Things that are not said are often more important than things that are said," Udall declared, "and Albert's silence speaks volumes."

With five candidates in the field and several others in the wings, factional politics became wondrously arcane. Much would depend on two tactical factors: Would caucus voting procedures make it possible for the various factions to work out a winning coalition during the balloting? How would the Whip's post be used to enlarge the bargaining arena? Whips had always been appointed jointly by the Speaker and the Majority Leader, but some members thought that the caucus should elect them. In either event candidates for Majority Leader were bound to try to enlarge their coalitions by making deals for the Whip job.

Ground rules for the voting were set at a luncheon meeting of the five announced candidates, called by caucus chairman Rostenkowski. After assuring the others that he himself would not be a candidate, Rostenkowski proposed a "drop-off plan": Two ballots would be held with all the candidates participating; then, if no one had mustered a majority, the candidate receiving the lowest number of votes on each successive ballot would be dropped until one of the surviving candidates gained a majority. The plan would allow votes to shift among candidates by ensuring that no faction would lose all its candidates on a single ballot. All five candidates agreed to the plan. The Udall and O'Hara camps, at first suspicious of anything that Rostenkowski might suggest, soon saw the plan's advantages to them. One liberal observed: "We're less capable than the power brokers are. The drop-off diminishes the possibilities of that kind of power brokering." Boggs would have preferred a runoff between the top two men. Such an arrangement would pit him against Udall; and in such a contest he thought that he could not lose. But he went along with the other candidates because he feared being accused of a power play if he insisted on the two-man runoff.

Another Rostenkowski proposal would have kept the nominations open after the balloting began. Not surprisingly, all five candidates vetoed this idea: Why should they let some bystander claim the prize that they had all fought for? Although Rostenkowski disavowed any desire to run, several candidates suspected that he merely wanted to keep the door open to enter the race in the event of a deadlock. Under solid pressure Rostenkowski had to back down. During the two-hour meeting it was also agreed that balloting would be secret and that reporters would be excluded from the caucus. As all five announced candidates backed these rules, the caucus later ratified them without dissent.

Once the secrecy of the vote and the possibility of caucus-day shifting among ballots were ensured, the trust relationships so crucial in the normal legislative bargaining process became very tenuous. Many representatives, indeed, found it useful to conceal their intentions or to give differing impressions to the various camps. Boggs considered himself the front runner and reported in early January that he had been assured 117 votes on the first ballot. Boggs and his staff had also identified 50 "undecideds," of whom about 30 were "our kind of votes" (that is, not liberals). Udall's supporters claimed 80 to 90 votes on the first ballot. O'Hara supporters said that they had 42 "hard commitments," and Sisk claimed "as many as anybody." As Congress was not in session for three weeks before the caucus, reporters and other observers had to rely on the rival candidates' claims and head counts, which were shown around clandestinely. More than a few names appeared on two or more lists, and everyone acknowledged that there were 50 to 60 votes still unpromised. As one veteran reporter mused, the race had all the markings of "the biggest con game in town."[16]

The one piece of impartial data proved seriously misleading. It was a straw poll conducted by *Congressional Quarterly* in December and released a week before the caucus,[17] to which about half (129) the Democratic members responded. Udall emerged as the leader with 46 votes; other totals were Boggs 30, Sisk 28, O'Hara 11, Hays 6, other candidates 6, and undecided 12. On closer inspection, however, the responses came disproportionately from westerners and low-seniority members, both tending to be heavy Udall supporters. In fact, Udall and his colleagues had quietly encouraged their forces to make a strong showing in the poll. In any event the poll confirmed the view that Udall was the man to beat. This view was turned to advantage by Boggs and his associates, who remained convinced that animosity against Udall would make him a certain loser in a two-man race against Boggs. They thus encouraged the impression that Udall was close to victory and had to be stopped on an early ballot.

Although the poll was widely considered a Udall coup in the face of mounting rumors that Boggs was picking up strength, it included one bit of intriguing information that was soon noticed by the Boggs camp. Of the 16 freshmen who had responded, Udall of course had the largest number of votes (9). But surprisingly, Boggs had drawn 7 votes from the newcomers—and in a "stacked" poll, at that! Almost everyone had conceded the newcomers to Udall, but this datum prodded Boggs to redouble his efforts among newly elected members. Here Boggs' experience and leadership status were put to good use: One of the first tasks of a new congressman is to lobby for a committee assignment that will help him to retain his seat, and of all the candidates Boggs was in the best position to help. Reminding each newcomer of his own place on Ways and Means, Boggs discussed the problem of a committee assignment and offered to do what he could. The implication could not be lost on the neophytes.

Another focus of speculation was the position of Whip, and its importance as a bargaining counter for candidates seeking to broaden the bases of their support. Rumors continually linked Boggs and Rostenkowski, and subsequent events suggest that there was indeed some sort of tacit agreement between them. Other bids seem to have been initiated by men hoping to be chosen Whip: Boland announced for Udall and Jack Brooks (Tex.) for O'Hara. Sisk apparently sought in vain for a northeastern Roman Catholic to balance his candidacy. All candidates insisted, however, that no deals had been made, and it is impossible to know how explicit the arrangements were.

As caucus day approached, Boggs' drive clearly picked up steam. Most of all his campaign profited from the candidate himself, who, in the words of one member, "swallowed his pride and went out and campaigned." Soon after the November elections Udall was admitting privately that "Boggs has done an amazing thing" in building the image of a bandwagon campaign. "People as wise as____and____both told me that Boggs was ahead and might already be so far ahead that it would be impossible to catch up." Although rival candidates did their best to minimize the bandwagon rumors, they soon recognized that the rumors themselves were a powerful force in Boggs' favor. Later Udall was to concede that "Hale ran a magnificent campaign—perfectly orchestrated and masterfully directed."

Boggs' comeback effort had been badly jarred by Sisk's entrance into the campaign, but again the Whip and his supporters fought back. The Sisk boomlet faded around Christmas, partly because conservatives decided that Sisk was no more attractive than Boggs—who was, after all, a southerner. Soon it was learned that Wilbur Mills, pressed by a newsman, had denied reports that he was backing Sisk and had revealed that he would vote for Boggs. At the news a small celebration broke out in the Whip's office, and Boggs' press secretary offered a prediction: "Gentlemen, I think it may be ultimately said that Sisk's march through Dixie was halted just outside Atlanta."[18]

Caucus Day

The Democratic Caucus met at 10:00 A.M., January 19, in the House chamber. All the candidates were suffering from the jitters, more acute because of flurries of last-minute rumors. O'Hara, Hays, and Sisk had pondered quitting the race but had decided to stay in.

A number of business items preceded the election of the Majority Leader. The first vote produced a startling result; Rostenkowski—generally acknowledged as an unusually skillful presiding officer—was deposed as caucus chairman in favor of Olin (Tiger) Teague of Texas, chairman of the Veterans Affairs Committee. Just before the caucus the Texas delegation had decided to put up Teague for Rostenkowski's job. They recalled the tradition that a caucus chairman serves only two terms, which Rostenkowski had just completed. They also circulated the rumor that Rostenkowski had agreed to support Boggs in exchange for appointment as Whip. Teague therefore received support not only from fellow southerners but also from liberal northerners eager to spike a Boggs-Rostenkowski axis and to take an indirect potshot at Mayor Daley. When the results were announced, new tremors were felt among the candidates for Majority Leader. But things soon returned to normal, and Carl Albert was overwhelmingly ratified as candidate for Speaker by a 220 to 20 vote, after a last-minute challenge by John Conyers, Jr. (Mich.), chairman of the Black Caucus.

Once the nominations for Majority Leader were declared open, two hours of nominating and seconding speeches were delivered by members, reflecting the breadth of each candidate's support. In seconding Boggs' nomination Mills gave an eloquent defense of Boggs' record as a "national" Democrat. Boland, a last-minute recruit to the Udall banner, observed that "we need leaders who can speak to the country, and who are articulate and effective." Charles C. Diggs, Jr., dean of the Michigan delegation and a Black Caucus leader, offered O'Hara as a man of intelligence and wisdom—"not a superman, but one whose perception matches that of the Speaker nominee." Sisk was nominated by Holifield, Hays by Thomas Morgan (Pa.).

It was mid-afternoon before the balloting began. Members cast votes secretly on colored slips of paper and deposited them in a wastebasket borne by

House Doorkeeper William M. (Fishbait) Miller, who then counted the ballots. The first ballot showed Boggs in the lead:

Boggs	95
Udall	69
Sisk	31
Hays	28
O'Hara	25

Boggs was only 30 votes short of the 125 needed to win. After the results were announced, Hays withdrew in support of Boggs; it was later revealed that the two candidates had agreed privately to support each other if necessary to stop Udall. Then O'Hara withdrew without supporting anyone. Some Udall supporters resented O'Hara's silence, but characteristically O'Hara thought that, though most of his supporters would certainly back Udall, he could not "deliver" their votes and would appear condescending if he made the attempt. On the second ballot Boggs went over the top with 15 votes to spare:

Boggs	140
Udall	88
Sisk	17

Boggs had picked up 45 votes on the second ballot, mainly from Hays and Sisk. O'Hara's strength had shifted mainly to Udall, but the combined Udall and O'Hara votes were far short of a majority. O'Hara bitterly called the result "a vote of confidence for the status quo."

Boggs had succeeded in mobilizing two of the three factions of the Democratic Party in the House: the southerners and the big-city representatives. Udall was left with the third element of the party—the issue-oriented liberal faction—and proved unable to broaden his appeal into Boggs' areas of strength. O'Hara, for his part, had not succeeded in combining the liberal and big-city factions in a winning coalition. Nor were Sisk and Hays successful in undermining Boggs' strength.

The dominant southern-big city coalition was consolidated when Albert and Boggs selected as Whip Thomas P. O'Neill, a big, jovial Irishman from Massachusetts. (Originally Albert and Boggs had let it be known that they were willing to have the caucus elect the Whip, but after strong protests from senior Democrats they decided to make the appointment themselves to ensure geographic balance and loyalty within the leadership ranks.) Boggs' original choice, Rostenkowski, was vetoed by Albert; then they settled on O'Neill, who had worked for Boggs' selection when no New England candidate had appeared.[19]

The voting procedures had failed to ensure a slow attrition of candidates and exploration for a compromise choice. Rather, there had been a quick rush to the leading contenders. Because the balloting had been secret, members were not likely to have voted for the winner just to be able to say, "Hale, I voted for you today." They could do that anyway, and many of them said similar things to more than one candidate. Why, then, was the conclusion reached so quickly?

Despite his liabilities, Boggs had staged a well-orchestrated campaign, making expert use of his resources as Whip and as a member of Ways and Means. He had been the model of diligence, persuading many skeptical colleagues that he deserved a chance as Majority Leader. And while Congress was in recess, he had been able to call upon friendly journalists to spread the impression that he had the inside track but that Udall was a major threat. As the presumptive successor to Albert, he had fostered the effect of a bandwagon and had convinced his colleagues that they should jump on board.

As it turned out, the issue-oriented liberals lacked a candidate who could attract enough anti-Boggs southern and big-city votes. Udall quickly emerged as the front-running liberal, but he suffered insurmountable liabilities. Although his earlier challenge to Speaker McCormack had made him a leader of the insurgent forces, it had also won him the unrelenting animosity of the retiring Speaker and his allies. The liberal activists who conducted his campaign formed an impressive inside lobby, but they doubtless frightened off more "establishment" types. Every report of Udall's strength had the effect of propelling votes in Boggs' direction and discouraging the search for alternatives. Whether or not some other candidate could have attracted broader support remained untested, but the indisputable fact is that the *combined* votes of the insurgents in the caucus fell far short of victory. The liberals had greatly overestimated the sentiment for new leadership.

The liberals' miscalculation can be illuminated by recalling the factional building blocks of the House Democratic Party: the northern New Deal liberals, the newer change-oriented liberals, and the southern conservatives. The national party has come to represent a coalition of the first two elements, which normally join in voting for economic and social legislation on the House floor. But internally the House has for two generations been controlled by the New Deal liberals and the conservatives. With their seniority and party posts these Democrats are used to following the rules of the game in the House and see no reason to alter them. The newer liberals, almost by definition less senior, are more apt to push for reform, if not radical alteration, of the system—not excluding the established House ways of doing things. From extensive research on Capitol Hill, Robert L. Peabody has estimated that, of the Democrats who attended the January 1971 caucus, 146 were "establishment" types, 64 were "change-oriented," and 45 were somewhere in between (either unknown or unclassifiable).[20] The programmatic liberals thus entered the contest at an enormous disadvantage.

Insofar as these categories pertain to matters of internal House structure and procedure, they are ill reflected in conventional voting measures. But even with such measures the new liberals' strategic problem clearly emerges. The major leadership candidates' party unity and "liberalism" voting records for the 91st Congress are shown in Table 2.

TABLE 2 Party Unity and "Liberalism" Voting Scores of
Democratic Leadership Candidates

Candidate	Party Unity* (1969-1970)	"Liberalism" (1970) †
Albert (Okla.)	85%	61%
O'Hara (Mich.)	87	93
Udall (Ariz.)	86	88
Hays (Ohio)	82	63
Boggs (La.)	79	62
Sisk (Calif.)	77	60
Averages		
Northern Democrats	81%	81%
Southern Democrats	52	21
All Democrats	71	58

*For a definition of the party unity score, see note 11. We have recomputed the scores from *Congressional Quarterly* to eliminate the effect of absences from roll-call votes.

† As a crude indicator of "liberalism," we have used *Congressional Quarterly's* "opposition to conservative coalition" score—the proportion of times that legislators voted negatively on conservative coalition issues (floor votes on which majorities of Republicans and southern Democrats were ranged against majorities of northern Democrats). We have recomputed the scores to eliminate the effect of absences from roll-call votes. The figures are found in *Congressional Quarterly Almanac,* Washington, D.C.: (1970), pp. 1144-1147.

The party unity scores all exceeded the average of their Democratic colleagues and ranged within a few percentage points of the average for northern Democrats. But on "liberalism" the contenders scored rather differently. Along with speaker-designate Albert, Boggs, Hays, and Sisk were close to the Democratic average, falling between the averages of southern and northern wings of the party. From a factional point of view, the party's House leaders were most likely to occupy such a position. In contrast, Udall and especially O'Hara were considerably to the left.

All the candidates ran essentially inside campaigns. But the behavior of the constituency was significantly affected by the *image* of the race projected by the candidates themselves and by the news media. The media depicted a two-man fight between Boggs and Udall. "I don't remember reading anywhere," Udall declared, "any in-depth story saying what the candidates stood for, or how they expected to operate as Majority Leader should they win." This simplistic image of the contest provided a strong incentive for members to line up behind one or the other of the front-runners, rather than exploring alternatives. A large number of representatives supported Boggs as the lesser evil, in order to prevent the election of a programmatic liberal and of Udall in particular.

Boggs' election had at least two significant effects, one immediate and one long-range. The first was to produce a Democratic leadership team relatively unchanged in philosophy, style, and even personnel from the one preceding it. The urban and southern wings of the party retained the reins of leadership; the programmatic liberals were in the minority, as they had been for more than a decade. Boggs' election in the face of a serious challenge could, in addition, only strengthen the presumption of advancement from one leadership post to the next, from Whip to Majority Leader to Speaker. This tradition was already well established for the speakership, but practice in relation to the majority leadership had been quite variable. Future aspirants will find it more difficult to avoid the powerful presumption of promotion along the established ladder. Udall summed up the problem: "The leadership ladder bit—tradition, promotion, seniority—was stronger medicine than I originally thought. This House apparently just insists on people getting in line, serving time."[21]

It is notable that the lowest rung of the ladder, the Whip's post, remains appointive rather than elective. David S. Broder's pronouncement is only slightly exaggerated: "Afterwards," he wrote, "no one will be able to say how the choice was made, or why, but the whole country will live with the consequences."[22]

Internal Democracy in the Senate

In contrast to their counterparts in the House, Senate Democrats have found the yoke of leadership easy to bear in recent years. The smaller size of the Senate is perhaps the most important variable: With fewer members the Senate can afford to allow each individual more latitude and to structure the leadership hierarchy less steeply. Leadership posts can also be distributed more broadly. At least in the twentieth century, therefore, Senate leadership has tended to be fragmented, varying according to such passing factors as the personality of the incumbent leader. Leadership is simply less institutionalized in the Senate than in the House.

A period of relatively centralized Senate leadership occurred in the 1950s, coincident with the majority leadership of Lyndon B. Johnson (1955-1961). Johnson, a highly effective legislative leader, helped to foster an atmosphere of consensus that encouraged senators to pay deference to certain "folkways"—for example, seniority, specialization, courtesy, and institutional loyalty.[23] There was nothing immutable about these techniques of leadership, however. A close observer of Johnson reported at the time that his chief technique was persuasion—of a highly personal brand at that. The successful Senate leader, Ralph K. Huitt has concluded, is one who "(1) can and does help individual senators to maximize their effectiveness in playing their personal roles in the Senate, and (2) structures roles and alternatives so that a maximum number of senators can join in support of the proffered solution of an issue."[24]

Both ideology and leadership style contributed to the unique character of the Senate in the 1950s. Most of the party and seniority leaders were conservative, and most of the liberals elected before 1958 found themselves relegated to the roles of "outsiders"—attempting to appeal to public opinion over the heads of Senate elders. Notable among the outsiders of the 1950s were such men as Wayne Morse of Oregon, Paul H. Douglas of Illinois (see Chapter 6), and Joseph S. Clark of Pennsylvania. When their ranks were augmented in the 1958 and subsequent elections, their influence over Senate procedures lagged behind their numbers. The notion of a tight, conservative ruling clique, or "inner club," soon became an obsession with liberals who perceived themselves as on the outside looking in.[25]

Slowly the picture changed. An informal policy of assuring each new Democratic senator of at least one major committee assignment—the so-called "Johnson rule," initiated by Majority Leader Johnson—resulted in more equitable distribution of desirable committee seats. As the seniority system worked its inexorable way, many of the "young Turks" of the 1950s became the "old Turks" of the 1960s and 1970s. Meanwhile, many of the older conservative leaders retired or died. Succeeding elections added to the Senate Democratic Party a group of young, activist liberals unimpressed by old rules about the sanctity of seniority. "We don't feel there's time to waste on that old seen-and-not-be-heard business," one of them explained. "After all, if a man manages to get to the Senate, he must have something to contribute."[26] In 1965 Clark, a vocal outsider, concluded: "The old times have changed. The Senate establishment is gone. Democracy is now pretty much the rule in the Senate."[27]

The new Majority Leader, Mike Mansfield (D.-Mont.), epitomized the changed atmosphere. "We've had a dispersal of responsibility," Mansfield explained. "I'm not the leader, really. They don't do what I tell them. I do what they tell me."[28] Later he summarized his philosophy for dealing with his colleagues: "Senators realize that they are treated as I'd like to be treated—as mature men. Their independence is not infringed upon. They know that everything is on the table. They know all about our moves ahead of time. There are no surprises."[29]

About the much-repeated advice that freshman senators should be seen and not heard he commented, "I have told all the new senators—North and South—that I expect them to be seen and heard if they have something to say." Although Mansfield himself has spoken out strongly on the issues, opposing his own party's President on the issue of the Vietnam war, his fairness in dealing with all factions of the party has been universally conceded.

In 1969, when the Democrats became the opposition party, Mansfield began to pull together the scattered elements of the Senate's majority party. Recognizing that the Democrats were in a precarious state—their forces divided by the 1968 campaign, their party coffers empty, and their House leadership weak—Mansfield determined to weld Senate Democrats into a national party voice. He was both aided and hampered by the fact that most of the 1972 presidential contenders—men like Edmund Muskie of Maine, George McGovern of South Dakota, Birch Bayh of Indiana, Harold Hughes of Iowa, and later Hubert Humphrey of Minnesota—were sitting in the Senate.

Mansfield began by reviving the Senate Democratic Policy Committee. The fourteen-member body, created by the 1946 Legislative Reorganization Act, had met only sporadically and, during the Kennedy-Johnson years, had refrained from issuing statements, on the theory that party policy should emanate from the White House. After 1969, however, it convened at least twice a month while Congress was in session to consider a wide variety of topics and occasionally to hear outside experts. During the first two years of the Nixon administration the group passed seventeen resolutions on such subjects as the income surtax, the economy, American troop levels abroad, and Senate rules reform. With one exception, the pronouncements were approved without active opposition. The exception was a resolution, approved February 22, 1971, that Senate Democrats "should work to achieve . . . [an] end to the involvement in Indochina and to bring about the withdrawal of all U.S. forces and the release of all prisoners at a time certain." The next day the Democratic Conference (composed of all Democratic senators) ratified the resolution by a 37 to 13 vote.[30] It was the first time in memory that a leadership initiative had split party ranks.

Those least eager to build up the Policy Committee's role are, of course, the chairmen of the standing committees. As one of them explained, "Around here, committee chairmen are tribal chiefs to be bargained with, not lieutenants to be commanded. The persons who are least enthusiastic about a strong policy committee . . . are the chairmen themselves, who have no desire to trade their sovereignty for a vote in council."[31] In order to keep channels of communication open, Mansfield has conferred with the chairmen of the Senate's seventeen standing committees on a regular basis, usually over lunch in his office. Pressure, when applied, has been of the gentlest sort.

Another locus of Mansfield's leadership was the Senate Democratic Conference, to which all Democrats belong. Like the Policy Committee, the conference had fallen into disuse. At the prodding of Fred R. Harris of Oklahoma, former chairman (1969-1970) of the Democratic National Committee, Mansfield agreed early in 1971 to convene the conference whenever any of its fifty-five members requested a meeting. He also established the precedent that the conference may nullify by a majority vote (by secret ballot) any committee assignment, including that of a committee chairman. The seventeen-man Democratic Steering Committee, which serves as a committee on committees, has under Mansfield's direction broadened its membership base, even accepting a freshman senator in 1971. Mansfield's ability to orchestrate the work of these committees is enhanced by the fact that he is chairman of all of them. Each title adds to his influence and the size of his staff.

Another leadership post that is emerging as distinctive is that of Majority Whip, a job held since 1971 by Robert C. Byrd of West Virginia. Byrd is the quintessential Senate insider, known to the larger world mainly as the man who, as chairman of the District of Columbia Appropriations Subcommittee, hounded welfare recipients.[32] After having been raised in relative poverty in Appalachia, he once served eighteen months as a kleagle (organizer) for the Ku Klux Klan ("It was a mistake," he has since confessed), and in 1970 he had the third most conservative voting record of any Democratic senator outside the South.[33]

Inside the Senate, however, he soon won recognition by rendering innumerable minor favors to his colleagues, taking on the unpleasant duty of presiding over the Senate for countless hours,[34] and writing notes of greeting on senators' birthdays. He was elected secretary of the conference in 1967, but that body met infrequently, and the job did not amount to much. He soon found a role to play, however. Majority Leader Mansfield disliked remaining on the floor during debate, and Russell Long (La.), then Whip, did not like to substitute for him. So Byrd made himself available on the floor, keeping a pocket notebook in which he jotted down requests from colleagues for help on the floor. For example, he was asked to keep them informed when matters of interest came up and to schedule debates at their convenience.

Byrd's functions continued after 1969, when Edward M. Kennedy won the Whip's job away from the erratic Long. Although more a Senate man than his two elder brothers had been, Kennedy also became impatient with floor routine and preoccupied with his own problems: the misfortune at Chappaquiddick Island in the summer of 1969 and his reelection campaign the following year. "Bob Byrd would do even the smallest chores for senators," one of Kennedy's friends said. "Ted Kennedy didn't do a damned thing for anybody." Still Kennedy wanted to retain the position, and the patient Byrd began to chafe at doing the work while Kennedy received the glory.

Byrd's challenge to Kennedy started slowly when a few of his friends quietly encouraged him to run for Whip. When Kennedy heard about it he telephoned Byrd in October 1970 to try to learn the latter's intentions. "Oh, that's pure speculation, Ted," Byrd said. "I've given it some thought, but it's premature." When Kennedy asked point-blank about Byrd's plans, the West Virginian merely said, "I can't make any kind of assurance." Kennedy flew off to a North Atlantic Treaty Organization conference in Belgium, and Byrd returned to Washington to look at the situation more closely. He made discreet phone calls, mainly to potential supporters, in order to avoid alarming Kennedy and his "national constituency." The weekend before the caucus vote was to be taken Byrd stepped up his efforts. He arranged for a friend, Georgia's Herman Talmadge, to visit the dying Georgia patriarch, Senator Richard Russell, and to obtain his signature to a proxy.

The caucus was scheduled for January 21, two days after the House caucus that had elected Albert and Boggs. It was only forty-eight hours away when Kennedy finally grasped that he was in trouble, but in the end Byrd's carefully kept tally sheet showed twenty-eight names, including that of Russell—exactly the number that he needed to win. When further efforts to line up some in-surance votes proved fruitless, Byrd was unsure whether or not to risk the challenge. After the caucus was called to order, he slipped out briefly to learn that Russell was still alive. When he returned to his seat, he nodded to fellow West Virginian Jennings Randolph, who by prearrangement placed Byrd's name in nomination. (Byrd later claimed that he would not have gone ahead with the challenge without knowledge that Russell's vote was still valid. Russell died three and a half hours later.) Most senators understood instantly that Byrd would not have acted without having made a meticulous count; actually he was three votes off, for he won with three votes to spare, 31 to 24.[35]

Kennedy and his staff—who thought they had enough pledges for vic-tory—pondered the reasons for the upset. As with everything else connected with the Kennedy name, the press strained to read global implications into the event. In fact, the internal business of the Senate was the heart of the matter. Byrd had shown himself indispensable to his colleagues in a hundred different ways; Kennedy had lagged in his Whip duties. Other factors may, of course, have contributed to the result. Some conservative senators were happy to vote against a Kennedy whenever they had an opportunity. Speculation also centered on several of the presidential contenders: Although most professed to have voted for Kennedy, all could have profited from his defeat.

Byrd plunged into his new duties with his usual energy and devotion to detail. With the blessing of Mansfield, Minority Leader Hugh Scott, and a bi-partisan group of senators, Byrd set about implementing a series of procedural changes designed to help the Senate to conduct its business more efficiently. Each day the Senate arranges its business so that short speeches come first, routine business next, and long speeches and controversial bills after other work is completed. During debate a "germaneness rule" is operative. In major debates each side has fifteen minutes to sum up its arguments before the vote. A blinking light has been installed to warn senators that a roll call is in its final five minutes. The Senate has also experimented with rearranging its legislative schedule to permit preplanned recesses so that senators can plan trips away from the capital without missing vital votes. On the other hand, votes are less frequently delayed to accommodate individual senators.

These changes in Senate procedure are minor in themselves, but they are designed to avoid the kind of stalemate for which the Senate has been criticized in the past. Byrd has not originated all the changes, nor could he have imple-mented them without the support of others. But as Majority Whip he has spent more time on the Senate floor than has any other senator. And as chairman of the relevant subcommittee of the Senate's Committee on Rules and Administra-tion (a housekeeping committee, paralleling House Administration more than House Rules) he is a pivotal figure in further reforms of the Senate. His innate conservatism has prevented him from going beyond housekeeping matters to embrace more sweeping changes, but at the same time he has shown himself willing to conform to the Mansfield leadership team.

REPUBLICANS: GUARDING THE CHANGE

When Richard M. Nixon took the oath as President on the steps of the Capitol on January 20, 1969, the late Senate Minority Leader, Everett McKinley Dirksen, presided at the ceremonies. Dirksen's presence on the inaugural stand symbolized the changed relations of the minority party Republicans with the White House during the 91st and 92nd Congresses. The Republicans, accustomed to opposing Democratic Presidents during the 1960s, now found themselves in a supportive role. The discussion here will center primarily on the activities of House Republicans—particularly the leadership—within this changed political environment. To gain a better perspective on the relations between the Nixon administration and Congress, it is necessary first to review the activities of House Republicans during the years before 1969.

House Republicans during the Kennedy-Johnson Years

During the Kennedy administration the minority Republicans in the House had no partisan responsibility for passing administration programs and were free to pursue various strategies, depending upon the nature and circumstances of each issue. The House GOP during this period had strong and experienced leadership. Minority Leader Charles Halleck (Ind.) had built a reputation as a tough, partisan "gut fighter," quick and frequently caustic in debate, often abrasive in manner, but willing to act quickly and decisively. Whereas the GOP had a strong and aggressive leadership, the Democrats in the House did not. Speaker Rayburn, who had been less effective in his later years than in previous times, died in November 1961. His successor, McCormack, never commanded "Mr. Sam's" influence and was forced to lead in a more collegial manner.

Traditionally more conservative than the Senate, the House had been the major battleground for domestic issues during the Kennedy years. The administration could not depend upon the weakly led and frequently disunited majority Democrats to pass its programs, and the GOP could therefore frequently play a decisive role in policy making. With the assistance of defecting Democrats (usually southerners) Halleck's troops could periodically defeat major administration proposals—for example, the first Kennedy farm bill, an attempt to create a Department of Housing and Urban Affairs, and federal aid to education.

At other times, as during House consideration of the Area Redevelopment Act (see Chapter 6) in 1961, the GOP had attempted unsuccessfully to gain House approval for what it considered constructive alternatives to administration-backed bills. Occasionally, Republican-sponsored alternatives had won House approval, as did certain innovations in the Manpower Development and Training Act of 1962. It was also possible for Republicans to support the Democratic administration, as they did that same year in defeating liberal Democratic attacks on the Communications Satellite Act.

Clearly, the GOP, with strong leadership and unhampered by partisan responsibility for supporting the President's legislative program, found itself free in the early 1960s to adopt a wide range of strategies in response to various issues.[36] Despite Halleck's flexible approach, there were rumblings of discontent within the party, particularly among the junior members, many of whom complained about the party image projected by the "Ev and Charlie Show"—Dirksen and Halleck's weekly press conference.[37] Junior members also complained that they were not playing a sufficiently important role in party decisions and that the party was not developing positive and attractive alternatives to the proposals of the Democratic administration.

Halleck also found it difficult to satisfy the diverse points of view within his party. The underlying discontent with the GOP House leadership was crystallized in the 1964 election disaster, when the GOP suffered a net loss of thirty-eight seats in the House. The 1964 election dealt most harshly with the more senior and conservative Republicans who could have been expected to be firm supporters of Halleck, leaving the House GOP membership with a pronounced youthful cast. Representatives Charles Goodell (N.Y.) and Robert Griffin (Mich.) seized upon this situation and, in conjunction with a group of their more activist and junior colleagues, persuaded Representative Gerald Ford (Mich.) to be a candidate for Minority Leader against Halleck.

The Halleck-Ford contest was an intense struggle waged over the Christmas and New Year's holiday season in 1965. The closeness and tension of the situation can be gathered from the fact that one day before the election in the GOP Conference (caucus), Ford's supporters could count only sixty-seven "sure" votes; seventy-one were needed to elect.

On January 4 the Republicans met in a mood of anticipation. The first action of the conference was to elect Melvin R. Laird as conference chairman, the post being vacated by Ford. Early in his House career Laird, like Ford, had been identified as a potential leader and had been assigned to the important Appropriations Committee, where he had gained a reputation for doing his homework while specializing in health, welfare, education, and defense matters. He was acknowledged as an astute legislative tactician, as well as an experienced national political leader. After nominating speeches, during which it was claimed, on one hand, that Ford would give the party "new energy and a forceful fresh image" and, on the other, that Halleck had been an effective leader, the congressmen cast their ballots. The vote was a narrow 73 to 67 win for Ford.

Leading a band of relatively independent political entrepreneurs like those in the House of Representatives is a difficult task. The new GOP leader was hardly accorded even a brief honeymoon before the reality of the congressional party's decentralized character and the leader's limited resources of influence were made apparent.

Ford's margin of victory had been slim, and Halleck's supporters were not won over suddenly. In addition, such rewards as patronage appointments, party-leadership posts, and committee assignments were in short supply in the minority party and not entirely Ford's to dispense. He therefore found himself challenged when he sought to change the nature of GOP patronage appointments to gain research and public-relations positions for the leadership. He was also defeated in his attempt to have Representative Leslie Arends (Ill.) replaced as Minority Whip.

Even with these setbacks, Ford was able to institute significant changes in GOP House organization. Under new rules, he was given the power to appoint seven members to the Policy Committee. The role of the Republican Conference was also strengthened. Its officers were all formally designated as members of the House Republican leadership. In addition, the conference became the main research arm of the party. Minority patronage positions were allocated to the new Conference Research Committee, which resulted in a small professional staff for the leadership. In addition, a series of issue-oriented task forces was created under the Research Committee to develop GOP alternatives to administration programs and to engage in criticism of the Democrats.

Because they did not have responsibility for enacting the legislative program of Democratic President Johnson, the new Republican leadership, like Halleck, had considerable freedom in selecting strategies. On some issues, like the Water Quality Act of 1965, Republican leaders cooperated with the administration. At other times they endorsed alternatives to majority programs (for example, changes in the Omnibus Crime Control Act of 1968). Open opposition to the Democrats' program was difficult during the 89th Congress, when GOP ranks were thin, but more effective after the gain of forty-seven seats in the 1966 election.

The electoral successes of 1966 not only gave the GOP a stronger voice in policy making but also strengthened Ford's position as leader, for he received partial credit for them. Indeed, it was acknowledged that Ford had spent a great deal of his own time campaigning and raising funds for Republican candidates.

Learning To Work with the White House

The vast majority of Republicans elected to the 91st Congress had never served with a Republican President. Nixon's election was therefore greeted with anticipation. Congressional expectations, however, were varied. Some members saw an opportunity to gain influence in the selection of key administrative officials. Others saw at long last a chance to play a more significant role in shaping policy by working closely with the new administration, for most believed that administrative decision makers would be more receptive to their requests. Finally, there were expectations of a policy shift. Some hoped for repeal of New Frontier-Great Society programs, and others anticipated a series of fresh Republican policy initiatives that would reorient the policies of previous decades.

When the Republicans met in January 1969 to organize for the 91st Congress, concern over the respective roles of Republican congressmen and the Nixon administration in policy development surfaced immediately. At issue was the fate of the Research Committee, which had been headed by Goodell before his appointment to the Senate seat formerly held by the late Robert F. Kennedy (D.-N.Y.). This committee and its task forces had generated continuing criticism of the Johnson administration and had devised GOP policy alternatives. But at times they had formulated and publicized positions at variance with those of ranking Republican committee leaders who would normally have had major responsibility for minority-policy development within the jurisdiction of their respective committees. This fact, combined with displeasure at Goodell's frequently abrasive, aggressive, and ambitious manner and conservative doubts about the need for the committee, had created a sizable bloc of votes against continuing it. In addition, some members believed that major policy research and development should be the function of the new administration and that House Republicans should not have a separate policy operation competing with that of a President of their own party. There were unconfirmed reports that the White House supported this view.

Ford and other members of the leadership, however, argued for continuation of the committee on the grounds that the minority would still need a professional research staff and the ability to take occasional independent initiatives. By a narrow margin the committee was renewed, and Representative Robert Taft (Ohio), who unlike Goodell, had not engendered intense personal antagonism during his House service, was elected chairman.

The most immediate impact of the new administration on House GOP leadership was the President's nomination of Laird as Secretary of Defense, which removed one of the most skillful and influential members from GOP ranks in the House. Laird was replaced as conference chairman by Representative John B. Anderson of Illinois (see Chapter 3).

The Role of Minority Leader

Recent history suggests that House leadership posts among the minority have not been particularly secure. The Minority Leader has fewer rewards to dispense among his colleagues than does the Speaker, and his colleagues are likely to develop a sense of frustration because their minority status denies them formal positions of influence or impact on policy. When matters go badly (as in the 1964 elections) or there is a shift in the composition of the party in the chamber, the Leader is a convenient target for those who are discontented.

Republican leadership from 1965 to 1968 was collegial in character, and Ford did not even attempt one-man rule. As noted earlier, his margin over Halleck had been paper-thin and his opponents' ability to defeat him on internal party issues had been clearly demonstrated. He therefore found it necessary to share policy and strategic decision making with other leaders—particularly Laird—and ranking Republican committee members.

Ford's position and influence, however, were significantly enhanced by Nixon's election. Presidents have traditionally found that they must work through their parties' leaders. They have insufficient time, energy, and detailed knowledge of the constantly changing legislative scene for direct and personal leadership. In addition, the President has responsibilities far beyond overseeing the fate of his legislative program in Congress. His diverse yet interrelated legislative program is scattered among scores of committees and subcommittees. To gain even partial approval of this program he needs the help of other generalists like himself, the party leaders.[38] Furthermore, as Donald R. Matthews has pointed out, working primarily with party leaders "minimizes the consequences of legislative defeat" and saves "his personal credit on the Hill for use in major crises."[39]

As had his immediate predecessors, President Nixon adopted this pattern of White House-congressional relations. In the House the President and his legislative-liaison staff worked most frequently and directly with Ford, who thus became the principal presidential spokesman in the House. He was also the prime source of information for House members—Democrats and Republicans alike—on the views, strategies, and priorities of the President. As Minority Leader, Ford had little formal authority, but his leverage among his colleagues was significantly increased by his easy access to the White House.

All members of the GOP House and Senate leadership attended the regular Tuesday morning meetings with the President in the Cabinet Room of the White House, but because of the size of the group and time limitations it was often extremely difficult to have in-depth discussions of administration policy. Many of the most significant strategy sessions had to be held in smaller groups, and then it was Ford who was most often and thoroughly consulted on matters pertaining to the House.

Ford and his Senate counterpart, Senator Hugh Scott (Pa.), were accorded each week a platform at the White House from which to summarize for the press corps the nature of their weekly meetings with the President. Ford also acted as chief defender of the administration during House floor debate, particularly during the opening minutes of the House sessions each day, when Democratic leaders frequently leveled their most partisan attacks on the Nixon administration.

As White House-congressional communications are reciprocal in character, Ford's Republican colleagues have relied upon him to convey their views to the White House. For example, after the President vetoed the Office of Education appropriation for fiscal 1971, some House Republicans complained about how the veto had been handled at the White House. The vast majority had voted by roll call for the conference report on the bill, thus helping to send the legislation to the President for his signature without, they claimed, sufficient advance warning that a veto impended. When the veto message came, many members were unhappy about not having been warned so that they would not have to appear inconsistent by first voting for the bill and then sustaining the President's veto.

Acting in his capacity as legislative leader, rather than as administration spokesman, Ford carried the message to the White House and asked forcibly for assurances that they would not again find themselves in such a situation.

Ford's status as the preeminent House Republican was further enhanced by the appointment of Laird as Secretary of Defense. With Laird gone from the House there was no visible rival (though Laird and Ford, contrary to some press reports, worked closely together). New and less experienced men serving as conference chairman and Research Committee chairman meant less need to share decision making—though the need for a broad base of support still dictated frequent consultation.

Although Ford's position had been made more secure by the 1968 election, the options open to him and his minority party were more restricted. As long as the Democrats had controlled both Congress and the executive branch, House Republicans had enjoyed maximum flexibility in their strategy on any given issue. The 1968 presidential election had changed this situation. Even though Republicans still did not control Congress, they understood that, as the party of the administration, they were likely to be held responsible by the electorate for whatever happened while Nixon was President.[40] They were therefore constrained, as they had not been since the Eisenhower period, by responsibility for passing the President's legislative program. How this new obligation influenced GOP behavior in the House is a major focus here.

The Role of the Policy Committee

Since its activation in the late 1950s the Policy Committee had been a vehicle for partisan attacks on the opposition and an effective means for developing and communicating to rank-and-file Republicans official party points of view. There is evidence that Policy Committee statements helped to increase GOP unity on roll-call votes.[41] After the election of Richard Nixon, however, House Republicans faced a problem more difficult than maintaining maximum party unity. They were charged with winning House approval for administration legislation, a responsibility that would inevitably require support from some Democrats. If the Policy Committee made a statement vigorously supporting administration-backed legislation, it might inject added partisanship into the issue and endanger needed Democratic support. Believing that their success was linked with that of the administration, House Republicans recognized that the role of the Policy Committee would be different after 1968.

legislation extending the surtax was to come before the House in the summer of 1969, the ranking Republican on the Ways and Means Committee, John Byrnes of Wisconsin, advised against a Policy Committee meeting because such a meeting and the ensuing statement might alienate badly needed Democratic support for this high-priority administration bill.

On other issues, however, the Policy Committee took strong stands— usually when unified Republican support for an administration proposal was absolutely essential *and* when substantial Democratic support seemed either certain or not required. In the summer of 1969 the Policy Committee endorsed the highly controversial Nixon welfare-reform proposal—the Family Assistance Plan (FAP). FAP aroused little enthusiasm among some House Republicans and in many instances provoked outright opposition. The Policy Committee was used to help gain support among more conservative members of the President's party. Similarly, it was used to consolidate GOP support to sustain the President's veto of the Labor-HEW appropriations for fiscal 1970. Because of White House criticism of House and Senate actions increasing HEW appropriations above the administration budget and because of Democratic attacks on the administration in return, the issue had already become highly partisan by the time of the veto in January 1970. The Policy Committee's urging of Republican support for the veto did not therefore endanger the limited support that the administration could expect from House Democrats.

The Nixon Administration Confronts the House: Three Examples

Box scores on the extent to which Congress supports a President can lead to a false impression that all administration-endorsed measures are equally important to participants in the legislative struggle. As the three examples to be discussed here show, however, the priority and the nature and level of activity among White House and Democratic and Republican Party leaders vary from issue to issue.[42]

Bipartisanship: The Surtax Extension, 1969

As a result of budgetary pressures occasioned by the Vietnam war and Great Society domestic programs, plus the developing inflationary momentum of the late 1960s, President Johnson after much controversy—within both Congress and his administration—succeeded in winning congressional approval for a measure adding a 10 percent surtax to the federal income tax for one year. Faced with continuing inflationary pressures, the Nixon administration, in March 1969, asked Congress to extend this surtax for an additional year. In his message to Congress the President also expressed his support for tax-reform legislation and promised forthcoming recommendations in this area. Even as a remedy for inflation, taxes are unpopular, and Congress quickly sensed the lack of public support for surtax extension. The House Ways and Means Committee, however, reported the legislation favorably with the support of its chairman, Wilbur Mills (D.-Ark.), and of Hale Boggs (D.-La.), then Democratic Whip and ranking Democrat on the committee.

The basic administration strategy on this bill was twofold—to seek unified GOP support and to win substantial Democratic support by working through the leadership and senior members of the Ways and Means Committee. This strategy naturally involved a bipartisan approach and characterization of the measure as essential for the nation's economic stability.

Such a strategy had worked well during the Eisenhower years when the Republican President and his key aides had sought bipartisan cooperation from Democratic leaders of Congress—Speaker Rayburn and Senate Majority Leader Johnson. Mutual accommodations between the White House and these legislative leaders could invariably produce a legislative majority in the Congress. Because of his experience as Vice-President in the Eisenhower administration and the parallel circumstances of divided government during his own administration, Nixon sought to employ a similar technique.

On June 12 the President invited Speaker McCormack and other Democratic House leaders to the White House to discuss surtax extension. After the meeting the Speaker and his colleagues pledged their support of the President's proposal and, more important, 100 Democratic votes. Legislative experts in the White House and Treasury saw little reason to doubt the promise. But an actual head count taken one week before the scheduled vote in the House showed that only twenty-five House Democrats were in agreement with their leaders.

There were several reasons for this lack of support on the Democratic side—beyond the obvious lack of enthusiasm for voting a tax increase. Neither individually nor collectively did Speaker McCormack, Majority Leader Albert, and Whip Boggs command the prestige and influence of the late Rayburn. Their failure to consult with the rank and file before making a commitment to the White House had also infuriated many of the foot soldiers on the Democratic side. Despite appeals by Nixon and Secretary of Labor George Shultz, their position was further weakened by the opposition of the AFL-CIO, the most important single source of campaign support for Democratic candidates. Also the unusually skillful chairman of the tax-writing Ways and Means Committee, Wilbur Mills, was ill during committee consideration of the surtax, and Boggs, his replacement, was less effective. The auxiliary issue of tax reform raised by liberal activist Democrats of the Democratic Study Group also made it difficult to muster Democratic support for the bill. DSG members of Ways and Means charged that tax reform was badly needed and that the surtax should not be renewed until it was coupled with such reform. The administration, though endorsing tax reform, argued that the surtax was urgently needed in the battle against inflation and could not be postponed while Congress wrestled with a complex and controversial tax-reform bill. Tax reform, however, became the issue around which Democrats opposing their leaders rallied.

That there was not a Democratic President to whom loyalty was owed contributed to the lack of Democratic support for the surtax. Democrats had given President Johnson reluctant support on the surtax in 1968 but felt less need to support Nixon. Approximately half the House Republicans had also supported the original surtax measure in 1968. The price extracted for their support had been inclusion in the surtax bill of a relatively strict ceiling on federal expenditures, which the Johnson administration had grudgingly accepted.

The Democratic leadership had originally hoped to call up the surtax bill for House consideration before the Fourth of July recess. But, sensing an acute shortage of votes on the Democratic side of the aisle, the Speaker postponed consideration of the bill.[43] Labor lobbyists and liberal Democrats opposed to the bill believed that the delay would demonstrate that the bill was not as important as the administration claimed and that the additional time would permit the opposition to convince more congressmen to vote against the bill. Some activist and antileadership Democrats privately conceded that they viewed the surtax and its possible defeat as a "three-bagger": an anti-Nixon vote, an antitax vote, and an anti-McCormack vote.

Sensing that support for the bill was eroding, Ford forced the Speaker's hand by claiming 170 Republican votes for the bill. Such a claim by the GOP made the Speaker's postponement of the bill difficult to justify unless he and his colleagues had totally failed to pick up Democratic votes. The Speaker rescheduled the bill for consideration before the recess. But, having forced an early vote on the bill through a somewhat exaggerated report of committed GOP votes, especially in view of the known lack of support on the Democratic side, the House Republican leadership had to supply a much larger than originally anticipated number of GOP votes.

Surtax extension was viewed by administration and House GOP leaders as the first critical test of the Nixon administration—a test of its ability to influence the Congress and to carry out its economic program. They therefore engaged in an intense effort to pass the bill, while avoiding public expressions of partisanship in order to hold the limited Democratic support that they had. Byrnes, the senior Republican on the Ways and Means Committee, as noted previously, recommended not holding a GOP Policy Committee meeting on this issue.

Whenever possible, however, meetings of Republican members were used to reinforce the committed and to influence the uncommitted and opposed. At a breakfast of Republican members called to discuss the distribution of patronage connected with the 1970 Census, Secretary of Commerce Maurice Stans spent more time talking about the surtax than about patronage. He noted that economic stability required the extension and that the nation's resolve to fight inflation was being watched by both domestic and international economic leaders. Stans further warned that, if the surtax was defeated, the world prestige of the Nixon administration would suffer severely.

Later, when about 115 House Republicans gathered in the House chamber for a Republican Conference to discuss the surtax, they heard a series of appeals from their colleagues for support of the President. Conferences are normally called by GOP leaders when they believe that a meeting of the membership will encourage party unity. In an emotional speech Minority Leader Ford recited the economic arguments for the legislation, but the bulk of his statement was a call for party unity and presidential support. The prestige of the President was on the line, he declared, leaving no doubt that this vote was more important than any that had yet been taken that session and many that would follow. Clearly this vote counted and would be remembered. Byrnes and Elford Cederberg (Mich.) of Appropriations then spoke, stressing economic issues. A particularly effective statement came from Arends, the usually easygoing Minority Whip. He reminded his colleagues—pointing to them and calling many by name—that they had helped to hatch Nixon's presidential candidacy in the cloakrooms of the House. It was now their responsibility to support him. Some members who had voted against the surtax in 1968 also spoke in favor of the bill. In this instance the Republican Conference was clearly used to rally partisan support for leadership policy.

In both the conference and informal discussions there were rumblings of unhappiness about the surtax. Some members simply feared taxpayers' wrath at the polls. Others reflected a more conservative point of view: disappointment with the Nixon administration for not having moved swiftly to reverse and even to repeal much of the New Deal-Great Society legislation. They resented voting for taxes to support the continuation of programs that they opposed. A preliminary Republican head count showed only 130 Republican votes for the bill—well below what would be necessary for passage even if the Democratic leaders could pick up a few more votes.

Before the vote on June 30 the leadership worked tirelessly to persuade GOP colleagues to support the bill. There were even press reports that Appropriations Committee members had told colleagues not to expect backing of bills that they considered politically important unless they voted for the surtax. At the same time administration officials sought to influence both Democrats and Republicans. The most celebrated of these attempts was a White House breakfast for twenty-six Republicans who had told party leaders that they opposed the bill. After the breakfast an Alabama Republican commented, "When the President of the United States tells you how much he is interested, it makes you think. He gave us something to chew on and I'm chewing on it as hard as I can right now." Eventually eighteen of the twenty-six, including the Alabaman, voted for the bill.

Floor debate centered around the issue of tax reform. The Democrats claimed that the administration was dragging its feet and that the only way to achieve tax reform was to combine it with surtax extension. Ford, seeking to answer this charge, read a letter in which the President said: "I want to remove any vestige of doubt as to the commitment of this Administration to prompt and meaningful tax reform. . . . There is no reason why a far-reaching tax reform bill cannot be put before the House of Representatives this summer." During the debate Ford was extremely active in buttonholing members to gain their votes.

During the roll call on the bill the outcome appeared extremely close. Late in the roll call Boggs held up four fingers to signal that four additional Republican votes would be needed if the bill was to clear the House. Ford immediately sought out four Republican members and personally accompanied them into the well of the House, where each asked the clerk to change his vote from nay to aye. When the vote switching had been completed, the bill had passed 210 to 205. The partisan breakdown was as follows:

	For	Against
Republicans	154	26
Democrats	56	179
Total	210	205

A reporter for *The New York Times* described the first lesson of the surtax vote:

> The technique so successfully used in similar political circumstances by the Eisenhower Administration—and plainly imitated this time by Mr. Nixon's political lieutenants—is not going to work . . . negotiation and compromise with Democratic leaders of Congress . . . does not work when the leadership cannot produce the votes . . . or even count accurately the number of votes it has.[44]

The weakness of the Democratic leadership was illustrated by the failure of Majority Leader Albert and Majority Whip Boggs to pick up even one vote in their respective Democratic state delegations from Oklahoma and Louisiana. Apparently Mayor Daley of Chicago was more successful. His House spokesman supplied five votes for the surtax from among Illinois Democrats.

Partisanship and the Veto: Labor-HEW Funding

The surtax bill involved cooperation between the leaders—Democratic and Republican—and the White House. Division on the Democratic side, however, forced the administration to make extraordinary efforts to pick up Republican support. The Labor-HEW appropriations battle of 1969-1970 involved a slightly different set of circumstances, which again forced GOP leaders and the White House to exert maximum influence on Republicans. This time, however, the GOP was more partisan.

On January 25, 1970, evening viewers witnessed the first televised veto of an act of Congress. Before a nationwide audience President Nixon first explained his reasons for vetoing the Labor-HEW appropriation for fiscal 1970 and then affixed his signature to the official veto document. The stage for this dramatic exercise of presidential authority had, however, been set six months earlier in the House.

When the Labor-HEW appropriation was reported by the House Appropriations Committee, it contained significantly less money for federal aid-to-education programs than the education lobby believed necessary. It reflected a tight administration budget and the committee's tendency to frugality in funding government programs. Sensing that the Democrats would feel none of the constraints that they had previously felt about supporting the general budgetary limitations recommended by a Democratic President and knowing that education had considerable popular appeal, education interest groups sought to persuade the House to overturn the committee recommendation and to add nearly $1 billion to the bill.

Education interests had previously been badly divided. But in 1969, led by the National Education Association, more than eighty educational organizations, corporate suppliers of educational materials, and the AFL-CIO organized a catalytic group—the Emergency Committee for Full Funding—to lobby for additional money. Through local organizations they sought to influence congressmen at the grass roots, while a professional staff of lobbyists personally spoke with members of Congress on behalf of the Joelson amendment (named for Democrat Charles Joelson of New Jersey), which would add almost $900 million to the bill.

The House Appropriations Committee has been particularly successful through the years in having its bills approved by the House without major change.[45] The halls of the Capitol were filled with educators, librarians, school-board members, and union officials, and the galleries were packed with people intent on knowing how each representative would vote on the unrecorded "teller votes," when, on July 31, 1969, the House approved the Joelson amendment 242 to 106 and thus added $895 million to the bill. Representative Robert Michel (R.-Ill.), the ranking Republican on the Labor-HEW Appropriations Subcommittee, commented after the vote, "Our committee on Appropriations has been 'rolled' for more money than I can recall in my fourteen years as a member."

Although last-minute attempts were made by Michel and the Republican leadership to head off the Joelson amendment by proposing smaller increases in education funds, these (apparently less attractive) amendments were defeated, as a substantial number of Republicans broke ranks and supported the Joelson amendment. It was particularly attractive because $400 million of the increase was for the popular impacted-aid program. Successive Republican and Democratic administrations have denounced this program—which gives federal aid to school districts with high concentrations of federal employees—as a boondoggle. But, because it provides aid to 355 congressional districts, it is to most congressmen an almost irresistible program. As the education lobby's chief strategist put it: "We beefed up impacted aid for an entirely pragmatic reason. This is where you can get the votes." Another important strategic decision was including an additional $131.5 million for vocational education, a program popular with Republican congressmen.

The intensive drive by education groups caught the administration and GOP leadership inadequately prepared, and they suffered a major setback in their attempt to hold the line on expenditures. There was no recent precedent for such dramatic "rolling" of the prestige-laden Appropriations Committee. There was no Republican Conference on the day of the vote and no attempt to rally forces through the Policy Committee.

The education groups had little difficulty securing passage in the generally more liberal Senate for a slightly higher level of appropriations than the House had approved. After a conference committee had approved a compromise between the House and Senate versions of the legislation, both chambers passed a bill containing almost $1.3 billion more in education funds than the President had recommended in his budget.

The President, in his televised veto message, stressed what he considered the inflationary impact of the bill and said that the bill "increases spending for the wrong purposes. . . . The increased spending ordered by Congress for the most part simply provides more dollars for the same old programs without making the urgent new reforms that are needed if we are to improve the quality of education and health care in America." He singled out the impacted-aid program for criticism, noting that the bill as passed provided $6 million in aid for the richest county in the nation and only $3 million for the three million people who live in the 100 poorest counties in the United States. Finally, he criticized the timing of the legislation. The bill provided funds for a fiscal year that would end on June 30, 1970. As Congress did not finish action on the bill until January 1970, the President believed that appropriating in excess of his budget would result in a wasteful rush to spend the money before the fiscal year ended.

Democrats in Congress were highly critical of the President's action and launched an all-out drive to override the veto. Indeed, it was charged that they had purposely pressed for a bill that would provoke a veto in the hope that the Nixon administration and congressional Republicans could be portrayed as anti-education.

In their efforts to override the veto, the Democratic leaders were assisted by a massive lobbying campaign conducted by the Emergency Committee for Full Funding. From across the country education personnel descended on the Capitol to engage in direct, personal persuasion of legislators. Although members of Congress were impressed with this mobilization of grass-roots support for the appropriations bill, the lobbying effort stirred resentment as well. Legislators resent overt threats, and when some of the amateur lobbyists threatened congressmen with defeat at the polls if they failed to support the bill, the interviews were sometimes terminated abruptly, occasionally with harsh exchanges of words.

Veto politics are unique. Passage of the surtax extension had required a majority. For the President and the Republican leaders this requirement meant playing down partisanship in order to pick up approximately one-fourth of the Democratic vote. By the time of a veto confrontation, however, partisan lines have normally hardened, and each side tries to portray the other in the most unfavorable light possible. The other big difference is that the President needs only one-third of the House membership to sustain his veto (a maximum of 145 votes). The administration and Republican leaders therefore concentrated on their own party.

As with the surtax, they staged an intensive campaign to win support among Republicans. Again the President's prestige was on the line. If he lost, it was argued, Joelson-type amendments would be approved for every major appropriations bill, sending federal expenditures out of control at a time when it was necessary to control inflation. It was also alleged that waste would mount as school systems sought to spend the funds in the limited time before the end of the fiscal year in June. Furthermore, Republicans claimed that it was not inconsistent to have supported the Joelson amendment the previous July, when inflation did not appear to be as serious, and then to oppose it in January. Efforts were made to convince members whose districts received large impacted-aid grants that even they must forgo constituency pressures and support the party and the President.

Because of the partisanship surrounding the issue, the formal party-leadership mechanisms were used fully. The Policy Committee met and issued a sharp statement supporting the presidential veto as essential to control inflation. This statement was sent to each GOP member. A Republican Conference was also held. As with the surtax, the conference was basically a rally for the administration position. Appropriations Committee members and the leaders urged their colleagues to take the side of the President and fiscal responsibility. A leading GOP spokesman on education matters and an advocate of federal education programs, Albert Quie (R.-Minn.) refuted the claim that sustaining the veto would mean no federal school aid for fiscal 1970. He said that, if the veto were sustained, a new bill could be quickly passed, one that the President would sign, for he had already indicated a willingness to compromise. Quie's statement was considered important because of his long advocacy of educational programs. At the Conference a few members complained at being cast in what could be construed as an antieducation role, but for the most part the meeting did encourage unity behind the President.

The GOP leadership argument was well summarized in a letter sent by Ford to each Republican:

... What is really at stake here is the ability of a Republican President to carry out a responsible fiscal program and resist the budget-
busting pressures of a Democrat-controlled Congress in an election
year.
  We number 189 in the House. Just 145 votes will sustain President Nixon's position. Obviously, a Republican President can only
be defeated in this showdown by the defections of his own Republican colleagues. . . . I think they [the American people] expect us, as
Republicans, to support him when the chips are down.
  This isn't going to be a vote for or against education. It's going
to be a vote of confidence, or no confidence, in the President. I'm
going to vote to stand by Richard Nixon. I hope you will too.

The White House believed that televising the President's speech would help to
mobilize both congressional and public support for the President. The administration also sought to reassure members that adequate education appropriations
would be supported and spent in fiscal 1970 if the veto were sustained. In a
letter to Congress, HEW Secretary Robert Finch pledged that, if the President
were given discretionary spending authority, he would spend $450 million of the
$1.26 billion added by Congress and that he would spend $440 million for
impacted aid (his original budget had recommended $202 million, whereas the
congressional measure provided $600 million).

  On the final head count before the vote the administration and GOP
leaders found themselves ten votes shy of the necessary total. But last-minute
efforts to persuade those who had remained uncommitted resulted in a relatively
easy victory for the administration. The final vote was 191 to 226, with 156
Republicans and 35 Democrats voting to sustain the President and 199 Democrats and 27 Republicans voting to override. The President's concern over the
issue was demonstrated after the vote when he invited the 191 members who
had supported him to the White House for a reception to thank them personally
for their support.

Party Fragmentation: Extension of OEO

  The surtax and the HEW veto were matters to which both the administration and the Republican House leaders attached great importance and on which
they engaged in maximum effort. In the former instance they worked closely
with the Democratic leadership; in the latter a bipartisan approach was out of
the question. The extension of the Office of Economic Opportunity, however,
revealed a quite different pattern of behavior on the part of the administration,
Democrats, and Republicans.

  As part of his legislative program President Nixon had announced in 1969
that he was requesting a straight two-year extension of the OEO (for a detailed
account of the agency's history see Chapter 7). This announcement drew a
generally favorable response from Democrats, but reaction was mixed within the

President's own party. Many Republicans had campaigned against what they considered excessively militant or partisan political activities by OEO-funded agencies. In previous years many had supported proposals, sponsored by Representative Quie, to provide more state control of OEO programs. Although the Nixon administration and OEO Director Donald Rumsfeld (a former Republican congressman from Illinois) had promised major administrative reform to meet most of these complaints, many GOP House members believed that the desired reforms could come about only through basic changes in the authorizing legislation.

Republicans on the Education and Labor Committee were divided over the two-year extension bill. A few opposed any bill. Some, like William Steiger of Wisconsin (see Chapter 2) and John Dellenback of Oregon supported the extension with some amendments. Quie and the ranking committee Republican, William Ayres (Ohio), continued to advocate far-reaching changes, but they declined to offer amendments to the two-year extension bill during committee consideration because previous experience had taught them that such a move would not only be defeated in committee but would also raise a chorus of adverse publicity and heavy lobbying among supporters of existing OEO operations. Even in the absence of amendments by Quie the committee became mired in controversy. Chairman Carl Perkins (D.-Ky.) refused for five months to schedule committee action on the bill until the Republicans would give assurances that they would not offer what he called "crippling" amendments to the bill on the floor. Such assurances were not forthcoming, and each side blamed the other for stalling the legislation.

When the committee finally reported the legislation, with an increase in funding of $295 million, it was scheduled for floor consideration in early December 1969. Attention then centered on the strategy that Quie and his supporters would follow. Quie indicated that he would offer a series of amendments to increase state control over OEO programs and to strengthen Rumsfeld's hand in dealing with what Quie called "bomb throwers" who had been blanketed into the program by civil service. He indicated that his amendments would be available in time for careful consideration before House action on the bill, but he would not tip his hand before that and allow the opposition to mobilize its lobbying and publicity forces.

While Quie and his committee associates were drafting their amendments to the extension legislation, Rumsfeld sought to shore up support for it among Republican members. Having gained no assurances of help from the Minority Leader or Minority Whip, Rumsfeld appealed to his former Illinois colleague, Republican Conference Chairman John Anderson (see Chapter 3 for a detailed account of Anderson's activities in the House), who ranked third in the House GOP hierarchy. Anderson hastily assembled a group of eighteen mainly younger members who were sympathetic to Rumsfeld's position. In a meeting with the group Rumsfeld stressed that the administration favored a straight two-year extension, that he was making significant administrative changes in the agency, and that it would be unwise for the GOP to be caught in a position in which it could be portrayed by the Democrats as opposed to the "war on poverty." Members of the Anderson group made an unofficial count of votes on the Republican side and also sought support for Rumsfeld among their colleagues.

In early December at a Policy Committee meeting on OEO, Quie was able to provide his colleagues with a summary of the amendments that he intended to propose. Lengthy discussions in the Policy Committee revealed substantial divisions on the issue among Republicans: Many members supported Quie, but others supported Rumsfeld, which meant that it was impossible for the Policy Committee to release a statement.

One of the most revealing aspects of the issue was the position of the leaders. Ford announced his support of the Quie amendments. Indeed, Anderson was the only member of the leadership to support the OEO position publicly.

After meetings among Quie, White House personnel, Rumsfeld, and Ford had failed to produce compromises, Rumsfeld publicly criticized the Quie amendments as "crippling." But support for them was building. Quie and Ayres quickly found bipartisan support and sponsorship for their amendments. This time the coalition that they formed included Edith Green (D.-Ore.), who had led many battles on education and who believed strongly in the need for more state control of OEO programs; Robert Giaimo (D.-Conn.); and the skillful leader of the southern Democrats, Joe Waggonner of Louisiana.

This coalition of Republicans (including most of the leaders), some northern Democrats, and southern Democrats was aided by the fact that the White House itself did not lobby for the straight extension, leaving Rumsfeld and his staff to carry the administration lobbying responsibility themselves. In a news conference the President endorsed the straight two-year extension and stressed his support of Rumsfeld. He also remarked that he hoped that Rumsfeld would "be able to work out with the [Republican] leadership of the House . . . and some Democrats . . . some kind of accommodation. . . ."

Rumsfeld's intense lobbying and the more restrained stance of the White House reflected different judgments within the administration on the importance of a straight extension of OEO. The agency, faced with a potential major change in its mode of operations forced upon it by Congress, responded to the external threat with vigor. While supporting the director, the White House staff apparently did not have the same stake in the congressional struggle. OEO was a controversial legacy of the Johnson administration with only limited support among Republicans. Many of its programs had already been transferred to other departments, and its primary role was being changed to one of research and handling special projects. Whatever Congress might do would not be as significant for the overall domestic programs of the administration as were the outcomes of the surtax and HEW-appropriation issues. The White House did not, therefore, involve itself in lobbying for OEO extension. Sensing these divergent views within the administration, GOP congressmen (including the leaders) believed themselves free to pursue relatively independent courses on this issue.

Rumsfeld, his GOP supporters, and Democrats favoring the committee bill were not at all confident when it was scheduled for floor action on December 3. Reluctantly and under extreme pressure from liberal Democrats on the Education and Labor Committee, Speaker McCormack agreed to postpone consideration so that liberal Democrats could muster their forces against the Quie amendments. When the House convened at noon that day Perkins therefore made a surprise announcement: He would not call up the bill for consideration. Ford immediately responded that he was shocked at Perkins' "arbitrary action" and declared that the "House has a right and a responsibility to work its will on this legislation as we have in the past." The following colloquy then ensued:

> MR. PERKINS: If the gentleman will make the commitment that he will carry out the President's wishes and Mr. Rumsfeld's wishes, I will get up there and immediately reconsider.

> MR. GERALD R. FORD: May I make this observation and comment. The President wants the present Economic Opportunity Act extended without crippling amendments and the Quie-Green-Giaimo-Ayres substitute is not a crippling proposal. . . . I will abide by a final decision of the majority. But you do not solve the problem by ducking and running, as apparently the chairman today wants to do. . . .

For a long period both sides traded charges about who was endangering OEO, who was stalling and refusing to negotiate, and whether or not the Quie substitute was a crippling amendment. But the Speaker's decision held, and the forces of Rumsfeld, Anderson, and the Democrats had time to try for the votes to kill the bipartisan substitute.

Anderson's group continued to work for GOP support of a straight extension. It argued that Rumsfeld and the President deserved a chance to clean up OEO in their own way without restrictive statutory language.

The AFL-CIO, the Urban Coalition's Action Council, and the nation's mayors lobbied for straight extension. They declined, however, to collaborate with OEO officials in the agency's drive to defeat the substitute because of distrust of the Nixon administration.

A vote on the critical Quie substitute was scheduled for December 12. First, on an unrecorded teller vote the House rejected the substitute 166 to 183. On a recorded roll call the plan was rejected by a wider margin, 163 to 231. The party breakdown was

	For	*Against*
Republicans	103	63
Democrats	60	168
Total	163	231

What had first looked like an extremely strong coalition for changing OEO had been defeated. There appeared to be several reasons for the House decision. First, Rumsfeld's intensive personal lobbying among former colleagues had paid off. In addition, he had received help from younger activists like Anderson and Steiger. Second, liberal, labor, civil rights, and urban interests had mounted an active drive to continue OEO in its existing form. Third, the delay in consideration of the bill had given time to gather votes against the substitute.

A final factor contributing to the defeat of the substitute was the failure of substantial southern Democratic support to materialize. Perkins was able to round up border-state Democrats with the argument that they should not vote to give Republican governors control of antipoverty funds. The governors themselves manifested little support for the substitute, despite the fact that it would give them more control over antipoverty programs. One was reported to have said: "Hell, who wants to have the Statehouse blamed for OEO's problems. It's much easier to blast Washington."

Administration Strategy and Congressional Response

These three examples of administration-congressional relations reveal something of the complexity of legislative strategy and coalition building, not to mention the various responses of the White House, administrative agencies, and party leaders to different pieces of legislation. Clearly not all bills are equally important to these sets of participants, who therefore respond differently, depending upon circumstances. The examples also illustrate how any administration that does not control Congress can encounter difficulty in forging majorities from among two diffuse and fragmented political parties. Of particular note is the difference in the flexibility of strategy enjoyed by leaders of presidential and nonpresidential parties. The GOP felt that it had to act in accordance with White House legislative priorities, whereas the Democrats were free either to support or oppose the administration, depending upon the issue.

SENIORITY: ATTACKING THE SYSTEM

Committee leaders are not usually considered party officials, but committee assignments (including the designation of chairmen and seniority rankings on committees) are the responsibility of the congressional parties. At the beginning of each new Congress both chambers elect the members of their respective standing committees. These elections, however, are merely pro forma affairs because the Senate and the House simply ratify decisions previously made by the Republican and Democratic Parties.

Slightly different procedures are followed in making committee assignments. In the Senate the Democratic Steering Committee, headed by the floor leader, performs this function, whereas in the House Democrats rely on their fellow partisans of the Ways and Means Committee. Senate Republicans have their Committee on Committees, composed of eighteen members. In the House the Republican Committee on Committees includes one representative from each state that has a Republican delegation in the House. This representative has as many votes in committee as there are Republicans in his state's delegation. The real work of the committee is done by an executive committee, which tends to be dominated by representatives of large states.

A legislator's initial committee assignment is made in accordance with various considerations, including the legislator's personal preferences, the support that he can muster among more senior members, geographic balance, his policy views, and the type of district that he represents.[46] Elected party leaders exercise considerable influence on assignments, but in no sense do they control them. Once given an assignment, the legislator is considered to have a right to it as long as he remains in Congress.[47] Equally by convention, committee members advance in seniority—defined by continuous terms of committee service—with the most senior majority member being named chairman. The most senior minority member, who is called the ranking minority member, becomes chairman if his party seizes control of the chamber. This is the substance of the much-debated "seniority system."

No feature of congressional practice has drawn as much criticism as has seniority. It is ironic to reflect that in the House the practice of seniority received its greatest impetus from two reform measures. In the revolt against Speaker Joseph G. Cannon (1910-1911) seniority was considered a way to wrest control of appointments from the Speaker's hands. Clause 2 of House Rule X (adopted April 5, 1911) directs that "at the commencement of each Congress the House shall elect as chairman of each standing committee one of the members thereof. . . ." The Legislative Reorganization Act of 1946 reinforced seniority by drastically reducing the number of committees and therefore available leadership positions. Before 1946 it had been possible for party leaders to persuade certain members to step aside from some chairmanships by assuring them of influential posts on other committees.

Another factor that has strengthened the seniority system, particularly in the House, is the professionalization of the congressional career. As length of service has increased and being a senator or representative has become a full-time job, legislators have attached more importance to seniority.[48] It assures those who stay long enough of important roles on their respective committees.

Although the seniority system denies to political parties flexibility in choosing committee leaders, the system has the advantage of providing an impersonal and automatic ("first come, first served") basis for making important personnel decisions. It eliminates some prolonged and bitter intraparty wrangles, not an insignificant advantage for political parties as lacking in agreement on policy and as loosely organized as are those in the United States. Indeed, it may be that the seniority system helps to hold the congressional parties together by assuring even those who represent minority points of view within their parties (like the southern Democrats) of important committee posts.

Political scientists do not agree about the exact effects of seniority, but it seems reasonable to conclude that in the recent past it has contributed to some unrepresentativeness in leadership, because longevity in office is associated with homogeneous, one-party districts.[49] In the 92nd Congress, for example, southerners constituted about a quarter of the members of both houses yet controlled the chairmanships of ten of the seventeen Senate standing committees and twelve of the twenty-one House committees. Advanced age impairs the ability of some of these committee leaders to perform their task, but physical unfitness takes less toll than does the psychological inertia of many years in the same job.

Committee leaders are frequently at loggerheads with the policies of their national parties. In March 1969 the Democratic Study Group issued a study of the voting records of the 114 House committee or subcommittee chairmen in the 90th Congress (1967-1968).[50] Of these committee leaders 42 had voted more frequently in opposition to party policies than in support of them. Their votes had provided the margin of defeat on nine, or better than half, of the losses sustained by the Democratic majority. The study concluded, "On many of the most crucial votes of the 90th Congress, one-third of Democratic committee chairmen voted against the Democratic Administration, Democratic party principles, and the majority of their Democratic colleagues—and were responsible for the defeat of many Democratic programs."[51] The Democrats, incidentally, have no monopoly on this problem: President Dwight D. Eisenhower had trouble in dealing with some chairmen in the Republican 83rd Congress.

Although the "rule" of seniority (which is nowhere written down) is almost never circumvented, it persists only at the sufferance of the party caucuses. The question is therefore how the respective parties have dealt with mounting criticism leveled at the seniority system.

The Democrats: Intense Generational and Ideological Conflict

House Democratic reformers in the 1960s strove to strengthen the caucus so that it could exercise its undoubted authority to depose chairmen who deviated repeatedly from declared party policies. One of these caucus reformers, Representative Bolling of Missouri, believed that "the implied threat of party discipline . . . would give pause to the member who would bolt his party's program."[52] Other critics have called for a frontal attack on seniority, proposing, for example, rotation in office or election of chairmen from among the three top-ranking majority members of each committee. Such proposals have little chance of adoption because the very leaders who are most threatened by them have the most power to prevent their passage.

Reformers worked to establish precedents for caucus modification of seniority privileges. In 1965 House Democrats removed the seniority of two southerners who had supported GOP presidential nominee Barry Goldwater in the 1964 election. John Bell Williams of Mississippi and Albert Watson of South Carolina were placed at the bottom of their committees' seniority lists.[53] (The liberals, who were in control of the caucus during the 89th Congress, had threatened to deny seating to defectors but decided not to press that course of action.) "It was a wise, new, fresh precedent," one liberal commented at the time. "We wanted to make the Democratic Party count for more."

In subsequent years, spurred by the Democratic Study Group, House liberals have sought to reinforce the precedent for caucus ratification of seniority lists presented by the Ways and Means Committee. In 1967 the caucus voted to rescind the seniority of Adam Clayton Powell of New York, then chairman of the Education and Labor Committee. Powell had been investigated and found guilty of misusing House funds, and the move was designed to forestall an effort on the floor (later successful) to refuse to seat him altogether. Early in 1969 liberals again succeeded in disciplining a member for party disloyalty, though only after two close caucus votes. This time the loser was John Rarick of Louisiana, who had supported George Wallace in the 1968 campaign.

A challenge to the seniority of the five-man Mississippi House delegation was turned back two years later. In 1970 the five had been candidates of the segregationist "regular" Democrats headed by Governor John Bell Williams, the same former representative who had been stripped of his seniority in 1965. But the 1968 national convention had voted to seat as the state's legitimate Democratic Party delegation an integrated group led by Aaron Henry, a civil rights leader. Henry became state chairman because he was recognized by the national party, but state officials steadily refused to certify the group. Henry therefore appealed to House Democrats to discipline the congressional delegation. This course of action had little chance of success: It is one thing to discipline one or two unpopular members but quite another to move against an entire state delegation, three of whose members are committee or subcommittee chairmen. Furthermore, one ground rule for making such challenges—one that goes back as far as 1960, when such action was considered against southerners who had supported unpledged slates of presidential electors—is that the errant legislators be amply forewarned before action is taken.

Negotiations between the Democratic Study Group and Speaker-designate Albert were proceeding toward a compromise: an official, party-sponsored study of the Mississippi loyalty question. Suddenly Chairman Conyers of the Black Caucus stepped in and insisted that the five be stripped of their seniority. When Albert refused to commit himself, Conyers announced that he would run for the speakership in the caucus. The negotiations collapsed, and Conyers' resolution, though nominally supported by DSG, was defeated in the caucus 55 to 111. Some members, however, sought to gain support for a similar challenge two years later; by that time the Mississippians would have been warned of the consequences of abandoning the national party.

Tampering with seniority is hardly an everyday occurrence. In successful instances, action has been directed against men who have been personally unpopular in the House and who have by their own behavior generated strong pressures for some form of discipline. In most instances the challenges have been precipitated by formal acts of disloyalty like support of another party's presidential candidate. No one has yet attempted, for example, to discipline committee leaders for consistently voting against party positions.

Institutional changes in the operation of the seniority system, however, promised to keep the issue alive during the 1970s. Some of the earliest stirrings came as a result of House Democrats' leadership conflicts. Early in 1970, DSG Chairman Donald M. Fraser (Minn.) and nine other DSG liberals announced their intention to raise in the party caucus "the subject of organization of the House of Representatives." Later Fraser was joined by sixteen DSG colleagues in circulating a resolution for caucus adoption. The resolution avoided use of the word "seniority"; as the practice is nowhere embodied in written rules, some leaders had claimed that it did not exist! The responsibility of the caucus for organizing the standing committees, the resolution declared, "is not relieved and cannot be evaded by simply following custom and tradition." The resolution would have directed the caucus chairman to

> appoint a committee of the caucus to review, consider and recommend ways in which the caucus may assure itself that those it selects as chairmen of standing committees will, in such capacity, be responsive to the caucus and to the Democratic leadership, and ways in which chairmen can be assured of working majorities on their committees who will support Democratic programs and policies. . . .

When the matter finally came up, the resolution was approved with modifications. Fraser had originally called for the committee report within sixty days so that its recommendations could become an issue in the ensuing election campaign. Many Democrats objected to this feature, and by a 110 to 46 vote the caucus voted to instruct the committee to report to the January 1971 caucus.

Few committee chairmen wanted the study launched in the first place, but the caucus action had the effect of taking a potential issue away from both the young GOP reformers and the DSG insurgents. The new study committee—officially designated the Committee on Organization, Study, and Review—was therefore carefully selected by caucus chairman Rostenkowski to reflect various points of view and to give sufficient weight to the leaders' interests. Julia Butler Hansen (Wash.), a respected six-termer and the first woman to head an appropriations subcommittee, was made chairman of the group.

The committee rejected a frontal assault on either the seniority system or the method of making committee assignments. A suggestion to require chairmen to retire at age seventy was turned down, Mrs. Hansen said, because it would violate federal law forbidding discrimination in employment because of age. Some members thought that committee assignments should be transferred from Ways and Means to a committee directly responsible to the caucus, but this suggestion was also rejected. Also voted down was O'Hara's proposal to increase the membership of the Committee on Committees by eight, adding the Speaker, Majority Leader, and six others to be appointed by the leadership. O'Hara argued that the Democrats on Ways and Means were unrepresentative, for seven of the fifteen were from the South.

On December 16 the Hansen committee issued a brief report consisting of twelve unanimous recommendations.[54] The report clarified the procedures for making committee assignments. Recommendations for chairman and membership of each committee were to be made to the caucus "and . . . need not follow seniority." The report of the Committee on Committees was to be presented one committee at a time, and any ten members could demand a separate vote on any portion of the recommendations. Forty minutes for debate would then be allotted. If the challenge were successful the committee list would be recommitted. An individual member could be nominated for a committee assignment by submitting a letter signed by a majority of his state's Democratic congressmen. Committee ratios were to ensure "firm working majorities" on each committee—at least three Democrats for every two Republicans. The effect of these provisions would be to ratify and extend nearly a decade of precedents for caucus supervision of committee assignments.

Equally important were the Hansen committee's proposed restrictions on the number of committee assignments that a single individual could hold: No legislator could be a member of more than 2 legislative committees, no member could head more than 1 legislative subcommittee, and no chairman could head more than 1 subcommittee within his own committee. At the end of the 91st Congress there were 141 subcommittees of House standing committees, and some representatives were heading as many as 3. The Hansen report freed about 30 subcommittee chairmanships for junior members.

Once the Hansen report had been issued, DSG began to fear that senior leaders would try to amend it in the caucus. They therefore devised a series of six strengthening amendments, including one that enunciated these considerations for choosing committee chairmen: "fitness, ability, length of service, past performance as chairman, support of Democratic programs and principles, cooperation with the leadership, and responsiveness to the will of the caucus." Four of these amendments were presented at the January 20, 1971, caucus, but all were rejected. On the other hand, the Hansen report was adopted without any modifications.

Once the new procedures were operative, critics of the seniority system had two courses of action open to them. One was a pro forma vote on every committee chairman. Ten members could simply call for a vote on each chairman in order to avoid singling out a particular one. This approach would further legitimize the caucus-review procedure and might eventually lead to the defeat of one or more chairmen. The other approach was to select one or more controversial chairmen for attack. As it happened, this second course of action was adopted.

For several years a storm had been brewing in the District of Columbia Committee. The nation's capital, whose population was more than 70 percent black by 1970, had long been controlled in the House by a southern-dominated group presided over by John McMillan of South Carolina, whose twenty-two years as chairman exceeded the tenure of any committee chairman in the history of Congress. Early in 1969 the committee's fourth-ranking Democrat, Charles C. Diggs, Jr., a black from Detroit, charged that McMillan was using his powers in an arbitrary and dictatorial manner: For example, no bills had been referred to Diggs' subcommittee after he had become chairman. In the fall of 1970 another committee member, Fraser, charged that three committee reports criticizing District affairs were biased, had been inadequately investigated, and had been issued before all committee members had had a chance to review them.

When the 92nd Congress convened, therefore, Fraser launched a campaign to replace McMillan with Diggs. The charges against McMillan were essentially procedural, though age and racial bias lurked in the background. Although Diggs was not in line for the chairmanship, the election of a black would be meaningful.[55] Fraser issued a call for Diggs' selection and by the time of the February caucus had gathered seventy-three signatures on his letter of intent. Outside support came from Common Cause, which was publicizing the entire seniority question and now called for the removal of McMillan, who "has almost single-handedly kept Washington, D.C., in colonial bondage."[56] The National Committee for an Effective Congress also vowed to work for the defeat of unresponsive committee chairmen.

McMillan enjoyed the dubious distinction of being the only chairman challenged during the February 3 caucus, but he won reinstatement by a 126 to 98 vote. Fraser, Diggs, Andrew Jacobs (Ind.), and Brock Adams (Wash.), all District

Committee members, detailed the charges against McMillan, who was defended by Ways and Means Chairman Mills and several other colleagues. The day before the caucus it had been announced that Mills, Speaker Albert, and Majority Leader Boggs had thrown their support behind the embattled chairman. What was not revealed was that Albert and Mills had privately extracted a promise from McMillan that he would mend his ways.

The attack on McMillan went to the House floor, where a bipartisan group tried to force a separate vote on his appointment as chairman. Rather than accepting the Democratic committee rosters en bloc, Jerome Waldie of California proposed an amendment that would have dropped McMillan from the chairmanship. On a procedural question (a motion for the previous question on the rosters, H. Res. 193), Waldie's move was defeated by a vote of 32 to 258, with more than 100 members not voting and 42 voting "present." Leaders of both parties opposed the move as a precedent by which, as Boggs noted, "if the majority party voted unanimously, we could displace any ... or every committee member nominated by the minority." Minority Leader Ford agreed that "we on our side should not get into the procedures and prerogatives of the majority party."[57] Also opposed were many caucus reformers who, though having no love for McMillan or the seniority system, were unwilling to tamper with the parties' control of such matters.

In the aftermath McMillan's powers were trimmed somewhat by a majority of his committee during the 92nd Congress, but he continued to be as arbitrary as ever in handling his subcommittees.

On the Senate side of the Hill Democrats were also making inroads on seniority. Largely at the prodding of Fred R. Harris of Oklahoma, Senate Majority Leader Mansfield established that the Democratic Conference can nullify (by majority secret ballot) any committee assignment, including that of a chairman. Mansfield confirmed that the conference "is empowered to decide all questions of committee membership, including chairmen, ratios, distribution and the basis on which assignments are made." At the initial conference of 1971 Mansfield took steps to implement this dictum. Instead of simply announcing the names of chairmen, as had been done previously, he read them as a proposal subject to ratification. Although there was no objection, Mansfield declared that "the fact that there was no challenge ... does not render these procedures any less effective." Mansfield also read off committee assignments, including those of newly elected or returning senators who had been given fresh assignments by the Steering Committee. "If there had been a request for a roll-call vote, it would have been granted," he said later.[58]

Other steps were taken to modify the seniority system in the Senate. Within the Democratic Conference Mansfield appointed a committee to study the system, credentials of senators who seek to join the conference but who do not run on the party's ticket, and assignment procedures for Senate members of conference committees. Mansfield also gave his blessing to a proposal for revising

Senate Rule XXIV to require the Senate to elect, one by one, the chairmen and ranking minority members of committees.[59] Already Rule XXIV made such votes discretionary, and when the names of committee chairmen for the 92nd Congress came to the Senate floor Harris asked for a voice vote on every one.[60] No negative votes were heard.

The Republicans: Generational Tension and Procedural Change

Republicans, too, have been wrestling with the seniority system, but in the House it does not pose quite the same problems for them that it does for the Democrats. First, the stakes are not so great because Republicans are not the majority party and therefore do not have chairmanships at issue; rather what is at stake is the influential position of ranking minority members. Second, the Republicans are more homogeneous than are the Democrats (the three wings of the Democratic Party have been discussed earlier in this chapter), and there are therefore fewer ranking committee members who are radically out of step with the point of view of the party as a whole. Third, the Republican Party suffered serious electoral setbacks in 1958 and 1964, which severely reduced the number of senior members (the Democrats have suffered no comparable thinning of their senior ranks). As a result, the overall seniority of the GOP is relatively low, and Republicans elected as recently as 1966 had by 1971 become ranking minority members on various subcommittees. Even so, many Republicans have been critical of the seniority system.

In March 1970 Minority Leader Ford and Research Committee Chairman Robert Taft, Jr., announced the appointment of a special Task Force on Seniority to make recommendations on party rules for the selection of committee leaders. The creation of the task force was brought about through the urging of junior members (those elected since 1966 constituted an unusually high 40 percent of House Republican membership) restless about the operation of the seniority system, criticism of several ranking Republican committee members who were frequently at odds with their party or who had cultivated comfortable relations with Democratic committee chairmen, and the unfavorable public image of the seniority system.

The eighteen-member task force was balanced in terms of junior and senior members, geography, and ideology. It included two ranking committee members—John Byrnes (Wis.) of Ways and Means and William Springer (Ill.) of Interstate and Foreign Commerce; leaders of the legislative-reform movement—William Steiger (Wis.) and Barber Conable (N.Y.); liberals like Paul N. (Pete) McCloskey (Calif.); and conservatives like Durwood Hall (Mo.) and Jack Edwards (Ala.). Despite the balanced membership and the influential positions given to ranking committee members, many senior members were extremely unhappy that Ford had allowed the task force to be appointed at all and hoped that no action would be taken on seniority.

The task-force members conceived the basic problem as how to foster flexibility in the selection of committee leaders and accountability from those leaders without tearing the party apart in a scramble for key legislative positions. Their work was skillfully directed by Conable, a respected upstate New York representative who had first been elected in 1964. Conable impressed party leaders early in his career and in his second term was assigned to the important Ways and Means Committee. He was also active in efforts to achieve legislative reform. (For an account of his role in the passage of the Legislative Reorganization Act of 1970, see Chapter 8.)

Conable presided over task-force meetings weekly between March and June 1970. The group considered proposals for committee selection of chairmen, Conference election, appointment by the leadership, and a variety of other methods of selection. All House GOP members were asked to give their views to the task force both orally and in writing. They were also given an opportunity to express themselves through an anonymous questionnaire; when seniority is at issue many members are reluctant to challenge committee elders.

Although many senior Republicans hoped that the task force would bury the issue, the Conable group believed that a failure to make a proposal would stimulate further unhappiness among junior members and would damage the public image of the party.

The plan finally accepted by the task force was proposed by Byrnes, himself the senior Republican on Ways and Means. Fearful of the harm that could result from intense intraparty contests for committee posts, not to mention the inevitable activities of lobbyists anxious to influence such selection, Byrnes proposed that the Republican Committee on Committees nominate candidates for the positions of committee chairmen or ranking minority members, depending upon whether the GOP was the majority or minority party in the House. In making its nominations, the committee would not be restricted to selecting the most senior members, though there would be a presumption that they would normally be nominated. The Republican Conference would then be required to vote separately on whether or not each nominee should be either chairman or ranking minority member. The party would thus have to take formal action to approve GOP committee leaders. In the event that a nominee were rejected by the conference, Byrnes proposed that the Committee on Committees be required to submit another name. This procedure was designed to prevent wide-open and potentially disruptive struggles for leadership posts.

The Byrnes proposal was in the congressional tradition of compromise. It did not go nearly as far as some of the younger members wished, but on the other hand, it was not as severe as many of the senior members had feared. Conable and his colleagues won early endorsement from Ford and the GOP leadership, who believed that the proposal would not endanger their essential working relationship with senior members but would at the same time introduce flexibility that had previously been absent from the selection process.

Anticipating opposition to the task-force plan from both those who preferred wholesale change and those who feared losing their own positions, members of the task force were assigned lists of colleagues whose support they were to try to enlist for the plan. The task force made a careful canvass of the vote and determined that it had enough support to bring the matter before the organizational conference in January 1971. After the conference had approved the report of the Task Force on Seniority, Conable declared that the new procedure would make ranking Republican committee members "in fact leaders and not just survivors."

At a later conference, when the Committee on Committees submitted its nominations, the list of nominees included no changes from those who would have been selected strictly by seniority. When the actual voting on the nominees occurred, however, a significant number of votes were cast against several ranking members, a reminder to each that from now on the party would wield sanctions against seniority leaders. This registering of opposition to senior leaders was not organized, because those interested in changing committee leaders believed that the Conable task force's recommendations would be endangered if a campaign were simultaneously mounted against any ranking committee members.

On the Senate side of the Capitol the Republicans also changed their seniority procedures. At the organizational conference of Republican senators in January 1971 a proposal by Mathias that no senator could be a senior member of more than one regular committee was adopted 35 to 2. This change had the immediate effect of forcing each of three senators—Margaret Chase Smith (Maine), George Aiken (Vt.), and Wallace F. Bennett (Utah)—to give up one of their two ranking committee positions. Three additional senators were thus elevated to positions of ranking members. Before adoption of the Mathia proposal, a move to let a senator serve as the senior member of two standing committees (which would have vitiated his proposal) was defeated by a 17 to 19 vote. Mathias and his supporters said afterward that they viewed their victory as only the first move toward loosening the Senate GOP seniority structure.

A Concluding Note

More will be heard of the issue of seniority. Newly formalized methods for exercising caucus control over committee assignments provide a legitimate tool for those who wish to challenge an assignment, even a chairman. No one expects wholesale replacement of seniority leaders, but the existence of the threat will usually be sufficient to encourage more cautious exercise of seniority powers in committee. Meanwhile, various new procedures (to be discussed in Chapter 8) are beginning to circumscribe the powers of committee chairmen. And new provisions for publicity, both in committee proceedings and in debates of the Committee of the Whole, promise to make the machinations of congressional committees more accessible to the larger public.

NOTES FOR CHAPTER 4

1 Randall B. Ripley, *Majority Party Leadership in Congress* (Boston: Little, Brown, 1969), pp. 166-168.

2 *Ibid.*, pp. 6-7. See also Ripley, *Party Leadership in the House of Representatives* (Washington, D.C.: Brookings, 1967).

3 Richard L. Lyons, "The Next Speaker," *Washington Post*, December 5, 1961, p. E-4.

4 The impact of the challenge on congressional-reform legislation is discussed in Chapter 8.

5 See Norman C. Miller, "John McCormack: Speaker under Fire," *Wall Street Journal* (February 17, 1970), p. 10.

6 William Chapman, "Carl Albert: Winning with a Waiting Game," *Washington Post* (January 10, 1971), p. B-3.

7 As are the other chapters in this book, this account is based largely on personal observations, interviews with participants, and inspection of private documents. These observations have been supplemented by press accounts, particularly Andrew J. Glass' reporting: "Uncommitted Democrats Hold Key to Choice of New House Majority Leader," *National Journal* (January 9, 1971), pp. 68-76, and "House Democrats Back Establishment in Electing Boggs Floor Leader," *National Journal* (January 23, 1971), pp. 186-190. Helpful reports were also published in *Congressional Quarterly Weekly Report*, November 27, 1970, pp. 2867-2870, and *Congressional Quarterly Weekly Report*, January 22, 1970, pp. 176-179. An interesting account appeared in Larry L. King's "The Road to Power in the House," *Harper's* (June 1971), pp. 39-63. The definitive account is Robert L. Peabody's "The Selection of a Majority Leader," in Peabody, *Congressional Leadership Change* (Boston: Little, Brown, forthcoming). Although the account and interpretation presented here generally agree with those of Peabody, in recognition of the independent research efforts involved, the authors have refrained from relying on his study, with the exception cited in note 20.

8 A brief discussion of the history and internal politics of the DSG is included in Chapter 8.

9 Nelson W. Polsby, "Two Strategies of Influence: Choosing a Majority Leader, 1962," in Robert L. Peabody and Polsby (eds.), *New Perspectives on the House of Representatives* (2d ed.; Chicago: Rand McNally, 1969), p. 356.

10 For one reason, Udall was acquainted with various scholarly studies and was determined to avoid the pitfalls of an ousider's stance. And some of Boggs' most useful allies were on the outside.

11 *Congressional Quarterly Almanac* (Washington, D.C.: 1969), pp. 1065-1069; *Congressional Quarterly Almanac* (Washington, D.C.: 1970), pp. 1139-1143. The party-unity score, as measured by *Congressional Quarterly*, represents the percentage of roll calls on which each legislator has voted in agreement with a majority of his party and in opposition to a majority of the rival party. This score is often used as a crude measure of party loyalty.

12 Joseph Alsop, "Durable Hill Monsters," *Washington Post*, January 15, 1971, p. A-24.

13 Donald G. Tacheron and Morris K. Udall, *The Job of the Congressman* (2d ed.; Indianapolis: Bobbs-Merrill, 1970).

14 Quoted in King, "The Road to Power in the House," p. 48.

15 Quoted in Glass, "Uncommitted Democrats," p. 71.

16 Lyons, "House Caucus Day: They All Talk Like Winners," *Washington Post,* January 19, 1971, p. A-1.

17 *Congressional Quarterly Weekly Report,* January 15, 1971, pp. 141-146.

18 Quoted in King, "The Road to Power in the House," p. 49.

19 In an effort to broaden the base of the leadership, Albert and Boggs announced creation of two new positions as floor Whips, whose major job would be to keep members on the floor. They were John Brademas (Ind.), a liberal O'Hara backer, and John McFall (Calif.), a Boggs supporter. The completed slate gave representation to the Northeast, Midwest, and West—for Albert and Boggs were from the same region. Udall backers were conspicuously absent from the leadership ranks.

20 Peabody, *Congressional Leadership Change,* pp. 1-23.

21 Quoted in King, "The Road to Power in the House," p. 62.

22 David S. Broder, "Picking a House Majority Leader," *Washington Post,* January 14, 1971, p. A-20.

23 Donald R. Matthews, *U.S. Senators and Their World* (Chapel Hill: University of North Carolina Press, 1960), chap. 5.

24 In Ralph K. Huitt and Peabody, *Congress: Two Decades of Analysis* (New York: Harper, 1969), p. 158.

25 See Joseph S. Clark, *The Senate Establishment* (New York: Hill + Wang, 1963).

26 Quoted in Dan Cordtz, "The Senate Revolution," *Wall Street Journal,* August 6, 1965, p. 8.

27 U.S., Congress, Senate, *Congressional Record,* daily ed., 89th Cong., 1st sess., September 13, 1965, 111, 22636.

28 Quoted in *The New York Times,* July 17, 1961, p. 11. To early attacks on his leadership, Mansfield delivered a fascinating reply in U.S. Congress, Senate, *Congressional Record,* daily ed., 88th Cong., 1st sess., 27 November 1963, 109, 22857-22866.

29 Glass, "Mansfield Reforms Spark 'Quiet Revolution' in Senate," *National Journal* (March 6, 1971), p. 509.

30 For a discussion of the Policy Committee's changing role, see *ibid.,* pp. 499-512.

31 *Ibid.,* p. 510.

32 Two portraits of the West Virginian can be found in Robert Sherrill, "The Embodiment of Poor White Power," *The New York Times Magazine*, February 28, 1971, pp. 9 ff; and Spencer Rich, "Outside South, Whip Byrd is Senate's Number 3 Conservative," *Washington Post*, February 14, 1971, p. E-5.

33 *Congressional Quarterly Almanac* (Washington, D.C.: 1970), pp. 1144-1147.

34 The Senate is usually presided over by junior senators. The constitutional presiding officer is, of course, the Vice-President, but he is rarely present. He appears mainly for special occasions and when a tie vote is likely. The President Pro Tempore is largely an honorific title, conferred automatically upon the senior majority senator.

35 Accounts of Byrd's election can be found in "The Tortoise and the Hare," *Newsweek* (February 1, 1971), pp. 18-20; "Russell's Proxy Kept Byrd in the Race," *The New York Times*, January 22, 1971, p. 1; and James Doyle, "Kennedy Men Assess Defeat," *Washington Evening Star*, January 22, 1971, p. A-1.

36 See Charles O. Jones, *The Minority Party in Congress* (Boston: Little, Brown, 1971), esp. pp. 108-112.

37 The head of *The New York Times'* Washington Bureau, for example, had drawn painful comparisons between the youthful President Kennedy and Dirksen and Halleck, who, he said, looked "like a veteran Shakespearean actor and W. C. Fields." See James Reston, *Boston Herald*, January 9, 1963, p. 17.

38 David B. Truman, *The Congressional Party: A Case Study* (New York: Wiley, 1959), p. 298.

39 Matthews, *U.S. Senators and Their World* (Chapel Hill: University of North Carolina Press, 1960), p. 142.

40 A study conducted by the Survey Research Center in 1958 showed that only 47 percent of the public knows which party controls the Congress. See Donald E. Stokes and Warren E. Miller, "Party Government and the Saliency of Congress," *Public Opinion Quarterly*, 26 (1962), 531-546.

41 Jones, *Party and Policy-Making: The House Republican Policy Committee* (New Brunswick, N.J.: Rutgers University Press, 1964).

42 For a discussion of the circumstances under which party leaders are most effective in leading their colleagues, see Lewis A. Froman, Jr., and Ripley, "Conditions for Party Leadership," *American Political Science Review*, 59 (1965), 52-63.

43 The tendency of party leaders not to bring legislation to the floor unless they know they have the votes to win is common, as this perceptive comment by the late Congressman Clem Miller of California shows:

> . . . they [the leadership] lead, but they lead only because they win. . . . If they cannot be certain of winning, they don't want to go. Latent power, negative power, is so much better than power committed that lacks victory as a capstone. . . . Hence, the great time lags for the consideration of legislation, stretching into years in many cases, while the leadership waits for the pressure to build—pressure that will produce success.

See Clem Miller, *Member of the House* (New York: Scribner's, 1962), pp. 91-92.

44 Eileen Shanahan, "Nixon and the House," *The New York Times*, July 2, 1969, p. 24.

45 For an excellent analysis of this committee and its relations with the full House of Representatives, see Richard Fenno, *Power of the Purse* (Boston: Little, Brown, 1966).

46 See Nicholas A. Masters, "Committee Assignments in the House of Representatives," *American Political Science Review*, 55 (June 1961), 345-357.

47 Infrequently a junior member may be "bumped" from a committee if his party loses enough seats in the chamber to require changing the party ratio on the committee. Even more rarely members change their party affiliations and are then at the mercy of their new parties for their assignments.

48 See Polsby, Miriam Gallaher, and Barry S. Rundquist, "The Growth of the Seniority System in the U.S. House of Representatives," *American Political Science Review*, 63 (September 1969), 787-806.

49 Barbara Hinckley, *The Seniority System in Congress* (Bloomington: Indiana University Press, 1971); Raymond S. Wolfinger and Joan Heifetz, "Safe Seats, Seniority, and Power in Congress," *American Political Science Review*, 59 (June 1965), 339; and George Goodwin, *The Little Legislatures* (Amherst: University of Massachusetts Press, 1970).

50 "Voting in the House" (March 10, 1969), reprinted in U.S., Congress, House, *Congressional Record*, 91st Cong., 1st sess., 18 March 1969, pp. E2108-2111. Because of some multiple assignments 114 chairmen headed the 21 standing (or full) committees and 141 subcommittees.

51 *Ibid.*, p. E2109. Among these 42 mavericks were 8 of the 21 standing-committee chairmen: Colmer, Mills, Richard Ichord (Mo.), Mendel Rivers (S.C.), John McMillan (S.C.), W. R. Poage (Tex.), George Mahon (Tex.), and Teague.

52 Richard Bolling, *House Out of Order* (New York: Dutton, 1964), p. 241.

53 Williams had been second-ranking Democrat on the Interstate and Foreign Commerce Committee, and the resignation of the committee's chairman later that year meant that without caucus action, Williams would have been chairman. Watson, a freshman, later changed his party affiliation.

54 A review of the Hansen committee's history and deliberations is included in Neal Gregory, "House Democrats Seek to Limit Powers of Chairmen, Senior Members," *National Journal* (January 2, 1971), pp. 16-24.

55 Ahead of Diggs on the committee roster were Thomas Abernathy (Miss.), who was already chairman of a key subcommittee for his district, the Agriculture Subcommittee on Cotton, and John Dowdy (Tex.), who was under federal indictment for bribery.

56 Common Cause, *Report from Washington*, January 1971. The other targets were Rules Chairman William Colmer, "a man who has life or death power over most legislation and has used it to kill important consumer protection and equal employment legislation," and Agriculture Chairman W. R. Poage (Tex.), "who promotes the interests of influential farmers and blocks legislation to feed hungry Americans." Neither of these two was challenged in the caucus, however.

57 U.S., Congress, House, *Congressional Record*, daily ed., 92nd Cong., 1st sess., 4 February 1971, 175, H428-434.

58 Glass, "Mansfield Reforms," p. 501.

59 S. Res. 17, cosponsored by Harris and Charles M. Mathias (R.-Md.), was later reported adversely by the Senate Committee on Rules and Administration.

60 U.S., Congress, Senate, *Congressional Record*, daily ed., 92nd Cong., lst sess., 28 January 1971, 117, S405-406.

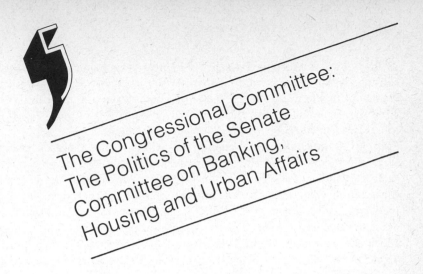

The Congressional Committee:
The Politics of the Senate
Committee on Banking,
Housing and Urban Affairs

Congress is an example of what Robert A. Dahl has called the "coalition of chieftains" leadership pattern: Individuals, each with significant political resources, accommodate one another, despite their various competing interests, in order to achieve integration of policy through negotiation and bargaining.[1] Foremost among the congressional "chieftains" are the chairmen of the standing committees (twenty-one in the House and seventeen in the Senate, plus the Joint Committee on Atomic Energy). With varying styles of leadership and degrees of control, they preside over the congressional subunits that, while technically only creatures of Congress, in reality dominate many of its decisions. The final decisions made on the floor of the House and Senate are frequently ratifications, perhaps with minor modifications, of previous judgments made in the standing committees.

These powerful subsystems of Congress all function differently. Some, like the House Appropriations Committee, operate with minimum internal conflict and effectively serve as arenas for the resolution of conflict.[2] The manner in which the Appropriations Committee does its work also enables its members to exercise considerable influence within the House as a whole. In contrast, the House Education and Labor Committee works in a highly charged atmosphere of partisan and ideological conflict, and its decisions are frequently overturned by the parent chamber.[3] Still other committees, like the House Interior Committee, deal with large volumes of locally oriented and relatively noncontroversial legislation that is considered by committee members important to their reelection.[4] A distinctly different pattern of committee operation is illustrated by the Senate Committee on Government Operations, which lacks significant legislative jurisdiction but has broad investigative authority, which makes it a sought-after assignment for senators interested in developing national issues while gaining maximum publicity for themselves. (For a description of how Senator Abraham Ribicoff, [D.-Conn.,] has exploited the investigative authority of this committee, see Chapter 3.)

Although congressional committees exhibit a wide range of behavior patterns, the functioning of all committees is influenced by a number of common factors including the chairman and his style of leadership, the subcommittee organization, the staff, the committee's recruitment patterns, the degree of member interest in committee work, the members' work orientation, the degree of committee integration, and the configuration of issues and agencies with which the committee deals. These factors have affected the operations of the Senate Committee on Banking, Housing, and Urban Affairs. In the analysis of this committee that follows, particular attention is directed to the manner in which these factors have limited the committee's performance of the oversight function.

An Overview of the Committee

In January 1971 the name of the Senate Committee on Banking and Currency was changed to the Committee on Banking, Housing, and Urban Affairs. This change reflected no alteration in the committee's jurisdiction. Rather, the title now reflects more accurately the actual subject matter of the committee and the topics of greatest concern to its members in recent years. Jurisdiction over urban-oriented programs is scattered among several committees because committee jurisdictions reflect traditional practices, past and present power alignments in the Senate, and the complexity of national issues and federal programs.[5] Nevertheless, the Senate Banking, Housing, and Urban Affairs Committee controls a significant array of urban programs. For example, programs of the Department of Housing and Urban Development for model cities, urban renewal, community facilities, public housing, housing for senior citizens, and low- and moderate-income housing are all referred to the committee. These and other programs (such as Federal Housing Administration mortgage insurance, veterans' housing, and college housing) are the subject of omnibus housing bills that are nearly always controversial because of their impact on sensitive areas of the economy. Urban transportation has also become a major concern of the committee, and it claims jurisdiction over the programs of the Urban Mass Transit Administration in the Department of Transportation.

As the committee's name implies, it also has jurisdiction over legislation dealing with financial institutions. It handles all banking legislation, encompassing the operations of national banks, the Federal Reserve System, the Federal Deposit Insurance Corporation, the Comptroller of the Currency, the Home Loan Bank Board (the federal regulatory agency for savings-and-loan associations), credit unions, the Federal Savings and Loan Insurance Corporation, and the Export-Import Bank. Matters pertaining to the Securities and Exchange Commission and the regulation of the sale of securities also fall within its purview. Small Business Administration (SBA) assistance programs and the depressed-areas programs of the Commerce Department are under the jurisdiction of this committee, as is legislation related to consumer credit, export control, defense production, and the striking of commemorative medals.

The political salience of Banking, Housing, and Urban Affairs' subject matter has fluctuated with economic and political conditions over time and with the forces controlling the committee. During World War II and immediately afterward the committee's activities connected with price and rent controls, government reconversion policy, and the Employment Act of 1946—a landmark in the government's commitment to sustain a prosperous economy—made the committee a center of intense conflicts over the future of the American economy. Also attracting widespread attention were postwar housing bills that were (and continue to be) important in terms of both assisting the housing-construction industry and performing broad social-welfare functions. During the Eisenhower years these housing bills became a central issue in the struggle between the Republican President and the Democratic Congress. In 1959 President Dwight D. Eisenhower twice vetoed major housing bills developed by committee Democrats working with liberal and labor interest groups. As is recounted in Chapter 6, the committee has also been more recently the locus of much of the battle over depressed-areas legislation. Currently community development, model cities, minority enterprise, price and wage controls, and urban mass transit have been among the more salient issues on the committee's agenda.

Because of price control, reconversion policy after World War II and the Korean war, housing and depressed-areas legislation, and defense-production policy during the cold war, the committee was until the mid-1950s a sought-after assignment. More recently, however, the issues under the committee's jurisdiction have been less prominent, reducing the attractiveness of assignment to this committee. The following discussion dramatizes the impact that this decline in attractiveness has had on the committee's operations.

The diminished desirability of the Banking, Housing, and Urban Affairs assignment is reflected in the reduction of its size in 1965 from fifteen to fourteen members, whereas more coveted committees like Commerce, Foreign Relations, and Judiciary were expanded. In 1969, however, the committee was restored to its earlier complement of fifteen members, in order to accommodate the increased number of Republicans serving in the 91st Congress.

The ratio of Democrats to Republicans on the committee has through the years reflected fluctuations in party strength within the Senate itself. Since the 83rd Congress party ratios on Banking, Housing, and Urban Affairs have been as shown in Table 3.[6]

TABLE 3 Party Ratios on the Senate Banking Committee, 1953-1972

Congresses	Party Ratios Democratic	Republican
83rd (1953-1954)	7	8
84th (1955-1956)	8	7
85th (1957-1958)	10	5
86th (1959-1960)	10	5
87th (1961-1962)	10	5
88th (1963-1964)	10	5
89th (1965-1966)	10	4
90th (1967-1968)	9	5
91st (1969-1970)	9	6
92nd (1971-1972)	8	7

The committee has a full complement of subcommittees whose respective jurisdictions cover the range of its activities. In 1961-1962, for example, there were five subcommittees: Housing, International Finance, Production and Stabilization, Securities, and Small Business. In 1963 a sixth, Financial Institutions, was added. Subcommittee chairmanships are awarded on the basis of seniority and interest among majority-party members. From 1961 to 1972 the committee's six senior Democrats each chaired a subcommittee.

The Chairmanship

Most commentaries on Congress emphasize the tremendous power of committee chairmen because they can call meetings and set agendas, appoint subcommittees and fix their party ratios, appoint staff members, refer bills to subcommittees, control committee funds, act as floor managers of committee bills, and make recommendations on appointments to conference committees.[7] Although these powers must be used within the limits that a committee majority will tolerate, challenges to the prerogatives of a chairman are rare and only reluctantly made. The leadership styles of chairmen vary, but they dramatically affect the capacity of committees to perform such legislative functions as oversight, as can be seen in a comparison of the operations of the Senate Banking Committee under the chairmen: J. William Fulbright (D.-Ark.), from 1955 to 1959; A. Willis Robertson (D.-Va.), from 1959 to 1966; and John Sparkman (D.-Ala.), from 1967 to the present.

A "Service Chairman"

When the Democrats regained control of the Senate in 1955, Fulbright assumed the chairmanship of the Banking Committee from Senator Homer Capehart (R.-Ind.). During his brief tenure (1953-1954) Capehart had demonstrated a consuming interest in committee work and had run the committee in a highly centralized manner. Subcommittees existed on paper but had little real power, for major legislative proposals (on housing and defense production) were handled in the full committee, where Capehart was personally in charge. Capehart also personally supervised much of the work of the committee staff.

By contrast, Fulbright's main interests were not with the Banking Committee, but rather with the work of the Foreign Relations Committee where he was the second-ranking Democrat. His method of running the Banking Committee reflected this preoccupation. He was a "service chairman"; that is, he permitted his committee colleagues relatively free rein and normally assisted them whenever possible. For example, under Fulbright each Democratic senator was given a subcommittee chairmanship. Instead of handling major bills in full committee, he permitted each subcommittee chairman an opportunity to assert leadership in shaping legislative proposals within the sphere of his jurisdiction. Thus, Senator Paul Douglas (D.-Ill.) used his Production and Stabilization Subcommittee as a forum to develop support for his depressed-areas bills (proposals for which Fulbright demonstrated no enthusiasm; see Chapter 6).

A further indication of Fulbright's assumption of the service chairman role may be seen in his treatment of the Subcommittee on International Finance. Fulbright himself had initially served as its chairman; when, however, Senator Mike Monroney (D.-Okla.) conceived of the need for an International Development Association as an affiliate of the World Bank, Fulbright surrendered his chairmanship of the subcommittee to Monroney, who was not even a member of the subcommittee. Monroney was allowed to take the initiative in the matter and was given assistance by Fulbright, including the services of a staff man assigned to the subcommittee. In the housing field, Fulbright was quite willing to let the Housing Subcommittee under Senator John Sparkman (D.-Ala.) assume the massive burden of handling the almost annual omnibus bills. He delegated this authority, even though most participants in committee activities believed housing to be the most important and politically rewarding phase of their work because it benefited such a wide array of interests, including the National Association of Home Builders, the National Association of Real Estate Boards, the Mortgage Bankers Association, the U.S. Conference of Mayors-League of Cities, the Americans for Democratic Action, and the AFL-CIO, to name only a few.

Fulbright's decentralized and permissive style of leadership meant that his committee colleagues, particularly the subcommittee chairmen, were able to engage in oversight activities if they wished. It was during that period, for example, that Sparkman's Housing Subcommittee became extremely active in studying the performance of the Housing and Home Finance Agency (HHFA)[8] and in pointing out housing problems. Despite his essentially favorable attitude toward the Federal Reserve Board (FRB) and its policies, Fulbright also showed more willingness than his successor, Senator Robertson, to permit committee members the opportunity to criticize its actions publicly. For example, because there was dissatisfaction regarding FRB policies in the committee in 1958, the chairman authorized a public hearing for the purpose of critically reviewing FRB monetary policies. At this hearing the FRB and its chairman, William McChesney Martin, were subjected to hostile questioning by members of the committee. After the hearing Fulbright commissioned an economist from the Library of Congress to study further the FRB's recent credit policies. The ensuing report was extremely critical and was believed by close observers to have been disturbing to the FRB.[9]

Fulbright further facilitated the activities of the members by making funds available for hearings (including field hearings outside Washington, D.C., like those that Senator Douglas held to mobilize support for a depressed-areas bill) and for travel (for example, to study foreign-lending operations of government agencies abroad). In addition, he both maintained the committee's tradition of employing a well-qualified and able staff and permitted the senior committee members, Capehart, Sparkman, and Douglas, to appoint staff members who would work primarily for them. Fulbright was anxious to keep the staff abreast of administrative developments and readily accepted the suggestion of his chief of staff that the FRB staff present to the committee annually the same report on the projected outlook for the economy that it gave to the Federal Reserve's Open Market Committee.

Since Fulbright's main interests were not with the committee and he operated as described, he was not considered an aggressive leader. He and his committee could, however, be extremely forceful when his interest was aroused. In 1955 he became concerned about the potential dangers of rising stock-market prices and the related policies of government regulatory agencies. After careful preparations by the committee staff Fulbright launched the Stock Market Study of 1955, which thoroughly and aggressively examined and criticized the agencies charged with regulating the stock exchanges.[10] Following the hearings the FRB raised its margin requirements (tightened the credit terms under which stocks can be purchased). Within the committee it was believed that these critical hearings had directly influenced this decision.

This incident was, however, an exception. Mainly Fulbright was a service chairman who kept the facilities of his committee open to the membership, permitting initiative to pass to other members and staff. One member of the committee summarized his chairmanship: "I always thought that Fulbright's main interests were in Foreign Relations. While he was chairman, the committee pretty much ran itself."

A "Minority and Restraining Chairman"

Senator Robertson, by contrast, can be characterized as a "minority and restraining chairman"; that is, his policy preferences put him in a minority position within his committee, and he used his prerogatives as quiet and subtle restraints on its activities. His reputation was that of a mild-mannered man.

Columnists Rowland Evans and Robert Novak described him: "As oligarchs go, Robertson is relatively benign. Though unmistakably a foe of the New Frontier [President John F. Kennedy's legislative program], he has never been as ruthless as some of his fellow southerners in blocking liberal legislation."[11] A staff assistant to a liberal committee member said: "He is an amiable and benevolent chairman who doesn't believe in using his power in an unfair or abusive manner. He's not an obstructionist so much as a drag. He won't obstruct, but he won't help." Because Robertson used his powers and prerogatives to restrain the committee in quiet and seemingly innocuous ways, the members did not consider his actions worth the cost of challenging and possibly alienating him. Senator Joseph Clark (D.-Pa.) explained that in 1964 he did not press for adoption of a change in the rules of the committee that would have limited the powers of the chairman because Robertson took the proposal as a personal affront. Clark did not want to work in an atmosphere of personal antagonism within the committee and so he withdrew the proposed rules changes.

Robertson's restraining influence left a clear mark on the operation of the subcommittees. He continued the eight subcommittees that he had inherited from his predecessor until 1961, when there was a substantial turnover in committee membership and Senator J. Allen Frear (D.-Del.), chairman of the Federal Reserve Subcommittee, was defeated for reelection. In the 1961 organizational meeting of the committee Robertson announced that the subcommittees on Banking and the Federal Reserve were being eliminated and that their work would henceforth be handled in full committee. The reason given for this action was that these were subjects of general interest to the membership, and that therefore, even if they were first considered in subcommittee, the full committee would want to take them up. The committee's work would thus be expedited if the first step in subcommittee were eliminated. Most observers, however, placed a different interpretation on the decision. It was known that both Senators Clark and William Proxmire (D.-Wis.) wanted the chairmanship of the Federal Reserve Subcommittee and that either would undoubtedly have used it as a forum for vigorous criticism of the Federal Reserve Board. Abolition of the subcommittee kept the Federal Reserve sheltered from such criticism and brought Federal Reserve and banking matters under the tight control of Chairman Robertson, a firm supporter of the Board and its policies.

Although it is a commonplace on Capitol Hill that committees carefully guard their jurisdictions, Robertson did not zealously protect that of the Senate Banking Committee. For example, for twelve years after passage of the Legislative Reorganization Act of 1946 the committee had exercised jurisdiction over foreign lending institutions through an informal agreement with the Foreign Relations Committee (which technically had been given the jurisdiction in the act). When Fulbright resigned as Banking Committee chairman in 1959 to assume the chairmanship of Foreign Relations, however, jurisdiction over foreign lending was quietly returned to Foreign Relations. This came as a surprise to certain members, including a senior Republican, and was regretted by the chairman of the International Finance Subcommittee, for it left his subcommittee with no meaningful jurisdiction. None of the members thought that this matter was worth objecting to, however, since foreign lending had traditionally been Fulbright's domain.[12] Nevertheless, the result has been reduction of the committee's power.

Similarly, as chairman, Robertson took pride in his efforts to reduce the cost of government, and his frugality with committee funds had a restrictive impact on the committee. Until finally outvoted in 1963, for example, he successfully prevented expenditure of committee funds for field hearings designed to build support for Douglas' truth-in-lending bill. This measure, which Robertson vigorously opposed, required lenders to disclose full interest rates in any transaction. Robertson also showed reluctance to print staff studies that he thought might be used as supporting evidence in pleas for expanded government housing programs. Similarly, the committee staff was kept small, with the result that few staff men were available for oversight or legislative work.

Such restraints severely limited the capacity of the committee to engage in oversight activities. This was acceptable to the chairman, however, since his concept of the proper function of a committee placed little emphasis on oversight. In his view the purpose of committees was to legislate. A colleague summarized the chairman's attitude by saying that Robertson thought that committees should "not be poking around the agencies and stirring things up." This attitude was illustrated by an incident at the organizational meeting of the committee in 1962, when one member suggested that the committee attempt to persuade the Small Business Administration to correct its administration of an existing program. Robertson replied that if the senator desired to change administrative policy he should introduce a bill. With that the matter was removed from consideration.

A "Consensus Chairman"

Senator Sparkman, who assumed the chairmanship in 1967 after the 1966 primary defeat of Robertson, can be characterized as a "consensus chairman." Sparkman is neither doctrinaire nor dogmatic, but he is skilled in building majorities and muting conflict. A staff assistant has described his guidance of housing legislation in committee executive sessions:

> I've watched him in executive sessions, and he will be there quietly presiding. You almost think he is asleep at times. People will begin to argue and be getting nowhere and be about to take unalterable stands. Then he will start to move. He has the benefit of long experience in the work of the committee and has been through similar arguments before. He will discuss past problems on this issue and possible solutions, and then he will suggest a little for both sides, and the matter will be settled. He is very effective—a real statesman.

In keeping with this consensus style of operation, Sparkman has gained a reputation for fairness in dealing with his committee colleagues. As one Republican put it: "He's a good chairman—not as partisan as some I could mention. He doesn't try to play a partisan angle on everything."

In contrast to Robertson, Sparkman has never been identified with the most conservative elements of the Democratic Party, and he has not attempted to restrain the committee as Robertson did. For almost two decades Sparkman has been the senator most prominently identified with federal housing programs. As chairman he has continued to dominate the work of the committee's most active and politically significant subcommittee, the Subcommittee on Housing and Urban Affairs. While exerting a strong influence in his field of expertise, however, Sparkman has guided the committee with a relatively loose rein, allowing subcommittee chairmen considerable autonomy in their respective operations. The committee has therefore been more active in legislation and in oversight than it was under Robertson. Furthermore, Sparkman's skill in playing the "middleman" and achieving consensus within the committee has meant that in the Senate he is considered a very effective chairman.

Comparison of committee operations under Senators Fulbright, Robertson, and Sparkman further substantiates the Capitol Hill dictum that committee functioning depends heavily upon the chairman's style of leadership. Through his loose control of the committee, Fulbright, the "service chairman," provided an atmosphere conducive to legislative innovation and oversight activities by others; the leadership of Senator Robertson, a "minority and restraining chairman," had exactly the opposite effect; Sparkman's "consensus" style, though not conducive to generating publicity for new causes, does tend to produce compromise legislation with excellent chances of passing the full Senate.

Subcommittees

The different treatment accorded to subcommittees under successive chairmen underscores the findings of George Goodwin that, like its parent committee, subcommittee organization reflects "to a great degree the nature of the chairman—his personality, his political ideology, and his concept of his role"—and that "a conservative chairman will not generally want to see much development of subcommittees."[13] The Banking Committee experience also reveals that, when subcommittees are given prominent roles in policy making and permitted to operate relatively free of restraints from the chairman, they can be extremely active legislative and oversight units. This observation has certainly been true of the Housing Subcommittee, which both Fulbright and Robertson allowed to function virtually as the personal domain of Sparkman. Fulbright had little interest in housing matters and tended to follow Sparkman's leadership (he frequently left his proxy with the Alabama Senator). Robertson, though opposed to the liberal omnibus housing bills emanating from the subcommittee, did not try in a serious way to limit its activities. There were close ties between Sparkman and Robertson, and Sparkman (who normally supported the chair on procedural issues within the committee) was accorded considerably more freedom than was any other subcommittee chairman. A committee majority in favor of more liberal housing legislation than Robertson preferred also buttressed Sparkman's position.

The autonomy of the Housing Subcommittee was also strengthened by the fact that it had more money available than any of the other subcommittees. Financed by special annual resolutions to which there had ceased to be significant opposition, its greater resources enabled it to build up a larger and more specialized staff than any of the others.[14]

The Housing Subcommittee became an active overseer of the Housing and Home Finance Agency, particularly during the later years of the Eisenhower administration, when most of the subcommittee Democrats thought that the agency was unduly restrictive in its administrative practices. It had an aggressive chairman who justified the existence of the subcommittee because of its oversight responsibilities, a majority of its membership firmly committed to expansion of housing programs, a moderate-sized staff, and adequate financing. The subcommittee engaged in studies designed to review agency performance and to point out areas calling for agency action. As the 1960 election approached it also bombarded the public with criticism of HHFA policy. At a lower policy level the subcommittee staff carried a heavy casework load as it checked complaints regarding HHFA actions, ranging from individual home owners' complaints about shoddy construction in FHA-approved homes to criticisms from large interest groups like the National Home Builders and the National Association of Housing and Redevelopment Officials.

While Robertson was chairman, other subcommittees of Banking were never accorded the autonomy of the Housing Subcommittee and never approximated it in extent of oversight activity. All operated under limitations of budget and staff. In addition, unlike Senator Sparkman, the other subcommittee chairmen seldom used their positions to develop their subcommittees into active oversight units. Senator Clark, for example, did not do so because the bulk of his International Finance Subcommittee's jurisdiction had been lost to the Foreign Relations Committee and also because he had no regularly assigned staff assistance. His, therefore, was a virtually meaningless subcommittee. Senator Douglas did not view the function of his Production and Stabilization Subcommittee as being one of oversight. Instead, he considered it a forum useful in agitating for and producing new legislation. Despite the prominent role he played in the enactment of the depressed-areas bill of 1961, therefore, Douglas failed to offer any guidelines to the Area Redevelopment Administration on how the act should be administered. When pointedly asked by his staff whether he wished them to keep a careful eye on the agency's activities, he replied in the negative.

The Committee Staff

When a committee has recruited a sizable and competent staff, which the chairman directs to scrutinize agency activities carefully, even to the extent of knowing more about them than the agency's own staff does, the committee staff can become a valuable source of information for committee members. With committee support it can also actively interject itself into agency policy deliberations, as the staff of the Joint Committee on Atomic Energy has done in Atomic Energy Commission decisions. The Banking Committee staff, however, has not operated under such a mandate. Staff members have not been made to understand that surveillance of agency behavior is expected of them, but feel their prime function to be assisting the processing of legislation.

The impact of the committee's staffing practices on its performance of the oversight function is revealed in a comparison of the functioning of the Housing Subcommittee staff with that of the full committee staff. The Housing Subcommittee has more available staff assistance than any other Banking subcommittee. The subcommittee staff men constitute the core of Senate expertise in housing matters and are the only committee staff personnel instructed to oversee actively agencies under the committee's jurisdiction. As a result, the HHFA has been subjected to greater surveillance than other Banking Committee agencies.[15] Studies prepared by the staff have been used to prod the agency into adopting policies preferred by a majority of the subcommittee. The staff assisted in preparing for hearings that were highly critical of the Eisenhower administration's handling of housing programs. It also acted as a communications link between the HHFA and members of the committee. During the Eisenhower years HHFA officials operated under the assumption that the staff had such excellent sources of information in the agency that there was little that the subcommittee did not know about its activities. The staff continued to be an important information conduit during the Kennedy administration. For example, HHFA took pains to explain its actions and proposals to the staff and relied heavily on the staff to explain the agency's actions to committee members.

Nevertheless, although the Housing Subcommittee staff has engaged in more oversight activity than any other staff personnel of this committee, it was not as active between 1961 and 1969 as it was during the Eisenhower years. In 1961 initiative for developing and pressing for adoption of new programs shifted from the subcommittee to the HHFA. In addition, the staff was reduced (with some key people having moved to administrative jobs). Chairman Sparkman assumed greater responsibility for the work of the Foreign Relations Committee, which left him less time to devote to Housing Subcommittee work.

There was no other specialized staff in the Banking Committee available to oversee the work of the nonhousing agencies under the committee's jurisdiction. As a result, committee review of these agencies was severely restricted. For example, Senator Proxmire, chairman of the Small Business Subcommittee, attempted to oversee the Small Business Administration carefully, but because he had only minimal staff assistance, his activities were limited in both scope and effectiveness.

Although the general orientation of the committee was against staff activity in overseeing administrative agencies, the full committee staff acknowledged a responsibility to "keep up to date" with administrative developments. Staff members believed that they should maintain a high level of professional competence in the subject matter and at the same time be alert for new developments, so that committee senators would not be embarrassingly surprised. They also professed a desire to "cover themselves," that is, to have sufficient information at their fingertips to answer senators' questions on short notice. Staff members also hoped to be able to demonstrate that they had taken appropriate action on any matter likely to cause controversy, so that neither they nor the committee would be accused of administrative mismanagement. Appropriate action, however, frequently meant merely obtaining an agency explanation for any complaint lodged against it by such an organization as the General Accounting Office.

The principal sources of staff information on agency performance were informal contacts within the agencies and complaints received from pressure groups and the constituents of subcommittee members. If there were no complaints about an agency, the staff believed that little could be seriously wrong with its performance.

Despite the Banking Committee staff's desire to "keep up" and "cover itself," its small size and the extensive number of agencies under the committee's jurisdiction forced it to concentrate on those few agencies in which committee members (especially those who controlled staff appointments) had demonstrated interest: the HHFA and, to a much lesser extent, the Small Business Administration.

Committee Recruitment Patterns

A committee's behavior is, of course, affected by the quality of the legislators that it attracts to membership. For example, the tendency of the House Education and Labor Committee to attract both Republican and Democratic congressmen with strong and frequently conflicting ideological commitments has made consensus building extremely difficult. Similarly, the recruitment pattern of the Senate Banking Committee has influenced its capacity to perform legislative oversight. The committee's work has been held back by the fact that the Banking Committee is not considered an attractive assignment. Indeed, it has been difficult to get members to serve on the committee. Senator Clark, a former member of the Democratic Steering Committee, which makes party committee assignments, commented: "When we came to the Steering Committee this year [1963], we couldn't get anybody to volunteer to go on Banking and Currency—it was a vacancy—we had to shanghai young Tom McIntyre (D.-N.H.) and put him there. He wouldn't volunteer." Republicans, too, have not viewed the committee as a good assignment. A senior GOP member has said: "When I came to the Senate, I didn't know much about the committee system and seniority. My whole life was in business. So I asked for Finance and Banking and Currency.... I often wonder why I stay on this Committee, but now that I'm here, I guess I'll stay. I'd hate to lose my seniority."

A more objective measure of the relative lack of appeal of the Banking Committee assignment is provided in Table 4, which records the number of times between 1947 (when the Legislative Reorganization Act took effect) and 1965 that senators switched committee assignments to join Banking or to leave it for some other committee. A record of which committees have had the greatest gains in membership from other committees provides an index of the committees that senators consider the most attractive assignments. Table 4 indicates that Banking had a net membership gain from only three committees.

TABLE 4 Net Membership Gains and Losses of Senate Banking Committee, 1947-1965

Committees Showing a Net Gain in Members from the Banking Committee

Appropriations	+3	Judiciary	+3
Armed Services	+3	Commerce	+2
Foreign Relations	+3	Finance	+1

Committees Showing a New Loss in Members to the Banking Committee

Post Office and Civil Service	−2	Rules and Administration	−2
District of Columbia	−2		

SOURCE: Appropriate volumes of the *Congressional Directory*.

A basic reason for the committee's low appeal has been its subject matter. Although the actions of agencies under its jurisdiction (like the HHFA, the Federal Reserve Board, the Export-Import Bank, the Federal Deposit Insurance Corporation, and the Home Loan Bank Board) have been far-reaching, the committee has not been considered on a par with Appropriations, Armed Services, and Finance in terms of power. Nor has it had the prestige and publicity value of a Foreign Relations assignment.

The composition of the Banking Committee has also affected its attractiveness in the past. Liberal Democrats believed that the committee would not be active as long as Senator Robertson was chairman and tried to avoid it, even though Senator Douglas urged junior Democratic colleagues to request the assignment. The committee has tended to be composed of first-term senators receiving their first assignments: 74 percent of the members appointed from 1947 to 1962 held such initial appointments.[16] As Table 5 demonstrates, the number of initial appointments to the Banking Committee was substantially higher than for the Commerce and Finance Committees, the other two Senate committees dealing with commercial, financial, and monetary matters. Members of Banking had shorter average length of service in the Senate before appointment to the committee than did senators on the other two committees, though not significantly less than that of Commerce Committee members (see Table 5).

TABLE 5 Comparison of Length of Senate Service before Appointment to Committees on Banking, Commerce, and Finance, 1947-1962

	Banking	*Commerce*	*Finance*
Size	15	17	15
Total membership	43	47	38
Average length of service prior to appointment (in years)	1.4	1.5	3.5
Number of initial appointees	32	21	7
Percent of initial appointees	74.4	44.7	18
Number of initial appointees, 1962 membership	14	9	3
Percent of initial appointees, 1962 membership	93.3	52.9	20
Average length of service prior to appointment, 1962 membership (in years)	1.5	1.1	4.2

SOURCE: Appropriate volumes of the *Congressional Directory*.

In addition to a membership with low seniority and therefore little experience in the Senate, the committee has also tended to recruit a substantial number of persons without prior experience in major elective office. Half the committee members during the 87th Congress were in this category, compared with less than one-third for the Senate as a whole or for the Senate exclusive of its Banking members (see Table 6).

TABLE 6 Comparison of the Political Experience of Banking and Currency Members and the U.S. Senate as a Whole, 87th Congress, 1961-1962

	Prior Service in House		Prior Service in Major State or Local Elective Office		Prior Service in Major Elective Office	
	Number	Percentage	Number	Percentage	Number	Percentage
Banking and Currency Committee (16 members)	5	31.3	4	25	8	50
U.S. Senate (105 members)	44	41.9	31	29.5	73	69.5
U.S. Senate, exclusive of Banking and Currency members (89 members)	39	43.8	27	30.3	65	73.03

Data taken from *Congressional Directory*; *Current Biography*; *Congressional Quarterly Weekly Report*, 20 (June 2, 1961), p. 934; 20 (January 12, 1962), p. 53. Percentages in the Banking and Currency Committee and U.S. Senate categories do not add up to 100 because senators are listed both as having served in the House and as having held major state or local office.

Because of this recruitment pattern, at the beginning of each new Congress the committee has normally had many members without training in the committee's work, the folkways of the Senate, or the work load of a high elective official. The number of members prepared and available for demanding committee oversight work has therefore been severely restricted. Of the four senators appointed to the Banking Committee during the 87th Congress, for example, none was sufficiently interested or prepared to use committee resources for oversight work.

Member Interest in Committee Work

The job of a legislator is much more complex than merely deciding how he will vote. More important, he must decide how and where to allocate his scarce and precious resources: time, money, staff, information, goodwill. Ideally, these resources are expended to maximize his opportunities to secure the goals that he has set for himself in the legislative process. As an institution of decentralized authority, the Senate permits each member to choose from a variety of roles and allows considerable freedom in deciding when and how to use his resources. A senator's interests—his "time-choice pattern"—thus become extremely important in explaining his behavior and that of the committees on which he serves.

A senator must automatically accept membership on standing committees, but how interested or involved he becomes depends primarily on his own interpretations of the senatorial role. Most committees have their "formal" members, who remain essentially passive toward committee work, and their active and "efficient" members, who do the real work of the committee.[17] Because Banking is not considered a good assignment, a substantial number of its members remain essentially formal, rather than efficient, members. Some have stayed on the committee only until more desirable assignments have opened up for them. For example, four senators transferred from the committee at the opening of the 92nd Congress in 1971. Edmund S. Muskie (D.-Maine), with twelve years of committee seniority, moved to Foreign Relations; Ernest Hollings (D.-S.C.) and Charles Percy (R.-Ill.) became members of Appropriations; and Harold Hughes (D.-Iowa) joined Armed Services. Between 1947 and 1971 approximately one-third of the members of the Banking Committee transferred to other committees.

Interviews with members and their staffs have indicated that for most members the work of the committee is not a matter of overriding importance. This attitude has contributed to the general lack of oversight activity. The committee has tended to become intensely interested in the activities of agencies under its jurisdiction only in special circumstances like a major scandal (for example, the investigations into the work of the bank-regulatory agencies following disclosures of banking irregularities in Illinois) or controversial administrative developments that generate complaints. (An example of such a situation was the lengthy study of the Export-Import Bank in 1953-1954 that the committee made after it had received complaints that an administrative reorganization of the agency had resulted in a cutback in loans made by the bank.)

Most members, however, have felt that investment of their valuable time, staff, and goodwill to oversee agencies under the committee's jurisdiction has not been worthwhile. Note the following comments from Democratic senators:

> I suppose we should do more in this area [legislative oversight]. But I have so many other irons in the fire that I don't do it. To do anything would probably just be frustrating and would be apt to involve a fight in the committee. I'd prefer not to have that.

> It's hard to expect that people will get very interested in the work of agencies that regulate the economy. It is technical, complicated and dry. . . . Unless a person has background in the field or a special interest, it is not likely he will give it much attention. There are too many other demands on a person's attention—such as subcommittees that are very active—to let a person really get into this field.

Senior members of the Banking Committee, those in the best position to make the committee active in oversight, had often yielded to alternative demands on their time. These members have had important and compelling duties outside this committee. Former chairman Robertson, for example, was an active member of the Appropriations Committee, having served as acting chairman of the time-consuming subcommittee on the Department of Defense and as chairman of the Treasury, Post Office, and Executive Office Subcommittee. Senator Sparkman, the present chairman, is the second-ranking majority member of the prestigious Foreign Relations Committee. In addition, he is a senior member of the Select Committee on Small Business, the Joint Economic Committee, and the Joint Committee on Defense Production. Such outside responsibilities, in conjunction with senior members' lack of compelling interest in committee business, has restricted the committee as an oversight unit.

Work Orientations of the Members

Committee performance of oversight has also been affected by the manner in which members have viewed their committee responsibilities. The members and staff tend to have legislative orientations: they view the function of the committee primarily in terms of processing legislation. This was the attitude of Senator Robertson and most of the subcommittee chairmen. Accordingly, when asked to describe their duties, staff members have spoken primarily in terms of preparing for hearings on bills, making digests of bills, drafting reports, and perhaps suggesting amendments and strategy.

Changes in the laws affecting an agency are certainly one method (and probably the most effective ultimate method) of bringing about changes in administration policy; and exercising some scrutiny of agency operations is usually required before acting upon agency legislation. Indeed, some longtime observers of the committee believe that the major stimulus for interest in agency operations comes from agency requests for new legislative powers or renewals of existing authority. Members and staff frequently have asserted that oversight was most frequently practiced, and certainly most regularized, at hearings on the legislative requests of the agencies.

Because of this legislative orientation and the only periodic need of agencies to seek new legislative authority, members had not necessarily have continuing interest in the workings of existing or newly enacted programs. For example, the committee's 1962 approval of extension of the Defense Production Act was criticized on the grounds that past performance under the act had not been examined with sufficient care. Although Chairman Robertson agreed that committee consideration had been less thorough than was desirable, he offered as an explanation the failure of the administration to send Congress its proposals for renewal of the act until shortly before it was scheduled to expire.[18] The need to renew an agency periodically had thus failed to stimulate continuing interest in its activity.

Committee Integration

As does every social system, committees have to solve the problem of integrating their various components. They must control conflict and organize themselves so that members can reach substantial numbers of their objectives by participating in committee work. Committees characterized by high degrees of integration have been shown to be effective in gaining support for their policy preferences both when legislation reported from the committee is being considered on the floor (as in the example of the House Appropriations Committee)[19] and when dealing with administrative agencies under their jurisdiction (note, for example, the decisive influence that the Joint Committee on Atomic Energy has exerted over the Atomic Energy Commission).[20] Integration is, then, an important ingredient of committee influence.

Committee integration is encouraged by attracting to membership legislators who readily fit into the committee group and who consider the assignment desirable. Such members are apt to remain on the committee for long periods, thereby giving the committee stability and the opportunity to develop informal behavioral norms that will encourage relatively smooth operation. Members recruited under such circumstances are also likely to have an intense interest in the work of the committee. The nature of a committee's subject matter also affects its capacity to meet the problem of integration. For example, a committee dealing with nonideological and nonclass issues is not apt to be wrenched by serious internal splits. Also the integration problem of the appropriations committees is somewhat easier than that of subject-matter committees, partly because they deal with specific dollar amounts to be spent by the government and not directly with the substance of policy. It is therefore possible to work out compromises by splitting budgetary differences mathematically.[21]

Informal behavior norms within a committee may also work for or against committee integration. For example, the House Appropriations Committee has a norm of minimal partisanship under which members are expected to keep their party-motivated behavior to a minimum. The sheer size of the appropriations job, encompassing, as it does, virtually all government agencies, encourages specialization by subcommittees. This is one means of resolving conflict. The committee also has an informal rule requiring that subcommittees present a unified front when reporting bills to the full committee. The committee is then expected to respect the decisions of its subcommittees. Once the full committee has made its decision on a bill, there is a further expectation that committee members will not file minority reports dissenting from the action. Integration is also facilitated because committee members specialize in the work of their own subcommittees and do not interfere with the work of others.

Integration-producing conditions have not been present in the Senate Banking Committee. It has been shown that the committee has not been a highly desirable assignment, that its membership has been unstable and characterized by a high rate of turnover, and that it has not been a consuming interest for most of its members. Furthermore, there has been no conscientious attempt to recruit members whose styles would be readily adaptable to the group. Indeed, in recent years it has included among its members such maverick senators as Proxmire, Douglas, Clark, Jacob Javits, and Charles Goodell.

Nor is the subject matter such that it has stimulated committee unity and compromise. The committee must decide thorny issues: whether or not there will be expansion or even continuation of public housing, how the costs of urban renewal will be shared, whether or not there should be federal rent subsidies for people whose incomes are too high for them to gain admission to public housing, whether or not there should be federal assistance for depressed areas and for mass-transit facilities in metropolitan areas, whether or not creditors must inform customers of the full interest rates being charged. These issues do not readily lend themselves to compromise by devices like splitting budgetary differences. Nor are they the types of issues that are relieved of their controversial impact by falling under the protective banner of national security. Instead, the Banking Committee is responsible for a field in which traditional divisions on domestic policy can easily assert themselves with intensity.

The norm of minimal partisanship has not been practiced in the committee; on the contrary, partisanship has frequently been strong. In the late 1950s the Banking Committee was the battleground for a major partisan conflict: The committee's Democratic majority twice attempted to override a presidential veto of the 1959 housing bill before finally compromising with the

Eisenhower administration on a third bill; and in 1958 and 1959, it passed a "Democratic" depressed-areas bill, actually courting a presidential veto.

The committee also has lacked the norm of strict specialization in subcommittee work and the willingness to accept readily the decisions of its subcommittees. The committee has had its specialists, like Sparkman in housing, but virtually all members have maintained interests outside the domains of their particular subcommittees. For example, practically all have taken part in deliberations on housing legislation, and the decisions of the Housing Subcommittee have been given careful scrutiny in the full committee. At times, important bills have been considered in full committee without having been referred to subcommittees.

Because it deals with issues that are controversial and operates in an environment devoid of norms encouraging integration, the Banking Committee contains well-defined blocs that are normally aligned against one another on issues coming before the committee. This was brought out by interviews conducted in 1962 with committee members, staff, and other close observers. The interviewees were asked with whom they most often worked and which members most frequently worked and voted together in committee. The results are presented in Figure 3, which shows the existence of two blocs—called "liberal" and "conservative"—that can normally be found in opposition to each other. The four senators designated as on the liberal fringe were considered by those interviewed to be less liberal than were the members of the liberal bloc and apt from time to time to side with the Republicans and Chairman Robertson. They were believed, however, to give the committee a liberal majority on most issues, though that majority was never certain. Republicans Capehart, J. Glenn Beall (Md.), and Prescott Bush (R.-Conn.) constituted a category whose members displayed considerable independence and whose votes were frequently in doubt, though they had a tendency to side with the conservatives. Although the committee is a small group, ease of communication has often been lacking among its members; some have been reluctant even to call one another on the telephone. Instead, communication has often been more indirect, with committee and office staff acting as conduits for information or as tools for probing other members' thinking.

Senator Sparkman has been consistently identified as the middleman of the committee, the person who can bridge the gaps and frequently bring differing individuals together. He is acknowledged as a man with considerable influence over his colleagues. Republicans, Democrats, administration officials, and many lobbyists believe that, in order to win in the Banking Committee, it is best to have Sparkman on one's side.

Figure 3 also shows that in their committee behavior neither Democrats nor Republicans were particularly stable in 1962. Neither was considered to have strong leadership: Chairman Robertson was not in a position to lead his more liberal Democratic colleagues; Senator Capehart, the senior Republican, though

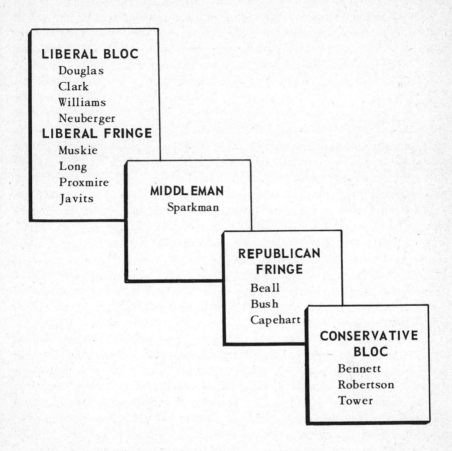

Figure 3
Internal Structure of the Senate Committee on Banking and Currency, 1961-62.

energetic, was not able to act as a strong leader of his party. Senator Javits could not be counted on to vote with the Republicans, and during the later Eisenhower years Capehart himself was at odds with the administration on housing matters and worked actively to override the President's vetoes of two housing bills in 1959.

The Banking Committee has thus lacked the conditions that might make it a well-integrated committee. Its recruitment pattern, subject matter, and lack of integrating norms have frequently split it. Unable to present a united front to either the Senate or the administrative agencies it has sought to influence, when it has engaged in oversight activities, its power has been limited. This, in turn has contributed to its general passivity toward this function.

Conclusion

Although the standing committees of Congress are generally thought to be active and aggressive, our analysis has shown that they can exhibit a quite different behavior pattern of inactivity and passivity.

This is a finding worthy of more than passing interest, because most discussions of the modern Congress stress that legislative oversight has become the most important function of Congress. Other committees, of course, may have very different relationships with the agencies under their respective jurisdictions, and in the future relations between Banking, Housing, and Urban Affairs and the relevant agencies may change as the political and economic significance of agencies and programs shifts with the times. The operations of the committee are likely also to be affected by changes in membership, particularly among those in leadership positions.

Something of the wide range of behavior patterns open to congressional committees has been shown here. The particular pattern of Banking, Housing, and Urban Affairs is but a part of the spectrum of committee operations. Its experience, however, indicates that the following variables have strong impact on how a committee will function: the committee chairman and his style of leadership, subcommittee operations, staff, recruitment patterns, members' interest in committee work, members' work orientations, committee integration, and the structures of the issues and agencies with which the committee must deal.

NOTES FOR CHAPTER 5

1 Robert A. Dahl, *Who Governs? Democracy and Power in an American City* (New Haven: Yale University Press, 1961), pp. 186-187.

2 Fichard F. Fenno, Jr., "The House Appropriations Committee as a Political System: The Problem of Integration," *American Political Science Review*, 56 (June 1962), 310-324.

3 Frank Munger and Fenno, *National Politics and Federal Aid to Education* (Syracuse: Syracuse University Press, 1962), pp. 106-136.

4 For an excellent comparative analysis of committees, see Fenno, "Congressional Committee: A Comparative View" (Paper read at the Annual Meeting of the American Political Science Association, 8-12 September 1970, at Los Angeles).

5 The extent to which urban-oriented issues are scattered among various congressional committees is illustrated by Frederic N. Cleaveland, *Congress and Urban Problems* (Washington, D.C.: Brookings, 1969). The seven issues considered in the book fell within the jurisdiction of six different Senate committees.

6 The analysis that follows deals with the operations of the committee during the late 1950s and the 1960s.

7 The most detailed analysis of a committee chairman's behavior and leadership style is John F. Manley's study of Chairman Wilbur Mills (D.-Ark.) of the House Ways and Means Committee. See Manley, *The Politics of Finance: The House Committee on Ways and Means* (Boston: Little, Brown, 1970), pp. 98-150.

8 Through an executive reorganization in 1966 the HHFA became part of the new Department of Housing and Urban Development.

9 U.S., Congress, Senate, Committee on Banking and Currency, *Federal Reserve and Economic Stability*, 1951-57, 85th Congress, sess., 1958, S. Rept. 2500. [This report was prepared by Asher Achinstein.]

10 U.S., Congress, Senate, Committee on Banking and Currency, *Hearings, Stock Market Study*, 84th Cong., 1st sess., 1955.

11 Rowland Evans and Robert Novak, "Inside Report: Mr. Robertson's Summer," *Washington Post*, July 23, 1963.

12 Robertson also failed to assert the committee's claim to jurisdiction over nominations to the Office of Emergency Planning other than to write a perfunctory letter to Chairman Richard Russell (D.-Ga.) of the Armed Services Committee that successfully claimed jurisdiction. As with the question of jurisdiction over foreign lending institutions, most members did not feel strongly enough about the matter to challenge the chairman. The exchange of letters between Robertson and Russell is reprinted in U.S., Congress, Senate, Committee on Banking and Currency, *Hearings, Defense Production Act Inventories*, 88th Cong., 2d sess., 1964, pp. 42-44.

13 George Goodwin, Jr., "Subcommittees: The Miniature Legislatures of Congress," *American Political Science Review*, 56 (September 1962), 598.

14 During the 87th and 88th Congresses the subcommittee had a staff of seven people, whereas the remaining subcommittees had no more than two staff assistants who normally devoted only part of their time to subcommittee work.

15 Even after the advent of the Kennedy administration, when it was assumed that the new HHFA administrators would be sympathetic to the objectives espoused by a majority of the subcommittee, Sparkman warned the staff to maintain an arm's length relationship with agency personnel and to remember that the staff's first responsibility was to the subcommittee and not the HHFA.

16 This pattern continued into the 92nd Congress (1971-1972). Five (33 percent) of the fifteen committee members were freshmen.

17 Holbert Carroll, *The House of Representatives and Foreign Affairs* (Pittsburgh: University of Pittsburgh Press, 1959), p. 28.

18 U.S., Congress, Senate, *Congressional Record*, 87th Cong., 2d sess., 1962, 108, 11707.

19 Fenno, "The House Appropriations Committee," pp. 313-315.

20 See Harold P. Green and Alan Rosenthal, *Government and the Atom: The Integration of Powers* (New York: Atherton, 1963).

21 Fenno, "The House Appropriations Committee," pp. 312-313.

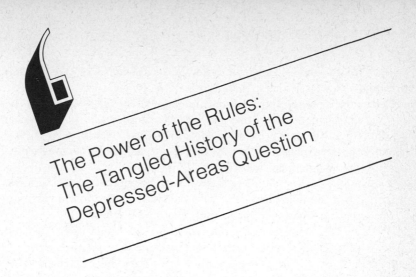

The Power of the Rules:
The Tangled History of the
Depressed-Areas Question

An omnipresent feature of the legislator's environment is the complex set of rules and procedures under which he must operate. Congress is no different from any other elaborate organization in its need for regular procedures, and the U.S. Constitution clearly provides that "each House may determine the rules of its proceedings."[1] In a legislative body rules and procedures are intimately related to the political conflicts among individuals and interests. That is, the rules are not neutral; rather they encourage certain types of actions and discourage others. Mastery of the rules can be a formidable resource in the "legislative struggle" and constitutes part of the influence of a John Stennis (D.-Miss.), a Wilbur Mills (D.-Ark.), or a George Mahon (D.-Tex.).

Some differences between the House and the Senate are reflected in their rules. Both houses have derived their procedures from three sources: *Jefferson's Manual* of parliamentary laws, the rules of each house, and precedents derived from rulings of the chair in each house. The House of Representatives has forty-three complicated rules, supplemented by *Hinds' and Cannon's Precedents*, an eleven-volume compendium of interpretations by various Speakers and chairmen of the Committee of the Whole House. For the average congressman the 500-page synopsis, *Cannon's Procedure in the House of Representatives*, is sufficient for daily needs. The operation of the House is necessarily more complex than sis that of the Senate because of its size. The House has therefore evolved a tight system of procedures that leaves little room for dilatory tactics on the floor. Yet during debate on most bills flexibility is obtained by resolving the House in the Committee of the Whole. With this device debate can actually be regulated by agreement between the managers and the chief opponents of the bill. This procedure will be discussed more fully in this chapter.

In the smaller and more leisurely Senate the rules are simpler and more lenient. The last general revision of its forty rules was completed in 1884. Debate is typically fixed by unanimous consent, and, as in the House, the standard practice is to divide and control time between proponents and opponents of the bill by prior agreement. The Senate cherishes its privilege of free and unfettered debate. Recently the Senate adopted a "rule of germaneness," which directs that debate after the "morning hour" (the daily period before consideration of pending legislation) must be relevant to the business at hand. Attempts at forcing compliance have met with confusion and irritation, and the rule has not so far altered the pace of senatorial business.

Detailed description of congressional rules would be tedious and, for the most part, pointless. (Fortunately for most members and their legislative aides, a telephone call to the Parliamentarian will clarify most entanglements with the rules.) The role of procedures in legislative politics can be illustrated by turning to the history of a specific policy question.

The Area Redevelopment Act of 1961 occupies a special niche in the recent history of public policy: In the Employment Act of 1946 Congress declared it the government's duty "to promote maximum employment, production, and purchasing power." For the next fifteen years little was done to make good this promise, as liberals and conservatives quarreled over how, and even whether, the federal government should intervene to promote high employment. The major battleground proved to be the depressed-areas question. Economic liberals argued that direct aid—in the form of subsidies, training, and rehabilitation—should be given to unemployed people and to the communities where unemployment is concentrated. Conservatives countered that government should limit its efforts to fostering a healthy business climate. It was not until the Kennedy and Johnson administrations of the 1960s that the economic liberals won politically.

In their struggles to provide direct governmental assistance to depressed areas a hard core of legislators from areas of chronic joblessness found themselves pitted against the prevailing influence structure on Capitol Hill, not to mention the relatively conservative Eisenhower administration. During the six years before its passage, therefore, the depressed-areas bill encountered most of the procedural hurdles common to social-welfare legislation of the 1950s and 1960s: what one writer called the "obstacle course on Capitol Hill."[2] In a sense the Area Redevelopment Act serves as a concrete illustration of some of the frustrations of congressional liberals that led to agitation for the rules changes described in Chapters 4 and 8. In a broader sense it demonstrates the role that Congress can play in the gestation of public policy by providing a forum where legislators can struggle, sometimes successfully, to publicize and gain acceptance for their "bright ideas."

When the Area Redevelopment Act was finally passed in 1961, it became the first New Frontier law and the first measure to give concrete substance to the pledge included in the Employment Act. There followed in the 1960s scores of new federal programs designed to enhance the skills, employability, and welfare of those who were encountering difficulty in competing in our economic system. The "war on poverty," whose origins are described in Chapter 7, was one of these programs, all of which owe their form to the debate first outlined in the depressed-areas controversy.

The account here does not include the *whole* story of the enactment of Public Law 87-27; it is simply a synopsis of its legislative history, focusing on congressional rules and procedures.

Committee Referral

The original depressed-areas legislation was hastily introduced in the summer of 1955 by Senator Paul H. Douglas (D.-Ill.). Despite general postwar prosperity, it was apparent that long-term unemployment in certain declining industries and localities was creating persistent "pockets of poverty." This hard-core unemployment was especially visible during periods of economic slack, and during the 1954-1955 recession legislators began prodding the Eisenhower administration to devise a solution for the problem. Douglas, concerned about the plight of southern Illinois' depressed coal regions, introduced a $390 million package proposal for financial and technical aid—including preferential treatment in government contracts, technical assistance, vocational retraining, and loans and grants to help communities lure new industry.

Six months later the Eisenhower administration sponsored a modest $50 million bill. Republican leaders gave lukewarm support to the administration's proposal, but the focal point of discussion during the next six years remained "the Douglas bill," in its various and evolving forms.

A combative liberal with a mercurial temperament, Douglas typified the Senate "outsider." His theory was that he would have influence *on* Congress later, if not *in* it now, and his heroes (their pictures adorned his office walls) were such former legislators as George W. Norris (R.-Nebr.) and Robert M. LaFollette, Sr. (Prog.-Wis.). He was used to having the rules used against him, and when the Area Redevelopment Act became law in 1961 it was the first to bear his name in his twelve years as a senator.

Yet Douglas was strategically positioned to lead the fight for his legislation: In addition to serving as rotating chairman of the Joint Economic Committee (which does not handle legislation), he held a seat on two other Senate committees, Banking and Labor and Public Welfare. As it turned out, the former committee had the best claim to consider the measure, but for several reasons S. 2663 was referred to Labor and Public Welfare. In the Labor Committee Douglas headed his own subcommittee, and committee chairman Lister Hill (D.-Ala.) allowed him free rein. Liberal majorities in both the subcommittee and full committee were favorable and ultimately passed the Douglas bill to the floor with only minor changes. The other claimant for jurisdiction over the measure, the Senate Banking Committee, presented no such bright prospect. Douglas did not have a subcommittee there, and the committee's membership seemed less favorable to "welfare" measures like S. 2663.

It thus seemed merely good politics for Douglas to request and receive referral of his bill to Labor and Public Welfare. On jurisdictional grounds, however, this referral was questionable. On the other side of Capitol Hill, the House Banking and Currency Committee had taken charge of the legislation. Senate Rule XXV declares that the Banking Committee shall have jurisdiction over "financial aid to commerce and industry, other than matters relating to such aid which are specifically assigned to other committees. . . ." It was not long before this rule began to raise trouble for Douglas.

On January 5, 1956, Banking Committee Chairman J. William Fulbright (D.-Ark.) wrote to Hill, warning that his committee would be "compelled to reserve the privilege of requesting an opportunity to consider the bill." The letter apparently went unanswered, and Fulbright refrained from playing his hand until June 28, the day after Hill's committee had reported S. 2663. At that time Fulbright wrote to Majority Leader Lyndon B. Johnson (D.-Tex.) that he intended to ask that the bill be referred to the Banking Committee. At such a late date in the session this action could only kill the bill. "I felt that it was necessary . . . to raise this question," Fulbright explained later, "because I believe it is my duty to protect the jurisdiction of that committee under the rules." Fulbright's real motives, however, lay deeper: As a southerner, he regarded the area redevelopment bill as an effort to preserve "old and worn-out" industrial regions at the expense of such expanding areas as his own state of Arkansas. A jurisdictional dispute could serve as a lever to halt the Douglas bill or at least to force its revision. (Contrast this move with Fulbright's usual attitude toward his committee, as described in Chapter 5.)

Fulbright's move caught the Douglas forces at an inopportune moment. Douglas had just resigned from Labor and Public Welfare to take a long-coveted seat on Finance, and his old subcommittee was no longer active. Furthermore, there was no way to sidestep Fulbright's impeccable parliamentary position so late in the congressional session. Johnson and Hill therefore arranged for Senator John F. Kennedy (D.-Mass.), the ranking member of Douglas' former subcommittee, to bargain with Fulbright. At a series of meetings staff aides hammered out three amendments favoring rural areas of unemployment and designed to render the bill more acceptable to southern senators. The amendments, accepted "reluctantly" by Kennedy during the brief floor debate, were Fulbright's price for dropping his jurisdictional objections. In addition, Fulbright received assurances that his committee would assume jurisdiction over the bill in the future. The deal having been consummated, S. 2263 passed the Senate easily, by a vote of 60 to 30.

This incident illustrates the importance of "the politics of referral and jurisdiction."[3] Most often referral is routine and thus beyond the legislative struggle, but complex or borderline bills may straddle several committee jurisdictions, rendering referral an important tactical consideration. A miscalculation like this one may have costly consequences.

The End-of-Session Squeeze

While Fulbright was exacting his concessions in the Senate, the bill's advocates in the House were waging a hopeless battle against time. At the center of the controversy was the House Rules Committee, which, through exercise of its broad scheduling powers, stands between the legislative committees and the House floor.[4] For a controversial measure that cannot be disposed of by more automatic parliamentary devices, the Rules Committee must grant a "rule" under which the bill is to be considered on the House floor. When a rule is requested by the legislative committee, Rules must first decide whether or not to hold hearings; if it does, it may then vote on whether or not to grant the rule.[5] A negative action by Rules (refusal to schedule hearings or a negative vote on granting a rule) usually serves to kill the bill, because the methods of circumventing the Rules Committee are cumbersome and time-consuming. Under the time pressure at the end of a legislative session, alternative procedures are even more difficult to apply.

As early as June 29 the depressed-areas bill had been reported by the House Banking and Currency Committee, but the Rules Committee, working through the end-of-session logjam, showed no inclination to clear the bill for floor debate. To complicate the situation further, the bill was caught in the cross fire of a feud between Rules and Banking and Currency over housing legislation. At the insistence of the Democratic leadership and friendly Rules members, a hearing was finally held on July 21—six days before adjournment! The committee merely voted to defer action on granting a rule, apparently killing the bill for the 84th Congress.[6]

One last chance for House passage that session remained. As adjournment was imminent, the House was operating under an agreement by which the Speaker would recognize members to move passage of bills under suspension of the rules (such a motion requires a two-thirds vote to pass). According to precedent the Speaker will recognize a member to move the suspension of the rules only with the consent of both the Majority and Minority Leaders. Speaker Sam Rayburn (D.-Tex.) and Majority Leader John McCormack (D.-Mass.) agreed to allow the depressed-areas bill to be called up, but Minority Leader Joseph Martin (R.-Mass.) said that he would have to consult with administration officials "downtown."

The Senate sent S. 2663 to the House early on the afternoon of July 26. The involved process of extracting a definitive answer from the administration occupied the remainder of that day and most of the next. Finally, Representatives Ivor Fenton and James Van Zandt, two Pennsylvania Republicans who had authored depressed-areas bills of their own, were enlisted to help obtain administration approval. It soon became apparent that the White House was leaving the decision to the Commerce Department. Secretary Sinclair Weeks, who was known to be skeptical about the legislation, dispatched Assistant Secretary Frederick H. Mueller to the Capitol to negotiate with Fenton and Van Zandt. After two hours of discussion, during which congressional supporters even offered to substitute the Eisenhower bill, the two Pennsylvanians emerged to inform their colleagues that the administration was opposed to having any bill whatever brought to the floor. In view of the administration's position, there was no hope for last-minute passage of the bill.

This story was repeated publicly by Democrats throughout the 1956 presidential campaign. For their part administration spokesmen never bothered to deny the incident. Running on the slogan of "peace and prosperity," they were content to let the issue ride. Administration officials argued privately, however, that they had been victimized by a trap play: Had they consented to House passage of the President's bill, the Douglas forces would have used the House-Senate conference as a lever to restore the provisions of the original S. 2663, thus driving the administration into an even more awkward position. Needless to say, their suspicions were not without foundation. The lesson of this incident was that the end of the session places a premium on time, especially if the niceties of the rules are to be observed. If the rules are to be sidestepped, there must usually be an interparty comity that is not obtainable when controversial legislation is involved. A special challenge then confronts legislative tacticians.

Power Play in Committee

Early in 1957 Douglas reintroduced the depressed-areas bill as S. 964. This time it was referred to Fulbright's Banking Committee and Douglas' new Production and Stabilization Subcommittee. For more than a year the bill was stalled, confirming the sponsors' original fears about the Banking Committee.[7] (The alignment on the committee at that time is shown in Table 7.) Douglas charged that his subcommittee was "stacked" against him, whereas Fulbright insisted that nothing of the kind had been intended. The only hope lay in bringing the bill to the full committee, which could be done either through an informal agreement with Fulbright or a formal vote of the full committee.

For a time Douglas failed to perceive this latter solution to his dilemma, preferring futile negotiations with Fulbright on dislodging the bill from the subcommittee. These negotiations were perfunctory, for the two men had never been close associates. For his part, Fulbright was still suspicious that the bill would disadvantage the new industrial areas, which depended upon low wages to lure industries from older, heavily unionized areas. Furthermore, he was not generally disposed to favor federal intervention in such problems.

TABLE 7 The Banking Committee Positions on the Douglas Bill, 1957-1958

	Against	For	Doubtful
Subcommittee	Fulbright (D)	Douglas (D)	
	Frear (D)	Sparkman (D)	
	Capehart (R)		
	Bricker (R)		
	Bush (R)		
Total	5	2	0
Full Committee	Robertson (D)	Monroney (D)	Payne (R)
	Bennett (R)	Clark (D)	Beall (R)
		Proxmire (D)	Case (R)
Total	7	5	3

The impasse was broken in early 1958 when Senator Frederick Payne (R.-Maine) let it be known that he favored a compromise. Payne faced a tough reelection fight that fall in a state in which hard-core unemployment in the Saco-Biddeford-Sanford textile region was a major issue. Douglas and Payne quickly reached an accord: Payne would introduce a new bill, which would be substituted in full committee for the Douglas bill. Senators Clifford Case (R.-N.J.) and J. Glenn Beall (R.-Md.) would go along to make the 8 to 7 majority.

On March 11 Payne introduced his bill, S. 3447, in what he called "a sincere effort to compromise the differences between the Douglas and Administration bills. . . ." Beall and Case were cosponsors, along with Senator Margaret Chase Smith (R.-Maine). The bill was, of course, referred to the Banking Committee, and Payne asked Fulbright to schedule S. 3447 for early action by the full committee.

The step of placing Payne's bill on the full committee's agenda was accomplished a week later, when hearings opened on Fulbright's own antirecession measure, the ill-fated community-facilities bill (S. 3497). According to plan, as soon as Fulbright called the meeting to order, Payne moved that the committee go into executive session. Fulbright refused to bring the motion to a vote, and for thirty minutes witnesses waiting to testify were treated to a rare display of verbal fireworks.[8] Payne led off by observing that, in view of the speedy consideration accorded to Fulbright's own bill, the depressed-areas proposal ought to be considered promptly. Fulbright countered by reminding the committee that Douglas was chairman of the subcommittee and "in no way inhibited from holding a meeting of his subcommittee at any time he wants to, and submitting the matter to a vote." Instead, he declared—glaring at Douglas—"you only talk about it."

To this Douglas retorted that he had not dared bring the issue to a vote "in view of the membership . . . selected for that subcommittee by the Senator from

Arkansas." Moreover, he had been trying to negotiate with Fulbright, but the latter's "unyielding determination to kill the bill" had prevented agreement. Fulbright elaborately denied both charges.

An acrimonious free-for-all ensued. Douglas called Fulbright a "deep-freeze artist," and the latter replied that Douglas was "derelict in his duty." Soon the entire committee was hopelessly entangled in parliamentary procedure. Then Payne inquired whether or not his own bill had been referred to a sub-committee. It was discovered that it had not; that is, the bill was still technically before the full committee. Douglas then moved that the bill be declared the "pending order of business" of the full committee. After some further haggling Douglas' motion was adopted 8 to 5.[9]

Having forged a winning coalition in the committee, Douglas and Payne had used a power play to overcome their bill's major obstacle in the Senate. The "clean bill" (a new bill embodying the original bill and the proposed altera-tions)—so favorable to Douglas' goals that he refused to call it a compro-mise—soon cleared the full committee. The unhappy episode in the committee shows that a chairman's prerogatives may border on the arbitrary and that to control the exercise of these prerogatives may require a determined majority willing to risk confrontation. Fulbright could not have been expected to make concessions until Douglas had enough votes in full committee to pass the bill. Once his bipartisan coalition had been fashioned, Douglas could force Fulbright to back down, either through informal agreement or a committee showdown. That the latter course was followed was probably a function of the somewhat tenuous relationship between the two men.

Judge Smith Enters

Once out of the Senate Banking Committee, the Douglas-Payne com-promise readily passed the Senate 46 to 36. The House Banking and Currency Committee trimmed the bill somewhat and reported it on July 1, 1958. This move shifted the arena to the often troublesome House Rules Committee. And, as in 1956, the end-of-session problem began to loom.

With an eye to the fall congressional elections, House Democratic leaders let it be known that they wanted the Douglas-Payne bill brought to the floor. They reasoned that President Eisenhower might be induced to sign the bill as a "bipartisan" solution to the depressed-areas problem. If he vetoed the bill, Democrats would have a ready-made campaign issue. A midyear economic reces-sion added urgency to the situation.

After some delay Rules Chairman Howard W. Smith (D.-Va.) scheduled a hearing, during which his committee forced the bill's sponsors to agree to offer a floor amendment eliminating a direct Treasury-borrowing ("back door financ-ing") provision. (Strongly favored by Douglas and the liberal advocates of the bill, this feature would have allowed the agency to draw authorized funds directly from the Treasury, rather than submitting expenditures through the annual appropriations process. Liberals argued that this device would permit agencies to make long-range financial commitments, but many legislators, especially in the House, considered it a threat to the prerogatives of the appropriations committees.) The Rules Committee forced the deletion of back door financing and then cleared the bill by a 6 to 5 vote on August 7, nearly six weeks after Banking and Currency had reported it.[10] By that time it was late in the session, and under pressure of time Judge Smith's prerogatives might be sufficient to prevent debate. After the vote Smith told reporters that "a rule was ordered reported on the depressed-areas bill." He had three legislative days in which to file his report; then seven more legislative days could elapse before the rule was called up on the floor. If he did neither of these things within the prescribed time, there would be further delays, any of which could be fatal to the bill in the closing days, even hours, of the session.

Because adjournment was set for Labor Day, Representative Daniel Flood (D.-Pa.) led a delegation of congressmen to Smith's Alexandria, Virginia, home. By agreeing to delete a section of the bill providing subsistence allowances for unemployed workers while they were being retrained, the group was able to persuade him to promise that he would report the rule by August 12. Smith was as good as his word, and the Douglas-Payne bill—complete with the amendments that Smith had extracted—passed on a standing vote. On the eve of adjournment the revised bill was sent to the White House.

Even when operating within the confines of the rules such holders of institutional power as Judge Smith have considerable latitude of action. Their prerogatives may be enhanced by a time shortage at the close of each session. As we have seen, a price may then have to be paid to ensure that the rules are meticulously observed.

Calendar Wednesday

President Eisenhower vetoed the Douglas-Payne bill—a move that some commentators held partially responsible for Republican losses in the congressional elections that fall. (Senator Payne himself was defeated for reelection.) Both the administration and the Douglas camp introduced new bills when the 86th Congress convened, and by the end of March the Senate had passed the Douglas version (S. 722). Two months later the House Committee on Banking and Currency reported the bill, which brought it again into the hands of the Rules Committee, where it languished for a full year.

The "depressed-areas congressmen," bolstered by the newly formed liberal Democratic Study Group,[11] attempted to enlist Speaker Rayburn's help in dislodging the bill from Rules. Rayburn had to exercise caution and refrain from expending credit on hopeless legislative ventures. The task of the depressed-areas coalition was to convince the Speaker that the bill was needed in their districts, that it would have favorable consequences for the Democratic Party, and—perhaps most important—that it had enough votes to pass on the House floor. The late Clem Miller (D.-Calif.), then a freshman congressman and an active member of the Democratic Study Group, has provided an engaging account of the confrontation with Rayburn:

> Groups cluster in the big antechamber outside his "official" office just off the floor of the House. Six or eight of us crowd about, ushered into the half of a railway car by his quite correct and unassuming aides. The Speaker is very friendly. The mouth, so down-curved for public ceremony, turns up readily and warmly in private. We range ourselves on the edges of chairs and sofas. The conversation begins all brisk and rapid-fire, about this and that and the other. The Speaker answers easily, and in good humor. His eye flicks over the group. He is a coachman for a poorly harnessed team. When will we begin? As I am the only freshman, he singles me out for special comment. This is simply delightful. Finally, a senior member of the group says, "Now, Mr. Speaker, about the Depressed Areas Bill."
>
> The joviality evaporates. But just as easily as before, the Speaker responds, "When are you boys going to do something about them upstairs?" He gestures towards the ceiling, above which the Rules Committee has its rooms.
>
> "That's what we came to see you about." The Speaker tries another tack. "With everything going well in the country . . . this bill . . . I don't see any great need for it." At once a chorus of anguish. We are ready for him on this. In rapid salvos everyone present, each experienced in the science of telling words, fires off bits—his reasons why this bill is needed now. There is even a scattering of shot—about aircraft shutdowns in Texas. We had received reports of the Speaker's doubts about the urgency of this bill, and to be forewarned is to be forearmed. So many problems of Congress are of such long standing that, many times, the basic issues get clouded with the passage of time. Everyone had presumed that the Speaker knew the facts about the depressed areas legislation. He had heard the story retold over so many years. Actually, his information was out-of-date.
>
> Round the room we went, each adding a fast reappraisal of the need for this legislation.
>
> The Speaker saw this was no group to go through the center with, so he tried his first move again. When were we going to do something with the Democratic members of the Rules Committee? And what could we do, we asked? We were asking the help of the Speaker with the gentlemen upstairs. The ball remained in midfield. The interview limped to a close.
>
> Had there been achievement? Perhaps. Perhaps a fresh understanding by the Speaker of a perplexing national disgrace. Perhaps a word would go out "upstairs." Perhaps he would not put in a fatal

objection should we try something on our own. The question, as always, boiled down to an appraisal—did we have the votes? Yes, the Speaker was interested in the currency of the problem itself. He was interested in the connection between chronically depressed areas and the areas of automation and technological change. But—but, he asked, could we produce the needed votes when and if we got to the Floor?

To this, we had chorused assent. Yes, we had the votes by a wide margin if we could only go to a test.[12]

Rayburn promised help but seemed in no hurry: As Eisenhower had already vetoed a bipartisan bill, there was no reason to press the House for a more liberal measure until the 1960 presidential campaign was closer at hand. It was not until March 1960 that Rayburn induced Smith to hold a hearing; on April 21 the committee turned down the rule by a 6 to 6 vote.[13] (When he had the necessary votes to withhold a rule, Smith was a particularly tenacious opponent.)

The leadership had to settle on a means of circumventing the committee. Of the available alternatives, suspension of the rules (see the earlier section on the end-of-session squeeze) was out of the question because the consent of the Minority Leader, Charles Halleck (R.-Ind.), could not be secured. A more feasible method, the discharge petition, was considered but discarded. Under the rules any committee that refuses to report a piece of legislation may be discharged of its responsibility by a motion signed by a simple majority (218) of the House. If the petition is successful the bill is printed on the Discharge Calendar and taken up on the second and fourth Mondays of each month. House norms discourage discharges, which represent votes of "no confidence" in the committee system. Only two laws in modern times have been enacted via the discharge route.[14] Seven days after the Rules vote, therefore, Majority Leader McCormack notified the House that S. 722 would be brought to the floor under a third procedure, Calendar Wednesday.[15]

In this procedure the names of standing committees are called alphabetically by the clerk each Wednesday. The chairman of a committee desiring immediate action on a bill stalled before Rules may call it up when his committee's name is reached. Action on such a bill must be completed by the end of the calendar day, under a two-hour limit for general debate. This feature of the rule makes users of Calendar Wednesday vulnerable to delaying tactics by the opposition. The procedure is therefore normally dispensed with by unanimous consent, and the most recent use had been ten years before, in 1950.

On Wednesday, May 4, an objection to dispensing with Calendar Wednesday by unanimous consent was to have launched the festivities. But, at 12:02 P.M., when the final "amen" of the chaplain's invocation had hardly been uttered, one of the two "sentries" stationed on the floor by Republicans and southern Democrats opposed to the bill—John C. Davis (D.-Ga.)—raised a point of no quorum, and the quorum bells rang out. Twenty-one minutes were spent calling the roll, and 379 members were found present.[16] Then the Speaker moved that "further proceedings [rounding up all absentees] under the roll call be dispensed with" by unanimous consent. When the anticipated objection was heard from John Bell Williams (D.-Miss.), McCormack moved to dispense with further proceedings and called a "previous question" on his motion. Davis countered by moving to table McCormack's motion of previous question and demanding a roll call. Davis' motion was defeated after a twenty-three minute roll call. Similar roll calls to approve McCormack's two motions (previous question, then the main motion) took another half hour. By this time the House had consumed one hour and thirty-eight minutes in satisfying everyone that a quorum was present.

Rayburn then moved to dispense with reading of the journal—normally a routine means of facilitating business. On that afternoon, however, Davis insisted on a full reading. Members were heard to groan audibly as they disappeared for lunch. Four minutes later Davis, noting that the chamber was emptying, made a point of no quorum. Twenty-two minutes were required to reassemble a quorum, after which the round robin of roll calls began again. Three roll calls were completed. Up to that point the House had spent three hours and fifteen minutes on quorum calls.

The clerk resumed the reading of the journal while members drifted away once more. Twenty minutes later Williams looked around at the empty chairs and raised a point of no quorum. And so it went for most of the afternoon.

In the end Davis and Williams relented and allowed the House to consider the bill. After the journal had been approved Rayburn ordered the call of the committees under the Calendar Wednesday procedure. When the clerk reached Banking and Currency, Chairman Brent Spence (D.-Ky.) called up S. 722 for consideration. Minority Leader Halleck called for a test vote on the bill, demanding a roll call on whether or not the House wanted to consider it. The motion carried comfortably, 221 to 171. With this vote the House was automatically transformed into a Committee of the Whole. This relatively informal procedure has the effect of easing the fight against dilatory tactics, for only 100 members are required for a quorum, and time-consuming roll calls are prohibited. When substantive debate finally commenced at 5:08 P.M., the House had consumed almost four and a half hours in calling the roll twelve times.

Only two hours were devoted to general debate, but even then dilatory tactics were employed by the bill's opponents. When Chairman Spence offered an amendment to substitute a committee-approved $251 million measure for the Senate's $389.5 million bill (S. 722), Congressman James Haley (D.-Fla.) forced a thirty-minute reading of the thirty-two page substitute. When Representative William Widnall (R.-N.J.) offered the administration's $53 million version, it too had to be read verbatim. The committee substitute was accepted, but the Widnall version was rejected by a standing vote of 77 to 152.

As the deliberations proceeded, Halleck and his southern allies closely watched the quorum calls to ascertain their level of strength. As the day dragged on the opposition support dwindled when members drifted away. Because the depressed-areas bill obviously had the necessary votes, its opponents finally relented. Some southerners were prepared to fight on, but the effort seemed futile, especially as it seemed likely that Eisenhower would veto the measure anyway.

The decisive vote—on a motion to recommit the bill to committee—came at 9:30 P.M., and the margin was 223 to 162 against recommittal. The Committee of the Whole then dissolved and reported its decision to the full House so that the House could vote final passage of the bill.

The obstruction of the southern sentries, Davis and Williams, demonstrates the risky nature of Calendar Wednesday, for the rules specify that it can consume no more than a single day. The majority victory in this instance depended not entirely upon the exhaustion of the minority's dilatory weapons; it was also influenced by the deliberate minority decision to relent. Nevertheless, a price must be paid when extraordinary legislative channels are invoked. The price for passing S. 722 under Calendar Wednesday was the time-consuming series of roll calls.

Conference Committee Politics

As predicted, President Eisenhower vetoed the 1960 depressed-areas bill, thus presenting the Democrats with a prime campaign issue. A recession had set in during mid-1960, and the issue of unemployment was salient in the depressed areas of New England, Appalachia, and the Midwest. The new Democratic administration that assumed office in January was committed to the passage of a Douglas-type bill for the relief of such areas. As a senator Kennedy had been cosponsor of area redevelopment legislation from its inception, and his campaign in the West Virginia primary of 1960 had left on him an indelible impression of the joblessness and poverty that he had found there.

The passage of a Douglas-type bill was thus a forgone conclusion. The six-year impasse between a Republican administration and Democratic majorities on Capitol Hill was at an end. Negotiation now focused on several important details of administering the program. Douglas lost several of these skirmishes, the chief one being a fight over where to locate the new agency in the executive structure. Douglas favored creation of a new independent Area Redevelopment Administration (ARA) that would presumably be free of the "vested interests" embodied in the regular departments. He was especially suspicious of the Eisenhower administration's insistence on placing the program in the Commerce Department, for he feared that its "business clientele" would sabotage the program. When the Kennedy administration came out for this alternative, Douglas realized that he was "surrounded" and accepted defeat.

A second major skirmish centered on the perennial issue of back door financing. Douglas had always favored Treasury financing over the customary annual appropriations process in order to permit the agency to make long-range financial commitments. It was not clear, however, what position the administration would take. In fact, two depressed-areas bills introduced in 1961 could claim to have administration "sponsorship." One was Douglas' own bill, which had been recommended by the pre-inaugural Task Force on Unemployment appointed by President-elect Kennedy and chaired by Douglas. This bill had been awarded the honor of being numbered S. 1 and, in accordance with Douglas' thinking, included Treasury financing. The actual administration bill (H.R. 4569), prepared downtown in February, was obligingly introduced by Chairman Spence under his own name. It called for financing by appropriations.

Douglas successfully steered the Treasury-financing provision of S. 1 through the Senate, but the House, always more sensitive to appropriations committees' prerogatives, accepted the Spence bill without even a test vote on the financing issue.

When the two chambers pass different versions of the same bill, a conference must be held to resolve the disparities before the measure can go to the President. Conference politics are as complex as any on Capitol Hill, and are undoubtedly the least understood of all aspects of congressional procedure. Conferences had been involved earlier in the history of depressed-areas legislation, in 1958 and 1960; but an ingenious twist in parliamentary maneuvering made the 1961 conference particularly noteworthy.

White House aides sent word to Chairman Spence that the administration would prefer Treasury financing—an obvious gesture to appease Douglas. Spence, with ill-concealed feeling, remarked to his fellow House conferees that he wished the White House would make up its mind. But Spence remained loyal to the administration's wishes, as did the rest of the House Democratic conferees: Wright Patman (Tex.), Albert Rains (Ala.), and Abraham Multer (N.Y.).

The problem then became how to induce the House to accept Treasury financing. As chairman of the conference, Douglas gave considerable thought to the question and came up with an adroit parliamentary maneuver: Because the House had acted on the legislation more recently, it was the Senate's decision to ask for a conference.[17] The Senate did so, and the House acquiesced. The distinction was important, for, if precedent is to be honored, "a conference report is made first to the house agreeing to the conference," in this instance the House of Representatives.[18] If the House were allowed to pass on the conference report first, it would undoubtedly decline to approve the back door financing feature and send its conferees back to the bargaining table, probably with instructions not to "recede" on that issue.

But *Cleaves' Manual*, which governs conferences, is based on precedent and not on rule. Accordingly, Douglas directed the Legislative Reference Service to prepare a lengthy memorandum outlining his rights as conference chairman and citing relevant precedents. Several precedents were turned up that were at variance with normal practice. Armed with this information and with the consent of the House Democratic conferees, Douglas refused to turn over the conference papers (records) to the House conferees and instead delivered the report directly to the Senate floor, where it was approved.

The House was thus confronted with a take-it-or-leave-it choice: It had to accept the report with Treasury financing, or there would be no bill at all. It chose to pass the bill, 223 to 193; observers estimated that only about twenty-five votes were lost because of the financing provision. But the incident provoked an outburst from Appropriations Chairman Clarence Cannon (D.-Mo.). "What a way to run a business—any business from a peanut stand to a bank," he exclaimed. "And yet that is the way we are running the greatest government on earth. Let us close the back door."

Douglas was very proud of his victory. Along with many liberals, he had long viewed the rules as silent partners of the conservative bloc. Now he felt the weight of the rules on his own side. With a mastery of the rules—and the connivance of relevant individuals—much is possible on Capitol Hill. Without these resources little can be accomplished.

Epilogue

In the end Douglas' master tactical stroke was of doubtful value. In the final bill of the 1961 session, a supplemental appropriations bill, a piqued Cannon and his colleagues wiped out back door financing for the Area Redevelopment Administration simply by appropriating it $170.75 million for fiscal 1962. On September 27 the House debated the bill (P.L. 87-332), approved it, and then adjourned for the year.

Even as the House was acting, the Senate was debating the appropriations bill, and when the senators discovered that the House had adjourned, they were enraged. Even such fiscal conservatives as Everett Dirksen (R.-Ill.) and Karl Mundt (R.-S.D.) decried this "affront to the Senate." "An outrage is being perpetrated on the Senate," Minority Leader Dirksen declared. "Are we a coordinate branch of the legislative establishment, or are we not?" Although the senators sullenly approved the bill, they indicated that the interhouse dispute had not ended. This incident contributed substantially to a spectacular 1962 feud between the House and Senate appropriations committees.

On the other hand, observers noted that the House bill included all the funds that ARA had requested. It was conceded that Douglas' earlier coup may have served the negative function of inducing Cannon to exercise caution in overruling the conferees' decision.

The lesson to be gleaned from this epilogue is that the arenas for legislative maneuvering are numerous and continuous, and that tactical defeats of the moment may be turned into victories in other arenas and at other times. Or, as in this case, a victory may be nullified by subsequent action. In commonplace idiom, "He who laughs last, laughs best."

Conclusions: The Rules and Legislative Politics

The Area Redevelopment Act of 1961 (P.L. 87-27) was signed into law by President Kennedy on May 1, 1961—as the first major legislative accomplishment of the New Frontier. A seven-year struggle for depressed-areas assistance on the part of an unwieldy coalition of liberal legislators, trade unionists, economists, city planners, and farm progressives had thus ended. There are many "nooks and crannies" in the history of P.L. 87-27 that are germane to students of politics. This account has not done justice to this history, for the purpose has been simply to illustrate the role of rules and procedures in legislative politics.

Several themes have recurred throughout this analysis: First, "the rules" have influence over legislative outcomes. They are resources, and mastery of them is a form of power in Congress. Senator Douglas' absence from the Senate floor when southerners speedily referred the 1956 civil rights bill to the Judiciary Committee, a traditional graveyard for such legislation, was an unfortunate miscalculation that resulted in pigeonholing of the bill, within the rules. Douglas' actions as chairman of the 1961 conference committee on the depressed-areas bill, on the other hand, constituted a shrewd use of the rules for his own advantage.

Second, the rules are nevertheless not independent of the power struggle that lies behind them. There is very little that the houses cannot do under the rules, so long as the action is backed up by votes and inclination. Yet votes and inclination are not easily obtained, and the rules persistently challenge the proponents of legislation to demonstrate that they have both resources at their command. There is thus little to prevent obstruction at every turn, except the tacit premise that the business of the house must go on.

Third, the rules cannot always be invoked with impunity. If they are used indiscriminately or flagrantly, there is a risk that they will be redefined and prerogatives taken away or modified. Fulbright was made to recognize this point during the 1958 Banking Committee fight;[19] Judge Smith certainly understood it in the 1958 incident, though repeated flirtations with the marginal extremes of his authority in 1960 led to its redefinition in 1961, when Speaker Rayburn was able to "pack" the Rules Committee.

Finally, a corollary principle is that rules and precedents often develop a life of their own. They may be valued for their own sake and may not be subject to cynical machinations of the moment. There are two reasons. First, routinization itself has value in such a conflict-laden body as a legislature, for it confines conflict and settles many questions that might otherwise be troublesome. Second, a member who breaches the rules today may expect to have them used against him at some future date. It is this ghost that haunts senators when they are confronted with the issue of cloture and that reinforces the congressional folkway of deference to the rules.

NOTES FOR CHAPTER 6

1 Article I, Section 5.

2 For an overview of these policy debates, see James L. Sundquist, *Politics and Policy: The Eisenhower, Kennedy, and Johnson Years* (Washington, D.C.: Brookings, 1968).

3 Another example of referral politics, involving the accelerated public-works bill, is discussed in Chapter 5.

4 For a thorough analysis of the operations of the Rules Committee, see James A. Robinson, *The House Rules Committee* (Indianapolis: Bobbs-Merrill, 1963).

5 The type of rule granted may also have important consequences for the bill's fate on the floor. "Open rules" permit floor amendments; "closed rules" either prohibit them or allow only specialized types of amendments. Some rules waive points of order against bills when there may be some parliamentary objection. In addition, rules typically specify time limits for debate.

6 Votes in the Rules Committee are seldom recorded. It appeared that, had a final vote been recorded, the bill would have lost 5 to 6.

7 For a comprehensive analysis of the Senate Banking Committee, see Chapter 5.

8 Transcripts of hearings, as well as of floor debates, are "revised" by members and their staffs before publication,—ostensibly to clear up grammatical errors but often more extensively. Even the "sanitized" version of this incident makes zesty reading, however. See U.S., Congress, Senate, Committee on Banking and Currency, *Community Facilities Act of 1958*, 85th Cong., 2d sess., 1958, pp. 1-13.

9 Senator Bennett (R.-Utah), who would have voted with the minority, was absent. Senator Frear (D.-Del.) was subject to conflicting pressures and voted "present." The following colloquy illustrates his dilemma:

FREAR: I am in favor of following the rules of the committee. I am in favor of having the chairman . . . exercise the rules. I have no objection, personally, to having the full committee act on the bill of the Senator from Maine but I do not desire to place myself in the position of voting against what the chairman has the authority to do. Nor do I want to vote against the Senator from Illinois [Douglas], because I think he has a right to ask that. I therefore ask I be excused from voting.

ROBERTSON: With all due deference, I do not think the gentleman is correct. I was in the same position. I did not want to go against the chairman, and had no personal feeling, but I voted and I think you should too. You have no personal reason except a little embarrassment.

10 The "usual" liberal-conservative division on the Rules Committee at that time was 6 to 6, with Chairman Smith and Representative William Colmer (D.-Miss.) voting with the four Republicans. On this bill Representative Hugh Scott (R.-Pa.), who was running for the Senate, provided the pivotal vote by voting for a rule. Another "liberal," James Trimble (D.-Ark.), was absent.

11 The Democratic Study Group is discussed in some detail in Chapters 4 and 8.

12 Clem Miller, *Member of the House*, ed. by John W. Baker (New York: Scribner's 1962), pp. 90-91. Reprinted by permission.

13 Representative Scott had moved to the Senate in 1959, and the conservative coalition of Smith, Colmer, and the four other Republicans remained firmly opposed to the bill.

14 The Wage and Hours Act of 1938 and the Federal Pay Raise Act of 1960.

15 Another device for circumventing the Rules Committee, the so-called "21-day rule," was not operative during this period. The rule, first enacted by the Democratic 81st Congress in 1949, provided that, if the Rules Committee reported adversely on a bill or failed to report it favorably within 21 days, the Speaker might recognize the chairman of the legislative committee to call up the bill for House consideration. The rule was repealed in 1951, reinstated in 1965, and again dropped in 1967. A proposed 31-day rule (a 21-day rule with a 10-day waiting period) was defeated in 1971.

16 A quorum of the House is a simple majority, or 218. For the Committee of the Whole, a quorum is only 100—one reason this device is so convenient for substantive debate.

17 "The request for a conference must always be made by the house in possession of the papers." *Cleaves' Manual*, section 3.

18 *Ibid.*, section 35.

19 Fulbright's successor as Banking chairman, A. Willis Robertson (D.-Va.), proved less successful in controlling his committee. His repeated use of the chairman's prerogatives against Douglas' "truth in lending" bill resulted in serious challenges to his authority during the 88th Congress (see Chapter 5).

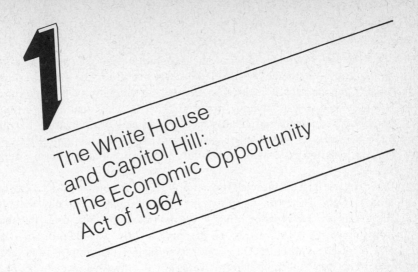

Nine months after his sudden succession to the presidency, Lyndon B. Johnson signed the Economic Opportunity Act of 1964[1]—one of the most controversial of the Great Society programs. Earlier Johnson had declared an unconditional "war on poverty," and now he reemphasized the significance of this decision. "Today for the first time in all the history of the human race," he remarked expansively, "a great nation is able . . . and willing to make a commitment to eradicate poverty among its people."

The Economic Opportunity Act actually consisted of several distinct programs, loosely tied together in the enabling legislation and placed under the aegis of a new agency, the Office of Economic Opportunity (OEO). The act's six substantive titles included several work and training programs for youth and people on relief; self-employment loan programs for marginal farmers and would-be small businessmen; a "domestic Peace Corps" under the name of Volunteers in Service to America (VISTA); and an open-ended program for federal grants to community organizations designed to stimulate and coordinate a variety of local social and welfare services. Few people thought that the first-year price tag of $962.5 million was adequate to relieve that one-fifth of our nation living below the poverty threshold, and more than one economist called the act a "band-aid program."

Few pieces of legislation in recent years, however, have generated more publicity or promised more revolutionary changes in the structure of communities and their social services. The Economic Opportunity Act signaled the elevation of poverty to a major public issue for the first time since the New Deal. "When did poor people ever make the headlines before?" asked the program's first director, R. Sargent Shriver. The emergence of poverty as a public issue was all the more remarkable because it occurred without the goading of a public "crisis" and because it involved a clientele with relatively little political voice. The language of the act also suggested that the poor themselves would be regarded as permanent participants in planning and implementing the programs and not merely as recipients of government largesse. This explosive issue was to threaten existing patterns of community leadership, welfare services, and federal relations.

The original Economic Opportunity Act was notable because it was "legislated" largely within the executive branch and, indeed, virtually without prodding from congressional or other "outside" clienteles. The draft bill that President Johnson sent to Congress on March 16, 1964, was the product of almost a year of discussions and negotiation among high-level administrators and economists. The process culminated in five weeks of intensive work by a special task force headed by Shriver. In this respect the "war on poverty" forms an instructive contrast to the Area Redevelopment Act of 1961, a measure that, though designed for an adjacent policy area, had been initiated and refined largely by Congress (see Chapter 6).

After the war on poverty was launched, however, Congress did not long remain on the sidelines. The idea of giving money to groups organized by or for poor people turned out to be a scandal-prone business; and the militance and disruptive tactics of some poverty warriors appeared threatening to local officials like mayors and councilmen. For their part, senators and representatives turned into anxious kibitzers and critics as they became familiar with the political implications of the antipoverty programs. Congress thus soon began to assume full partnership in the legislation, revising and amending the act in 1966, 1967, 1969, and 1971. As in many of the newer domestic programs, the congressional role was enhanced by the practice of writing authorizations for limited numbers of years and requiring agencies to return to Congress for renewal.

The Economic Opportunity Act thus offers an example of "executive legislation" followed by congressional recovery of initiative. It also illustrates the life cycle of a government policy from birth to maturity (and, some may say, old age).

Rediscovering the "Invisible" Poor

"There is an ugly smell rising from the basement of the stately American mansion," Swedish economist Gunnar Myrdal wrote in 1963, referring to the paradox of poverty within an affluent society.[2] But, though about one-fifth of the nation's population may be classified as impoverished, its plight is strangely invisible to wealthier citizens. General prosperity itself operates to dull concern for the poor. The poor are politically invisible also. They are notorious nonparticipants in politics, tending to vote less often and to join fewer political groups than the nonpoor. Few lobbies therefore work for the interests of impoverished citizens. As John Kenneth Galbraith wrote in 1958, "any politician who speaks for the poor is speaking for a small and also inarticulate minority."[3]

Recent political history had seemed to reinforce Galbraith's point. Although the spectacle of massive unemployment had formed the background for an impressive array of New Deal legislation, poverty had not been a conspicuous political issue in the 1940s and 1950s. Widespread fears of anticipated manpower surpluses following post-World War II demobilization had led in 1946 to passage of the Employment Act, with its goals of high employment, production, and purchasing power. But general prosperity had prevailed during the postwar years, and the act had remained largely unimplemented.

Two developments encouraged the rediscovery of poverty. As we have seen in the instance of depressed areas, it became apparent during the 1950s that certain geographic regions were not sharing in the nation's prosperity. These areas of hard-core unemployment showed up strikingly in the Labor Department's labor-market statistics, especially during periods of general economic slack. The "depressed-areas congressmen," naturally sensitive to these problems, soon became an identifiable bloc and evolved the series of loan and grant proposals described in Chapter 6. Although the intellectual community had been slow to take an interest in problems of poverty, by the early 1960s a growing stream of articles and books had begun to appear—most notably Michael Harrington's *The Other America* and a scholarly study by economist Leon Keyserling.[4]

Another development, more pervasive in its impact, was increasing national preoccupation with the problems of black citizens. Although initially fought in terms of social and political rights, the civil rights issue inevitably led to consideration of poverty. Not all blacks were below the poverty threshold, and not all the impoverished were black. But burgeoning statistics on the race question made it transparently clear that a disproportionate number of blacks were to be found in the ranks of the unskilled, the unemployed, and the poverty-stricken. The riots that broke out in ghettos of northern cities in the mid-1960s were widely interpreted as protests against general deprivation. The race problem was thus gradually recast as the "poverty problem"—a transmutation that somehow seemed to lessen the tensions implicit in racial warfare.

Kennedy and Poverty

The vagaries of politics propelled Kennedy into the West Virginia presidential primary to do battle with Senator Hubert Humphrey in 1960. Kennedy knew of the depressed regions of his native Massachusetts, and in the Senate he had been an early supporter of Senator Paul Douglas' area redevelopment bill. But to this wealthy young Bostonian the first-hand view of poverty in West Virginia was nevertheless a new and jarring experience. Kennedy's political debt to the voters of that state, who had so strategically aided his drive for the presidency, was partially repaid with passage of the Area Redevelopment Act and a regional development program for Appalachia. But the memory of the deprivation that he had seen in West Virginia was never completely erased from Kennedy's mind.

His early economic program emphasized the expansion of overall demand, on the theory that prosperity would reduce hard-core unemployment and alleviate poverty through the creation of new jobs. During 1963 Kennedy and his advisers devoted their attention to a comprehensive tax reduction designed to invigorate the economy further by placing more dollars in the hands of consumers. The tax cut was pending before Congress when Kennedy died, but under pressure from President Johnson it was enacted the following year. As early as May 1963 presidential aide Kenneth O'Donnell was assuring Walter W. Heller, the Minnesota economics professor who was serving as chairman of the President's Council of Economic Advisers, that "the tax cut is going to pass—and pass big. So worry about something else."[5]

Meanwhile, Kennedy was showing interest in the general problem of poverty. As early as December 1962 he asked Heller for copies of several books, including *The Other America*. (Heller never got them back.) He then gave tentative approval to the theme of "widening participation in prosperity" for his 1964 legislative program. In mid-1963 Heller and the council had thus turned their attention from the expansion of demand to programs aimed directly at the poor.

The considerations behind this interest in poverty were both political and intellectual. Kennedy was casting about for new programs for his 1964 legislative package. If a "war against poverty" (Kennedy had used the phrase in the 1960 campaign) proved to have public appeal, it would be an important weapon in his reelection campaign. Such an issue could be especially effective if, as Kennedy hoped, conservative Senator Barry M. Goldwater (Ariz.) were the Republican nominee.

Meanwhile, many liberal economists were expressing dissatisfaction at what they interpreted as the administration's preoccupation with improving the overall "business climate." Such demand-expansion measures as the tax cut, they argued, would aid only those workers prepared to enter the labor market and would not "trickle down" to help the hard-core poor. As Galbraith had written, "growth is only for those who can take advantage of it."

Objectively, the problem of poverty was becoming increasingly stubborn, despite general prosperity, a point especially urged by Robert Lampman, a University of Wisconsin economist serving on the council staff during 1962-1963. According to a memorandum forwarded to the President on May 1, there had occurred "a drastic slowdown in the rate at which the economy is taking people out of poverty." An estimated one-fifth of the population was living below the poverty threshold (defined at first as $3,000 income per family per year but later refined by government economists). This figure represented some improvement over the "submerged third" mentioned by President Franklin D. Roosevelt but was nonetheless alarming in conjunction with overall prosperity.

As Heller expressed it, "This led to some basic soul-searching" by the council during the summer of 1963. How much would the poverty problem yield to a tax cut and full employment? The answer was encouraging up to a point. Projected long-term economic growth, the council staff believed, would reduce poverty at a faster rate than during the 1957-1961 period. But the recognition that many of the poor would be untouched by overall growth led to further queries. What antipoverty measures were already in operation? What lines of action might be proposed for 1964? And what new types of data would be necessary to measure the extent of poverty and the impact of federal programs? Throughout the summer and fall the council generated a flurry of papers on these questions, drawing upon the White House and Budget Bureau staffs when necessary.

In early November Heller issued a formal request to members of the "domestic Cabinet"[6] in order to generate program suggestions. Departments and agencies were asked to examine their existing programs to suggest new programs or redirections of old ones, and to estimate the additional funding or reorganization that would be necessary. The agencies were to range widely in suggesting a framework for a program variously termed "human conservation and development," "access to opportunity," and "attack on poverty."

"When a President wants a 'new' program," Nelson W. Polsby has written, "desk drawers fly open all over Washington. Pet schemes are constantly being fished out, dusted off, and tried out on political leaders."[7] Although the council had intended to report back to the White House in short order, by mid-November it was inundated with proposals from the agencies, including a 150-page document from the Labor Department. The Bureau of the Budget was called in to process and evaluate these papers, an operation similar to its normal annual budgetary review. Predictably, each agency was preoccupied with its own bailiwick: Labor with training and employment, HEW with health and welfare, Agriculture with rural development, and so on. But the sheer number of ideas (more than 100 distinct proposals) was impressive. As one staff aide put it, "they snowed us under with an agenda for social programs which would keep Congress busy for a decade."

The size of the task made it unlikely that the council and the bureau could submit a definitive report by Thanksgiving, but time was short. Proposals for new legislation could be delayed until early 1964, but any references to a poverty program in the President's mid-January budget message or Economic Report would have to have White House clearance sometime in December. Heller needed a definite commitment from the President. Before departing with the Cabinet for a trip to Japan he had a hurried interview with Kennedy and asked whether or not work should go forward on the assumption that an antipoverty measure would be included in the 1964 legislative agenda. Kennedy's answer was immediate: "Yes, and let me see your proposals in a couple of weeks." The interview was on November 19, as Heller and the Cabinet departed for Japan and Kennedy for Dallas.

Three days later a Budget Bureau group was meeting to continue its evaluation of the departmental proposals when news of Kennedy's assassination reached Washington. Having no heart for further discussion, the group silently drifted out of the conference room. Like most other governmental affairs on that November 22, the poverty program was suspended, awaiting the instructions of the new Chief Executive.

Johnson Declares War on Poverty

Any doubts about the new President's interest in the poverty question were soon removed. On the evening of November 23—the Cabinet members had turned back from their trip in mid-flight—Heller briefed Johnson on the current work of the council. When the pending antipoverty program was mentioned Johnson responded quickly: "That's my kind of program. It will help people. I want you to move full speed ahead on it."

Spurred by this assurance, the council embarked on what Heller described as "a most intensive period of hammering the program into shape." In mid-December a section on poverty was inserted in the President's Economic Report and a "line item" of $500 million included in the draft budget for fiscal 1965. The council-bureau task force had, however, temporarily no specific legislative proposal. Limited by time and preoccupied with their own policy concerns, the departments and agencies had proposed only limited-purpose programs for their own areas. Many of the suggestions appeared to have merit, but, with only half a million dollars in new funds, which programs should be recommended? And, even if the best suggestions could be pulled out, would they constitute an integrated war on poverty?

At this point a Budget Bureau official hit on the idea of a limited number of general-purpose grants to help localities develop their own community-wide poverty programs. The idea of this Community Action Program (as it came to be known) had actually originated in the 1950s as a means of dealing with juvenile delinquency through concerted action in deteriorated neighborhoods. The Ford Foundation had supported broad-based community organizations in the "gray areas" of several northern cities; and President Kennedy's Commission on Juvenile Delinquency and Youth Crime, created in 1961 in the Justice Department, had sponsored a limited program of demonstration grants aimed at developing neighborhood attacks on juvenile delinquency. It was the latter program that intrigued the Budget Bureau official, who immediately asked a staff member of the President's Commission on Juvenile Delinquency to prepare papers on how the concept might be applied to the poverty question.

Others in the task force bought this idea, and it soon became the keystone for the evolving poverty program. By December 17 an initial proposal had been transmitted to the White House and various Cabinet members. The key element in a realistic attack on poverty was to be a series of grants aimed at local poverty areas and relying on organized local initiative; in the words of a Labor Department aide, "a pot of money which local people could ask for."

The community-action concept was attractive for at least two reasons. First, it was a way to experiment on the poverty problem with limited funds and within the traditional framework of "grass-roots initiative." Second, it suggested a new way of coordinating and funding federal programs: Multipurpose grants to community organizations could bypass agency jurisdictions and avoid duplicating federal programs and personnel at the local level. These grants could be used for a variety of purposes suggested by local officials; educational upgrading, job-creation and work-training, health services, consumer counseling, and urban renewal and public housing.

The departments and agencies were not happy with this solution. It was true that much of the $500 million allocated for the community-action programs would eventually be spent through existing federal programs. And, to boost the new programs to a "really dramatic" figure of $1 billion, the council was proposing that an extra amount of up to $625 million be reallocated to the war on poverty from the agencies' current budget requests. The agencies, however, wanted to retain control of their own funds and programs, and the intervention of a poverty council posed a threat to their autonomy. Moreover, most agencies thought that their own proposals had gotten short shrift from the task force. One official who was not happy with his own department's contributions remarked wearily, "We didn't come up with anything very useful, and what we proposed wasn't accepted."

The agencies thus exhibited a certain ambivalence toward the war on poverty: They wanted to be included, but they feared that their own programs would be submerged in the new arrangement. The Labor Department, for example, wanted more emphasis on youth employment but thought that too much emphasis might jeopardize the prospects for its own youth-employment opportunities bill, then pending before Congress. The Department of Agriculture was interested in developing local leadership in rural poverty programs, and Commerce thought that the role of local business leaders had been inadequately stressed. HEW feared that local community-action agencies might bypass the department's important clientele groups, the state and national federations of teachers and social workers. Spokesmen for Interior protested that their Bureau of Indian Affairs was also in the poverty business and should be included.

These differences came to the surface during a White House meeting on January 23, 1964, to discuss a draft bill that the council had asked Health, Education, and Welfare to prepare. Labor Secretary W. Willard Wirtz bitterly attacked Heller over the entire proposal. He reasoned that the bill would elevate local educators and welfare workers, for whom HEW serves as the natural spokesman within the federal government. At the same time Labor's traditional interest in minimum wages, job training, and employment would, he thought, be difficult to emphasize within the community-action framework. Wirtz was able to couch his argument in general terms that Heller, Budget Director Kermit Gordon, and other officials found difficult to counter. He therefore had support when he argued that the proposal be "broadened out" to an essential expansion and redirection of existing federal activities to be administered by existing agencies.

The January 23 meeting showed that a stalemate was threatening the war on poverty even before it began. The task force had the general support of the White House, but short of direct presidential intervention it was clear that the two participating staff agencies could not force a resolution of the conflict. The Council of Economic Advisers and Budget Bureau staffs had long assumed that a "poverty czar," with a strong personality and direct access to the President would be necessary to coordinate the legislation once it had been enacted. This person, whoever he might turn out to be, would be needed sooner than anyone had anticipated.

The Shriver Task Force

On February 1 President Johnson announced that Peace Corps Director R. Sargent Shriver would lead the assault on poverty. Shriver's first job would be to hammer out the administration's antipoverty legislation. The reasons for the President's choice were not hard to fathom: A businessman, a school-board chairman in Chicago, and brother-in-law of the late President, Shriver had gained a reputation as a strong and innovative administrator since joining the New Frontier in 1961. In guiding the Peace Corps he had demonstrated acute political sense and an ability to charm conservative congressmen.

Shriver lost no time in starting to fashion the final bill. On the same day his appointment was announced in the newspapers he summoned a small group to his office to brief him on the work of the preceding four months. Two days later he convened a full-scale meeting of departmental representatives, personal associates, and a few nongovernmental observers.

At this meeting there was a reenactment of the conflict that had stalemated the task force proposal. In opening the session, Heller presented an hour-long report of the work to date, devoting most of his time to the community-action concept. Secretary Wirtz followed with a half-hour statement attacking both Heller and the task force proposal. The war on poverty, he declared, could hardly be fought with a single weapon in only a few "demonstration" areas across the country. More jobs were what was needed, for job scarcity caused unemployment that in turn produced poverty.

As the discussion went around the table, it became obvious that Wirtz' notion of a broad-based and multifaceted war on poverty had many supporters.

Spokesmen for departments whose proposals had been pushed aside in favor of the community-action concept expressed their unwillingness to wait another fiscal year before funding their program ideas. Shriver, acting as referee, presently indicated his view that the poverty program should have a scope and glamour equal to the concept of the war on poverty that was being sold to the public through the communications media.

When the meeting adjourned the notion that the war would be limited to a few community-action programs on a pilot basis had been completely destroyed. Clearly, the new poverty bill would be a "package" of several legislative proposals, some of which were already before Congress.

For the next five weeks a Shriver task force, working out of the Peace Corps Building, shaped the contents of this legislative package. The group had no legal status, and its staff members were either volunteers or on loan from their departments or agencies. Office expenses were covered from the White House contingency fund. The group used stationery emblazoned with "War on Poverty." Even after the administration's bill had been put together and sent to Capitol Hill, the task force continued in existence many months to plan for implementing the law. Finally, in August 1964, the remnants of the group were merged into the new Office of Economic Opportunity.

The task force was an extremely fluid group and consisted of many types of people. Representatives were detailed by their departments and agencies to work with the task force, focusing their attention particularly on matters of interest to their agencies. Not all were physically situated in the Peace Corps offices, where Shriver continued as director, and scores of others from various agencies were drawn in at various times to assist with certain sections of the bill. Another group, consisting of Shriver's personal friends and associates, was even more amorphous: in Shriver's words, "the kind of people you like to bat an idea against." A stream of businessmen, mayors, professors, and local welfare officials came to Washington to offer suggestions.

The Shriver task force represented a legislative work group nearly unique within the executive branch; its general structure is outlined in Figure 4. Generalists like Christopher Weeks of the Budget Bureau and Hyman Bookbinder of the Commerce Department provided overall coordination and kibitzing. Three intellectuals attached to the task force—Harrington, author Paul Jacobs, and Frank Mankiewicz of the Peace Corps—made no specific contribution to the act but explored long-range problems and produced a series of "philosophic memos" for Shriver. Decisions were reviewed by Shriver and Adam Yarmolinsky, a special assistant to the Secretary of Defense who was on loan to serve as Shriver's alter ego and chief of staff. Several major departmental disputes were referred to the President himself. About a week after the task force had begun its work, a legal drafting team was mobilized. This group, headed by Assistant Attorney General Norbert Schlei, was able to resolve a number of minor issues by consulting and mediating among the experts on the task force.

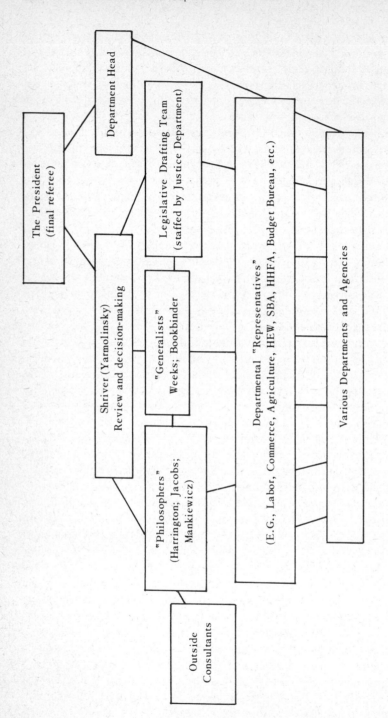

Figure 4
The Shriver Task Force: A "Legislative" Work Group in the Executive Branch.

Because Shriver wanted a broad-gauged and spectacular package, the task force recanvassed the agencies for suggestions, plowing over much of the ground covered earlier by the council-bureau group. Several pending administration bills were woven into the new legislation. The Job Corps camps and work-training programs in Title I, for example, had previously been embodied in the youth-employment opportunities bill, which had been passed by the Senate and reported by the appropriate House committee before languishing in the House Rules Committee. Another Title I provision, work-study programs for college students, had been considered but was dropped with the other National Defense Education Act amendments in 1963. The domestic Peace Corps, which naturally interested Shriver, had previously been proposed by the administration as the National Service Corps. In selecting such programs Shriver was alert to ideas that could be sold to Congress and the public and would yield visible results in a relatively short time.

The resulting legislative package therefore in no real sense originated with the Shriver task force, though the combination of these proposals was a feat of considerable political artistry. Without exception, the act's components had "been around" or "in the air" for some time.[8] The Job Corps had been proposed as the Youth Conservation Corps as early as 1959 by Senator Hubert Humphrey (D.-Minn.), who had in turn drawn on the Civilian Conservation Corps of the 1930s for inspiration. Not all the proposals had such lengthy antecedents, but with one exception they had all previously undergone some gestation on Capitol Hill. The single exception—the community-action agencies, with their "maximum feasible participation" clause—was to prove crucial indeed.

Many liberals distrusted Shriver's approach as too conventional, too parsimonious, or too permeated with middle-class values. Shriver continually emphasized that the bill would provide training and rehabilitation but not relief. "Let me tell you," he said to a reporter, "I'm not at all interested in running a handout program, or a leaf-raking program, or a 'something for nothing' program. I don't know what we're going to come up with, but when we do, it will be a practical program."[9] Outside economists criticized the task force for producing merely conventional federal services. Within the task force the three "philosophers" were equally critical. Harrington told Shriver that the program was "nickels and dimes" compared to the immensity of the problem. Staring in disbelief, Shriver answered: "Mr. Harrington, perhaps you've spent a billion dollars before, but this is my first time around." To his left-wing critics, Shriver had a stock response: "I don't want anybody to get the idea that [with this bill] we're going to cure the poverty problem in this country. Nobody thinks that. But we can do something."

Explicit attention was devoted to outside clienteles, for one of the task force's functions was to consult and win over numbers of businessmen, economists, local officials, and welfare workers. The working group was often forced to halt whatever it was doing to receive out-of-town visitors summoned by

Shriver. A few useful ideas were obtained in this way, but the main purpose was to make the visitors think that they had participated in the evolution of a practical and far-reaching piece of legislation. When the final draft bill was unveiled the White House released a list of 137 names, described as "a partial list of people Mr. Shriver has consulted in developing the poverty program." Shriver was especially proud of having consulted more than thirty business and farm leaders. ("Wait 'til I show them the list of businessmen who've helped us with this program," he remarked on the eve of the House hearings.)

In addition to screening a vast number of existing proposals, the task force was called upon to resolve several major conflicts. The first was over the importance to give to the community-action programs, which had been at the heart of the earlier bill. Many people believed them to be the only unique product of the poverty discussions—a sentiment not confined to the council or Budget Bureau. Shriver did not share their enthusiasm, preferring instead a limited number of specific-purpose programs. On the urging of people in the Budget Bureau and the Juvenile Delinquency Commission, however, Attorney General Robert Kennedy, who had taken an interest in the juvenile-delinquency approach, spoke to Shriver and persuaded him to emphasize the community-action programs as Title II of the new bill. No less than $315 million was allocated for them.

The task force also inserted the stipulation that community programs should be "developed, conducted, and administered with the maximum feasible participation of residents of the area and members of the groups served." Staff people from the President's Commission on Juvenile Delinquency proposed this wording in the clear understanding that it might serve as a wedge to pry loose existing local power structures. To most members of the task force, however, the provision simply permitted inclusion of black leaders in the planning of anti-poverty campaigns in southern communities. Whatever the motivations, the task force accepted the provision casually, few members recognizing its implication that the poor themselves were to participate in decision making.

The task force spent some time drawing up detailed specifications for the community-action programs, on the assumption that Congress would be reluctant to approve such a large amount of money for unspecified purposes. But the various welfare groups soon began jockeying to obtain high priorities for their own programs. There were too many claimants for the funds available. Finally, the legal-drafting team decided to resolve the issue by removing all the specifications from Title II. The lawyers were unhappy about this legal untidiness, but as it turned out Congress did not notice the omission.

Conflicts over administration of the legislation were not so subtle. Once it became inevitable that a special agency (presumably under Shriver's direction) would coordinate and administer portions of the package, the main question was which, if any, programs would be assigned to existing agencies. The Labor Department was most vocal on this issue; Secretary Wirtz held that the war on poverty should be implemented and coordinated through established agencies.

At the very least, Wirtz hoped to administer the youth-employment and work-experience programs himself. He had an established claim to the former, including the Job Corps, in the pending youth-employment bill.

Shriver himself decided to locate the Job Corps in the new Office of Economic Opportunity and to give the Neighborhood Youth Corps to the Labor Department in exchange. Apparently attracted by the potential glamour of the Job Corps camps, he determined to run them himself, along with the community-action programs and the domestic Peace Corps (VISTA). Wirtz was unhappy with this solution, and the final decision was referred to the President, who stood behind Shriver. It was informally agreed that other programs would be delegated to the relevant agencies under vaguely defined supervision by the new poverty office.[10]

If it were decided that the poverty office would have operating as well as supervisory functions, there would remain the question of whether it would be independent or part of the Executive Office of the President. Shriver opted for the latter alternative on the reasonable theory that he would need the weight of the presidential office to coordinate the activities of other departments and agencies. Budget Bureau canons, however, hold that operating and staff agencies should be separated, only the latter being located in the Executive Office. Again the final decision was taken to the President, who once more ruled in Shriver's favor.

On March 16 the President transmitted to Capitol Hill the draft bill for the Economic Opportunity Act, along with a message urging "total victory" in the war against poverty. He announced that he proposed to appoint Shriver "my personal Chief of Staff in the war" as head of the proposed Office of Economic Opportunity. In less than a year's time, the executive branch had launched a major domestic policy departure, in the virtual absence initially of expressed outside interest. It had canvassed the technical constituencies represented by the various federal welfare agencies and had endeavored to consult such external clienteles as local officials, social-welfare groups, businessmen, community developers, and the academic community. And it had combined a number of specific-purpose programs in a legislative package designed to draw support from most of the groups currently engaged in social-welfare activities. Finally, the administration had endeavored to sell the program as responsible and consistent with American traditions of local initiative, voluntarism, and self-help. The public appeared to be enthusiastic. It remained to see how Congress would react to such an initiative.

Congress Acquiesces

The process of shaping the poverty package was legislative in character, though executive in locus. Congress was thus asked not to draft a war on poverty but rather to ratify a fully prepared administration program; it was invited, though hardly encouraged, to propose marginal changes.

The Johnson administration constructed a favorable setting for the passage of this legislation. Shortly after assuming office, Johnson had begun to cultivate the image of frugality when he asked Defense Secretary Robert S. McNamara to cut defense-production costs, called for an overall curb on federal jobs, and underscored his point by personally turning out lights in the White House. He encouraged the notion that these savings might be used for social-welfare legislation. In announcing a billion-dollar slash in the defense budget late in 1963, for example, he suggested that the move would pay for the initial year of the war on poverty. Johnson told reporters that this program would cause a "redistribution in wealth," which would "come from those who have it to those who don't have it." Congressional constituencies were reminded of their stakes in the poverty program. Meanwhile, the administration dangled the prospect of forthcoming funds before mayors and other local officials.

Potential opponents had little time to gather their forces. Congressional hearings were launched on March 17, the day after the administration's draft bill (H.R. 10440) had been introduced. Major attention was focused on the House, where the most strenuous opposition was expected. Representative Adam Clayton Powell (D.-N.Y.), chairman of the Committee on Education and Labor, quickly named an ad hoc Subcommittee on Poverty, with himself as chairman, to hear testimony. Powell took an active interest in the bill, though he agreed to the administration's tactical suggestion that a respected southern moderate, Representative Phil M. Landrum (D.-Ga.), serve as the bill's principal sponsor.

The hearings were designed to advertise broad support for the poverty bill. Shriver appeared as the lead-off witness to outline the program; he described it as responsible, comprehensive, and the product of many individuals and groups. Then Heller presented the Council of Economic Advisers' statistics on the extent of the problem. Like Shriver, he stressed the program's self-help features, arguing that they would permit individuals to "earn" their way out of poverty. For the next two weeks the administration's top brass—the Secretaries of Defense, Labor, Commerce, Agriculture, Interior, and Health, Education, and Welfare; the Attorney General; and the administrators of the Housing and Home Finance Agency and the Small Business Administration—appeared before the committee to amplify the arguments for each provision. Later, spokesmen for an impressive range of civic, welfare, and religious groups appeared to endorse the bill. AFL-CIO President George Meany and the National Urban League's executive director, Whitney Young, Jr., led off, followed by representatives of such groups as the National Council of Churches, the National Catholic Welfare Council, the National Education Association, the American Public Welfare Association, the National Farmers Union, the National Grange, the American Friends Service Committee, and the General Federation of Women's Clubs. The administration also procured five mayors, five governors, and several local welfare officials to testify on the bill's behalf. Of the 139 "advisers" to the Shriver task force, no fewer than 33 appeared or filed statements with the House committee.

TABLE 8 Primary* Witnesses in the House Hearings on the Economic Opportunity Act of 1964

Category	Favored	Opposed	Advisory-No Opinion
Executive branch	12	0	2
State and local officials	14	0	1
Business groups	0	3	–
Business individuals	3	0	–
Labor groups	2	0	–
Religious and welfare groups	14	0	–
Farm groups	5	1	–
Scholars	3	3	–
Members of Congress	3	2	1
Totals	56	9	4

* Only the "primary" spokesman for each group or agency was counted. Secondary, advisory, and back-up witnesses were excluded.

The bill's opponents were hopelessly outnumbered in the hearings, as the figures in Table 8 demonstrate. Of the sixty-nine witnesses who appeared during the twenty days of House hearings only nine opposed the bill. Four of them were from groups traditionally opposed to government spending on social welfare: the U.S. Chamber of Commerce, the National Association of Manufacturers, the American Farm Bureau Federation, and a state manufacturers' association.

The pace of the hearings was accelerated by Powell and the two ranking subcommittee members, Landrum and Carl Perkins (D.-Ky.). Republicans complained that the sessions were scheduled at irregular hours and without proper notice and that members were being gaveled down before finishing their questioning of witnesses. One morning the Republicans were able to call as witnesses a group of statistical experts from the Labor Department and Census Bureau, in an effort to show the need for further study of the nature and extent of poverty. Powell's gavel became so heavy that protests of being "stampeded" came from Representatives Peter Frelinghuysen (R.-N.J.) and Charles Goodell (R.-N.Y.). "I am the chairman," Powell retorted. "I will run this committee as I desire."[11]

Committee Republicans probed for breaches in the administration's defenses, and several promising issues developed. Obvious targets were the bill's unique administrative arrangement and the broad authorization under Title II. Frelinghuysen, the ranking Republican on the full committee, asserted that OEO would be resented by existing agency heads and would duplicate their programs. Obviously feeling for a sensitive nerve, Frelinghuysen and others pursued the point vigorously, asking several Cabinet members their reactions to becoming subordinates to a "poverty czar." Even Labor Secretary Wirtz replied blandly that "I do not think of it in terms of any diminution or enlargement of the power in the department."[12] One by one Cabinet members pledged support for the new arrangement.

Another line of attack involved states' rights and the future of the American federal system. The Republicans noted that the poverty program would bypass the states and create new functional relationships between the federal government and public and private entities in communities. Fearing that poverty projects and the potential patronage that they embodied might be used to undermine the position of an incumbent governor (especially if he were a Republican), some congressmen argued that governors should at least have some review powers over projects in their own states. Because of the obvious relevance of the war on poverty to disadvantaged blacks, the bill also stirred traditional states' rights concerns. More broadly, Republicans charged that the bill was unnecessary; that inflation, not welfare, was the prime problem; and that in any event more research into the question was needed.

On April 28 Frelinghuysen introduced an alternative bill (H.R. 11050) reflecting Republican criticisms. The Frelinghuysen version would have authorized $1.5 billion for a three-year program run by the states and coordinated by HEW. Except for deletion of the Job Corps, the bill included many of the same programs as did the administration proposal but gave to the states more power for planning, implementation, and financing. The bill also authorized further research into the poverty question, including exploration of the feasibility of giving Selective Service examinations to sixteen-year-olds to identify those needing remedial education and training.

Committee Democrats were by that time encountering troubles in reaching agreement on the more than twenty proposed compromise amendments. On April 29 they held a lengthy caucus, after which Chairman Powell announced suspension of hearings for a week because of members' "other responsibilities." But the caucuses continued through the first week in May. The most troublesome issue was aid to sectarian schools under the community-action programs. The administration's drafting team had given much thought to this problem and had concluded that local programs should not be administered by parochial schools but that their pupils should be included in the programs of the public schools. This provision implied that parochial-school pupils would be included through a "shared time" arrangement, a position consistent with HEW's handling of the general school-aid problem. But Representative Hugh Carey (D.-N.Y.), a Roman Catholic, would not accept such a flat prohibition of funds to parochial schools. Finally, an acceptable compromise was reached; parochial schools would receive aid for nonsectarian "remedial noncurricular" programs. Other provisions that came under close scrutiny included a Title V program to train unemployed fathers, the method of allocating funds among the states, the inclusion of women in the Job Corps, and an adult-literacy program.

By the second week in May another series of hearings could be scheduled, and on May 26 the full committee approved, by a straight party-line vote (19 to 11), the Johnson Administration's bill, as amended by the Democratic Caucus. The committee omitted a Title IV program of incentive loans designed to encourage businesses to hire the hard-core unemployed, but two new programs had been added: aid for adult-literacy education (Title II) and assistance to migrant farm workers (Title III). And at the insistence of Representative Edith Green (D.-Ore.) the Job Corps was opened to women as well as men.

As minor concessions to Republicans and southern Democrats the committee bill included a formula for allotting funds among the states for certain programs, as well as a requirement that the OEO utilize existing federal agencies whenever possible. Still, every Republican on the committee voted against the bill, explaining that Republican amendments had been ignored—especially proposals for deletion of OEO, for revamping the domestic Peace Corps, and for sponsoring Selective Service examinations for sixteen-year-olds.

Landrum reported a "clean" bill (H.R. 11377), that is, one incorporating all committee amendments, to the House on June 3 and petitioned the Committee on Rules for a rule governing floor debate.[13] At a June 16 hearing Rules Committee Chairman Howard W. Smith (D.-Va.) indicated that he was "doubtful" about the legislation because it was "too vague and indefinite for me." Smith said he was worried that Job Corps camps would be coeducational and integrated. As for coeducation, Landrum replied that "common sense" would dictate separate camps for men and women, but under questioning he acknowledged that the camps would probably be integrated. He stressed, however, that enrollment in the camps would be voluntary, reminding Smith that integration was "a matter of law on which neither you nor I can prevail." But Smith allowed the bill to languish before his committee for another six weeks; on July 28 a rule for debate was finally granted by an 8 to 7 vote.

While the Rules Committee was temporizing, the Senate was considering and approving its version of the poverty bill. The administration bill (S. 2642) was introduced by Senator Patrick McNamara (D.-Mich.) and referred to a select subcommittee of the Labor and Public Welfare Committee. McNamara was chosen by Committee Chairman Lister Hill (D.-Ala.) to head the ad hoc group. After four days of hearings featuring many of the same witnesses who had appeared earlier before the House groups,[14] the full committee revised the measure and on July 7 ordered it reported. The vote was 13 to 2, with only Republicans Barry Goldwater (Ariz.) and John Tower (Tex.) opposed.

The Senate version was similar to the House committee bill (H.R. 11377), differing only in minor respects. Three of the Senate committee's contributions were especially noteworthy. Senator Jacob K. Javits (R.-N.Y.) had successfully sponsored an amendment permitting federal aid to state Job Corps camps. At that time several states were supporting their own Job Corps programs, but neither the administration nor the House committee bills had included an aid provision. Javits' goal, as he put it, was "to encourage and facilitate the full cooperation of the states, and the integration wherever possible of this program with existing state and community public and private agency activities."[15] A second amendment by the committee tightened up provisions for aid to local groups in the absence of community-wide antipoverty plans. And Senator Goldwater sponsored yet another formula for resolving the church-state issue—an amendment that made its way into the act. Other amendments were technical in nature.

For two days (July 22 and 23) Senate floor debate centered on the issues of states' rights and agricultural programs. In a series of close roll-call votes the administration forces turned back attempts to require the governor's approval of all poverty programs in each state. But two compromise states' rights amendments sponsored by Senator George Smathers (D.-Fla.) were accepted by the bill's floor manager, Senator McNamara. These amendments, which provided for a governor's veto of Job Corps camps and contracts with private agencies, were later accepted by the House and included in the final act. Two controversial farm provisions were eliminated.

The Senate passed S. 2642 on July 23 by a 61 to 34 roll-call vote. Among northern Democrats only the conservative Frank J. Lausche (D.-Ohio) voted "no." The southerners were evenly split, and ten Republicans crossed party lines to vote for the bill. The measure then awaited only final House action.

The three days of House floor debate (August 5-7) had a highly partisan flavor. Goodell charged that the administration was subjecting members to "unprecedented pressure" to gain votes, and other Republicans noted that they had been coerced. "We have been blackjacked, gagged, threatened, and bulldozed into accepting something that we know is not good," Frelinghuysen declared. For their part, Democrats accused Republican leaders of instructing their members to oppose the bill without even reading it.[16]

Both sides attempted to lure southern votes. Republican floor managers characterized the OEO's powers as an invasion of states' rights. The bill's proponents made a concession to this argument by offering a floor amendment permitting governors to veto community-action projects. Not all southerners were placated by this move. Referring to the "integrated camps" of the Job Corps, Judge Smith declared, "I want to say to any southerners who plan to vote for this bill, you are implementing the civil rights bill that you opposed." Landrum, the bill's floor manager, responded by describing the measure as "the most conservative I've ever seen."

The outcome of the debate was a forgone conclusion when, on August 7, Judge Smith's motion to "strike the enacting clause" (a routine motion to kill a bill) was defeated. The motion first carried by a 170 to 135 teller vote, but the administration hustled its forces to the floor to win the roll call 225 to 197. After this vote the Democratic floor leadership imposed tight controls on debate. In order to avoid a conference with the Senate, Landrum substituted for the committee bill (H.R. 11377) an amended version of the Senate-passed bill

(S. 2642). Before the final voting on August 8 Frelinghuysen moved to recommit the bill to the committee with instructions to report out the Republican version, but this motion was defeated 177 to 295 on a roll-call vote along party lines. On final passage the vote was 226 to 185. Every northern Democrat was recorded in favor of the bill, along with forty southerners and twenty-two Republicans.

Several significant amendments were accepted during House debate. In addition to the Senate's gubernatorial veto, the House approved without debate an amendment by John Bell Williams (D.-Miss.) requiring loyalty oaths or disclaimer affidavits of all aid recipients. In addition, two GOP amendments were adopted: one preventing solicitation of funds for political purposes from aid recipients and a "conservationist" amendment requiring that at least 40 percent of Job Corps enrollees be assigned to conservation camps.

Three days later the Senate approved the House changes by a voice vote, and the bill was sent to the White House for President Johnson's signature.

In retrospect the congressional contributions to the Economic Opportunity Act can hardly be considered of major importance. The governors' veto, though used only a few times, gained prominence after Alabama's Governor George Wallace used it as a weapon to substitute his own "lily white" poverty organization for an integrated group that had been established earlier. Governors of both parties regarded the veto as protection for their own political position and opposed its elimination in the 1965 amendments to the act. But, in light of the larger exclusion of state governments and the revolutionary provision for "maximum feasible participation" by the poor (not discussed on Capitol Hill), the gubernatorial veto paled in importance as an instrument for preserving established federal relationships.

Perhaps the most significant congressional contributions were the addition of three new programs: aid for migrant farmers, an adult-literacy education program, and an unrelated "rider" authorizing indemnity payments to dairy farmers whose milk had been ordered removed from the market by the federal government because of the presence of chemical residues. In addition, Congress vetoed two items in the administration's draft bill: Title IV business-incentive loans and the "socialistic" farmland corporations provision in Title III. The other controversies that occupied the legislators' time represented typical (though not necessarily trivial) "political" concerns on Capitol Hill: aid to church-related schools, the inclusion of women, solicitations for partisan political advantage, and loyalty to the nation. Some congressional amendments represented minor technical adjustments of one sort or another.

Congressional Recovery

President Johnson's "unconditional war on poverty" was thus launched in a flurry of favorable publicity. It caught the fancy of press and public; legislators dared not oppose it, for they, like everyone else, were opposed to poverty. The very luster of OEO's early publicity proved a liability, however, when it became apparent as time passed that the elimination of poverty is an elusive and demanding goal. The deepening involvement of the Johnson administration in Vietnam precluded the kind of budgetary support that had been expected. The appendix of the *Congressional Record* soon began to bristle with stories of OEO's shortcomings both large and small, inserted by critical legislators. (Before 1964 the word "poverty" did not even appear as a heading in the index to the *Record*.) Antipoverty programs are by nature prone to scandal. Recipients of aid are not usually solid middle-class citizens; they are often unemployed, uneducated, bitter, frequently with prison records. If they caused trouble while enrolled in OEO programs, their transgressions made easy targets for hostile politicians or journalists. Furthermore, many of those in charge of local OEO programs were, though well-meaning, often inexperienced and sometimes inept in handling federal money. OEO itself initially administered antipoverty funds relatively loosely without stringent policy guidelines.

More fundamentally, some local antipoverty workers saw the programs as opportunities to wage war on local governments, which they charged had been unresponsive to the needs of the poor. Sometimes the community-action agencies (CAAs) served as springboards for mobilizing poor people to militant action against the government agencies that had ignored them in the past (and, in the South, against segregation). As a 1968 OEO guideline declared, "The constituency of the Community Action Program and its grantees is poor people. CAP is based upon the recognition that poor people possess talents and resources essential to reducing the problems of poverty." Local CAAs forged cadres of disadvantaged citizens who became educated in their rights and knowledgeable about techniques of influence. By mid-1965 a number of influential mayors were having troubles with the agencies in their cities. Eventually the more militant antipoverty warriors were brought under control or left the programs, but the highly publicized conflicts left an aftertaste of distrust.

OEO's troubles distressed liberals on Capitol Hill and angered conservatives, inducing Congress to take a strong hand in refining or shaping the programs. In 1965 Congress held lengthy hearings and heard criticism of the antipoverty programs but took little action. The following year, however, Congress tried to tighten up the act by adding new restrictions and earmarking funds. The expensive Job Corps residential training program was brought under tight fiscal control, and new rules were devised to clarify the role of the poor in community-action agencies.

Although CAAs and local governments reached a déntente after 1966, congressional criticism of OEO continued. In the fall of 1967 the House voted to exclude OEO employees from a general salary increase for government workers, then refused the usual "continuing resolution" permitting OEO to operate on the previous year's budget pending new authorizations. For two weeks OEO was literally without funds and had to discontinue projects.

Because of pessimism over the outcome House Democratic leaders post-poned final action on extending OEO's authority until the closing days of the 1967 session. Two months before the House vote Representative Sam Gibbons (D.-Fla.), floor leader for the bill, admitted that "the outlook is really dis-mal . . . there will be better than 230 negative votes on any antipoverty bill we write." Republican spokesmen, led by Representatives Albert Quie (Minn.) and Goodell, were sponsoring an alternative program—the Opportunity Crusade—which would have curtailed OEO's work and transferred its programs to estab-lished government agencies.

Congressional harassment of OEO, however, encouraged the agency and its supporters to mobilize support for existing programs. As projects were termi-nated and local jobs eliminated, legislators began to hear from affected and interested constituents. And, as many of the popular Head Start (preschool) projects were imperiled, congressional inaction roused sympathy for the anti-poverty effort. One count found no fewer than 450 newspaper editorials favor-ing continuation of the act during the fall of 1967. Mobilization of businessmen, mayors, and other city officials to lobby for OEO also rallied support. Clients of the programs, once they had grown accustomed to their newfound voice in national policies, often proved effective spokesmen. A client group of CAA executives, the National Association for Community Development (NACD, or Naked), soon surfaced to lobby for authorizations and funds. OEO, in common with other government programs, was thus building a constituency, despite its short lifetime.

Supporters of the agency still had to break the hostile coalition of Repub-licans and southern Democrats which had been working effectively in the 90th Congress. The coalition was finally thwarted by acceptance of the so-called "Green amendment," sponsored by Edith Green, which redefined the com-munity-action concept to make it more palatable to local politicians. Essentially the amendment allowed local governments to take over CAAs if they wished (not many did). It allowed northern Democrats to persuade their southern colleagues that antipoverty programs would not be antagonistic to local elected officials. This concession satisfied many southern Democrats, who joined their northern colleagues rather than supporting the Republican position. Mrs. Green's amendment was quickly labeled the "bosses and boll-weevil amend-ment" because it enabled southern and big-city Democrats to join forces and stave off moves to alter OEO more drastically. On December 11, 1967, the House extended the Economic Opportunity Act for two years, with fewer sub-stantive changes than anticipated. The vote of 247 to 149 was an impressive show of strength for the act (the Senate had already voted to renew it).

When the Nixon administration took office in 1969, it proceeded to imple-ment its philosophy related to OEO. Antipoverty programs that remained with OEO (some had already been removed) were transferred after intensive inter-agency negotiation and bargaining to regular Cabinet departments—primarily Labor and Health, Education, and Welfare. OEO's mission was narrowed from program administration to research, demonstration, and special projects. In 1969 and again in 1971 the agency's authority was extended, however—indicating that poverty was to be a continuing concern of federal policies and programs. (See Chapter 4 for a description of the events in 1969.)

Besides debating periodic authorizations, Congress made many positive contributions to the antipoverty programs. Although many of the provisos reflected narrow perspectives, congressional review of programs grew more sophisticated as time passed. In 1965 Senator Gaylord Nelson (D.-Wis.) proposed the Nelson amendment, a program to hire the chronically unemployed for community-beautification projects (Operation Mainstream). Another congressionally sponsored amendment was New Careers, a 1966 program to train the poor as aides to professionals in such fields as education, health, and welfare. This amendment was sponsored by Senators Javits and Robert F. Kennedy (D.-N.Y.) and Representative James Scheuer (D.-N.Y.).

The Ebb and Flow of Legislative Initiative

Traditionally Americans have paid allegiance to the constitutional dictum that "all legislative powers . . . shall be vested in a Congress of the United States" (Article I, Section 1), yet an increasingly powerful springboard for legislative authority is another of the Constitution's provisions: The President "shall from time to time give to the Congress information of the state of the Union, and recommend to their considerations such measures as he shall judge necessary and expedient" (Article II, Section 3).

The emergence of the President as "chief legislator," primarily a twentieth-century phenomenon, has received almost continuous attention from commentators since the era of Theodore Roosevelt. Until well after World War II the President's legislative program was apparently a casual affair in which the Chief Executive merely lent his support to a few of the many proposals floating around Capitol Hill. Gradually the President's legislative role, not only in setting the congressional agenda but also in proposing the specific content of bills, became institutionalized.[17] Until 1961 the fiction was observed that the President himself did not sign the draft bills sent to Congress, and friendly members were solicited to introduce the administration's measures as their own. After 1961 the President's signature began to appear on draft bills, even though formal introduction must still be by a member of Congress.

The President's ability to function as chief legislator arises from the capacity of the executive branch to articulate and resolve many, if not all, of the demands pressed upon government in a particular policy area. In the modern "service state" the vast and diverse bureaucratic apparatus offers to outside interests multiple access to public policy. These interests often find that their points of view are faithfully represented by the executive agencies with which they normally do business. When this phenomenon is multiplied the interplay of outside clienteles and executive agencies generates a process of negotiation, bargaining, and conflict among the various agencies and groups.

An administration bill may therefore be viewed as a treaty among the several interested parties that has been negotiated within the executive branch. If the conflicts remain unresolved, the President or his political advisers may step in to effectuate a bargain or to select one alternative over the others. If the issue is too low in priority to warrant direct intervention, however, it may lie dormant until some kind of bargain can be reached. The Economic Opportunity Act of 1964 was a classic example of executive legislation. The bargaining process was originally sponsored and stimulated by the White House, acting through the Council of Economic Advisers. When the council (working with the Budget Bureau) proved unable to conclude the negotiations, the President intervened and appointed Shriver to act as a broker among the quarreling interests. With the force of the President behind him Shriver was able to resolve the conflicts and to hammer out a multipurpose bill.

The classic legislative function—bringing political combatants together to hear their claims and then resolving these claims—is performed in the complex modern polity with equal dexterity by Congress and the executive establishment. The ability of the executive to perform the traditional legislative functions has profound consequences for the future of Congress. As Arthur F. Bentley foresaw in 1908:

> If the group interests work out a fair and satisfying adjustment through the legislature, then the executive sinks in prominence . . . when the adjustment is not perfected in the legislature, then the executive rises in strength to do the work . . . the growth of executive discretion is therefore a phase of the group process.[18]

According to constitutional theory, political bargains will be struck by the legislature; executive agencies will ratify these bargains when the President signs them into law and when bureaucrats implement them. But when the bargains are struck within the executive branch, these institutional roles seem to be reversed. Congress becomes ratifier, modifier, lobbyist, and even court of appeals for policies originated by the executive.

Yet Congress remains an effective instrument for articulating and integrating the competing interests in domestic policy making. We have already seen this pattern in the history of the depressed-areas question. In the instance of the Economic Opportunity Act, the President acted as initiator because he (or, rather, those acting in his name) was able to bring the relevant interests together, combine a series of proposals into a "salable package," and ensure priority for the matter on the legislative agenda. It would be a mistake, however, to accord the President, or for that matter the executive branch, full credit for "originating" the antipoverty proposals, whose origins were scattered in many places. And, once the act was implemented, senators and representatives quickly became aware of its social and political implications. Although the executive had originally taken the initiative it turned out that the writers of the act were hardly more enlightened than were their congressional counterparts about the ways of eliminating or alleviating poverty. After 1965, in fact, it is fair to say that the bulk of innovations originated on Capitol Hill, rather than in executive agencies. Perhaps there is a lesson in these events for those who argue that the legislature has lost the initiative, or that, when it does not initiate, it does not have a piece of the action.

NOTES FOR CHAPTER 7

1 The history of the Economic Opportunity Act was first told, as far as we are aware, in the first edition of this book. Since then many books and articles on the subject have appeared. Especially useful are two narratives prepared by close observers of the program: James L. Sundquist, *Politics and Policy: The Eisenhower, Kennedy, and Johnson Years* (Washington, D.C.: Brookings, 1968), pp. 111-154; and Sar A. Levitan, *The Great Society's Poor Law* (Baltimore: Johns Hopkins Press, 1969), chap. 1. Details of certain crucial events can be found in Walter W. Heller, "American Poverty: Its Causes and Cures" (Address to the Seventh Annual Public Affairs Forum, 25 March 1965, at Indiana State College, Indiana, Pa.); and Lillian Rubin, "Maximum Feasible Participation: The Origins, Implications, and Present Status," *Poverty and Human Resources Abstracts*, (November-December 1967), pp. 1-23.

2 Gunnar Myrdal, *Challenge to Affluence* (New York: Pantheon, 1963).

3 John Kenneth Galbraith, *The Affluent Society* (Boston: Houghton-Mifflin, 1958), p. 328. See also Myrdall, *Challenge to Affluence.*

4 Michael Harrington, *The Other America* (New York: Macmillan, 1962); and Leon Keyserling, *Poverty and Deprivation in the United States* (Washington, D.C.: Conference on Economic Progress, 1962).

5 The Council of Economic Advisers consists of a chairman and two other members selected by the President. The council, created by the Employment Act of 1946, prepares annual reports on the state of the economy and advises the President on overall economic policy. The chairman has come to function as a personal adviser to the President, and the relationship between Heller and Kennedy was especially close. It is relevant that the council, along with the Bureau of the Budget (now the Office of Management and Budget) is organizationally part of the Executive Office of the President and that physically the two agencies are located in the Executive Office Buildings near the White House.

6 At that point it included the Secretaries of Commerce, Labor, and Health, Education, and Welfare; the administrator of the Housing and Home Finance Agency; and the director of the Bureau of the Budget.

7 Nelson W. Polsby, "Strengthening Congress in National Policymaking," in Polsby (ed.), *Congressional Behavior* (New York: Random House, 1971), p. 7.

8 The most thorough view of the antecedents of the act is found in Sundquist, *Politics and Policy*, esp. pp. 115-134. For a thoughtful discussion of the role of Congress in policy incubation, see Polsby, "Strengthening Congress," pp. 7-8.

9 *Newsweek*, (February 17, 1964), p. 38.

10 This so-called "delegate agency" concept, in which an agency will contract, or delegate, certain of its programs to another agency, permits, for example, rural poverty programs to remain technically under OEO's jurisdiction but to be in fact implemented and controlled by the Agriculture Department.

11 U.S., Congress, House, Committee on Education and Labor, *Hearings on the Economic Opportunity Act of 1964*, III, 88th Cong., 2d sess., 1964, p. 1150.

12 *Ibid.*, I, p. 201.

13 House Report 1458.

14 U.S., Congress, Senate, Committee on Labor and Public Welfare, *Hearings on the Economic Opportunity Act of 1964*, 88th Cong., 2d sess., 17, 18, 23, and 25 June 1964.

15 U.S., Congress, Senate, Committee on Labor and Public Welfare, *Report on S. 2642*, 88th Cong., 2d sess., 1964, S. Rept. 1218, p. 87.

16 The House floor debate can be found in U.S., Congress, House, *Congressional Record*, daily ed., 88th Cong., 2d sess., 5, 6, 7 August 1964, pp. 17610-17652, 17672-17739, 17932-18025.

17 See Richard Neustadt, "Presidency and Legislation," *American Political Science Review*, 48 (September 1954), 641-671, and 49 (September 1955), 980-1021; and Neustadt, "Politicians and Bureaucrats," in David B. Truman (ed.), *The Congress and America's Future* (Englewood Cliffs, N.J.: Prentice-Hall, 1965).

18 Arthur F. Bentley, *The Process of Government* (Chicago: University of Chicago Press, 1908), p. 359.

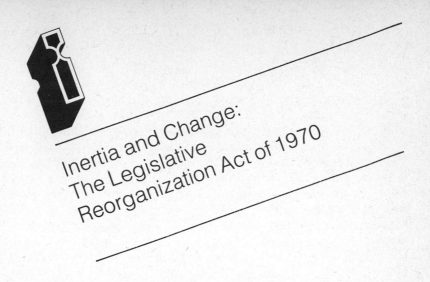

Inertia and Change: The Legislative Reorganization Act of 1970

Legislatures are creatures of conflict, and Congress is no exception. Uniquely exposed and intensely political, it is the object of the combined awe and denigration with which Americans view their elected officials. In the past few decades Congress has endured periodic criticism from both scholars and other citizens for its inefficient procedures, its undemocratic structure, and its political shortcomings, whether real or imagined. These criticisms, together with greater executive participation in legislative functions (discussed in Chapter 7), have called into question the very survival of our national legislature as a viable policy-making instrument.

Nor has Congress remained unmoved in the face of external challenges. In recent decades many institutional alterations—formal and informal, planned and unplanned—have occurred on Capitol Hill. The modern history of Congress probably begins with the landmark Legislative Reorganization Act of 1946, spurred by the extensive investigations of a joint committee chaired by Senator Robert M. LaFollette, Jr. (Prog.-Wis.), and Representative A. S. Mike Monroney (D.-Okla.). The act produced far-reaching innovations in congressional practices, especially in increasing staff resources and reducing the number of standing committees; some other reforms, particularly in fiscal procedures, fell by the wayside. Many minor innovations have occurred since World War II in response to the increasing work loads of individual members. Others have arisen from the ebb and flow of party fortunes: The advent of a Democratic administration in 1961 led late Speaker of the House Sam Rayburn (D.-Tex.) to take control of the obstreperous House Rules Committee; an outsized Democratic majority in the 89th Congress enabled liberals to enact a series of rules changes; disastrous defeats, especially in 1958 and 1964, eliminated so many elderly Republicans that the House GOP underwent a dramatic transformation. Some of these innovations were transitory, but others will leave their imprint on Capitol Hill for many years to come.

Formal changes in congressional organization or procedures are difficult to enact because they must emanate from Congress itself. Because Congress is a political institution, alterations in its structure are necessarily alterations in the distribution of power; and those who have the most power have nothing to gain from tampering with the status quo. At the same time, those who are unhappy with the status quo are likely to be motivated by various and often conflicting considerations: One person's reformism is another person's folly. The diverse goals of legislators therefore complicate coalition building for institutional reform.

Nor is there usually compelling public pressure for change. To be sure, citizens judge congressional performance, and their judgments are often harsh. But they cannot effect change themselves. More likely they will turn their backs on the institution and seek instruments more responsive to their will. The task of reform is thus almost always an internal matter, but the existing structure of Congress is not geared to make it an easy one.

The special problems of formal change are vividly illustrated by the history of the Legislative Reorganization Act of 1970. The first broad-ranging restructuring in a generation, it was itself the product of six years of debate, negotiations, and delay. With one notable exception, this history took place outside the view of the general public.

Senator Monroney's "Reform Mosaic"

The history of the 1970 reorganization law goes back at least to late 1964, when Monroney, by then Oklahoma's senior senator, announced that he intended to introduce a resolution creating a successor to the LaFollette-Monroney committee. He spoke particularly of the appropriations process and showed reporters piles of weighty documents that had to be digested by legislators in reviewing the annual federal budget. Congress was following "an obsolete system inherited from the Gay Nineties," he declared, comparing current procedures to "a group of farmers sitting around a cracker barrel and a pot-bellied stove and trying to run a $100 billion business." Monroney also said that he wanted to study changes in scheduling and in committee structures and work loads.[1]

Monroney's omnibus approach to reform was aimed at the practical goal of putting together a package with the widest possible appeal. "We will, I hope, not start out with one single purpose to achieve a single objective," he told reporters. "Such an approach, or suspicion thereof, has frustrated many well-intentioned efforts of the past to modernize Congress." Because meaningful changes would arouse stiff opposition, especially from the senior leaders, he reasoned that the omnibus approach would permit a few "ice cream" provisions to make the "spinach" provisions more palatable. He was fond of pointing out, for example, that the 1946 act had been approved partly because it had been accompanied by a pay raise and a retirement plan desired by most members.

According to Monroney's resolution (S. Con. Res. 2), the new joint committee, like its 1945 predecessor, would be prohibited from recommending changes in House or Senate rules. Obviously many of the innovations that Monroney had in mind, like reformulating committee jurisdictions, involved amending the rules, but these proposals could emerge from the joint committee's work and then (as had actually occurred in 1945-1946) be processed by the two houses separately. Monroney argued on the Senate floor that contentious rules fights, like that over the Senate's cloture rule, should be avoided. "The intent of this resolution," he told the Senate, "is to seek solutions to the problems of Congress on which there is a consensus that something should be done."[2]

Several reform senators, led by Joseph S. Clark (D.-Pa.), charged that reform would be meaningful only if the committee were free to probe what Clark called "our present iniquitous rules." "I find myself unable to agree," Clark declared, "that the resolution as [Monroney] has caused it to be drawn would accomplish what the body of the resolution purports to do." Those who drafted the resolution, he declared, "do not wish to put their support behind any investigation . . . which might conceivably overthrow the balance of power in the Senate." He went on to estimate that the limitation would cut out as much as three-fourths of the work that the committee ought to accomplish. During the previous Congress Clark himself had proposed no fewer than twenty-seven rules changes, and "not one of these . . . changes in the rules . . . could be the subject of recommendation by the joint committee under the resolution of the Senator from Oklahoma." Although Clark's position was supported by a few liberal colleagues from both parties, his amendment to the Monroney resolution was defeated 29 to 58 on a roll-call vote; on March 9, 1965, the Monroney proposal was adopted 88 to 0.

On the other side of Capitol Hill creation of a joint committee was one of a series of demands presented to Speaker John McCormack (D.-Mass.) by liberal Democrats, their ranks swollen by the 1964 elections and their organization spearheaded by the Democratic Study Group (DSG). McCormack saw to it that the resolution (H. Con. Res. 4) reached the floor under a no amendment rule. Two days after the Senate adopted the joint committee plan, the House approved it quickly by a voice vote.

The committee's twelve members (six from each chamber divided equally by party) underscored the complex political constraints under which it was to work. They were designated by the House and Senate Majority and Minority Leaders. Monroney, who headed the six-man Senate contingent, was a genial moderate acceptable to both conservatives and liberals. Representative Ray J.

Madden (D.-Ind.), who led the House delegation and was named cochairman, was chosen by Speaker McCormack because he was a "safe" liberal who was also a member of the House Rules Committee. The other members were chosen to represent faithfully the various ideological points of view in the two houses.

The joint committee's first action was to adopt unanimously a brief statement interpreting its scope of operations.[3] The statement was drafted specifically to answer the charge that the prohibition on considering rules changes would render the hearings meaningless before they even began. It noted that the joint committee had a mandate to study and take testimony on all aspects of Congress and was limited only in what it could recommend. As time went on, however, persistent quarrels among the staff members (who were divided according to political party and chamber) precluded the kind of cohesive research effort that had been completed single-handedly by scholar George Galloway for the LaFollette-Monroney committee.

Laboring under these handicaps, the joint committee inaugurated hearings on May 10, 1965. It relied mainly on hearings to gather information, hearing 199 witnesses—mostly congressmen, but also scholars, interest-group spokesmen, and a few executive officials. The printed testimony ran to 15 volumes and 2,322 pages. "I think just about every reasonable and constructive idea for the reorganization of Congress—plus a few silly ones—is in our files," Monroney reported. No fewer than 275 separate proposals were presented. They ranged from Senator Clark's demand that Congress reassess its role in society (buttressed by 70 pages of testimony on dozens of subjects) to one member's suggestion that the congressional restaurants improve their service. Most proposals in fact came from incumbent legislators, and typically they reflected their authors' particular institutional statuses.

After the hearings had been concluded Monroney's committee took ten months to negotiate its report. During this period scattered meetings were held, and members discussed the proposals freely and bargained for agreement on a final report. Essentially the deliberations represented a two-step process. First, those proposals were eliminated that were deemed actually undesirable. Next the committee had to agree on that combination of desirable proposals that would have the best chance of passage in both houses. Some of the ideas that fell by the wayside at this stage were included in supplemental views filed with the committee's final report.[4]

On July 21, 1966, the Monroney committee revealed the results of its deliberations. Sixty-six proposals received the unanimous backing of the committee, which immediately incorporated the provisions into the omnibus Legislative Reorganization Act of 1966. The heart of the report was a "committee bill of rights," designed to regularize committee procedures, prevent the arbitrary exercise of chairmen's powers, and protect minority-party rights. The bill of rights included such proposals as recognition of the majority's right to call meetings and report bills in the event that the chairman refused to do so, more frequent open hearings, broadcasting and telecasting of hearings at the committee's discretion, participation of all committee members in preparation of reports, and elimination of proxy voting in committees. Three staff positions on each committee would be allotted to the minority party, upon its request. An additional staff member, designated as a "review specialist," would be assigned to each standing committee to handle oversight functions. On the basis of an extensive study of congressional work loads and schedules, the joint committee also proposed to limit individual committee assignments and chairmanships in the Senate.

Fiscal controls and congressional review of the budget were also the focus of numerous proposals. Automatic data processing was favored to expand the amount of budget information available to members, and specific alterations in the presentation of the budget were suggested. Executive officers would appear before the appropriations committees within thirty days after the submission of the budget to discuss overall budget guidelines. The appropriations committees were enjoined to expand their study of multiagency programs and to hold more hearings. New operating units within the General Accounting Office were urged to assist committees in program evaluation. Such proposals and others reflected concern over inadequate attention to the oversight function (see Chapter 5).

One of the more far-reaching suggestions was creation of a permanent Joint Committee on Congressional Operations to undertake continuing inquiry into the organization of Congress and to protect legislative prerogatives. There were also proposals for an enlarged legislative research service (to be created from the existing Legislative Reference Service), a five-day work week for legislative business, a recess during August, and changes in the content and format of the *Congressional Record*.

The report included several "ice cream" provisions: the August vacation, additional individual and committee staffing, increased travel allowances and telephone facilities for members, and organizational streamlining of the Capitol police, pages, and guides.

The Monroney committee's report was a laundry list of relatively detailed items. Missing were discussions of issues that many dedicated reformers thought central: seniority, party responsibility, and Senate filibusters. In view of the committee's limited mandate and broad ideological mixture, not to mention its limited time and resources, the omissions were predictable. Indeed, the tone of the report reflected perfectly the approach of its cochairman, Senator Monroney. "A lot of little reforms add up to a big reform," he remarked during one of the hearings. "If we are going to get an up-to-date, modern Congress, it will be a mosaic you build from lots of little improvements." [5]

S. 355 Goes in the Refrigerator

Because the joint committee had not been authorized to report legislation, it was anticipated that both houses would create special committees to transform the recommendations into legislation or rules changes and report them to the floor of each house. In the Senate this course was followed. The Senate's Special Committee on the Organization of Congress was composed simply of the Senate members from the joint committee. But the resolution establishing the committee (S. Res. 293) provided one more day in court for the seniority leaders by requiring that "no report shall be made until the chairman and ranking minority member of each standing committee of the Senate shall have been given the opportunity to appear before the Special Committee and present their views." Several senators took advantage of this opportunity to plead for special dispensations for their committees, and the resulting bill, S. 3848 (introduced September 21, 1966), embodied a few of their demands. Because of the Senate's crowded agenda, no action was taken on the legislation before the 89th Congress adjourned.

On January 15, 1967, Monroney introduced S. 355 as a "clean bill," incorporating all committee amendments. It differed from S. 3848 by incorporating several new concessions to committee leaders. In accordance with Monroney's strategy of accepting modifications that would enhance the bill's chances of passage, these concessions were designed to counteract potential floor opposition. In opening floor debate on S. 355, Monroney repeated this philosophy: "The committee's goal was not simply to publish a thought-provoking group of recommendations. Rather, our objective has been to produce meaningful legislation based on those recommendations."[6]

In all, S. 355 consumed six weeks of debate (although the Senate transacted other business during this time); there were 113 proposed amendments and 30 roll-call votes. Nearly everyone, so it seemed, had something to say about how the Senate was run. Of the 40 proposed amendments that were defeated (no action was taken on another 34), no fewer than 24 came from Senator Clark and dealt with such matters as cloture, the selection of committee chairmen, and the Senate's rule-making power. All were easily defeated. On the other hand, Monroney had been authorized by his committee colleagues to accept amendments that would make the bill more acceptable to the Senate as a whole. Of the 39 amendments that were adopted, 33 dealt with committee procedures and came from Democratic committee leaders from the South and Southwest. The joint committee acquiesced to all but 1 of these amendments. The remaining 6 amendments were mainly "ice cream" provisions like Jacob Javits' (R.-N.Y.) voice-amplification system for the Senate floor and Hugh Scott's (R.-Pa.) automatic data-processing facilities for the Library of Congress. The pattern of accommodation represented by the 39 amendments was significant, for a similar process was to take place in the House—though the second time around would be in private.

The strategy of accommodation seemed to have paid off when, on March 7, the Senate adopted S. 355 by a vote of 75 to 9. Both Senate and House members of the joint committee agreed that their recommendations had survived virtually intact. S. 355 then moved to the House of Representatives.

Two days after the Senate had approved S. 355, Speaker McCormack referred the bill to the House Rules Committee. He was acting on the advice of veteran House Parliamentarian Lewis Deschler,[7] who argued that, after all, the bill did propose changes in House rules. The real reasons behind McCormack's and Deschler's decision were somewhat different, however. The committee bill of rights, which Senate committee leaders had succeeded in modifying somewhat, was still too potent for McCormack and the circle of senior committee chairmen around him. He would not, if he could prevent it, allow the bill to go to the House floor until these provisions were drastically diluted. The Rules Committee, composed mainly of senior and "safe" congressmen of both parties, provided a reliable tool for transforming the bill. Or perhaps the bill could be sidetracked altogether, for Rules Chairman William Colmer (D.-Miss.) was known to oppose the whole idea. As one member of the committee confided, McCormack had "put the bill in the refrigerator"—where, as it turned out, it would remain for more than three years.

Various attempts were made to revive the bill. Chairman Colmer began hearings on April 10, but they were suspended before the first day was over. There followed a fitful and more or less clandestine series of negotiations designed to reach an acceptable compromise. In all, seven "committee prints" (versions) of the bill were produced, mainly at the instigation of Representative Jack Brooks (D.-Tex.). All were designed, in the words of a staff member who helped to prepare them, to "write a bill the Speaker [or, more properly, his Parliamentarian] would allow to be reported out." Some reformers charged that the committee bill of rights was being so emasculated that "it would be worse than no bill at all." Republicans charged that Brooks and others were gutting the minority-staffing provision through requirements that the committees' majorities retain final control over staff decisions. Such conflicts occasionally surfaced in the press, as one side or the other attempted to gain support for its position.

In this atmosphere it is not surprising that the congressional reform issue took on a partisan flavor as 1967 wore on. It was obvious to everyone that the elderly cadre of Democratic committee leaders had decided to hold the reform measure in the Rules Committee, hoping that they could remove its committee-related provisions or even kill it altogether. For their part, many Republicans had long been resentful of unfair treatment at the hands of Democratic committee chairmen. Some chairmen allotted no staff assistance for minority-party members, and many tried to withhold information from the minority. When younger, activist Republicans first raised the issue in the late 1950s, they received little encouragement from their own party elders, who, as often as not, had reached comfortable accommodations with their Democratic counterparts and were perfectly content with the situation. When Ford had been installed as GOP Conference (caucus) chairman in 1963, it had been generally understood that he would bear down on the minority-staffing issue.[8] He had immediately appointed a Conference Task Force on Congressional Reform and Minority

Staffing, headed first by Fred Schwengel (R.-Iowa) and then by James C. Cleveland (R.-N.H.).[9] As more and more senior Republicans were retired, especially in the Johnson landslide of 1964, younger activists came to dominate the GOP apparatus in the House. They presented a striking contrast to the Democratic leadership, epitomized by the likable but aging Speaker McCormack.[10]

On May 10, exactly one month after the Rules Committee's one-day hearing, the House Republican Policy Committee issued a call for immediate action on the reorganization bill. On August 22 Cleveland reactivated the twenty-two-man task force "to put pressure on House Democrats to report out" the Senate-passed bill. "I want to make it clear," he emphasized, "that I am talking about the bill passed by the Senate, not some watered-down 'compromise version.' We have worked too hard on this legislation, and the need for modernizing Congress is too urgent for us to accept anything less than the modest reform package embodied in S. 355." Thereafter task force members arose almost daily on the floor to comment on the delay and to insert in the *Record* comparisons among the various committee prints. On October 11 the entire Republican Conference voted unanimously to ask the leadership to schedule floor debate on S. 355 under an open rule, but the session ended without any stirrings from the Rules Committee.

Republican sniping at the Democratic leaders resumed early in 1968 and continued throughout the year. In fact, Minority Leader Ford delegated a portion of the GOP response to the President's State of the Union message to young William A. Steiger (R.-Wis.), who spoke of the need for congressional reorganization. When pressed, McCormack and Majority Leader Carl Albert (D.-Okla.) said that, yes, they favored a reorganization bill and certainly hoped that the Rules Committee would come up with a report.

Meanwhile, the ultimate fate of the reform package was in jeopardy on another front. Monroney's strategy had dictated a number of "ice cream" provisions to accompany the necessary "spinach" in the bill. But, while S. 355 remained bottled up in the Rules Committee, both House and Senate found time to enact some of the more attractive provisions piecemeal. Representative Madden called this process "ho-dagging"—a Hoosier term that apparently means stripping the measure of its more attractive features. Some of the major "ho-dags" occurred when the Senate voted to increase each senator's clerk-hire allowance (Monroney opposed it on the floor as removing one incentive for enacting S. 355), to add to the Capitol police force, to consolidate telephone and telegram allowances for individual members, and to establish an ethics committee. Several House committees adopted rules to curb the chairmen's power and to protect minority-party rights. However laudable these moves may have been, they were correctly viewed as deterrents to the basic reform bill.

Late in the session a group of thirteen Republicans, led by Donald Rumsfeld (R.-Ill.), began to use delaying tactics on the House floor to publicize the congressional-reform issue and to protest the leadership's unwillingness to report S. 355. Although House rules prohibit filibusters, energetic legislators have at their disposal a few delaying tactics—for example, insisting on quorum calls and demanding roll-call votes. Such tactics have mainly nuisance value and cannot be carried too far lest they alienate colleagues. One day the GOP group, promptly dubbed Rumsfeld's Raiders, stalled the House consideration of the $72 billion defense appropriations measure for more than two hours. It gave up without any assurance from the leadership on the reorganization bill; none was really anticipated.

The activities of the Raiders stimulated a small group of Democratic liberals—determined not to have Republicans take all the credit for reform—to hold a press conference of their own and to begin efforts to dislodge S. 355. The Democratic reformers were mostly recruited from the Tuesday Group, a small, relatively informal group of hard-core liberals who met weekly for breakfast.[11] Together with the Raiders these Democratic reformers began circulating a petition to discharge S. 355 from the Rules Committee; more than 100 signatures had been secured by the time that Congress adjourned.

The more important objective of the Raiders—activation of public opinion and press comment—was not very successful. Although several editorial writers praised the group's efforts, most found it hard to paint the reform issue in a partisan light. True, Democratic leaders were to blame for pigeonholing the bill, but it was also a fact that some of the most forcible reformers were Democrats. A more fundamental problem was the general inattention of the press and public to matters of congressional structure and procedure. "Congressional reform is an issue without a constituency," Rumsfeld conceded. If it was hard to convert congressional reorganization into a partisan issue, it was hard to make it into a public issue at all. One congressman who had been active in reform efforts estimated that it would win him no more than fifty votes in his district. Needless to say, in the tumultuous party battle of 1968 the issue of congressional reform was hardly mentioned. The Republican platform included a call for congressional reform. The Democratic platform committee, headed by Majority Whip Hale Boggs of Louisiana, avoided mention of the issue.

The Leadership Begins To Move

As the 91st Congress convened, the pending congressional reorganization bill seemed all but forgotten. As often happens in politics the scene and the actors had shifted dramatically. Senator Monroney, the figure most identified with the measure, had been defeated for reelection; another reformer, Representative Thomas Curtis (R.-Mo.), was also absent, having left his safe seat to run unsuccessfully for the Senate. Even Representative Rumsfeld, the young activist who had assumed leadership of the GOP reform forces, was soon to be recruited by President Nixon as director of the Office of Economic Opportunity. Reform leadership was for the moment lacking.

Related events were taking place, however, that were finally to unlock the reform bill from the Rules Committee's deep freeze. The ferment centered on the House Democrats, who had returned as the majority party even though the voters had elected a Republican to the White House. The party clearly needed compelling spokesmen to challenge the administration in the coming years, but it was badly divided after the disastrous Chicago convention and the ensuing campaign. As Democratic legislators returned to Washington, they faced a disheartening prospect. The discontent and disillusionment that had been smoldering among young and middle-seniority members for at least a decade burst into the open. "The House is like the Black Hole of Calcutta," said one of the harsher critics. Freshman Congressman Allard K. Lowenstein (D.-N.Y.) agreed: "Nothing prepares you for its horrors."[12]

In a real sense, House Democrats were victims of their own past successes. Since 1932 they had controlled the House for all but four years, usually by substantial margins. Democratic incumbents, moreover, had until recently tended to come from less competitive districts than had their Republican counterparts. As a result, House Democrats were older on the average than Republicans: Their median seniority was 6.5 terms (thirteen years), compared with 4.6 terms (nine years) among GOP ranks. Their leaders, too, were older: House committee chairmen Averaged almost sixty-seven years of age, whereas ranking Republican members of those same committes averaged sixty-one years. And, whereas House Republicans had streamlined their party apparatus in the 1960s (see Chapter 4), middle-seniority Democrats—men in their forties and fifties, for the most part—were disenchanted and bitter at their minimal role in party affairs.

The disenchantment was manifested in many ways, but it naturally focused on seventy-seven-year-old Speaker McCormack. The day after Christmas 1968 Morris Udall (D.-Ariz.) announced that he would challenge McCormack for the speakership in the initial Democratic Caucus of the 91st Congress. That his challenge was doomed from the beginning was obvious to everyone (the story is related in greater detail in Chapter 4). What was telling, however, was the amount of discontent that Udall's candidacy uncovered. Under the circumstances, a vote of "no confidence" from virtually one-third of the party members was an unmistakable warning, and Speaker McCormack could not fail to heed it.

Although they lost their battle to oust McCormack, the challengers nonetheless won several concessions that promised younger members a larger voice in party and legislative affairs in the House. One was an agreement to hold regular monthly party caucuses. Another was to establish a holiday and vacation schedule to enable members, especially younger ones with school-aged children, to spend time with their families and plan trips to their districts. McCormack also agreed to support a study of electronic voting systems for installation in the House committee chairmen averaged almost sixty-seven years of age, whereas soon after, Colmer indicated that he would not try to pigeonhole S. 355 any longer. "Congressional reform has become a symbolic thing to many members, and it's awfully difficult to resist it under those circumstances," one of McCormack's associates confessed. "I think the Speaker has become reconciled to having a bill."[13]

Even with this informal understanding, progress was not immediate. It was not until April 22 that Colmer designated a special Rules subcommittee, to be chaired by Representative B. F. Sisk (D.-Calif.), to study the matter and to write an acceptable bill. Although not identified with the reform cause, Sisk was known as a fair and hard-working legislator, a moderate Democrat of southern extraction who enjoyed the confidence of the House leadership. Once having been given the assignment, Sisk persisted doggedly in the face of lukewarm leadership support and often conflicting directions. Soon he won the respect of even the most disgruntled reformers, who testified to his fairness in hearing them out. His counterpart, senior Republican H. Allen Smith (D.-Calif.), though never identified with congressional reform, also demonstrated determination to develop a meaningful bill. Of the remaining subcommittee members, only Richard Bolling (D.-Mo.) was known for his reformist sentiments.[14]

Sisk's group spent the summer and early fall poring over previous proposals and preparing a new draft bill. Additional staff help was recruited from the Legislative Reference Service, the Office of the Legislative Counsel, and the personal staffs of Colmer, Sisk, and Bolling. By late October a draft was ready to be presented in a series of seminars and then circulated to all members of the House. Meanwhile, the subcommittee opened eight days of hearings: First a Budget Bureau official discussed fiscal policy making; then media representatives expounded on the roles of radio, television, and newspapers; and finally thirty-five representatives spoke.[15] It was seven more months before the Rules Committee was ready to report its own revised bill.

H.R. 17654 as it was reported was somewhat bolder than the committee prints that had been circulating during the previous Congress. Title I, devoted to the committee system in the House, embraced a long list of specific provisions to regularize procedures for (among other things) calling meetings, broadcasting or telecasting hearings, respecting minority-party rights. The major goal, as the subcommittee put it, was "to strike a more judicious balance between the prerogatives of the majority and the minority parties while at the same time preserving the legitimate rights of individual committee members."[16] Beyond prescribing new rules, the bill was designed to promote equitable committee operations by more indirect means—by encouraging committees to adopt more detailed written rules for themselves and by giving the public more opportunities to scrutinize committee work. Other titles in the bill dealt with new congressional fiscal controls, increased sources of information (including additional committee staffs and an enlarged Congressional Research Service), and housekeeping matters like data processing, the Capitol Guide Service, Senate and House pages, and modernization of the House gallery facilities.

Although not intended to embody sweeping changes, H.R. 17654 was a well-drafted and surprisingly wide-ranging piece of legislation. It was primarily the handiwork of Sisk, Smith, and especially Bolling, whose commitment and legislative skill were responsible for many of the bill's artful compromises. Sisk's subcommittee approved the bill unanimously, as did the parent Rules Committee. The committee granted the measure an "open rule," except for changes in committee jurisdictions; that is, with the exception provided, the bill would be open for amendment once it had reached the House floor. Although the authors knew that the members would insist on proposing amendments, they feared that the bill would become so loaded down with revisions and additions that it would sink of its own weight.[17] "If they get into a whole lot of foolish stuff," Smith warned, "then I'm going to walk away from this bill." Sisk and Bolling expressed similar views. Their warnings were not idle, for a bipartisan reformist coalition was gathering momentum for the coming debate.

DSG and the Raiders

The core of the reform coalition consisted of relatively junior activists within the 125-member Democratic Study Group (DSG) and remnants of the Republican Rumsfeld's Raiders. In late May, as soon as the basic contents of H.R. 17654 were known, they were discussed at the regular Wednesday breakfast meeting of DSG's executive committee—composed of Chairman Donald M. Fraser (D.-Minn.), Vice-Chairman John Brademas (D.-Ind.), and Chief Whip James C. Corman (D.-Calif.). During the conversation the staff director, Richard P. Conlon, suggested that the group try to organize support for a provision to permit recorded votes in the Committee of the Whole, as well as several other "antisecrecy" amendments to the forthcoming bill. These issues had shown promise of stirring support among diverse elements in the House; and, as a former newspaperman, Conlon sensed an opportunity to interest journalists in the problem. The three leaders bought the idea, and the next Wednesday Representative Sam Gibbons (D.-Fla.), chairman of a DSG Task Force on Congressional Reform, was invited to join the group. Meanwhile, staff negotiations had begun with Republicans, and to the following week's meeting were invited Representatives John Dellenback (R.-Ore.) and Steiger.[18] A bipartisan coalition was beginning to form.

Both parties in the House have several informal organizations within their ranks.[19] The DSG is the largest, best-organized, probably best-known, and most powerful of these groups. It started in December 1956, when a young Minnesota representative named Eugene J. McCarthy circulated among a group of his friends a statement of aims that became known as the Liberal Manifesto. By January 8, 1957, the document had twenty-eight signers; when Representative Frank Thompson, Jr. (D.-N.J.), inserted the program in the *Congressional Record* three weeks later the list of signers had grown to eighty.[20] These liberal Democrats, many from urban areas, had found a chance to express their own ideas on the sort of measures they thought Congress should be considering. A rudimentary and informal whip system was soon established to implement these goals, and later the group—McCarthy's Mavericks, as it was called—acquired a staff assistant. Bolstered by an influx of young liberals known as the Class of '58, the group was formally launched in 1959 with Lee Metcalf (Mont.) as chairman (McCarthy had moved on to the Senate).

The formal House Democratic leaders at first feared that the new group might turn into an unfriendly rival. Nevertheless, as one student has remarked, "the attitudes of the House leadership toward the group which became the DSG might best be described . . . as benevolent neutrality that grew into tacit approval."[21] By the late 1960s the organization boasted several staff aides, a full-fledged whip system, and a fund-raising and publicity program to help liberal candidates campaign more effectively (a move designed to compensate for the ineffectual and crony-dominated Democratic Congressional Campaign Committee).

DSG's influence in the House naturally fluctuates with the electoral fortunes of liberal Democrats. In the 1964 Democratic landslide its membership swelled to about 175 and its influence reached a high-water mark. To exploit its strength, the group sponsored a list of reform proposals—all but one of which were ultimately adopted in the 89th Congress. One of them was the proposal for a joint reorganization committee, which dovetailed with Monroney's efforts in the Senate. Although the group urged its members to testify before the Monroney committee and later before the Sisk subcommittee, it played a relatively minor role in promoting the reform bill. Its members were badly divided over whether the Monroney and Sisk committees would produce meaningful proposals and even whether a reorganization bill would yield enough improvements to be worthwhile. Some younger members, however, suspected DSG's leaders—who by the inexorable process of seniority were approaching leadership status in the House—of becoming "soft" on reform.

In fact, the DSG as an organization was slow to mobilize on this issue. The reasons are not difficult to find. Once a fairly compact band of younger liberals, the group had grown by the late 1960s into a large body with its own internal factions. Some of its early leaders had been transformed by seniority into confirmed establishmentarians. An even more divisive factor in the liberals' ranks was the rise of new issues—particularly ecology and the Vietnam war—which threatened to redefine liberalism and often pitted traditional advocates of economic intervention against those who emphasized antiwar and conservation issues. By 1969 DSG's whip system was breaking down, and many of its members remained on the rolls primarily to receive the staff's informative fact sheets on measures under consideration on the floor—a service that supplemented the scanty information released by the Majority Whip's office. Staff Director Conlon estimated that, of DSG's members, about half were "core" supporters and the remainder "on the fringe."

Nonetheless, the DSG was a potentially powerful source of support for reform in the House. At first, agitation on the reform bill was concentrated among a few of the most liberal members, like those in the Tuesday Group. Once the Rules Committee seemed determined to produce a measure, however, the group's leaders were galvanized into action by the desire to build a broader coalition for reforms than the Tuesday Group and their GOP allies could hope to achieve. DSG's staff proved indispensable to the entire operation.

Although the DSG provided the broadest base for reform among Democrats, there was no lack of reform sentiment on the Republican side of the aisle. The minority-staffing issue aroused special energies, although that single issue by no means preoccupied Republicans. When the 91st Congress opened, the GOP lacked vigorous leadership on such issues, but Dellenback, Steiger, and Barber Conable (N.Y.) soon moved in to fill the vacuum. Even before lines of communication to DSG opened, they agreed among themselves to divide chores: Dellenback would keep track of proposed amendments, Steiger would handle press relations, and Conable would coordinate overall strategy.

Talks between Democratic and Republican reform leaders proved fruitful, for both sides had decided to avoid partisanship. "We decided we couldn't make this a political issue because we'd lose the reforms we sought, and they were more important than scoring some political points," Conable explained. In such a partisan institution as Congress, though, bipartisanship was not without its hazards. The collaboration was viewed with suspicion by some. "One has to be careful about how many things he gets into at one time around here," one Republican reformer commented. "Some of my colleagues are beginning to refer to me as 'the honorary Member of the DSG.' "

Throughout the 91st Congress, the GOP leadership felt intermittent pressure to take a more partisan stand on congressional reform—especially because the Democratic leadership was vulnerable on this score. Minority Leader Ford resisted these appeals, maintaining that Smith and the Rules Committee should be given a chance. Ford appeared to believe that a good bill would be worth more than an issue to the Republicans and to Congress. Turning reform into a partisan issue also had tactical drawbacks: Good working relations with Democratic leaders were necessary if President Nixon's legislative program was to have any chance of passage, and some senior Republicans, with whom Ford had to work closely, were themselves only reluctant supporters of reform.

At the initial mid-June breakfast session the two factions decided to draw up a bipartisan list of amendments to present during floor debate on H.R. 17654. Memorandums and telephone calls crisscrossed congressional offices for the next few weeks; lists of possible amendments were exchanged and their merits weighed. Many of the proposals emanated from such reformers as those in Thomas M. Rees' (D.-Calif.) breakfast group (the Tuesday Group), and Rees himself hired an extra staff assistant and drafted almost 100 amendments on a variety of subjects. Once the proposals had reached the DSG-Raider group for serious consideration, much of the background work was done by Linda Kamm, a DSG staff member.

The coalition was searching for ideas that would be potent yet also reasonably likely to pass. The bill's sponsors were apprehensive about what might happen on the floor; the reformers were equally worried. As they saw it, two eventualities were to be avoided. If too many "extreme" amendments were put forward, a wave of negative reaction might set in, and all the amendments would be defeated. On the other hand, if too many controversial amendments were successfully tacked onto the bill, the leadership might turn against it and try to defeat it on final passage. Rules Committee members Sisk, Bolling, and Smith repeatedly warned others that, if the bill were loaded down with amendments, Colmer would not hesitate to have the Committee of the Whole rise without reporting the bill ("Colmer will just fold his tents, and the Committee of the Whole will never report") or, failing that, would try to kill the bill in conference. The coalition convened in a Capitol room supplied by Majority Leader Carl Albert (D.-Okla.) and after a few sessions was able to agree on a basic reform package of ten proposals. Agreement on this bipartisan package served to focus the reformers' efforts, ensure more orderly floor debate, and dissuade many individuals from offering their own proposals. Because of this package, most of the 200 or so amendments being prepared were never offered on the floor. The DSG-Raider group also made certain that its package of amendments was widely circulated and understood in advance of floor debate; as the debate progressed a daily agenda put out by Gibbons' office became an essential guide for participants on all sides.

In formally announcing the bipartisan package on July 8, Gibbons and Conable noted in a joint statement that "secrecy undermines the democratic process and saps public confidence in the House as a responsive and effective legislative body."

Unquestionably the most important of the coalition proposals was one introduced by Charles Gubser (R.-Calif.) and Thomas P. O'Neill (D.-Mass.) to permit recording of teller votes on major amendments during House consideration of legislation. In a teller vote representatives file quickly past two tellers and vote "aye" or "nay," without any record of who voted which way. The device originated in the British House of Commons and has been used on this side of the Atlantic from the early days of the Republic. It is used only on amendments and only when the House is sitting as a Committee of the Whole.[22] But the House almost always sits as a Committee of the Whole for serious consideration of legislation, and so the most significant votes have often been cast in unrecorded teller votes. The technique has been attractive because it is quick and simple and allows members to vote without worrying about public repercussions. In the 91st Congress alone unrecorded teller votes were used on such key issues as the Senate-passed Cooper-Church amendment to limit the use of land troops in Southeast Asia; attempts to cut appropriations for military projects, including the antiballistic missile system; efforts to cut development funds for the supersonic transport; and controversial aspects of the D.C. crime bill.

Unrecorded voting in Committee of the Whole has represented much more than an exercise in secrecy. It also has buttressed the power of committees by making it more difficult for coalitions to oppose bills on the floor. Partly because votes were unrecorded, debates were often poorly attended and committee managers usually prevailed. There were few members who could not cite instances in which their own amendments had failed because too few of their allies had shown up on the floor. Indeed, amendments presented in Committee of the Whole usually failed; during the year immediately preceding debate on the reform bill, 53 of the 73 teller votes taken on the floor had represented defeat. During the same period 85 of 113 division (standing) votes had been defeats. These expeditious semipublic practices were part of the set of procedures that supported the committee system and fragmented power in the House of Representatives.

Almost everyone who wrote about the House—scholars, reporters, and even representatives themselves—had paid scant attention to the importance of Committee of the Whole practices. "It really shows how this place can get out of touch with itself," Gibbons remarked. For several years, however, interest in the matter had been building, and in May 1970 it suddenly burst into the open. Journalists and lobbyists in the galleries were beginning to try to record the votes of individual legislators. Although key congressmen were easy to identify, it was virtually impossible to keep track of large numbers of legislators. People not in the reporters' gallery were even more handicapped because of an inexplicable rule that gallery visitors may neither read nor take notes.

The issue came to a head as a by-product of House leaders' handling of mounting antiwar sentiment on the Hill. Criticism of the Vietnam war, not to mention foreign policy and military spending generally, had by that time become politically respectable. In 1966 a group called Members of Congress for Peace through Law had been created to coordinate efforts; by 1970 it had grown into a full-fledged organization of ninety-eight members with a staff of eight.[23] The group was bipartisan (one-third of its members were Republicans) and bicameral (including eighteen Senators and seventy representatives). Essentially the group performed back-up and coordination functions for individual legislators and their aides. It was also able to mobilize an outside lobby called the Coalition on National Priorities, a loose alliance of more than twenty church and peace organizations.

In spring 1970 this latter group stationed about forty "spotters"—mostly liberal House staffers—in the visitors' galleries to try to record individual votes on defense-related issues. Each spotter was charged with memorizing the facial and physical characteristics of four representatives so that he could tell from the gallery which were walking past which teller. During House debate over a $20.2 billion military appropriations bill, a series of key amendments that would have reduced military spending was defeated on teller votes. The anger of antiwar legislators reached its zenith on May 6, when President Richard M. Nixon's Cambodian offensive caused heated debate on Southeast Asian policy. Antiwar forces lost all the votes, but the coalition quickly prepared lists of these votes and sent them to all representatives, asking for any corrections before they were released to hometown newspapers. Howls of rage could be heard all over Capitol Hill. Members whose votes were recorded incorrectly or who had hoped their votes would not be publicized found it difficult to counter the adverse publicity. (The spotters, as it happened, were not overly scrupulous in recording members when they were unsure of the vote—the idea being to evoke just such an angry response.)

It soon became clear that many members had been stung by such incidents.[24] One of them was Gubser, who had earlier been attacked by an opponent in his district on the basis of misleading spotter information. The Gubser-O'Neill amendment had thus evolved just as the DSG-GOP coalition was forming, and it was a natural focus of reform sentiment. O'Neill, a member of the Rules Committee, first presented his proposal at a final committee session on the reform bill; it lost by a 6 to 6 tie vote, thus making it necessary to take the issue to the floor. Meanwhile, DSG's mid-June survey of its own members showed that this was by far the most popular of all the reform proposals; eventually 182 representatives of both parties cosponsored it.

Republicans found the teller-vote amendment attractive for reasons having to do with the prerogatives of the minority party. House rules provide that those opposed to a bill have the right just before final passage to offer a motion to recommit the bill to committee with or without instructions for revision. A successful motion to recommit ensures opponents of a chance either to defeat or to alter the pending measure, and the vote on this motion is often the most critical vote on a bill during House deliberations. Control of the motion to recommit rests with the minority party.

In efforts to have votes on matters acted upon in the Committee of the Whole recorded, liberal Democrats had started to use a maneuver that threatened to wrest control of the recommit motion from the minority party. On several occasions liberal strategists had sought to defeat (by roll call) the calling of the previous question on GOP motions to recommit, announcing that such votes would permit new recommit motions embodying amendments previously defeated in Committee of the Whole. Liberals advertised such votes as the equivalent of substantive votes on the rejected amendments. Sensing that this tactic threatened their traditional control over the motion to recommit and faced with substantive interpretations of procedural votes, many Republicans seized upon the notion of recorded teller votes in the Committee of the Whole.

The very fact of Gubser's sponsorship of the teller-vote amendment also encouraged GOP support. As one Republican leader commented, "When you get a respected conservative like Charlie Gubser working for a reform like this, then the boys know that it isn't just some scheme by the far-out crowd."

The teller-vote amendment promised to revolutionize legislative proceedings by stripping the semisecrecy from the most crucial voting on the House floor. But other amendments were important too. One proposal struck at closed committee meetings: 43 percent of all hearings and meetings held by House committees were closed to the public in 1969. The Appropriations Committee, for example, held every one of its 330 meetings that year behind closed doors.[25] Important sessions of such House committees as Ways and Means, Armed Services, Judiciary, and Foreign Affairs were also closed.[26]

The ten proposals were chosen from the scores being circulated because they were considered to have the broadest appeal and the best chance of passage. Many in the bipartisan group would have gone much farther. An attack on the seniority system was planned by Rees, Charles Vanik (D.-Ohio), and Henry S. Reuss (D.-Wis.), who drafted an amendment proposing that a committee chairman not be required to be the senior member of the committee. Others also had seniority amendments to offer. The DSG-GOP coalition avoided the seniority issue because it had no chance of being resolved on the floor and might weaken efforts to modify seniority through the party caucuses.

On the Republican side of the aisle related reform activities were taking place concurrently with the DSG-Raider negotiations. A 19-member House Republican task force (with Conable as chairman and including Steiger) had been set up by the GOP leadership to frame recommendations on the seniority system. From its inception in March until the Labor Day recess the task force met weekly in a conference room just off the House floor (next door to the room used by the DSG-Raider group). From the beginning, progress on the reform bill was of concern to the task force: Floor action on H.R. 17654 could create a hostile atmosphere for further reform efforts *within* the parties, and seniority amendments of the Rees-Reuss-Vanik type could drastically restrict the task force's scope. (A more complete account of the task force's activities is presented in Chapter 4.)

As plans for the floor challenges evolved, leaders of the coalition group checked with their respective party leaders. Retiring Speaker McCormack took a detached but bemused stance. "McCormack's real attitude is that this is none of his business," one leading Democrat confided. "This is Carl's business." As Majority Leader and the Speaker's heir apparent, Albert tried to placate both the reformers and the committee leaders. One DSG leader described Albert's role:

> We met with Carl early in the game as part of our staging operations. He was sympathetic but didn't commit himself. He's always weighing his position against that of the committee chairmen. He knows that if he wants to be a successful Speaker he has to play ball with them.

His Republican counterpart, though somewhat more committed to reform, struck essentially the same pose. One GOP reformer described Ford this way:

Jerry is genuinely interested in reform. But he can't afford to antagonize the barons. He's got to work with them on White House legislation all the time. Dellenback and Steiger went to see him and he agreed with their proposals right down the line. Yet, as the leader, he can't say so.[27]

The remaining top party leaders on both sides remained aloof, and some were hostile to the reform proposals.

Even though they lacked the Whip and organized communications resources of the DSG, the GOP Raiders worked to sell the proposals on their side of the aisle. Memorandums from Conable, Steiger, and Dellenback describing the amendments were sent to all House Republicans. Cosponsors were sought from within the party's ranks. Raider leaders formally presented their arguments at a meeting of the House Republican Policy Committee and at a well-attended Republican Conference (caucus) that stimulated unusual interest. The GOP reformers were eager that all members be informed about the proposed amendments to prevent opponents from claiming that the amendments had been unveiled without adequate notice.

The antisecrecy amendments made an attractive package that immediately put opponents at a disadvantage. But the DSG-GOP leaders recognized that they would stand little chance unless a bandwagon for support started rolling. In the weeks before floor debate on H.R. 17654 the DSG prepared an intensive campaign to publicize the amendments. The lobbying effort, Staff Director Conlon explained, followed "the classic two-pronged effort" of talking to representatives and persuading outside organizations to generate pressure.

A series of three meetings was called to acquaint lobbyists with the reform bill and the proposed floor amendments. The theory was that many lobby groups would profit from open sessions and votes. Not all the groups were interested, but a few were. "We got a big lobby effort going," Conlon said. "But it is what you would call a 'public interest lobby.' They understand that this bill, with our revisions, is really going to revolutionize this place." Actually, most of the help came from such liberal and labor organizations as the AFL-CIO, the National Education Association (NEA), Americans for Democratic Action, the National Committee for an Effective Congress, the National Farmers Union, and the Anti-Defamation League of B'nai B'rith. On July 10 AFL-CIO Legislative Director (and former representative) Andrew J. Biemiller wrote a letter to legislators saying that "the AFL-CIO urges you to be present on the floor when H.R. 17654 is before the House...." Letters on behalf of the antisecrecy provisions also went out from the National Farmers Union and the NEA.

Even more successful was the coalition's appeal to journalists around the nation. The antisecrecy theme was selected partly with this appeal in mind. As one leader of the drive said privately:

> We were extremely eager that the stakes be seen as being larger than
> merely a housekeeping matter of small concern to the public. The
> way this was done was to package our moves as "an antisecrecy
> drive." Since the press hates secrecy in all forms, this proved to be a
> highly productive technique.

A concerted campaign, designed by Conlon, was launched to catch the
attention of journalists, and the results were gratifying. DSG Chairman Fraser
wrote to the editors of 600 newspapers, as well as to national political columnists. A two-page letter, signed by 11 Republicans and 11 Democrats who
described themselves as "both liberal and conservative," was mailed to 2,000
editorial-page editors and news editors. Samuel J. Archibald, director of the
Washington office of the University of Missouri's Freedom of Information Center, alerted 770 daily newspapers and 600 radio and television stations in urban
areas; Sigma Delta Chi, the professional journalism society, issued a similar statement; and the chairman of the freedom-of-information committee of the American Society of Newspaper Editors issued a statement that "the more the public
knows about Congress, the better the Congress." The three-month-old Public
Information Center inaugurated its editorial service with a release entitled
"Making Congressmen Accountable," which in turn served as the basis for many
newspaper editorials.

No one knows just how many newspaper articles were generated by the
campaign, but dozens of editorials were introduced into the *Congressional
Record* by supporters of the amendments. Probably not since the revolt against
Speaker Joseph Cannon in 1910 had the nation's press taken such an interest in
congressional procedures. Whether or not the general public evinced any deep
interest in the question is doubtful; Rumsfeld's remark about the lack of a
reform constituency must be recalled. But this time, at least, a few influential
outside voices were heard.

Leisurely Floor Debate

The reform bill reached the House floor on Monday, July 13, under a rule
that permitted four hours of general debate, followed by consideration of
amendments under the "five-minute rule"—which permits each member to speak
no more than once or for no longer than five minutes on any single proposed
amendment. The House was to sit as the Committee of the Whole. In presenting
the rule for approval, Chairman Colmer issued a warning to the reformers:

> There will be some members who will be running off on different
> tangents wanting to change what your committee, in its wisdom and
> after long and deliberate consideration, has provided. . . . [T]hose
> who have been crying loudest for reorganization and reform, if they

want it, I would suggest to them [that] they stay pretty well within the lines of reason and not try to just revamp the whole Congress and the character of the legislative procedures now in existence.[28]

Other committee leaders echoed this warning. After a day of general debate, the amending process began, also in the Committee of the Whole.

The proceedings did not start auspiciously for the bipartisan coalition. Its first major proposal, presented by Representative William D. Hathaway (D.-Maine) and forty-two cosponsors, was designed to open more committee sessions to the public. It would have required that a quorum of committee members conduct an open roll call each day on whether or not that day's meeting or hearing would be open or closed to the public. The proposal actually involved two amendments, one covering hearings and another covering committee mark-up sessions (which are usually closed to the public). Hathaway asked for and received unanimous consent to have the two amendments considered together, a move that turned out to be a tactical error. The notion of open hearings might well have passed, but the thought of open mark-up sessions horrified many members.[29]

The error was not long in revealing itself. Representative Emanuel Celler (D.-N.Y.), veteran chairman of the House Judiciary Committee, followed debate on the reform bill from his usual seat in the front row. Then he asked, "Does the amendment provide for 'hearings' or for 'meetings'?" "Under the unanimous consent request, I will say to the gentleman, it applies to both," Hathaway replied. Later Hathaway argued that only lobbyists have access to committee members when secret meetings are employed. "Now just one minute," interjected peppery Wayne Hays (D.-Ohio). "If you want to write up a bill with a lobbyist sitting at every Member's elbow, some of you who like to proclaim yourself as ultra-liberals . . . are going to have a rude awakening."[30] Representative George Mahon (D.-Tex.), chairman of the prestigious Appropriations Committee, declared that, if open mark-up sessions were instituted, "the silent majority will not be there, but the special interests will be well represented." Representative L. Mendel Rivers (D.-S.C.), chairman of Armed Services, remarked that many hearings on national-security matters would have to be closed. He said that the proposed change "is not needed. We get along well now." A majority of his colleagues seemed to agree, for the Hathaway amendment was defeated by a 102 to 132 teller vote.

The Gubser-O'Neill proposal to permit recorded teller votes came up ten days later, and the result was more favorable. Introducing the amendment for the 182 cosponsors, O'Neill explained that although he did not think of himself as a reformer, he did think that "every member should report to his or her constituency as to how he or she votes, and the complete record should be available for public scrutiny."[31] He recited the familiar arguments against the unrecorded teller vote: the ubiquity of debate in Committee of the Whole, the

importance of amendments considered there, and the irresponsibility of legislators' voting secretly on such questions. "The secrecy of the Committee of the
Whole has allowed too many Members to duck issues, to avoid the perils of
controversial votes," he concluded, "but that is not the spirit of this nation, nor
of this Congress." Then O'Neill added a comment suggesting why some reformers had become so interested in his amendment. Referring to the many
unrecorded votes on crucial issues, he declared that if constituents had known in
the past how their representatives had actually voted, "I believe we probably
would have had some different results. Probably we would have passed more
pieces of legislation."

The principle behind the amendment drew very little criticism. The publicity had done its job, and few members were willing to go on record in favor of
secrecy. Most of the discussion was directed at several amendments to the
amendment (two were accepted and two rejected). Then the House passed the
Gubser-O'Neill teller-vote provision by voice vote, with "spotters" on duty in
the galleries.

The remaining eight amendments presented by the bipartisan coalition all
passed, most by voice votes. Perhaps the most controversial was the provision for
larger committee staffs for the minority party. Although by that time the idea
had become a rallying cry for Republicans, it was fiercely opposed by many
Democrats, including most committee chairmen. As Celler declared, "I have long
hoped that the committee staff would serve the members, not only along ideological lines, but along the lines of skilled professionals and craftsmen." [32] He
objected also to the rigid apportionment of staffs (that is, one-third for the
minority party). Other senior Democrats added their voices. Yet the amendment
was important to Republicans and a keystone of the bipartisan reform coalition.
As if to underscore the trade involved, a Democratic liberal was heard to comment wryly to a conservative Republican as they moved together through the
teller line, "And now what are *you* going to do for *me*?" The teller vote was 105
to 63 in favor of the amendment—though the committee chairmen did not let
the matter rest there.

The ten amendments on which the reformers had achieved consensus were
only a few of the attempts to modify the bill on the floor. A total of sixty-five
amendments were actually presented; thirty-six were accepted and twenty-nine
rejected. Only the threat of defeat for the entire bill prevented more from being
introduced.

Although most of the defeated proposals were technical in content, a few
struck at basic issues. One, presented by Representatives Schwengel and Dante
Fascell (D.-Fla.), would have eliminated the use of proxy votes in committee
meetings. The proposal passed the Committee of the Whole but was defeated on
reconsideration before final passage of H.R. 17654. Several amendments would
have modified the seniority system: a Fascell proposal to permit election of a
chairman if the incumbent chairman was unable to perform his duties, a

Schwengel proposal to allow a majority of committee members to elect their chairman from among the three senior majority members, a proposal by Jonathan B. Bingham (D.-N.Y.) to limit the tenure of committee chairmen to four terms (unless the House, by a two-thirds vote, made an exception to the rule in each individual instance), and the Rees-Reuss-Vanik proposal that seniority not be required as the only consideration in selecting committee chairmen.

This last suggestion was by far the mildest on the subject, and in fact represented no modification of existing rules, for seniority is nowhere mentioned in the rules. But Sisk, the bill's floor manager, warned that the seniority amendments, "if adopted, probably are going to be enough weight to sink this bill." [33] Bolling, a long time foe of seniority, also opposed the amendments: "The problem of seniority when the Democrats are in the majority is the problem of the will of a majority of the Democrats," he said. "If they choose to modify seniority, they have the power to do so." Republicans like Conable, and indeed most members, seemed to agree that the matter was properly the responsibility of the two party caucuses, both of which had subcommittees studying the matter (see Chapter 4). Some members, especially on the Republican side, also considered the Rees-Reuss-Vanik amendment a device to provide the Democrats with a means of attacking seniority without changing the way in which the House would be required to operate under the rules. The measure was defeated on a 73 to 160 teller vote.

During the debate, which was generally well attended, House leaders hovered in the background. Speaker McCormack took no part in the deliberations, but he was often seen roaming around the chamber and talking to his friends. When asked how he stood on the recorded teller-vote issue, he told a reporter: "It's all right with me. It would have been all right 20 years ago." Then, spreading his arms wide, he added with disbelief, "Why, it's the great utopia . . ." [34] Generally McCormack supported the Rules Committee, voting against attempts either to strengthen or to weaken the bill.

The Democratic leadership had obviously decided to let the debate proceed at a leisurely pace. "They're loving this bill to death," one reformer said caustically. Frequently the bill would be scheduled for consideration but then passed over in favor of substantive legislation. The long Labor Day vacation (between August 15 and September 9) intervened, as did many minor matters—like the annual House gymnasium party, a testimonial dinner for a retiring member, a campaign seminar for Democratic representatives, White House picture-taking sessions for Republican representatives, and a dental appointment for Colmer. As a result, almost ten weeks passed between the opening of debate and the final House vote (although it was true that the House devoted only eleven full days to the measure, whereas the Senate had required seventeen days in 1967).

Just before the August recess Representative Rees issued a caustic news release detailing delays in what he called the "ghost bill" of the year. [35] GOP

Conference Chairman John B. Anderson (Ill.) separately charged the Democratic leadership with "benign neglect" of congressional reform.[36] Other members expressed fears that the bill might be lost in the rush for adjournment after Labor Day.

The charges leveled by Rees, Anderson, and others were primarily preventive measures, for the leadership was still maintaining its stance of indifference. But the criticisms were not without effect, and Rees' news release generated a fair amount of newspaper publicity. Perhaps more influential than the reformers' criticisms was Sisk's issuance of what amounted to an ultimatum to the Democratic leadership. If the leadership could not promise to set aside time to finish the bill without interruption, Sisk said that he would abandon the effort altogether. He asked that consideration of H.R. 17654 be resumed on September 15 and continue for the next two days if necessary to complete action. The request was granted.

The Legislative Reorganization Act of 1970 was finally passed by a roll-call vote of 326 to 19. The six Republican dissenters were all conservatives; of the thirteen Democrats recorded against the bill, twelve were southerners, and six were senior committee leaders. Most representatives probably concurred with Anderson when he said:

> At a time when our institutions are under increasing attack from all directions for not being responsive, we have passed a bill that will make this Congress more responsive to its own membership and . . . to the people it serves. . . . I am proud to have been part of this most historic moment.[37]

The rest of the bill's history was anticlimactic. The Senate promptly scheduled the bill for consideration. During debate on October 5-6, the floor manager was Metcalf, who had been a member of the Monroney committee.[38] In presenting the bill to his colleagues Metcalf recalled that it had been former Senator Monroney who had started the history of the law six years earlier. Of the 16 amendments accepted by the Senate, thirteen were presented by Metcalf; all pertained to the Senate, and most were uncontroversial. One of the five defeated amendments was Senator Robert Packwood's (R.-Ore.) bid to eliminate the seniority system, which failed on a 22 to 46 roll-call vote. The final vote on the bill was 59 to 5 (the opponents were all conservative southern Democrats).

Two days after the Senate had acted, the House accepted the amended bill and sent it to the President. The leading Washington newspaper marked the event with only a two-inch story.

The Politics of Reform

Passage of the Legislative Reorganization Act (P.L. 91-510) proved that explicit reform is not impossible, given the right combination of discontent, persistence, shrewdness in mobilizing outside support, and at least six years of tortuous negotiations. "The doomsayers were wrong, and we were right," exulted one reform-minded representative. What direct impact the bill's provisions will have, only time will tell. Even the most thoughtful alterations in institutions often turn out quite differently from what instigators have planned—as the 1946 reorganization law had shown.[39] Sometimes reforms do not alleviate the ills for which they have been devised; sometimes they have effects undreamed of by the authors. At the same time, subtle and gradual alterations—often produced by long-range social and political forces—may come "like a thief in the night" and have far greater impact than any piece of legislation.

It did not take long for a few of the reform provisions to fall by the wayside. The Senate quickly ignored the provision of the act which limited to one the number of joint committee memberships a senator was entitled to hold. On at least one occasion, the House by unanimous consent waived the requirement that House-Senate conference reports be printed in the *Congressional Record* at least three days before the House considered the report. The streamlined quorum-call procedure was ignored by the House, with the Parliamentarian maintaining it was unworkable. And committees varied in complying with the mandate to publish the results of all record votes on reporting bills.

The most dramatic reversal of the act occurred when the House voted, the day after it convened in January 1971, to delete the provision that one-third of committee investigative funds be used to hire minority staff members. Instigator of the move was the new chairman of the Government Operations Committee, Chet Holifield (D.-Calif.). With the support of other seniority leaders, Holifield persuaded the Democratic Caucus to approve the rescission and, over the protests of some of the previous year's reformers, saw to it that the caucus vote was "binding"—that is, Democrats voting against the caucus position on the House floor would risk expulsion from the caucus. Two days later—after the Republicans had stalled for a day—the House by a straight party-line vote approved H. Res. 5, which included deletion of the minority-staffing reform.

Republicans were apoplectic at the Democrats' action. Steiger, after making a hasty survey of GOP committee staff resources, accused the Democrats of "tearing down the work of the bipartisan group." Cleveland branded it a "shocking breach of faith" and Minority Leader Ford said it was a "setback" for the cause of reform. On the Democratic side of the aisle, views were scattered. Obviously, a majority felt that the one-third apportionment had been too generous. (Some reformers, like Rees, argued that the DSG bargainers had offered the Republicans far more staff than his own Tuesday Group had earlier agreed upon with the Raiders.) Thompson, who had sponsored, with Schwengel, the bipartisan proposal, was placed in an embarrassing position and, along with a few others, voted "present" on H. Res. 5. But a separate vote was never taken on the minority-staffing issue.[40]

The 1970 law nevertheless promised to work significant changes—

especially in the larger House of Representatives, with its often hierarchical committee fiefdoms. Greater publicity on floor votes and committee sessions may alter the structure of power in the House. With the possibility of recorded votes on a large proportion of the amendments presented in the Committee of the Whole, attendance during floor debates will be higher than in the past, when most members spent most of their time in their offices, in meeting rooms, or in the House gymnasium. Furthermore, the presence of additional members on the floor to cast recorded votes will mean more challenges to the committee managers of bills, a development that may reduce committee influence over legislation. It may also mean some loss of "efficiency" in floor debate, as consideration of legislation becomes more protracted.

The recorded teller vote soon bore spectacular fruit. Committee decisions, which had seldom been overturned on the floor, were soon being challenged in the glare of national publicity. On March 30, for example, during discussion of Sidney Yates' (D.-Ill.) proposed amendment to delete funds for the supersonic transport from the Department of Transportation appropriation, Yates called out, "Mr. Chairman, I demand tellers with clerk." Tellers were ordered, and for the next twelve minutes members streamed onto the floor, picked up and signed green or red cards (signifying "aye" or "nay" on the amendment), and walked past the tellers to deposit the cards in ballot boxes on either side of the chamber. When the cards were counted, the House had voted 217 to 204 to reverse seven years' support of federal financing of the SST.

Political commentators were quick to credit the recorded teller vote. As veteran reporter Norman C. Miller put it, the recorded vote "substantially weakens perhaps the most effective carrot-and-stick power the committees hold." The rules change will, he said,

> force more meaningful votes in the House on issues that the Members, as a whole, have heretofore tended to let the committees decide. And the committees, for the most part, tend to be advocates for the interests whose bills they handle; any diminution of their influence thus should tend to reduce the influence of special interests.[41]

Of course, the precise impact of the innovation may change as time goes on, and other devices, like more frequent imposition of closed rules, may soften the effect of recorded teller votes. But it seems fair to conclude that "the reform makes the House a far more open political arena than it had been ..."[42] And that fact alone, as students of politics know, can serve to alter the power structure of an institution.

The recorded teller vote illustrates a central truth about the politics of reform. The proposal was widely accepted as a limited remedy for a problem that many members had faced in bringing amendments to the floor. Its capacity for altering fundamental power relationships was largely overlooked by the members, even many who stood to lose by it. O'Neill's remark during floor debate on the measure—that with this device "probably we would have passed more pieces of legislation"—seems to have been ignored by many of his colleagues. Had its full import been known—or for that matter, knowable—his amendment might very well have been defeated.

Most of the struggle over the legislative reorganization bill took place in private, with little public involvement. Except for the flurry of journalistic acclaim for the antisecrecy amendments, press coverage was almost nonexistent. Nor did the public demonstrate any abiding interest in the subject. "Congressional reform is an issue without a constituency." However painful it may seem, only the legislators themselves can engage in self-evaluation and "preventive maintenance." The 1967 and 1970 debates showed clearly that legislators had plenty to say about the structure and procedures of Congress. As might be expected, those who had gained most under existing practices were most fearful of change, and they had disproportionate power to resist these changes. The resulting measure was the product of many hands, some of whom were hostile to the notion of reorganization. But the Reorganization Act of 1970 remained a singular achievement; its impact will be felt for years to come.

NOTES FOR CHAPTER 8

1 *The New York Times*, November 26, 1964, p. 42.

2 The Senate debate on S. Con. Res. 2 can be found in U.S., Congress, Senate, *Congressional Record*, daily ed., 89th Cong., 1st sess., 8-9 March 1965, pp. 4223-4429.

3 U.S., Congress, Joint Committee on the Organization of the Congress, *Interim Report*, 89th Cong. 2d sess., 1966, pp. 5-6.

4 U.S., Congress, Joint Committee on the Organization of the Congress, *Organization of Congress*, 89th Cong., 2d sess., 1966, S. Rept. 1414. Although the committee's recommendations were unanimous, the House Republican delegates filed supplemental views urging, among other things, minority-party control of one investigative committee when a single party controlled both houses of Congress and the presidency, curtailment of lobbying by executive branch, disclosure of assets and income by members, and provisions relating to financing of political campaigns.

5 U.S., Congress, Joint Committee on the Organization of the Congress, *Hearings*, 89th Cong., 1st sess., I, p. 75.

6 U.S., Congress, Senate, *Congressional Record*, 90th Cong., 1st sess., 25 January 1967, p. S873. The Senate debates lasted from January 25 to March 7, 1967.

7 Since his appointment by Speaker Nicholas Longworth (R.-Ohio) in 1928, Deschler has worked loyally for each succeeding Speaker as an adviser on, and interpreter of, the House rules. See Prentice Bousher, "The Speaker's Man: Lewis Deschler, House Parliamentarian," *Washington Monthly*, (April 1970), pp. 22-27.

8 House Republican leadership changes are recounted in Chapter 4.

9 Although its activities were somewhat sporadic, the task force had played a valuable behind-the-scenes role in the joint committee's work and even wrote its own book on reform, *We Propose: A Modern Congress* (New York: McGraw-Hill, 1966).

10 One of the GOP activists, Donald Rumsfeld (R.-Ill.), delighted in pointing to his party's dominance of the annual congressional baseball game as evidence of Republican youthfulness.

11 Leaders of the Tuesday Group were Representatives Thomas M. Rees (Calif.), William Hungate (Mo.), Brock Adams (Wash.), William Hathaway (Maine), and Andrew Jacobs (Ind.).

12 Norman C. Miller, "Updating Congress," *Wall Street Journal*, March 27, 1969, p. 1.

13 Quoted in Miller.

14 Other members were John Young (D.-Tex.) and Delbert Latta (R.-Ohio).

15 U.S., Congress, House, Committee on Rules, Special Subcommittee on Legislative Reorganization, *Hearings on Legislative Reorganization Act of 1970*, 91st Cong., 2d sess., 1970.

16 U.S., Congress, House, Committee on Rules, *Report on Legislative Reorganization Act of 1970*, 91st Cong., 2d sess., 1970, H. Rept. 91-1215, p. 4.

17 By the time that general debate (the stage of consideration of legislation before action on amendments in the Committee of the Whole) had ended, more than 200 amendments had been drafted. By their sheer number they threatened to prolong consideration to the point at which the bill could not be acted upon.

18 A description of these events was written by Andrew J. Glass, *National Journal* (July 25, 1970), pp. 1607-1614.

19 These informal groups are explained in greater detail in Charles L. Clapp, *The Congressman: His Job as He Sees It* (Washington, D.C.: Brookings, 1963), pp. 36-45; and Miller, "Chowder and Marching Society Does More than Eat and Strut," *Wall Street Journal*, March 4, 1971, p. 1.

20 U.S., Congress, House, *Congressional Record*, 85th Cong., 1st sess., 30 January 1957, 103, 1324-1326.

21 Kenneth Kofmehl, "The Institutionalization of a Voting Bloc," *Western Political Quarterly*, 17 (June 1964), 272, provides a useful account of the Democratic Study Group's early history.

22 The Committee of the Whole is described on p. 218.

23 The work of MCPL is described in *Congressional Quarterly*, July 31, 1970, pp. 1952-1956.

24 Representative Steiger (see Chapter 2) found himself incorrectly recorded on five of six votes supplied by spotters for the Milwaukee papers.

25 The Senate Appropriations Committee opened 75 percent of its meetings, probably reflecting its somewhat different role. The House committee has normally considered its function as to cut the budget, whereas its Senate counterpart has normally acted as a "court of appeals" for executive agencies whose budgets have been cut in the House.

26 *Congressional Quarterly Almanac* (Washington, D.C.: 1969), pp. 1031-1032.

27 Quoted in Glass, *National Journal*, pp. 1610-1611.

28 U.S., Congress, House, *Congressional Record*, daily ed., 91st Cong., 2d sess., 23 July 1970, p. H6598.

29 At the time of the debate only one congressional committee—the House Committee on Education and Labor—opened its mark-up sessions (and verbatim transcripts of them) to the public. The committee had long been a liberal-conservative battleground, with jurisdiction over many of the more controversial domestic issues. Attending the sessions or even reading the transcripts is an eye-opening experience.

30 Debate on this amendment is found in U.S., Congress, House, *Congressional Record*, daily ed., 91st Cong., 2d sess., 14 July 1970, pp. H6671-6681.

31 U.S., Congress, House, *Congressional Record*, daily ed., 91st Cong., 2d sess., 27 July 1970, p. H7155.

32 Debate on this amendment, which was introduced by Frank J. Thompson (D.-N.J.), can be found in U.S., Congress, House, *Congressional Record*, daily ed., 91st Cong., 2d sess., 15-16 July 1970, pp. H6750-6756, H6845-6854.

33 Debate on the Rees-Reuss-Vanik proposal can be found in U.S., Congress, House, *Congressional Record*, daily ed., 91st Cong., 2d sess., 27-28 July 1970, pp. H7189-7193, H7251-7252.

34 Glass, *National Journal*, p. 1610.

35 Thomas M. Rees, news release, August 10, 1970.

36 Quoted in *Washington Evening Star*, August 11, 1970.

37 U.S., Congress, House, *Congressional Record*, daily ed., 91st Cong., 2d sess., 17 September 1970, p. H8893.

38 For Senate debate see U.S., Congress, Senate, *Congressional Record*, daily ed., 91st Cong., 2d sess., 5-6 October 1970, pp. S17122-17138, S17141-17182.

39 For a discussion of the politics of reform, see Roger H. Davidson, David M. Kovenock, and Michael K. O'Leary, *Congress in Crisis: Politics and Congressional Reform* (Belmont, Calif.: Wadsworth, 1966), esp. chap. 3.

40 The lively exchange of views on this point can be found in U.S., Congress, House, *Congressional Record*, daily ed., 92nd Cong., 1st sess., 22 January 1971, pp. H58-70. See also Richard L. Lyons, "House Opens with Squabble Over Spoils," *Washington Post*, January 22, 1971, p. A-7.

41 Miller, "House Reform Begins to Take Hold," *Wall Street Journal*, April 2, 1971, p. 8.

42 David S. Broder, "SST: Hill Reform Victim," *Washington Post*, March 23, 1971, p. A-19.

Congress and the Struggle for America's Future

Our nation was born and nurtured in an age of parliamentary ascendancy. "The energy of legislatures," Sir Henry Sumner Maine wrote 100 years ago, "is the prime characteristic of modern societies." In the United States the framers of the Constitution clearly viewed Congress as the keystone of the democracy: It is no accident that Article I is devoted to enunciating the powers of Congress. Reflecting upon the prolonged period of legislative ascendancy following the Civil War, Woodrow Wilson concluded that "Congress is the dominant, nay, the irresistible power of the federal system.... In a country which governs itself by means of a public meeting, a Congress, or a parliament, the only real leadership in governmental affairs must be the legislative."[1]

Hardly any observer in the mid-twentieth century would describe Congress in terms of "irresistible power." Its decline has been universally commented on—by friends as well as detractors, and by members themselves as well as by academic observers. The pessimistic assessment of George Galloway, written on the eve of passage of the Legislative Reorganization Act in 1946, would still be accepted by most observers: "Overworked and underpaid, often lampooned by the press and unfairly criticized by the thoughtless, our national legislature had fallen from its once high estate.... With Congress overwhelmed by its great responsibilities, operating under its ancient ritual, the streamlined age ..; seemed to have passed it by."[2]

As explained in Chapter 1, however, it is probably incorrect to assert that congressional powers have declined in any absolute sense. The twentieth-century Congress involves itself in a host of governmental functions that in earlier days were performed by local or private entities—or else not performed at all. As

President John F. Kennedy was fond of recalling, the legislative giants of the nineteenth century—the Henry Clays, John Calhouns, and Daniel Websters—could afford to devote whole generations or more to refining and debating the few great controversies of the Republic. The contemporary legislator cannot take such a leisurely approach; he finds himself beset daily by a staggering number and range of public problems, both large and small. And the growing size, complexity, educational level, and mass-media exposure of constituents have greatly increased the volume of communications handled by congressional offices (a phenomenon noted in discussion of the work loads of members in Chapter 3). The quantity and diversity of legislative business create their own frustrations for Congress, to be sure; and it is debatable whether congressional involvement is as decisive as it once was. But the fact of this involvement itself cannot be questioned.

It is in relation to the executive branch that the influence of Congress is most in jeopardy. Few would disagree with the judgment of Edward S. Corwin that, "taken by and large, the history of the presidency is a history of aggrandizement."[3] And in the past generation a quiet constitutional revolution has resulted in executive leadership in the initiation of legislation. The depressed-areas legislation, discussed in Chapter 6, was noteworthy in that the major impetus for its passage came originally from congressional representatives of the depressed areas. For six years these members sparred with the Eisenhower administration, which evolved more modest measures of its own and vetoed two Democratic bills. With the advent of a Democratic administration committed to passage of depressed-areas legislation, Senator Paul Douglas (D.-Ill.) and his colleagues were faced with a quite different problem. For, once passage was virtually assured, the executive branch assumed leadership in laying out specific provisions—sometimes in opposition to Douglas' objectives.

Whereas the Area Redevelopment Act illustrates the influence of executive leadership on a congressionally originated issue, the Economic Opportunity Act of 1964 demonstrates the full dimensions of executive "legislation." Here the intricate processes of interest articulation and consensus building were concentrated almost wholly within the executive branch. The stream of individuals and group representatives that poured through the Peace Corps Building during the Shriver task force's deliberations contributed to a legislative process in almost every sense of the term. Congress quickly ratified the resulting package, understanding little and altering less. This example is extreme, perhaps, but it suggests the direction that executive initiation of legislation can take.

Many of the controversies raging over the future of Congress center on its ability to compete with the executive establishment in the complex policy-making tasks of the modern age. Can Congress effectively process specialized economic and sociological data of the type involved in implementing the Economic Opportunity Act—not to mention hundreds of other social programs? Can Congress master the detailed and sensitive information necessary to conduct the foreign policy of a modern superpower? Can a legislature take concerted and coherent action on foreign and domestic policies?

The Cult of the Presidency

For more than thirty years after the Great Depression most careful observers of government would have answered "no" to these questions. The 1930s had demonstrated the need for sophisticated action to adjust to an increasingly interdependent national economy. Then came World War II and its aftermath, in which foreign affairs and national defense reached a new ascendance in public discussions and federal expenditures. Presidential initiative in these areas is specified in the Constitution and reinforced by historical experience. Because these concerns were enhanced by events, the President and the executive establishment were enhanced in turn.

Many, if not most, commentators during this period saw in executive institutions the embodiment of good policy-making practices. In the presidency and the executive branch of government were to be found such virtues as planning, decisive and speedy action, coordination, and efficiency. Bureaucratic institutions, at least in theory, represent the application of organized rationality to public problems. To those who were attracted to planning and orderly structure, therefore, the executive branch was a congenial focus.

Many observers, schooled in the management techniques of large-scale organizations, look with undisguised horror upon what they interpret as the messy inefficiency of Capitol Hill. As an overtly political body, Congress frequently engages in symbolic or even ritualistic behavior to facilitate the processes of conflict resolution. Coupled with the intensive personalism on Capitol Hill, these practices are jarring to efficiency-minded critics, who tend to overlook the ad hoc political character of such executive bargaining processes as were involved in producing the Economic Opportunity Act of 1964 (see Chapter 7).

Such considerations have motivated many critics to support executive domination of decision making. "The executive is the active power in the state, the asking and the proposing power," wrote Walter Lippmann, then a well-known proponent of this view. In turn, Congress was to be acknowledged as "the consenting power, the petitioning, the approving and the criticizing, the accepting and the refusing power."[4] Adherents to this point of view usually emphasized the oversight function of Congress, as expressed in the 1946 Legislative Reorganization Act's injunction that congressional committees exercise "continuous watchfulness" over executive agencies. To ensure that legislators would not "meddle" in the implementation of programs, however, it was usually specified that congressional review should be directed to general policy decisions, rather than to details.

Such were the procedural arguments buttressing executive authority. But few people choose their institutional loyalties by the criterion of efficiency; in fact, more fundamental forces have served to magnify the achievements and capabilities of executives and executive institutions.

Members of the liberal intelligentsia, for their part, had policy reasons for welcoming the growth of executive power in the years following the New Deal. Because of the pivotal power of large urban states in presidential elections and the importance of urban centers in the winner-take-all Electoral College, Franklin D. Roosevelt and his successors became spokesmen for urban interests, minority rights, social-welfare legislation, and internationalism—values associated with New Deal-Fair Deal liberalism. In comparison to the presidency, Congress appeared to many liberals reactionary, parochial, small-townish, and an impediment to the "progressive" policy objectives of the executive. James M. Burns, for example, argued that the congressional power system places leadership in the hands of "those members . . . least aware of the problems of industrial society and least equipped to deal with them."[5] Many such charges were well-founded, for congressional responsiveness was distorted by malapportionment and the seniority system. Clearly the dominant forces within Congress were attuned to a different and generally more conservative constituency than was the President.

For the majority of citizens focusing upon the executive was less a policy choice than a manifestation of a deep-seated desire to believe and trust in great men. "The American people are prone to place their Presidents—especially the dead ones—on a pedestal rather than under a microscope," Thomas A. Bailey has written.[6] Young children learn about the President before they learn about legislators (whom they sometimes identify initially as "the President's helpers"), and this disparity in information continues through adulthood. The President is the best-known figure in public life, and he usually ranks high on "most admired" lists.[7] Most people seem reassured by the image of a vigorous and revered person working actively to solve the nation's problems: from Doctor New Deal of the 1930s to Camelot of the 1960s, the modern presidency is replete with visions of personalized wish fulfillment.

Modern communications media, it must be added, magnify the heroic dimensions of the presidency. Journalists lavish attention on the President, his family, his entourage, and his activities; at the same time they sift out actual and potential presidential candidates. Even when reporters are ambivalent toward an incumbent, they often treat the office with undisguised awe. In contrast, Congress is a complex, faceless body, (except insofar as it harbors would-be presidents). The essence of "news" is simplified personal confrontation. The operations of Congress are designed to diffuse and obscure such confrontation; as a result, press and public alike apparently have difficulty in comprehending congressional activity.

Taken together, these factors have produced a highly idealized view of the presidency, comprising a mixture of values, legend, and reality that has been so prevalent in academic and popular literature that Thomas E. Cronin has called it "the textbook presidency." After surveying a large quantity of post-World War

II literature on the presidency, he summarized the major tenets of this conception:

1. The President is the strategic catalyst in the American political system and the central figure in the international system as well.
2. Only the President is or can be the genuine architect of United States public policy; only he, by attacking problems directly and aggressively, can be the engine of change to move the nation forward.
3. The President must be the nation's personal and moral leader—by symbolizing the nation's past and future greatness and by radiating inspirational confidence.
4. If only the right man is placed in the White House, all will be well—and, somehow, whoever is in the White House is the right man.[8]

Clearly these qualities are unattainable by any human being, much less by a political institution. And when Presidents proved unable to fulfill such an expansive mandate—as would surely occur—would not the dashed hopes of the citizens cause all the more bitterness? Having been the object of unreal expectations, would not the modern presidency also be the recipient of excessive blame when things went wrong?

Congress has not been without its defenders, but they have tended to be advocates of less rather than more governmental action. Willmoore Kendall expressed a typical conservative point of view when he urged Congress to stiffen its spine against "the ten thousand . . . drastic proposals cooking away in ten thousand bureaucratic heads in Washington,"[9] hardly a prescription for institutional growth. Many conservative lawmakers—the Republicans who spearheaded the minority-staffing struggle, for example (see Chapter 8)—have urged upon Congress the more expansive role of providing alternatives to administration policies, but, caught in cross fire between supporters of the executive branch and more traditional laissez-faire conservatives, they have not always been able to implement their ideas.[10]

For their part, senators and representatives of all political persuasions have watched with growing alarm as their prerogatives have seemed to be dissipated. Gloomy prognostications about the demise of Congress have become commonplace, and the wave of antiparliamentarism in other nations has seemed a harbinger of the fate of legislatures everywhere. "The cause of the opponents of a strong presidency," the late Clinton Rossiter wrote firmly, "is ill-starred because they cannot win a war against American history. The strong presidency is the product of events that cannot be undone and of forces that continue to roll."[11]

The Vital Partner

Like so many fragments of received wisdom, the theory of executive supremacy was severely wounded in the jungles and rice paddies of Southeast Asia. It is ironic that dissatisfaction over foreign policy should have unleashed opposition to executive power, for this realm is the one in which that executive power had been most unassailable. Historically and constitutionally the President was long acknowledged as the nation's sole representative in dealing with foreign powers.[12] Citizens were expected to rally around their President in his forays into the world arena, and after World War II politicians expended much rhetoric claiming that politics ought to stop at the water's edge. Public-opinion surveys in the wake of crises in American foreign policy between 1950 (when President Truman ordered American troops into Korea) and the 1964 Gulf of Tonkin incident show strong support for presidential initiatives, even when such policies have proved to be fiascoes (for example, the Bay of Pigs invasion of 1961).[13]

American involvement in Vietnam began in 1954, after the withdrawal of the French, who had been struggling unsuccessfully against Vietnamese nationalists since the end of World War II. It was mainly advisory until the mid-1960s, when combat troops were committed to the effort by President Lyndon B. Johnson; at the peak of American efforts there were approximately 800,000 civilian and military personnel in Vietnam. As the 1960s closed more than 40,000 Americans had perished there. Originally most citizens and politicians had supported the effort, no doubt confident that the Americans would make short work of the North Vietnamese. As the war dragged on, however, people became impatient at the apparent lack of progress and cynical about the assurances of successive Presidents and Cabinet officials that the end was in sight. Meanwhile, journalists, scholars, and returning veterans told of the debilitating effects of the war on the Vietnamese people, not to mention this nation's own troops. Soon a crisis of confidence extended to a very large segment of the American people, with consequences that will have profound effects on politics for generations.

The war's effect upon executive-congressional relations was epitomized by the Gulf of Tonkin resolution of 1964. In the first week in August of that year the Johnson administration reported that an American destroyer cruising in international waters off North Vietnam had been attacked by North Vietnamese torpedo boats; two days later other attacks upon American ships were reported. (Later, serious questions were raised about whether or not the attacks had ever taken place.) Retaliatory air action was ordered against North Vietnam, and both sides followed inexorably with retaliation and escalation.

Immediately after the Tonkin incident the President recommended that Congress pass a joint resolution affirming its support of "all necessary measures to repel any armed attack against the forces of the United States . . . to prevent further aggression . . . [and] to assist any member or protocol state of the Southeast Asia Collective Defense Treaty requesting assistance. . . ." Three days later, on August 7, the resolution passed the House by a 414 to 0 vote and the

Senate by an 88 to 2 margin.[14] Congress was ill prepared to deal with the crisis; indeed, it relied upon the executive's determination that there *was* a crisis. Once a crisis had been acknowledged, time seemed to be of essence, and any dissent was viewed as likely to weaken the President's position in the eyes of the adversary.

The Vietnam war remained undeclared, but Congress continued eagerly to provide moral and financial support for it. Indeed, during the early stages of American combat involvement in Vietnam, Congress as a whole tended to be more "hawkish" than was the President, who tried to resist demands for escalation from many in the civilian and military bureaucracy. The Gulf of Tonkin resolution, though it did not specifically endorse the broadening of the war in Southeast Asia, was cited by executive policy makers as evidence of congressional support. Some officials, like Undersecretary of State Nicholas Katzenbach, argued that congressional declarations are obsolete in wars like Vietnam and that the President has ample powers (through his treaty powers and his authority as Commander-in-Chief) to involve the nation in war without consulting Congress.[15] Postwar history has generally corroborated Katzenbach's contentions.

However sound the constitutional basis for these assertions of executive power, the exercise itself is tenable only when the policies prove viable in the long run. And, as dissent against the war mounted, the executive branch could not help but bear a large measure of responsibility. After all, executive decision makers enjoyed almost a monopoly of information on the Southeast Asian situation in the mid-1960s. The most advanced thinking of the cold-war intelligentsia and the most sophisticated management techniques had been marshaled to rationalize and then to implement the United States' role in the war.

Reassertion of congressional prerogatives occurred slowly. In 1966 the Senate Foreign Relations Committee held a series of highly publicized hearings on the war, and Wayne Morse (D.-Ore.) was able to muster five votes in support of his move to repeal the Gulf of Tonkin resolution. In the following year Congress continued to support extra appropriations for the war, but, through proposed amendments to a new authorization (P.L. 90-5), many legislators attempted to influence administration conduct of the war. A mild declaration of congressional support for efforts to prevent expansion of the war and to bring about an honorable negotiated settlement was approved. The Foreign Relations Committee again held hearings, this time to ascertain the extent to which American policy was bound by treaty commitments: Secretary of State Dean Rusk told the legislators that, in addition to its multilateral or bilateral treaties with more than forty nations, the United States would support victims of aggression around the world.

The result of the Senate hearings was a national-commitments resolution (S. Res. 187), declaring the sense of the Senate that no future commitment of American forces to hostilities abroad should be made without "affirmative action" by Congress. Although Foreign Relations Committee Chairman J. William Fulbright (D.-Ark.) did not push for immediate action, he hoped that the resolution might "provoke some very careful thought and analysis about the role of the Senate in the formulation of foreign policy in a democracy." Meanwhile, Vietnam dominated the events of 1968: with the savage Tet offensive early in the year, the abdication of President Johnson from the presidential race, the fierce split within the Democratic Party, and the election of Richard M. Nixon. The new President promised to "wind down" the war, and Congress responded by giving him latitude to do so, though it passed several minor resolutions on the war, including one calling for "peace with justice."[16]

Two events in spring 1970 marked the end of President Nixon's "honeymoon period" with Congress over the war. Details of American involvement in a clandestine war in Laos were given wide publicity, and late in April the President decided to dispatch American troops to Cambodia to clean out enemy sanctuaries along the Cambodian border with South Vietnam. In the uproar that followed the latter event Senators Frank Church (D.-Idaho) and John Sherman Cooper (R.-Ky.) introduced an amendment, eventually attached to a supplemental foreign-aid authorization (H.R. 19911), prohibiting military assistance or operations in Cambodia. A hotly debated "end the war" amendment authored by Senators George McGovern (D.-S.D.) and Mark Hatfield (R.-Ore.) would have eliminated military spending in Southeast Asia after a specified date.[17] And on two occasions the Senate approved repeal of the controversial Gulf of Tonkin resolution.

The year 1970 also marked the first time that the House had gone on record concerning congressional war powers, in a joint resolution (although the Senate took no action on it) defining the war powers of the two branches of government. The resolution (H. J. Res. 1355), which passed the House 288 to 39, reaffirmed the right of Congress to declare war and stated the sense of Congress that the President should consult with it, "whenever feasible" before sending troops into conflict. On January 21, 1971, a strangely unheralded event took place: President Nixon signed into law a foreign-military-sales law (H.R. 15628), which, among other things, repealed the Gulf of Tonkin resolution. The action, Senator Fulbright claimed, removed "the one legislative sanction which, though fraudulently obtained, nonetheless provided some facade of constitutional legitimacy to the war in Indochina."[18]

As the 1972 elections loomed on the horizon congressional pressure mounted for curtailing the war effort. A spate of new "end the war" proposals were debated, and presidential contenders grew bolder in attacking the administration. Periodic mass demonstrations in Washington, D.C., garnered increased congressional support. Part of the agitation could be charged to political opportunism, as antiadministration spokesmen sought issues to take to the voters in hopes of unseating President Nixon. It must further be noted that part of the antiwar sentiment, perhaps a very large part, was based on weariness and impatience at not having achieved victory, rather than on doubts of the wisdom or propriety of the American military venture. Yet, even so, the aftermath of Vietnam has raised the most basic issues of American purpose and of the concept of separation of powers.

The debate over the roles of President and Congress in determining policy is hardly novel, but the Vietnam war posed it anew. The crisis proportions of many problems in the modern world had seemed to dictate executive-centered government, but that solution was perhaps premature. In theory the executive establishment has the advantage of access to information and ability to focus action based on assessment of that information. Yet executive institutions suffer a fateful defect: Insofar as they are hierarchical (and they are by no means perfectly so, at least in our polity), there is tremendous pressure to limit and at times even to stifle free exchange of ideas and alternatives. The President himself can become a prisoner of this system, for his entourage often is more prepared to pay him homage than to give him the advice that he really needs. "The aura of reverence that surrounds the President when he is in the Mansion," former presidential press assistant George Reedy has written, "is so universal that the slightest hint of criticism automatically labels a man as a colossal lout."[19] Presidential egos, it seems, are as prone as any to such distortions.

There is even question about the efficacy of speed, coherence, and expert advice in formulating wise policies. To be sure, many observers continue to believe that perilous times demand swift and sure responses. Burns, a long time advocate of presidential power, told the House Foreign Affairs Committee, "I do not see how our executive leadership can deal effectively with totalitarian governments if our executive is encumbered by artificial restraints."[20] In contrast, Fulbright has warned that "a condition of permanent crisis must almost certainly lead any society to eventual dictatorship."[21] The alternatives are not attractive.

Vietnam was the major trigger for criticism of executive initiative, but discontent spread to domestic policies as well. When the New Deal was young there was much talk about the application of planning, rationality, and expertise to the solution of social and economic problems. Millions of people have been helped by federal programs since the 1930s—through education, health, training, and welfare programs, to name only a few. But four decades later more than 1,000 accumulated domestic-aid programs have come to resemble a formless jumble of inefficiency and duplication. And, in contrast to his power in foreign affairs, the President has limited capacity to straighten out the jumble. Whatever their merits, President Nixon's far-reaching proposals for revenue sharing and reorganization of federal agencies are testimony to the inability of the executive establishment to reorder its forces within conventional rules of the game.

There have been many, of course, who have concluded that "the system" is beyond repair; they have either dropped out entirely or struck out blindly in rage. For those who are determined to try to alter the course of events for the better, however, Congress provides an ideal focus of activity. Legislators who opposed the Vietnam policy—a small enough group to begin with but soon increased—had ready-made platforms from which to publicize their criticisms and make dissent respectable. Congressional committees, not to mention individual legislators and their staffs, can delve into scores of pertinent issues, from ecology to foreign policy to invasion of privacy. And, although legislators have frequently been brushed off by arrogant bureaucrats, the average citizen stands even less chance of emerging successfully from an encounter with the bureaucracy. Congressional elections prove an ideal focus for issue-oriented campaigns, and dissenters are more often seen in the halls of Capitol Hill office buildings than in the huge, monolithic structures "downtown." In an eloquent statement before the Senate Foreign Relations Committee, John F. Kerry, an organizer of Vietnam Veterans Against the War, told on April 22, 1971, why he looked to Congress for changes in policy:

> We are asking here in Washington for some action, action from the Congress . . . which has the power to raise and maintain armies, and which by the Constitution also has the power to declare war. We have come here, not to the President, because we believe that this body can be responsive to the will of the people, and we believe that the will of the people says that we should be out of Vietnam now.[22]

Thus the legislative branch has remained accessible to the people, a beachhead for criticism of established governmental policies.

At the very least, the events of recent years have demonstrated that the reports of Congress' demise were premature. Despite persistent and legitimate concern that Congress was simply deferring to the President (or that both were deferring to the bureaucracy), legislators individually and collectively have demonstrated their capacity to perform their historic roles as critics, goads, and ombudsmen. Through its extensive committee specialization the House of Representatives at its best performs as a persistent and often bothersome accountant for the activities of governmental agencies. Through policy entrepreneurship the Senate performs a somewhat different role; it is no accident, for example, that criticism of the Vietnam war is associated in the public mind with that body. Nelson W. Polsby has called the Senate "the crucial nerve-end of the polity": Its latent function as springboard to the presidency, coupled with its organizational flexibility, permits it "to incubate policy innovations, to advocate, to respond, to launch its great debates, in short, to pursue the continuous renovation of American public policy through the hidden hand of the self-promotion of its members."[23] In the halls of Congress outside opinions often find sympathetic hearings; and those halls offer a forum for dissenting views.

Despite their fascination with the presidency, average citizens are apparently ready to support a full partnership role in policy making for Congress. In a national survey conducted in 1968 a majority of respondents preferred partnership in three designated policy areas: foreign policy, economic affairs, and racial matters (see Table 9).

TABLE 9 Public Preferences for Policy Leadership in the U.S.

Policy Area	President	Equal	Congress	No Answer
Foreign Policy (n=1518)	14.1%	60.0%	22.9%	3.0%
Economic Policy (n=1514)	7.3	57.9	30.7	4.1
Racial Policy (n=1513)	10.6	62.8	23.2	3.4

SOURCE: Louis Harris and Associates, Study 1900 (December 1968). The question was: "Some people think that the President ought to have the major responsibility in making policy while other people think that Congress ought to have the major responsibility. In [making the nation's foreign policy] [making the nation's economic or welfare laws] [dealing with racial problems], who do you think should have the major responsibility—the President, Congress, or both about equal?"

Even more noteworthy, more respondents preferred congressional dominance to presidential dominance in these areas, though this preference was least marked in foreign policy. Other fragments of survey data suggest that the national legislature holds a more central place in the thinking of adult citizens than is usually supposed.[24] Whether or not these attitudes are products of the cynicism of the late 1960s or of more enduring attachments to the constitutional balance of powers, they represent a potentially significant resource for Congress in the years ahead.

Nor has Congress remained static in the conduct of its own affairs. The reforms described in detail in Chapter 8 were enacted only after six years of struggle, and continual vigilance will be required to preserve and extend these reforms. But the innovations are impressive to anyone familiar with the deliberate pace on Capitol Hill; and mounting frustration and anger have motivated legislators to exercise greater zeal in protecting their prerogatives. Furthermore, as demography and reapportionment alter the membership of Congress, even more fundamental changes in policy making will doubtless occur. The 1970 census eliminated approximately thirty-seven rural districts in the House and replaced them with an equal number of new suburban districts. Further changes are likely.

The grave constitutional debate of the 1960s and 1970s will not soon be resolved. Nor is it clear, in this age of runaway technological advances, what the shape of the eventual resolution will be. All the words expended in behalf of congressional reassertions of power have not added any tangible powers to the legislative arsenal. Nor is there much wisdom in reducing the President or the bureaucracy to the status of Gulliver. But recent events have demonstrated once again the continual relevance of the Founding Fathers' insistence that free competition among political institutions is the only defense (and no guarantee, at that) against error and tyranny. Corwin once observed that the U.S. Constitution is an open invitation to institutional warfare, and contemporary events are but the most recent manifestations of the truth of this statement. "The truth is," James Madison remarked, "that all men having power ought to be mistrusted." Or, as Thomas Jefferson testified, "In questions of power, then, let no more be heard of confidence in man, but bind him down from mischief by the chains of the Constitution."

The debate over policy leadership thus extends far beyond immediate policy controversies, important as they may be. A person's stance in the conflict between executive and legislative powers calls into play one's assumptions about the nature of political man, the styles and functioning of political institutions, and the priorities of traditional normative theory. Such a position, if it is to be useful, can be arrived at only through careful examination of one's own personal and political values. As long as the twentieth century continues to produce confusion and conflict over such values, the national legislature will remain at the vital center of a prolonged institutional dialogue.

NOTES FOR CHAPTER 9

1 See Woodrow Wilson, *Congressional Government* (New York: Meridian, 1955), p. 23.

2 George B. Galloway, *Congress at the Crossroads* (New York: Crowell, 1946), pp. 5-6.

3 Edward S. Corwin, *The President: Office and Powers* (4th ed.; New York: New York University Press, 1957), pp. 29-30.

4 Walter Lippmann, *The Public Philosophy* (Boston: Little, Brown, 1954), p. 30.

5 James M. Burns, *Congress on Trial* (New York: Harper, 1949), p. 59.

6 Thomas A. Bailey, *Presidential Greatness* (New York: Appleton, 1966), p. 3.

7 Fred I. Greenstein, "The Best-Known American," *Trans-Action*, 4 (November 1966), 12-17; and Hazel Gaudet Erskine, "The Polls: Textbook Knowledge," *Public Opinion Quarterly*, 27 (Spring 1963), 137-140.

8 Thomas E. Cronin, "The Textbook Presidency and Political Science," paper read at the Sixty-sixth Annual Meeting of the American Political Science Association, Los Angeles, September 1970.

9 Willmoore Kendall, *The Conservative Affirmation* (Chicago: Regnery, 1963), pp. 30-31.

10 Proposals of reform-minded Republicans, all members of the House Republican Task Force on Congressional Reform and Minority Staffing, are collected in Mary McInnis (ed.), *We Propose: A Modern Congress* (New York: McGraw-Hill, 1966).

11 Clinton Rossiter, *The American Presidency* (New York: New American Library, 1956), p. 151.

12 U.S. v. Curtiss Wright Export Corporation, 299 U.S. 304 (1936).

13 See Greenstein, "The Best-Known American"; and Nelson W. Polsby, *Congress and the Presidency* (2d ed., Englewood Cliffs, N.J.: Prentice-Hall, 1971), p. 45.

14 H. J. Res. 1145 (P.L. 88-408). The two dissenters were Senators Ernest Gruening (D.-Alaska) and Wayne Morse (D.-Ore.).

15 U.S., Congress, Senate, Committee on Foreign Relations, *Hearings on U.S. Commitments to Foreign Powers*, 90th Cong., 1st sess., S. Res. 151, 1967, 72-73 ff.

16 See p. 128.

17 See pp. 103-104.

18 U.S., Congress, Senate, *Congressional Record*, daily ed., 92nd Cong., 1st sess., 5 February 1971, S888.

19 George E. Reedy, *The Twilight of the Presidency* (New York: World, 1970), p. 80.

20 Quoted in *Congressional Quarterly Almanac* (1970), p. 968. The theory of executive dominance also gained many new adherents among the ranks of conservatives, including Senator Barry M. Goldwater (R.-Ariz.).

21 J. William Fullbright, "The Legislator: Congress and the War," address reprinted in U.S., Congress, Senate, *Congressional Record*, daily ed., 92nd Cong., 1st sess., 5 February 1971, P. S890.

22 Quoted in *New Republic*, May 8, 1971, p. 17.

23 Polsby, "Strengthening Congress in National Policymaking," in Polsby (ed.), *Congressional Behavior* (New York: Random House, 1971), p. 8.

24 See, for example, David Easton and Jack Dennis, *Children in the Political System: Origins of Political Legitimacy* (New York: McGraw-Hill, 1969), p. 119.

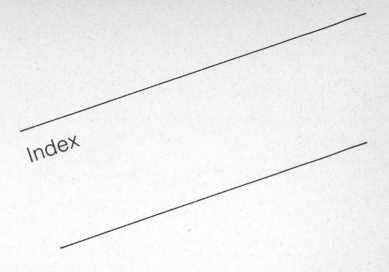

Index

37-302